CW00409626

GENDER IN HISTORY

Series editors:
Lynn Abrams, Cordelia Beattie, Pam Sharpe and Penny Summerfield

The expansion of research into the history of women and gender since the 1970s has changed the face of history. Using the insights of feminist theory and of historians of women, gender historians have explored the configuration in the past of gender identities and relations between the sexes. They have also investigated the history of sexuality and family relations, and analysed ideas and ideals of masculinity and femininity. Yet gender history has not abandoned the original, inspirational project of women's history: to recover and reveal the lived experience of women in the past and the present.

The series Gender in History provides a forum for these developments. Its historical coverage extends from the medieval to the modern periods, and its geographical scope encompasses not only Europe and North America but all corners of the globe. The series aims to investigate the social and cultural constructions of gender in historical sources, as well as the gendering of historical discourse itself. It embraces both detailed case studies of specific regions or periods, and broader treatments of major themes. Gender in History titles are designed to meet the needs of both scholars and students working in this dynamic area of historical research.

Elizabeth Wolstenholme Elmy and the Victorian feminist movement

Manchester University Press

ELIZABETH WOLSTENHOLME ELMY AND THE VICTORIAN FEMINIST MOVEMENT

THE BIOGRAPHY OF AN INSURGENT WOMAN

⊷ Maureen Wright ⊷

Manchester University Press

Manchester and New York

distributed in the United States exclusively by Palgrave Macmillan

Published by Manchester University Press
Oxford Road, Manchester M13 9NR, UK
and Room 400, 175 Fifth Avenue, New York, NY 10010, USA
www.manchesteruniversitypress.co.uk

Distributed in the United States exclusively by Palgrave Macmillan
175 Fifth Avenue, New York,
NY 10010, USA

Distributed in Canada exclusively by UBC Press
University of British Columbia, 2029 West Mall,
Vancouver, BC, Canada V6T 1Z2

British Library Cataloguing-in-Publication Data
A catalogue record for this book is available from the British Library

Library of Congress Cataloging-in-Publication Data applied for

ISBN   978 0 7190 8109 5   hardback
First published 2011

Typeset
by Toppan Best-set Premedia Limited
Printed in Great Britain
by CPI Antony Rowe Ltd, Chippenham, Wiltshire

Contents

List of plates

Abbreviations

ASS	Adult Suffrage Society
BL	British Library
CALPIW	Campaign for Amending the Law in Points Wherein it is Injurious to Women
CCNSWS	Central Committee of the National Society for Women's Suffrage
CDA	Contagious Diseases Acts
CNSWS	Central National Society for Women's Suffrage
ESPP	E. Sylvia Pankhurst Papers
EWE	Elizabeth Wolstenholme Elmy
HM	Harriet McIlquham
ILP	Independent Labour Party
JBP	Josephine Butler Papers, Women's Library
LBLB	Lydia Becker's Letter Book, Manchester Women's Suffrage Collection
LCTOWRC	Lancashire and Cheshire Textile and Other Workers Representation Committee
LNA	Ladies National Association for the Repeal of the Contagious Diseases Acts
LSEPS	London School of Economics and Political Science
MBS	Manchester Board of Schoolmistresses
MCEW	Manchester Committee for the Enfranchisement of Women
MEL	Male Electors' League
MNSWS	Manchester National Society for Women's Suffrage
MWPC	Married Women's Property Committee
NAPSS	National Association for the Promotion of Social Science
NESWS	North of England Society for Women's Suffrage
NSWS	National Society for Women's Suffrage
NUWSS	National Union of Women's Suffrage Societies
NVA	National Vigilance Association
PCWS	Parliamentary Committee for Women's Suffrage
PSF	People's Suffrage Federation
SDF	Social Democratic Federation

JOURNAL	Journal of the Vigilance Association for the Defence of Personal Rights, later the Personal Rights Journal
TRANSACTIONS	Transactions of the National Association for the Promotion of Social Science
UPS	Union of Practical Suffragists
VADPR	Vigilance Association for the Defence of Personal Rights
WEU	Women's Emancipation Union
WEUP	Women's Emancipation Union Papers
WFrL	Women's Franchise League
WFL	Women's Freedom League
WL	Women's Library
WLF	Women's Liberal Federation
WPP	Women's Penny Paper
WSPU	Women's Social and Political Union

Acknowledgements

I am indebted to the Arts and Humanities Research Council, without whose generous sponsorship during 2005–2007 this project may not have been accomplished. Further, I wish to thank the Josephine Butler Memorial Trust for funding the initial stages of my research.

Librarians and archivists of the British Library, the British Newspaper Library, Bishopsgate Library, the London School of Economics and Political Science, the John Rylands Library (University of Manchester), the Women's Library (London Metropolitan University), North-Western University (Illinois), Newnham College, St John's College, Girton College and the University Library in Cambridge, Manchester Central Library, the Mary Evans Picture Library, the Cheshire Archives and Local Studies Centre, Macclesfield Library, the University of Hull and the University of Portsmouth were all extremely helpful. Particular thanks go to Julie Weller of Portsmouth University library, whose talent for tracking down inter-library loans during the past six years was exceptional and deeply appreciated. At Manchester University Press I must thank my Editor, Emma Brennan and the anonymous readers, for their timely suggestions for revisions.

In Elizabeth Wolstenholme Elmy's home town of Congleton, I acknowledge the help and assistance I received from Jeremy Condliffe, editor of the *Congleton Chronicle* and his staff. The week spent researching the archives in the basement of the newspaper offices is one my husband and I will long remember. Thanks are due to Jean Squires and Lyndon Murgatroyd, whose local knowledge of Congleton also proved invaluable, and to the staff and researchers at Congleton Museum. Thanks are also due to Ruth Strong, archivist of Fulneck School, Pudsey for opening up some long hidden details of Elizabeth's childhood and to Mrs Janice McGrath for permission to publish from her late father's reminiscences of the village of Roe Green. In addition, grateful thanks go to Susan Talbot of the Independent Methodist Church, Roe Green for her help in locating an image of the 1855 chapel.

I owe much to June Purvis, who was the first to stimulate my interest in this project and fostered its development. Thanks also to June Hannam, Matthew Taylor and Brad Beaven for their comments on a preliminary version of this manuscript. To my colleagues at Portsmouth (who have lived with the production of this book now for numerous years) the word 'thanks' seems quite inadequate. From undergraduate days you have nurtured my enthusiasm for history and, significantly, have helped to foster a liking for the nineteenth century I would have wondered at a decade ago. To David Andress, Sue Bruley and Robert James I offer particular thanks, both for their friendship and for their insightful criticism.

An author's life is sometimes an isolated one and friends and family are crucial in keeping a knowledge of the 'outside world' alive. Thus I must express a profound debt of gratitude to my husband, Frank and to my mother, Muriel Smith for their constant and loving support. Both have 'lived' with Elizabeth as they have lived with me for, as is now universally acknowledged, biographers cannot and do not remain aloof from their subjects. Both have also read and commented extensively on my writing, equally in times of productivity and frustration and have developed a deep admiration for Elizabeth, both as an individual and as a social reformer. Another family, Marcia, David and Katrina Wright welcomed me into their home for extensive periods during the progress of my research, for which I offer my profound gratitude. For Anne Le Fevre, whose example I followed in returning to university as a mature student, thanks for the inspiration; and for so often providing a haven in which to put my thoughts on paper I send my love and appreciation to the Sisters of the Society of the Precious Blood at Burnham Abbey.

Dedications of books are always awkward for, after all those 'thank yous', who is to be the subject of these last words? I have chosen to look specifically to the future and to those students whose love of history I now help to foster. My former and current students, whose enthusiasm for this book has been (and is) infectious, have given me the energy to push the work to its conclusion. The challenge now is to maintain that delight in the study of history for years to come, both for them and for those who follow them. I hope, in some small measure, by dedicating this book to them, it will aid that ambition.

Portsmouth, 2010

The song of the insurgent women

We come! We are here at last!
Sisters, ye waited long.
But the cold dark night is past,
And the day breaks clear & strong.

What are the gifts we bring?
Hope, in the place of despair,
Truth in everything,
And justice everywhere.

These are the gifts we bring,
And their magical power shall last
Till the best in man is slain,
And man is Man at last.

Then Love, undying Love
Shall shape this old work anew,
Brighter than heaven above,
Fresher than morning dew.

And our beautiful human life,
Free from all sad annoy,
No space for empty strife,
Shall be charged to the full with joy.

We come! We are here at last!
Sisters, ye waited long.
But the cold dark night is past,
And the day breaks clear and strong.

Elizabeth Wolstenholme Elmy, 14 November 1906

Figure 1 Elizabeth Wolstenholme Elmy at her writing table
Source: Reproduced with the permission of Congleton Museum

Introduction

> When the history of the struggle of women for freedom and opportu-
> nity, in this country is written, no name will stand higher than that of
> Mrs. Wolstenholme Elmy (Margaret Sibthorp 1899)[1]

Elizabeth Wolstenholme Elmy was an ardent 'woman emancipator' from
the 1860s, and the most significant British feminist theorist of her generation. Her principal contribution to feminist ideology was made in 1895,
as honorary secretary of the Women's Emancipation Union (WEU), a
numerically small and short-lived parliamentary pressure group. Wolstenholme Elmy was the first woman ever to speak from a public platform on the sensitive topic of conjugal rape, and her pamphlet *Women
and the Law* refashioned the discourse surrounding female bodily autonomy in order to link the issue of 'consent' to maternity to 'consent' in
matters of government.[2] She argued that 'enforced maternity' should be
criminalised and, in addition, linked the potential sacrifice of life risked
by every mother in childbirth to that offered to the state by the male
citizen-soldier. The 'special dignity and worthiness' possessed by mothers
was '*superior* to that of the mere male faculty of fighting', she asserted,
and it was for this reason that women demanded the 'fullest opportunity
for self-development' and service afforded by the possession of national
citizenship.[3] Her meaning, succinctly, was that if laying down one's life
for one's country was the defining characteristic of citizenship then
women held the superior claim. Such an imagining of women's contribution to the state's future changed forever the grounds on which the
definition of a citizen was constructed and brought all women, regardless
of class, race, ethnicity or religion within its remit.

The publication of *Women and the Law* marked a high point in
Wolstenholme Elmy's long career. It came also at a moment when theories of citizenship and democracy were undergoing fundamental revisions in a turbulent intellectual and political climate.[4] Old certainties in
the power of liberalism to sustain 'progress' and to revitalise a nation
mired in the grip of moral depravity and social unrest were questioned.
Likewise, Darwinism, laissez-faire economics and increasing state intervention in individual lives had transformed views both of living and of
relationships of power. Discussions of patriarchy, its constraints and its
limits were also blatantly heard, though the group of 'active' feminists
working during the *fin de siècle* was small in comparison with the early
twentieth-century movement. Their message of emancipation, however,

by virtue of an expanded press and increased popular literacy, reached an audience of women who were increasingly receptive to its ideas. Wolstenholme Elmy, a prolific journalist, essayist and public speaker rejoiced, for she had already been engaged in the dynamics of women's emancipation for over thirty years.

An active worker in the signature 'single-issue' campaigns of the mid-Victorian era, Wolstenholme Elmy had long argued that the nature of women's socio-economic subjection was 'unnatural' and a bar to humanity's happiness.[5] She also pointed out that its roots lay in the very structures of heterosexual society; in the cultural codes and practices that had, hitherto, defined women merely as 'the sex' and in the laws that had enforced their oppression. Always the most radical of her contemporaries, in *Women and the Law* she constructed a rhetorical tour de force against these restrictions.[6] 'The right to labour and to live', she wrote, was a natural one, and only women's freedom, in its broadest sense, would help the evolution of an honourable world. Though deeply involved in evaluating the theories of social science and eugenics then current in intellectual thinking, Wolstenholme Elmy believed that evolution alone would not bring about the changes she yearned for. Her interpretation, rather, privileged the autonomous power of each individual-as-citizen and framed the terms of reference by which women everywhere could contest, by force if necessary, their exclusion from national affairs. She understood too that emancipation would be hard won. Only 'long years of agonising effort' would bring about a 'human' world, she asserted, and women themselves must 'strike the blow' for their own freedom.[7]

In the words of one who knew her well, Wolstenholme Elmy's vision and dynamism, both in their theoretical and practical aspects, set the tone for a 'new and aggressive' phase in women's suffrage activism.[8] Her part, though, in framing the tenets of 'militancy' has not received comprehensive historical attention. Assessing her life and her impact on feminist thought is therefore deeply significant for historicising early twentieth-century suffragism, and conclusively challenges the impression that she was purely the septuagenarian 'mascot' of the Edwardian struggle for the parliamentary vote.[9] Her views, in fact, significantly predated those of her ideological successors, the members of the Women's Social and Political Union (WSPU), on whose Executive she served, and the Women's Freedom League (WFL). She was not, as pictures of the 1900s show, a quaint elderly lady, but bitterly determined: and her time and talents were given to the WSPU in part because she perceived, in the organisation's feisty chief strategist, Christabel Pankhurst, a 'force and originality' that mirrored her own.[10] The younger woman respected her judgement and held her articulation of feminist ideals in high regard. For instance, when Miss Pankhurst argued that one of the principle objectives of feminist citizenship should be to free a woman from the necessity of making a 'permanent sex bargain for her maintenance' she was echoing Wolstenholme Elmy's earlier rhetoric as an 'insurgent woman'.[11]

When, in 1908, the militant suffragettes of the WSPU acknowledged Elizabeth as the 'Nestor' (wise one) of their movement it was an accolade she received with a curious mixture of pride and humility.[12] Though she found it hard to believe that the oration was for her, she nonetheless stood proudly on the platform of the Queen's Hall to receive it, writing that it indicated a spirit of 'fuller-cooperation' with her ideals.[13] Brave and stoic, sensitive and stubborn, critical, feisty and often pernickety, Wolstenholme Elmy's uniqueness among her peers lay in the twin attributes of inexhaustible energy and astounding intellectual prowess. Her work for women was not undertaken lightly, and her presence in feminist circles touched many lives – not always without controversy. It is the object of this book, the first full-length biography of Wolstenholme Elmy's life, to restore, explore and evaluate her significant contribution to 'first-wave' British feminism.[14] In so doing, it will open up the life of a significant suffragist to scrutiny, and shed further light on the complex and evolutionary nature of the definitions by which feminists engaged with what it meant to be both a woman and a citizen of the modern age.

By the time of her death on 12 March 1918, Elizabeth Wolstenholme Elmy had guided the cause of women's emancipation in Britain for over fifty years from her modest home in the hamlet of Buglawton, Cheshire (a suburb of the town of Congleton). She had held seats on the executives of over twenty organisations founded on a feminist agenda from 1865 to 1913. The diligent record-keeping and administrative labours for which she was renowned were first honed as honorary secretary of the Manchester Board of Schoolmistresses (MBS), founded by her in 1865 as an offshoot of the wider campaign for higher education for women. Later, from 1867 to 1882, she held the position of honorary secretary of the Married Women's Property Committee (MWPC), and she was the founder and honorary secretary of both the Women's Franchise League (WFrL) and the WEU. Her last recorded formal post was as honorary Vice-President of the Tax Resistance League in 1913. Tracing the development of her feminism today assimilates a range of sources which, though significant, recount only a portion of her labours. Her personal archive, including literally thousands of letters from friends including Josephine Butler, Emily Davies, F.W.H. Myers, Emmeline Pankhurst, Henry Sidgwick, Kate Sheppard and Esther Roper, was destroyed shortly before her death. While this is undoubtedly a loss, a significant corpus of correspondence remains, together with quantities of published commentary, articles, reports and other artefacts. These were not all written with a specific 'feminist' focus, but all are directed, in some measure, to the 'social condition' of humanity.

Such was Wolstenholme Elmy's grasp of the British legal and judicial system she acquired a formidable reputation as 'the parliamentary watch-dog' and few state officials escaped being drawn into the circle of her correspondence.[15] This numbered well in excess of 7,000 individuals worldwide and the mailings of the WEU, for example, were received in cities as far apart as Birmingham, Cape Town, Chicago, Glasgow and Wellington. Elizabeth revelled in the life she lived at the heart of this web of friendships, and her family's often strained financial circumstances in no way affected her feminist commitment. Diligent to the point of fanaticism in her labours for women's emancipation she could, however, be immodest, for she possessed a fine sense of self-worth and considered herself an 'initiator' of campaigns. The compliment that she supplied 'the grey matter in the brains of the women's movement' delighted her.[16] She may be forgiven, perhaps, a degree of self-publicisation in the texts through which she chronicled her experiences – for the conservative values of some contemporaries conspired for many years to deny this most progressive of radicals the place in history to which her labours entitled her.

Wolstenholme Elmy's egalitarian beliefs (influenced by the texts of Mary Wollstonecraft, Charles Fourier and 'utopian-socialist' Robert Owen) were always among the most forward-thinking of her peers – even though the shades her radicalism took changed over time. Although Helen Rappaport identifies her as 'a radical liberal in the early nineteenth century mould' she did, in fact, have strong connections to socialism – though her engagement with its ideals was rarely constant.[17] She wrote emphatically in 1903 that she had never supported Conservative ideals, and she considered it the duty of 'women working for justice . . . to do so outside [of] party' political constraints.[18] Women working from within politically allied associations such as the Primrose League or Women's Liberal Federation, therefore, sometimes found her too challenging and her remarks too astringent. Her quick intelligence and progressive thinking, combined with an intransigent approach to campaign strategy, ensured that while she was much admired by colleagues she was often at the centre of controversy. This was particularly the case after (and as a consequence of a profound intellectual and religious struggle) her political allegiances shifted away from the Methodist-inspired Liberalism of her youth towards an evolutionary, humanitarian and secular creed.

Her secularism placed her beyond the pale for some colleagues. Her wedding to secularist textile manufacturer Benjamin (Ben) Elmy in 1874 was the catalyst for a period of particular pain, and it made her a target for malice among those who argued that only 'religious people' could truly be relied upon to support the women's cause.[19] Though treated cruelly at this time, she believed no human being incapable of raising themselves to a 'new and better' creed of unselfish justice to others. She wrote that work to seek an egalitarian world should transcend any dogmatic belief system – either of religion or of party politics – and that society should seek only that path to the world's salvation which put at its heart the honouring of human life. In 1897 she argued that the increasingly statist institutions of British society had 'cripple[d] the weak and strong alike', and by 'restrictive laws . . . had identified itself with caucus, coercion, cloture and compulsion'. She viewed the modern state as unjust and as restrictive to human freedom as the institutions of Christianity which, she declared, had worked merely for their own aggrandisement and not for the salvation of the destitute.[20] Her concern for those society considered inferior was absolute, and likewise her condemnation for those who, with the means to secure 'justice' in their power, refused to exercise the privilege. Her admirers, including journalist and social reformer William T. Stead, demanded that she be revered as a feminist 'pioneer . . . a remarkable survivor . . . deserving of honour'.[21] Her detractors, on the other hand, voiced the opinion that she was uncooperative, autocratic and 'wholly impractical'.[22]

It is the object of this book to consider such dichotomous assessments in order to re-evaluate both her character and her valuable contribution to history. The purposes of the introduction itself are threefold: first, to outline the reasons for presenting a chronological biography, as opposed to a thematic or theoretical interpretation of her ideals; secondly, to offer a brief assessment of current historiography relating to Wolstenholme Elmy, and finally to submit a succinct account of the organisation of this study.

Wolstenholme Elmy and the biographical spotlight

Born in Eccles, Manchester on 1 December 1833, Elizabeth Wolstenholme was her parents' third child. Tragically, she was doubly orphaned before her twelfth birthday, when the responsibility for her care passed to her maternal grandfather Richard Clarke, a self-made textile mill owner. She lived in the Salford districts of Roe Green and Worsley and grew up rooted and grounded in the philosophy of non-conformist, northern radical-Liberalism – the Clarkes connected by both faith and commerce to the friendship networks of anti-Corn Law League hero John Bright.[23] As the daughter of an Independent Methodist minister, she might have been expected to have been influenced by the doctrines of social justice, human equality and pacifism that comprised the bedrock of the non-conformist creed. However, though she often acknowledged these character traits, she saw them not as imbibed but innate. Writing to her closest friend, Harriet McIlquham, she reflected that she would have had to have been 'hatched again and hatched different' in order to have been immune to the effects of human suffering – whatever its cause.[24] Her public work had been motivated by this impulse, and it was something she held in common with Emmeline Pankhurst, who considered her political career to have been shaped more by her 'character' than by 'heredity or education'.[25] Both women recalled their abhorrence of the lack of opportunities for growth and personal development available to women in the Victorian age, but Wolstenholme Elmy did not condemn men themselves for women's plight; merely the socio-cultural systems that dictated the limits of female existence. Her life's work was to raise awareness of, to challenge and, where possible, to undercut these systems to achieve a fair society. It is in order to capture and assess the complex nature of a feminist consciousness that evolved over almost three-quarters of a century that this book follows a chronological structure.

For scholars narrating the lives of the feminist forebears of the Western world the straightforward, chronological biography has long been a popular methodology.[26] There has, however, been increasing criticism of this 'spotlight' approach in recent years. Morley and Stanley, for example, point out that a tendency by authors to focus on a subject too intensely has obscured the complexities of the arguments in which feminists engaged – something which, in consequence, has sublimated history to *her*-story and polarised a complex narrative.[27] The nature of modern socio-cultural history demands more. It requires that biographers of feminists (and indeed feminist biographers) look beyond the spotlight into the shadows beyond, in order to seek out the multiple influences of both culture and circumstance which shaped their subjects' lives. Only by doing so can the evolutionary 'process' of a feminist journey be mapped and the subject's feminist consciousness 'read' through the textual trail that the researcher follows. Combining this 'kaleidoscopic' interpretational approach with research into the networks in which each feminist moved provides (in place of a narrative of a 'woman worthy') a way to map broader patterns and trends not otherwise visible – such as the relationship between suffragism and wider politics, or between feminism and the law.[28] In this way, as Karen Hunt suggests, the 'insights of biography' can prove immensely significant to our understanding of 'what the struggle for women's enfranchisement *meant*' for those who engaged in it – both women and men.[29]

Elizabeth Wolstenholme Elmy stated unequivocally what 'the cause' meant for her. Quite simply, it was 'a labour of love'.[30] It was a love, though, that sometimes demanded a high price, in money, in health and in relationships. Friendships fractured under the strain of campaigning, and this was something which affected Wolstenholme Elmy both personally and politically. Personality clashes were not uncommon, and she could bear a grudge, sometimes for many years, as her treatment of Florence Fenwick Miller and Dora Montefiore in Chapters 5 and 7 illustrates.[31] Sometimes too she refused to give credence to the fact that, as her own position shifted, the views of others evolved in different directions – something which offered fruitful possibilities for reading the complex and engaging narrative of the 'progress' of suffragism as a whole. In order for readers to appreciate the evolutionary nature of Wolstenholme Elmy's personal feminism, I have chosen to follow the chronological, rather than the thematic path as adopted by, for example, Patricia Romero and Carolyn Steedman in their respective studies of Sylvia Pankhurst and Margaret McMillan.[32] I have, however, been attentive to the fact that the presence of those many 'dear friends' who shared in Wolstenholme Elmy's labours did much to influence her patterns of thought and feeling.[33]

No nineteenth-century feminist led a static life – Wolstenholme Elmy least of all. Her political consciousness, for example, was developed, revised and re-fashioned in many subtle ways – though it can be argued that always at its core lay the humanitarian conception of 'justice': 'justice' in this context being the acknowledgement that women be legally designated as man's human equal. One of the most significant ways in which I charted the development of Wolstenholme Elmy's feminism was through the transcription of the exciting (and, to date, only partially exploited) resource of her correspondence with Gloucestershire suffragist and Poor Law Guardian, Harriet McIlquham. Lodged in the archives of the British Museum after McIlquham's death, the collection (which dates from 1881 to 1914) offers to researchers a resource that superlatively demonstrates the complexities, shifts, and (occasionally) bitter feuds that characterised British suffrage history. Drawn by Wolstenholme Elmy's distinctive, spider-like hand, the personalities of the late-Victorian feminist movement spring off the page – though they do so tinged often with an element of resentment or pique. Ursula Bright, W.E. Gladstone, Florence Fenwick Miller, and the 'ineffably silly' Mary Cozens, leader of the Parliamentary Committee for Women's Suffrage, are some of her favourite targets.[34] Although, as June Hannam has shown in the case of socialist-feminist Isabella Ford, convincing biographies can be written without the aid of a voluminous correspondence archive, there is little doubt that Wolstenholme Elmy's letters add much to the evaluation of her personal life-narrative.[35] It is particularly important, given the fact that the unpublished manuscript of her autobiography, *Some Memories of a Happy Life*, was lost in the destruction of her archive. What remains, however, is not a carefully constructed autobiography that might have chosen to be selective in what Wolstenholme Elmy chose to narrate, but a day-to-day account of events that is, by its nature, more spontaneous and direct.

While Wolstenholme Elmy's letters clearly have value as textual artefacts in their own right (and as products of contemporary culture), their principal worth for me as biographer lay as the means through which I could interact with her self-representation: the way in which she recorded her 'feminist life'. Other documentary sources were also significant in this way. While Wolstenholme Elmy did not write any book-length studies she was a prolific journalist, both in her own name and under her pseudonyms, Ignota (the unknown woman) and the more seldom used 'E'. In addition to evaluating the extended series of articles she submitted to newspapers and periodicals including the *Westminster Review*, the *Englishwoman's Journal* and *Shafts* (long established as important sources for historians of suffragism) this biography applies evidence from others, less well known. She wrote, for example, for W.T. Stead's pacifist-themed *War Against War* and *Review of Reviews*. She also authored a fortnightly column in Stanton Coit and J.A. Hobson's *Ethical World* in the early 1900s and, as shown in Chapter 5, her contributions to the *Journal of the Vigilance Association for the Defence of Personal Rights* were partly responsible for a schism in that organisation's ranks during the mid-1880s.

As such, these lesser known publications highlight both the varied audiences to which Wolstenholme Elmy addressed her feminist concerns, and her labours to ensure that women's subjection was seen as a socio-cultural (as opposed to simply a sexual or political) issue. Perceiving Elizabeth as a 'humanitarian', as opposed simply a feminist, makes a significant difference to understanding the radical mindset that prompted her labours. It also helps to explain why, in the manner of other late nineteenth-century progressives, she was able to seek cooperation from those outside of the party-political spectrum to search for 'collectivist solutions' to the problems of the age.[36] Ian Tyrrell has recently argued that the 'progressive voice' has been given but 'short shrift' in the era's historiography and this biography will be significant in extending discussions of a political stance most often associated with American feminists.[37]

Wolstenholme Elmy was deeply appreciative of her transatlantic friendships. For example, she proudly noted the presence of Charlotte Perkins Gilman (then Stetson) at the final meeting of the Women's Emancipation Union in July 1899, and wrote warmly of her friendship with the young Fabian, Harriot Stanton Blatch – daughter of abolitionist Elizabeth Cady Stanton – who was elected to the WEU's Executive in 1893.[38] These are only two examples of how both her letters, and the formal reports of the organisations for which she undertook administrative duties, yielded insightful nuggets of deeply personal information about her relationships. In *Three Years Effort*, for example, the voluminous report she wrote on the conclusion of the agitation for the passage of the Guardianship of Infants Act 1886 the reader learns of the significant financial contribution made by her husband to the campaign.[39] This is something which, in the absence of any extant letters between the couple, illustrated the depth of their commitment to both one another and to feminism. Likewise, and never shy of linking the personal to the political, Wolstenholme Elmy's awakening to political consciousness is recorded when she narrates (from a distance of forty years) her admiration for Liberal Free Traders when, as a twelve-year-old girl, she watched the procession through Manchester following the Repeal of the Corn Laws in 1846.[40] Her reflections are made in 1886 from the perspective of a 'Fair-Trader', something which suggests that her political activism was lived out more fully than a study of her feminism alone would permit. Justice in economics, trade and commerce was equally as important, in her eyes, as justice between the sexes and, to understand her sometimes deeply emotional responses to the world's ills, it is essential that her multi-layered appreciation of them is understood.

It would be hard to write of Wolstenholme Elmy's life without reaching towards her emotions. She struggles to understand, for example, why some colleagues were content only to offer 'their name' to the cause. Why would they not, she wondered, seek wholeheartedly to 'work' for justice by 'individual . . . influence and effort'; a dynamic, practical activism which also acknowledged from within an appreciation of what Mary Wollstonecraft termed the 'wrongs of woman'.[41] This concept, which Laura Nym Mayhall has defined as 'engaged citizenship', became crucial in shifting the patterns of feminist activism in the *fin de siècle*, when women of all classes rallied to the suffragist cause as the political climate broadened in the light of organised labour representation.[42] Certainly, Annie Kenney, Hannah Mitchell and many other working-class suffragettes of the WSPU and the WFL faced the terrors of hostile political hustings with courage and conviction, but such engagement had always been an integral part of Wolstenholme Elmy's activism. As an executive member of both the National and the Ladies National Association (LNA) for the Repeal of the Contagious Diseases Acts from 1870 to 1874, she had faced gatherings equally as intimidating, and had campaigned on behalf of Britain's prostitutes from a perspective of gender solidarity that overrode class. She termed the Repeal movement as 'the Moral Crusade of the Nineteenth Century', but a crusade not against men *as* men, but against the licentious culture that had sanctioned as commonplace man's abuse of woman.[43] She had taken this stance in a LNA meeting in York in 1871 and it formed the bedrock of her oratorical technique. She later recalled to McIlquham that when she spoke in the feminist cause she did so with 'indignant feeling, force and passion . . . straight to the heart' of her audience. She wrote, however, that she could not speak automatically, or 'to order' – and only if she felt the sympathy of spectators reach out towards her could she 'speak as [she] felt' and allow her audience to 'breathlessly follow' her message.[44]

Such a comment places emotional awareness at the heart of Wolstenholme Elmy's public life, but for a biographer to reach too intently towards such emotions is also to cast a 'shade' of their own presence on to the life of their subject.[45] The shadow cast by the overlay of evidence with interpretation surely is most prevalent when discussing a subject's emotional stance. This, without doubt, is the point at which authors are most likely to focus on texts prejudicially, in order to seek a knowledge of 'experiences' that the challenges of the linguistic turn have queried as 'truth'.[46] But how indeed can we know another's feelings? We can only, as Michael Roper argues, trust that our sources present us with 'an adequate sense of the material [and] of the practices of everyday life' to enable us to make sound judgements on our subject's thoughts and actions.[47] I have assessed Wolstenholme Elmy's emotions from this standpoint, and acknowledge that other interpretations are possible. My own engagement is, however, acknowledged by naming her as 'Elizabeth' in the pages that follow this introduction – for after almost a decade researching her life and achievements this is how I have come to think of her.

Much could be gained for the history of feminism by further research into Wolstenholme Elmy's life. To consider more deeply her theoretical construction of women's subjection would offer (as in the case of Judith Allen's recent work on Charlotte Perkins Gilman) an in-depth appraisal of how a woman at the heart of the British campaign sought to philosophise and historicise the nature of feminism – even before this French term came into widespread use in the 1880s.[48] Likewise, a project to edit and publish her voluminous correspondence would open up fascinating insights into the practicalities and mechanics (as well as the emotional commitment) of leading a suffragist life. A focused effort, too, on mapping the directions of her correspondence network would offer a fruitful path for a scholar of international suffragism. While, of necessity, Wolstenholme Elmy's own life-narrative is placed at the centre of analysis here, there is much in both her personal and her public textual legacy (and especially her largely anonymous contributions to the *Review of Reviews*) that would aid the evaluation of international feminist history.

Wolstenholme Elmy and suffrage history

The object of this biography is to argue that Elizabeth Wolstenholme Elmy was foremost among the Radical suffragists of her generation and to interpret that radicalism as a force for change. She wrote in 1898 that she was proud to have been one of the 'leaders of the [feminist] revolt', and she encouraged women to apply 'the tools' men had used to gain political freedom in order to secure their own.[49] From the platforms of countless political gatherings she urged women to apply what Jon Lawrence has termed the 'politics of disruption' to gain their objectives, and for her labours she was honoured by Emmeline Pankhurst as the 'first militant' of the WSPU in 1905.[50] The history of British women's suffragism, however, takes place on contested terrain and as both Sandra Stanley Holton and Krista Cowman have pointed out, the definition of the 'militant' feminist is one that is impossible to fix.[51] What influences prompted a 'radical' thinker to become a 'militant' was a matter for the individual's conscience, and women (and some men) moved fluidly between differing forms of protest, most often allied to more than one campaigning group.

Wolstenholme Elmy's activism during the *fin de siècle* shows the veracity of this view. Between 1889 and 1905 she was either formally allied or sympathetically connected to the labours of the WEU, the WFrL, the

Women's Co-operative Guild, the North of England Society for Women's Suffrage (NESWS), the Pioneer Club, the Union of Practical Suffragists and numerous organisations supporting the labour movement – including the Fabians and the Independent Labour Party (ILP). While she had been the driving force behind many of the single-issue campaigns by which Victorian feminists acquired social reforms (of education, employment and property rights) she also considered these to be mere 'scraps and shreds of liberty'.[52] She had a broader vision of emancipation than these campaigns allowed and it was expressed most forcefully through her challenge to male sexual dominance. Her resolve that women should have legal redress against sexual coercion, and that a woman's citizenship be determined on her bodily autonomy rather than any consideration of property, provided a fertile discursive environment which enabled the ideals used by Edwardian militants to flourish. But although she believed firmly in heckling and other forms of 'passive' militancy she did not countenance violence, and it was with bitter disappointment that she resigned from the executive of the WSPU in July 1912 as a consequence of the new tactics of arson employed by its 'young hot-bloods'. The sanctity of human life was, for Wolstenholme Elmy, beyond the price even of women's freedom and, in designating such actions a 'criminal folly', she queried how the extremists could 'be secure against hurting the innocent?'[53] Her life, above all, highlights that there is no simple dichotomy between the suffragist and the suffragette.

In the eyes of many, her pacifism, republicanism and secular adherence placed Wolstenholme Elmy outside mainstream society – a controversial figure upon whose person the nineteenth-century imperial patriots of her home town poured scorn (and on one notable occasion, mud and stones). She followed a creed of radicalism at its most extreme, and so great was her notoriety during the heated debates surrounding her marriage that Josephine Butler commented that she wished to remove the stain of her association with 'such people as the Elmys' from her character.[54] Though their friendship weathered this particular breach and lasted until Butler's death in 1906, such assessments contributed to Wolstenholme Elmy's exclusion from history – at least history as recorded by her peers.[55] Contemporary chroniclers, more cautious than she, shied away from heaping praise on a black sheep of suffragism – a woman who upheld consistently (and with the clear intention of making marital rape a crime), John Stuart Mill's premise that it was 'barbarous . . . that one individual could, under any circumstances, have a *right* to the person of another'.[56] Her constant, forceful appraisal of the sexual nature of women's subjection, her recommendation of extreme campaign tactics and her hectoring of those 'do-nothings' whose commitment was perhaps not as deep as her own, added to contemporaries' distaste.[57] Thus, while she was admired for her stoicism in the face of parliamentary intransigence, a multitude of reasons ensured many peers kept their distance. It is not, therefore, hard to find reasons why, in their important accounts of what is categorised as 'constitutional' or 'non-violent' suffragism, Helen Blackburn and Ray Strachey give her labours only cursory attention.[58] It fell to Ben Elmy, who believed her contribution to have been trivialised, to publish the first short biography of his wife in 1896 to highlight her 'indomitable efforts' in the women's cause.[59]

In some key narratives of militancy published during the inter-war years, Wolstenholme Elmy is revered as a feminist pioneer: as a partner in the mid-Victorian struggles for women's higher education and professional employment, but a worker obscured by the focus on the higher profiles of colleagues, including Josephine Butler, Anne Jemima Clough and Emily Davies. She is, however, sidelined by the fact that her life-narrative did not include the indignities of 'imprisonment, hunger-strike and forcible feeding' – the mantra of genuine militant activity upon which, Hilda Kean has suggested, so many suffragette accounts had been founded.[60] Sylvia Pankhurst's influential autobiography *The Suffragette Movement* is a case in point. Pankhurst paints a pathetic portrait of Elizabeth as a frail, diminutive 'Jenny-wren' – a care-worn though dedicated activist whose sad fate it had been to be married to an unpleasant and unfaithful spouse.[61] Dora Montefiore's *From a Victorian to a Modern* also offers an assessment which privileged the ethereal aspect of her friend's character. Montefiore wrote that Wolstenholme Elmy possessed an 'intense spiritual enthusiasm' and a soul which 'eventually moved the somewhat inert mass of suffrage activity and set it on the road' to militancy.[62] While kindly meant, these images of the leader of so many Victorian feminist organisations deny the forceful elements of Wolstenholme Elmy's practical activism and, crucially, the intellect and zeal that shaped it. While Montefiore was correct in assuming that her friend was responsible for the shift to militancy, her labours were, as Chapter 6 shows, far more tangible, and significant, than Montefiore's language indicates.

Other contemporary authors, though less illustrious than Pankhurst and Montefiore, point towards this different history. For example, Margaret Sibthorp, editor of the feminist periodical *Shafts*, claimed Wolstenholme Elmy as both 'prophetic' and a visionary.[63] While this might place her as being 'ahead of her time', she was, nonetheless, a product of her context and of its cultural influences. Ethel Hill and Olga Fenton Shafter understood radicalism in this light and saw no reason to denigrate the 'cool courage' of those who adopted a progressive stance. They argued that 'great suffragists' came in many guises and the inclusion of Wolstenholme Elmy in their 1909 volume of 'prominent leaders . . . writers, and thinkers' of suffragism went some way to mitigating her exclusion elsewhere.[64] Hill and Shafter concluded that they 'look[ed] upon the actions – the logical, well-thought-out actions – of any [campaigner] as so many means to the same great end', and saw progress in the deeds of both the 'suffragist' and the 'suffragette'.[65] Thus, in common with the late twentieth-century assessments of Sandra Stanley Holton and David Rubenstein, these earlier authors understood the necessity of placing the actions of the militants in the context from which they had sprung – the decade of the 1890s – rather than perceiving militancy as an aberration or divergence from tradition.[66]

As this introduction has shown, Wolstenholme Elmy's life can be interpreted as having being lived at the pivot of the suffrage narrative. She was not, however, designated as a luminary of the movement until the most recent times. Although included in four biographical dictionaries of women's suffragists to date, numerous calls for a full-length study have gone unheeded.[67] The research of Lee Holcombe and Mary Lyndon Shanley offered important perspectives on Wolstenholme Elmy's work in the single-issue campaigns between the 1860s and 1890s, but not until Holton's innovative research in *Suffrage Days* was her role placed centre stage.[68] Holton's objective was to highlight that those she termed 'Radical suffragists' were at the forefront of shaping, and putting into practice, a 'militant' agenda; and her methodology, the group biography, worked well in opening up neglected life 'stories that [had] become largely hidden in the patterns formed by previous history making'.[69] Significantly too, the book revealed that the decades of the *fin de siècle* were a far from tranquil period in the women's struggle – though one glance at Wolstenholme Elmy's correspondence for the early 1890s would negate Andrew Rosen's comment that these years comprised the 'nadir' of British suffragism.[70]

Investigating the shades and tones of conflict and friendship, of struggle, compromise and dispute help identify the still hidden depths within the movement for women's emancipation, and while this book follows *Suffrage Days* in that it explores Wolstenholme Elmy's relationship network, I extend its arguments in three key areas. First, I present new evidence that places Wolstenholme Elmy in her familial context and enables a deeper assessment to be made of the naissance of both her political and her feminist consciousness. Second, while Holton claimed the 'conscience of radical suffragism' lay at the heart of the WFrL (founded by Elizabeth and others in 1889), I argue this is a term which could be applied more perfectly to the WEU, whose willingness to engage in public debate on the matter of women's sexual subjection pushed discursive boundaries further even than the Franchise League's uncompromising attitude to securing married women's enfranchisement.[71] And finally, in making plain Wolstenholme Elmy's key role in organising and promoting the 1903 Convention in Defence of the Civic Rights of Women, I link the ideals at the heart of WEU rhetoric to the issue of autonomy and free choice and its implications for citizenship. The matter of making women's suffrage a 'test question' was at the heart of Radical suffragist thinking post-1893, but its importance for the narrative of militancy has been under-investigated. The adoption of the policy by the large audience at the Convention, however, significantly changed the terms of reference by which suffragists defined their activism. By their united refusal to canvass for a parliamentary candidate who may be opposed to the women's vote, these suffragists set the limits of their consent to government without representation. And, as the pages of Wolstenholme Elmy's *Women and the Law* had made clear in 1895, if women could refuse, they could also resist. The stage was set for a new form of action.

Exploration of the issues above will add much, both to an appreciation of Wolstenholme Elmy's life and of her importance within British suffragism. However, it was Holton's work, and Elizabeth Crawford's comprehensive narrative portrait in her 1999 *Reference Guide* to the struggle for the vote, which formed the starting point for my investigations.[72] To understand Elizabeth Wolstenholme Elmy's life convincingly, however, it is crucial that her theoretical interpretation of feminism be teased out from its practical application, and here the work of Laura Nym Mayhall was influential to my approach. Mayhall's book, *The Militant Suffrage Movement: Citizenship and Resistance* was the first full-length consideration of militancy as an expression of how suffragettes engaged with the theories of citizenship and democracy.[73] Expanding on previous studies by Holton, Jane Rendall and Stefan Collini, Mayhall claimed that for many of those she termed 'radical independent' suffragists an active involvement in political life was to be considered an essential factor of the kind of 'engaged citizenship' Wolstenholme Elmy encouraged.[74] The depth of these links between the personal and the political are amply illustrated by Elizabeth's comment that if the road to parliamentary representation lay before women 'moistened with blood and tears, and made rough with the bones of those who have fallen in it' then so be it – for only such a commitment would secure their rights and duties as citizens.[75] Thus, Wolstenholme Elmy's construction of citizenship, while head of the WEU and the WFrL, was important in setting the context for Mayhall's study. However, while the two organisations (together with the Union of Practical Suffragists) are comprehensively defined as the leaders of *fin-de-siècle* suffragist progressivism, *Citizenship and Resistance* fails to explore in depth the link between the WEU's formation and its key objective: the politicisation of motherhood and its meaning for militancy.

The detailed retrieval of organisations such as the WFrL and the WEU forms an important aspect of this study. It appears, though, that the juxtaposition of maternity and militancy made explicit in WEU ideology can also be argued to have contributed to Wolstenholme Elmy's lack of historiographical presence – for as Linda Martz has noted, even among the most recent assessments of militant ideology there lies a 'negation of the existence of any historical link between sexuality, feminism and suffrage.'[76] For Martz these twenty-first-century developments are a disturbing step away from the acknowledgement by feminist scholars of the 1980s and 1990s that the 'sex war' activists fought was not 'a titillating sidelight ... [but] ... the crux of the suffrage campaign.'[77] This is the opinion investigated in depth below, and it surely contradicts the view posed by Melanie Phillips in 2003 that Puritanism and an abhorrence of sexual activity in general characterised radical discourse.[78] While Wolstenholme Elmy's interpretation of sexuality is focused upon in short studies within the late twentieth-century feminist work by Lucy Bland, Susan Kingsley Kent and Sheila Jeffreys, it is most often explored with an emphasis on her published (as opposed to her personal) texts and those of her husband.[79] Ben and Elizabeth shared a deep, moral commitment to sexual abstinence and 'psychic love', and Ben, writing under his pseudonym of Ellis Ethelmer, penned a series of polemical works on sex education and women's sexual physiology which were published privately, under the auspices of the WEU, from 1893 to 1897.[80] These have been freshly assessed by Katharina Rowold as 'the most comprehensive [contemporary] argument that subordination had been imprinted on the female body', but to lay stress upon Ethelmer's work (and particularly his misconstrued beliefs surrounding menstruation) obscures the contextual importance of the WEU's membership as agents of progressive politics.[81]

Such discussions also place the organisation too firmly as a focus for middle-class, neo-Malthusian intellectualism, something which negates the considerable contribution made to its endeavours by the wider membership – those 'real workers' who, Wolstenholme Elmy believed, were the life-force of any great movement.[82] The interpretation presented here lays stress not only on how women's sexual subjection was challenged rhetorically, but also on the relationships between intellectuals and grassroots activists. Only by so doing can the organisation's attempts to collapse distinctions of class and to incorporate the voice of working-class women, be explored. The history of the WEU, the organisation perhaps dearest to Wolstenholme Elmy's heart, tells much more than the history of her interaction with it. Nonetheless, by reading this history through the medium of biography, the process of her politicisation, and that of her fellow workers, can be better mapped and understood.

The biographical structure

Wolstenholme Elmy's philosophy was that a person's duty was not to acquiesce to 'coercion by legislation' but to promote instead a 'nobler ideal of life and action' through the example of lives well lived.[83] This was a route to a humane, progressive society which lay open to all, not merely a propertied elect who had earned their citizenship by prudence, privilege and diligence. Such an opinion looked, ultimately, towards universal adult suffrage – the benchmark of socialist ideology. Elizabeth's relationship with socialism was, however, complex and contradictory. As Hannam and Hunt have pointed out, each woman activist negotiated a complex web of personal and political influences in the pursuit of her own socialist journey, often under pressure from socialist men who believed feminist issues to be divisive to the wider movement.[84] Elizabeth's marriage to Ben Elmy, who she described as an 'advanced socialist' built, in part, on the ways in which her ideas had been shaped by earlier friendships with those linked to the Owenite movement, and on her own egalitarianism.[85] Yet these influences were tempered by an enduring allegiance to the 'Liberalism of [her] youth', something she did not renounce (and then only in a fit of pique) until 1892.[86] Scholars must be cautious therefore of viewing her life simplistically via an association with particular political ideologies, for the picture that it paints is certainly opaque. She can, I contend, be rather better understood viewed through a lens of feminist humanitarianism – as the advocate of an ethic of active compassion for all human life. The structure of this book, outlined below, will show how Wolstenholme Elmy built a life of political action upon the principal that *all* women had a human right to equality with men on every issue: socio-economic, political, legal and sexual. She did not consider her own sex 'superior', but equal, and her unshakeable belief in this equality demanded of her, from her twenties, that she live a public life.[87]

This introduction has considered my reasons for writing Wolstenholme Elmy's life chronologically. Here I outline the main themes of the study. Chapter 1 presents an interpretation of the first thirty years of her life, and offers new evidence of both her familial context and her 'conversion' to feminism at the age of seventeen. It was her experiences as a bridesmaid that prompted her to understand that the 'immoral vow, "to love, honour and obey"' bound women for the rest of their lives in the condition of 'sex slavery'.[88] This revelation unlocked her feminist consciousness, but she wrote of it only once, briefly, in a letter to McIlquham – a gem almost lost in the mass of her correspondence. Wolstenholme Elmy's life was also shaped by her experience of double orphanhood, her desire for an education and for a life dedicated to the service of others. She showed a strong determination to carve out an independent life, and her career as headmistress of her own girls' boarding school both helped fulfil this desire and, in her determination to acquire pedagogical training for women in similar circumstances, precipitated her public work.

Elizabeth's childhood links to the northern-radical 'activist families' described by Philippa Levine were influential too – although her experience of guardianship after the death of her parents was fraught.[89] She shared with many contemporaries the restrictions on their lives that familial economic dependence made necessary, although as Chapters 2 and 3 demonstrate, she always refused to let precarious financial circumstances curtail her work. The theme of these chapters is to highlight the many and varied organisational affiliations through which she lived out her feminist life and to plot the shape of the friendship networks that supported her. This demonstrably highlights that, even from the 1860s, the path of woman's emancipation activism lay open to dispute and confrontation, as no two women's hopes and objectives truly followed identical paths. To restore Wolstenholme Elmy into this mid-Victorian campaign history is to include the deeds (and the words) of the first professional employee of the women's cause. As 'scrutiniser' of parliamentary practice for the Vigilance Association for the Defence of Personal Rights from 1872 to 1874, she both honed her skills in dissecting legal judgments and acquired a reputation as a fearsome lobbyist. Always controversial, she followed the most progressive path, but while the heckling of disruptive audiences left her unscathed, her health broke down under the stress of colleagues' criticism. This reached its apogee when, aged forty, and six months pregnant, this high-profile exponent of 'free love' capitulated to peer pressure and formalised her partnership with Ben Elmy in (what she later termed as) the less-than-dignified environs of Kensington Register Office.

The circumstances of, and reaction to, the Elmys' nuptials, form the topic of Chapter 4 – a narrative set, perhaps with a little irony, within the context of Elizabeth's work as honorary secretary of the MWPC. Though the birth of her only son, Frank, had restricted her ability to travel and speak on feminist issues she had, contrary to official evidence, continued administrative work for the MWPC. Seven years passed before the passage of the Married Women's Property Act 1882 saw her restored, professionally, to the spotlight. While the campaign she led exemplified a high point of reforming Liberalism, the Home Rule crisis soon precipitated an internal schism in the Liberal Party which had far-reaching consequences for the feminist agenda, as women began to seek more widely for effective ways to promulgate their message. Despite being honoured for her success at the head of the MWPC, Elizabeth never ceased to court controversy. Her nature was not conciliatory and her objectives, though she commented otherwise, rarely took the 'path of least resistance'.[90] Chapter 5 demonstrates this, and, by exploring her 'single-handed' campaign to secure guardianship rights for mothers to their own children, I illustrate Wolstenholme Elmy's broad challenge to every aspect of patriarchal dominion – even the effects on children of the 'dead hand' of their father's will. Her work on behalf of family relations demonstrates her deep understanding of the multi-layered nature of women's subjection: and although she believed that, with the suffrage, women would secure an effective voice to combat oppression, she recognised too that many women had only a dim appreciation of the many forms that oppression took.

Wolstenholme Elmy's drive and determination were effective in securing the passage of the Guardianship of Infants Act 1886, but her domestic life was increasingly influenced by both financial worries and her husband's indifferent health. Ben Elmy was seriously affected by the economic downturn in the northern textile industry, and though not left totally insolvent when the business collapsed, the family were henceforth partially supported by charitable bequests from Elizabeth's suffragist friends from the mid-1890s. Though a small coterie, including McIlquham, Frances Rowe (a former pupil of Elizabeth's), Louisa Martindale and Harriot Stanton Blatch gave willingly, the waves of the suffragist tide were once again turning stormy and the years 1888–99 were among the most difficult of Wolstenholme Elmy's life. They were also, however, the most significant, for it was then, using all her experience of family relations and the law, that she conceived and put into practice, via the work of the WEU, the doctrine which linked a woman's consent to maternity to her willingness to consent to government. Chapters 5 and 6 chart the implications of this theory for the future of the suffragist movement in the context of the fracture of some significant relationships in Wolstenholme Elmy's life – especially her friendships with Ursula Bright and Florence Fenwick Miller.

The correspondence that plots the breakdown of these 'Liberal alliances' is often painful and distressing to read. What follows, however, shows another aspect of the evolution of Wolstenholme Elmy's political consciousness, for in November 1905, aged almost seventy-two, she became a member of the Manchester Central Branch of the Independent Labour Party (ILP). Unfortunately, her letters recall nothing of her motivation for this formal alliance by a dedicated non-partisan, and indeed in many ways she can be considered idiosyncratic. For example, it was she alone of her middle-class contemporaries who initially appreciated the significance of bodily autonomy and free choice in relation to the citizenship debates. It was an issue her 'humble pupil', Dora Montefiore, of the Social Democratic Federation (SDF), made very much her own during the years of the Anglo-Boer War, with extensive commentaries in the magazine *New Age*.[91] The matter of 'choice' became a key feature of feminist politics at the turn of the century and in the WSPU, an organisation that eschewed party politics, Elizabeth found her 'natural' home.

The issues, however, were more complex and as Chapters 7 and 8 show, her life-narrative still exhibits signs of struggle and complexity – such as that of her interaction with socialism hinted at above and the triumph of her pacifism over her militancy. As an octogenarian she lived, cared for in a nursing home in Manchester, just long enough to know that the parliamentary franchise had been conferred upon women, though with certain qualifications, under the terms of the Representation of the People Act 1918. This biography restores Wolstenholme Elmy's life-narrative to suffrage history, but in so doing it acknowledges that her part in Victorian and Edwardian feminism did not exist independently of its context. The political culture of which she was a part and the influences of her colleagues on her thoughts and actions all had a role to play in shaping the circumstances and framework of her activism.

Notes

1 Anon. [Margaret Sibthorp], 'Women's Emancipation Union', *Shafts*, July–September 1899, p. 47.

2 Elizabeth Wolstenholme Elmy, *The Criminal Code in its Relation to Women* (Manchester: A. Ireland & Co., 1880). Elizabeth Wolstenholme Elmy will hereafter be referenced as EWE.

3 EWE, *Women and the Law* [a series of four letters from *The Western Daily Press* (Women's Emancipation Union, 1895), p. 6. Women's Emancipation Union Papers, British Library. Shelfmark 8416.h.40. (Hereafter WEUP and BL.)

4 Jon Lawrence, *Speaking for the People: Party, Language and Popular Politics in England, 1867–1914* (Cambridge: Cambridge University Press, 1998), p. 190; Duncan Tanner, 'Ideological Debate in Edwardian Labour Politics: Radicalism, Revisionism and Socialism', in Eugenio F. Biagini and Alistair J. Reid (eds), *Currents of Radicalism: Popular Radicalism, Organised Labour and Party Politics in Britain, 1850–1914* (Cambridge: Cambridge University Press, 1991), pp. 271–93; Susan Kingsley Kent, *Gender and Power in Britain, 1640–1990* (London and New York: Routledge, 1999), chapters 8 and 10.

5 Elizabeth Wolstenholme Elmy to Harriet McIlquham, 1/9/1903, 47453, fol. 161. Elizabeth Wolstenholme Elmy Papers, Add. Mss. 47449–47455. BL. (Hereafter referenced EWE/HM, by volume and folio number.)

6 For a full discussion see Chapter 6, and Maureen Wright, 'The Women's Emancipation Union and its place in radical-feminist politics in Britain, 1891–99', *Gender and History*, Vol. 22, No. 2, 2010, pp. 382–406.

7 EWE, *Women and the Law*, p. 10. Maroula Joannou, '"She who would be Free Herself must strike the Blow": Suffragette Autobiography and Suffragette Militancy', in Julia Swindells (ed.), *The Uses of Autobiography* (London: Taylor & Francis, 1995), pp. 31–44.

8 William T. Stead, 'Woman's Suffrage in the Ascendant', *Review of Reviews*, July 1911, p. 18.

9 Helen Rappaport, *Encyclopaedia of Women Social Reformers*, Vol. 1 (Santa Barbara: ABC-Clio, 2001), p. 753.

10 EWE/HM, 30/03/1904, 47453, fol. 263.

11 Christabel Pankhurst, *The Great Scourge and How to End It* (London: The Women's Press, 1913), p. 115, quoted in Elisabeth Sarah (1983), 'Christabel Pankhurst: Reclaiming Her Power', in Dale Spender (ed.), *Feminist Theorists: Three Centuries of Women's Intellectual Traditions* (London: The Women's Press 1983), pp. 256–84, p. 271.

12 In Greek mythology Nestor, King of Pylos, was renowned as an elder statesman. Although too old to fight in the Trojan Wars his experience and wisdom was nevertheless held as an example to younger soldiers. EWE/HM, 26/6/1908, 47455, fol. 186.

13 EWE/HM, 26/6/1908, 47455, fol. 186.

14 Though the term 'feminism' was a new and evolving one in the 1890s, Wolstenholme Elmy's circle were among the first to apply it theoretically, for example, Ellis Ethelmer (pseudonym of Benjamin Elmy), 'Feminism', *Westminster Review*, Vol. 149, No. 1, January 1898, pp. 50–62.

15 Ellis Ethelmer, 'A Woman Emancipator: A Biographical Sketch', *Westminster Review*, Vol. CXLV, 1896, pp. 424–8, p. 427.

16 EWE/HM, 29/4/1908, 47455, fol. 170. W.T. Stead, 'Honour to Whom Honour is Due', *Review of Reviews*, September 1910, p. 223.

17 Rappaport, *Encyclopaedia*, p. 750.

18 EWE/HM, 14/8/1903, 47453, fol. 157.

19 I. Whitwell Wilson to Henry Wilson, 20/12/1875, 3/JBL/14/11, Josephine Butler Papers, Women's Library, London Metropolitan University. (Hereafter JBP and WL.)

20 EWE, 'The New Priestcraft', *Shafts*, September 1897, pp. 245–9, p. 245.

21 Stead, 'Honour', p. 223.

22 EWE/HM, 17/9/1904, 47454, fol. 6.

23 Sandra Stanley Holton, 'From Anti-Slavery to Suffrage Militancy: The Bright Circle, Elizabeth Cady Stanton and the British Women's Movement', in Caroline Daley and Melanie Nolan (eds), *Suffrage and Beyond: International Feminist Perspectives* (Auckland: Auckland University Press, 1994), pp. 213–33. For Wolstenholme Elmy's early life see Maureen Wright, '"An Impudent Intrusion": Assessing the Life of Elizabeth Wolstenholme Elmy, First-Wave Feminist and Social Reformer (1833–1918)', *Women's History Review*, Vol. 18, No. 2, 2009, pp. 243–64.

24 EWE/HM, 21/11/1901, 47452, fol. 221.

25 Emmeline Pankhurst, *My Own Story* (London: Eveleigh Nash, 1914), p. 5.

26 See, for example, Ray Strachey, *Millicent Garrett Fawcett* (London: John Murray, 1931); Paula Bartley, *Emmeline Pankhurst* (London and New York: Routledge, 2002); Jane Jordan, *Josephine Butler* (London: John Murray, 2001).

27 Liz Stanley with Ann Morley, *The Life and Death of Emily Wilding Davison* (London: The Women's Press, 1988).

28 June Purvis, 'From "Women Worthies" to Poststructuralism? Debate and Controversy in Women's History in Britain', in June Purvis (ed.), *Women's History: Britain, 1850–1945* (London and New York: Routledge, 1995), pp. 1–22.

29 Karen Hunt, 'Journeying Through Suffrage: The Politics of Dora Montefiore' in Claire Eustance, Joan Ryan and Laura Ugolini (eds), *A Suffrage Reader: Charting Directions in British Suffrage History* (London and New York: Leicester University Press, 2000), pp. 162–76, pp. 172–3. (My emphasis.)

30 WEU, Final Report, 1899, p. 30.

31 Hunt, 'Journeying Through Suffrage'; Rosemary Van Arsdel, *Florence Fenwick Miller: Victorian Feminist, Journalist and Educator* (Aldershot and Burlington: Ashgate, 2001).

32 Patricia W. Romero, *E. Sylvia Pankhurst: Portrait of a Radical* (New Haven and London: Yale University Press, 1990); Carolyn Steedman, *Childhood, Culture and Class in Britain: Margaret McMillan, 1860–1931* (New Brunswick: Rutgers University Press, 1990).

33 EWE/HM, 25/11/1896, 47451, fol. 21.

34 EWE/HM, 22/2/1894, 47450, fol. 84.

35 June Hannam, *Isabella Ford* (Oxford and New York: Basil Blackwell, 1989).

36 Laura E. Nym Mayhall, *The Militant Suffrage Movement: Citizenship and Resistance in Britain, 1860–1930* (Oxford: Oxford University Press, 2003), p. 23.

37 Ian Tyrrell, 'Transatlantic Progressivism in Women's Temperance and Suffrage,' in David W. Gutzke (ed.), *Britain and Transnational Progressivism* (Basingstoke: Palgrave Macmillan, 2008), pp. 133–48, p. 133.

38 WEU, Final Report, 1899, p. 32. WEU, Third Report, 1896, Appendices.

39 EWE, *The Infants' Act, 1886: The Record of Three Years' Effort for Legislative Reform, with its results* (London: Women's Printing Society, 1888). (Hereafter TYE.)

40 EWE, 'A Woman's Plea to Women', *Macclesfield Courier*, 20 November 1886.

41 EWE, 'Women's Suffrage', *Shafts*, July and August 1897, p. 209.

42 Mayhall, *Citizenship and Resistance*, p. 11.

43 EWE, 'The Moral Crusade of the Nineteenth Century', *Shafts*, March and May 1897, pp. 85–8 and 153–5.

44 EWE/HM, 27/4/1890, 47449, fol. 111.

45 Carolyn Steedman, *Past Tenses: Essays on Writing Autobiography and History*, London: Rivers Oram, 1992), p. 163.

46 With particular reference to women's biography, see Mary Spongberg, 'Female biography', in Mary Spongberg, Barbara Caine and Ann Curthoys (eds), *Companion to Women's Historical Writing* (Basingstoke: Palgrave Macmillan, 2005); Liz Stanley, *The Auto/biographical I: The Theory and Practice of Feminist Auto/biography* (Manchester: Manchester University Press, 1992); J. Burr Margadant (ed.), *The New Biography: Performing Femininity in Nineteenth-century France* (Berkeley and Los Angeles: University of California Press, 2000).

47 Michael Roper, 'Slipping Out of View: Subjectivity and Emotion in Gender History', *History Workshop Journal*, Vol. 59, No. 1, 2005, pp. 57–72, p. 62.

48 Judith A. Allen, *The Feminism of Charlotte Perkins Gilman: Sexualities, Histories, Progressivism* (Chicago and London: University of Chicago Press, 2009).

49 EWE/HM, 30 May 1898, 47451, fol. 215.

50 Jon Lawrence, 'Contesting the Male Polity: The Suffragettes and the Politics of Disruption in Edwardian Britain', in Amanda Vickery (ed.), *Women, Privilege, and Power: British Politics 1750 to the Present* (Stanford: Stanford University Press, 2001), pp. 201–26, p. 208.

51 Sandra Stanley Holton, *Suffrage Days: Stories from the Women's Suffrage Movement* (London and New York: Routledge, 1996), p. 2; Krista Cowman, *Women of the Right Spirit: Paid Organisers of the Women's Social and Political Union (WSPU) 1904–18* (Manchester: Manchester University Press, 2007), pp. 121–2.

52 Anon. [EWE], 'The Emancipation of Women', leaflet reprinted from an article published in the *Cambrian News*, 2 October 1885, p. 4, WEUP.

53 EWE/HM, 1/7/1908, 47455, fol. 187.

54 Josephine Butler to Millicent Garrett Fawcett, 8/12 [1875], 3/JBL/14/04, WL. For discussion of the Elmy marriage see Chapter 4, and Sandra Stanley Holton, 'Free Love and Victorian Feminism: The Divers Matrimonials of Elizabeth Wolstenholme and Ben Elmy', *Victorian Studies*, Vol. 36, 1994, pp. 199–222.

55 EWE/HM, 18/9/1906, 47455, fol. 312. Josephine Butler died on 30 December 1906.

56 John Stuart Mill, *The Subjection of Women* (1869), quoted in EWE, 'The Marriage Law of England', in *Women in Industrial Life: The Transactions of the Industrial and Legislative Section of The International Congress of Women*, London, July 1899 (London: T. Fisher Unwin, 1900), pp. 115–19, p. 118.

57 EWE/HM, 11/10/1907, 47455, fol. 121.

58 Helen Blackburn, *Women's Suffrage: A Record of the Women's Suffrage Movement in the British Isles* (London and Oxford: Williams & Norgate, 1902); Ray Strachey, *'The Cause': A Short History of the Women's Movement in Great Britain* (London: Virago, 1978). For an explanation of the four key categories of British suffragism, see Sandra Stanley Holton, 'The Making of Suffrage History', in June Purvis and Sandra Stanley Holton (eds), *Votes for Women* (London and New York: Routledge, 2000), pp. 13–33.

59 Ellis Ethelmer, 'A Woman Emancipator: a Biographical Sketch', *Westminster Review*, CXLV, 1896, pp. 424–8.

60 Hilda Kean, 'Searching for the Past in Present Defeat: The Construction of Historical and Political Identity in British Feminism in the 1920s and 1930s', *Women's History Review*, Vol. 3, No. 1, 1994, pp. 57–80, p. 73. See also Laura Nym Mayhall, 'Creating the "Suffragette Spirit": British Feminism and the Historical Imagination', *Women's History Review*, Vol. 4, No. 3, 1995, pp. 319–44.

61 E. Sylvia Pankhurst, *The Suffragette Movement: An Intimate Account of Persons and Ideals* (London: Virago, 1977), pp. 31–4. (Hereafter TSM.)

62 Dora B. Montefiore, *From a Victorian to a Modern* (London: E. Archer, 1927), pp. 43–4.

63 Anon. [Margaret Sibthorp], 'Women's Emancipation Union', *Shafts*, July–September 1899, p. 47.

64 Ethel Hill and Olga Fenton Shafter (eds), *Great Suffragists and Why: Modern Makers of Future History* (London: Henry J. Drane, 1909), pp. 11–13 and 66–70.

65 Hill and Shafter, *Great Suffragists*, p. 13.

66 Holton, *Suffrage Days*, chapter 5; David Rubinstein, *Before the Suffragettes: Women's Emancipation in the 1890s* (Brighton: Harvester, 1986).

67 Olive Banks, *The Biographical Dictionary of British Feminists* (Brighton: Wheatsheaf, 1985), p. 288; Elizabeth Crawford, *The Women's Suffrage Movement: A Reference Guide 1866–1928* (London and New York: Routledge, 2001), pp. 188–206; Rappaport, *Encyclopaedia*, pp. 750–3; Sandra Stanley Holton, 'Elizabeth Wolstenholme Elmy', in *Oxford Dictionary of National Biography* (Oxford: Oxford University Press, 2004), pp. 302–4.

68 Lee Holcolmbe, *Wives and Property: Reform of the Married Women's Property Law in Nineteenth-Century England* (Toronto and Buffalo: University of Toronto Press, 1983); Mary Lyndon Shanley, *Feminism, Marriage and the Law in Victorian England, 1850–1895* (London: I.B. Tauris, 1989).

69 Holton, *Suffrage Days*, p. 2. See also, Fran Abrams, *Freedom's Cause: Lives of the Suffragettes* (London: Profile, 2003), pp. 1–15. I follow Holton in applying the term Radical suffragists to those who 'adhered to a political current outside the women's movement' and adhered 'to more inclusive forms of the suffrage demand.' Holton, *Suffrage Days*, p. 255, fn. 1.

70 Andrew Rosen, *Rise Up, Women!: The Militant Campaign of the Women's Social and Political Union 1903–14* (London and Boston: Routledge & Kegan Paul, 1974), p. 3.

71 Sandra Stanley Holton, 'Now you see it, Now you don't: the Women's Franchise League and its Place in Contending Narratives of the Women's Suffrage Movement', in Maroula Joannou and June Purvis (eds), *The Women's Suffrage Movement: New Feminist Perspectives* (Manchester and New York: Manchester University Press, 1998), p. 25.

72 Crawford, *Women's Suffrage Movement*, pp. 188–206.

73 Mayhall, *Citizenship and Resistance*, chapter 1.

74 Mayhall, *Citizenship and Resistance*, p. 11; Jane Rendall (ed.), *Equal or Different: Women's Politics, 1800–1914* (Oxford: Blackwell, 1987); Stefan Collini, *Public Moralists: Political Thought and Intellectual Life in Britain, 1850–1930* (Oxford: Clarendon, 1991); Sandra Stanley Holton, *Feminism and Democracy: Women's Suffrage and Reform Politics in Britain, 1900–1918* (Cambridge: Cambridge University Press, 1986).

75 Anon. [EWE], *The Emancipation of Women*, p. 5, WEUP.

76 Martz is especially critical of Martin Pugh's *March of the Women* (2000) and *The Pankhursts* (2001) for failing to engage with the importance of the discourse of sexual

subjection in the texts of Christabel Pankhurst on the grounds that suffragists who engaged in the 'sex war' were only a tiny minority of the total. Linda Martz, 'An AIDS-Era Reassessment of Christabel Pankhurst's *The Great Scourge and How to End It*', *Women's History Review*, Vol. 14, Nos 3 and 4, 2005, pp. 435–46, p. 441. Martin Pugh, *The March of the Women: A Revisionist Analysis of the Campaign for Women's Suffrage* (Oxford: Oxford University Press 2002), p. 29. Martin Pugh, *The Pankhursts* (London: Penguin, 2001), pp. 271–2.

77 Martz, 'Christabel Pankhurst', p. 441. Susan Kingsley Kent, *Sex and Suffrage in Britain, 1860–1914* (Princeton: Princeton University Press, 1987), p. 5.

78 Mona Caird, *The Daughters of Danus* (London, 1894), quoted in Kent, *Sex and Suffrage*, p. 112. Melanie Phillips, *The Ascent of Woman: A History of the Suffragette Movement and the Ideals Behind it* (London: Little Brown, 2003), p. 12.

79 Bland, *Banishing the Beast*, pp. 135–9, 141–3, 155–6 and 215–16: Sheila Jeffreys, *The Spinster and her Enemies: Feminism and Sexuality 1880–1930* (London and New York: Routledge & Kegan Paul, 1985), pp. 28–35. Kent, *Sex and Suffrage*, pp. 92–3, 110, 206–13 and 219.

80 Ellis Ethelmer, *Woman Free* (Congleton: Women's Emancipation Union, 1893); Ellis Ethelmer, *Life to Woman* (Congleton, 1896); Ellis Ethelmer, *The Human Flower* (Congleton, 1894); Ellis Ethelmer, *Baby Buds* (Congleton, 1895); Ellis Ethelmer, *Phases of Love: As it was, As it is, As it may be* (Congleton, 1897). There has been some historiographical debate regarding Ethelmer's true identity. Sheila Jeffreys and Barbara Gates suppose the pseudonym to be that of Wolstenholme Elmy alone, as does the British Library cataloguing system. Susan Kingsley Kent claims Ethelmer to be a nom de plume of the Elmys jointly. Lucy Bland and Sandra Stanley Holton suggest that Ethelmer's texts are the work of Ben Elmy, but acknowledge that Elizabeth Wolstenholme Elmy's ideals influenced his writing to varying degrees. This biography follows Wolstenholme Elmy's own acknowledgement that her husband was Ethelmer, but acknowledges that both her views, and their shared life, impacted on his textual production. Jeffreys, *Spinster*, p. 29; Barbara T. Gates, *Kindred Nature: Victorian and Edwardian Women Embrace the Living World* (Chicago and London: University of Chicago Press, 1998), pp. 131–3; Kent, *Sex and Suffrage*, p. 110; Bland, *Banishing*, pp. 339–40; Holton, 'Free Love', p. 219; Ignota [EWE], 'Pioneers! O Pioneers!', *Westminster Review*, April 1906, pp. 415–17, p. 415.

81 Katharina Rowold, *The Educated Woman: Minds, Bodies and Women's Higher Education in Britain, Germany and Spain, 1865–1914* (New York and Abingdon: Routledge, 2010), pp. 59–60.

82 Holton, *Suffrage Days*, p. 83; EWE/HM, 29/12/1895,47450, fol. 240; EWE/HM, 11/12/1892,47449, fol. 310.

83 EWE, 'English and French Morality', *Journal of the Vigilance Association for the Defence of Personal Rights*, May 1885, p. 50. (Hereafter *Journal*.)

84 June Hannam and Karen Hunt, *Socialist Women: Britain 1880s–1920s* (London and New York: Routledge, 2002). See also, Karen Hunt, 'Rethinking Activism: Lessons from the History of Women's Politics', *Parliamentary Affairs*, Vol. 62, No. 2, 2009, pp. 211–26.

85 Wolstenholme Elmy classified Ben Elmy by this term in his obituary. Ignota, 'Pioneers!', p. 415.

86 EWE/HM, 3/7/1892, 47449, fol. 280.

87 EWE/HM [n.d.], probably mid-December 1896, 47451, fol. 35–6.
88 EWE/HM [n.d.], probably mid-August 1897, 47451, fol. 129–30.
89 Philippa Levine, *Feminist Lives in Victorian England: Private Roles and Public Commitment* (Los Angeles: Figueroa, 2003), chapter 1.
90 WEU, Final Report, 1899, p. 2.
91 See, for example, Dora Montefiore, 'The Woman Question', *New Age*, 6 and 20 July 1899.

I

The making of a feminist: 1833–61

A past concealed

The most well-known portrait photograph of Elizabeth Wolstenholme Elmy presents an image of a petite, frail-looking elderly woman.[1] Her hair is dressed in a cascade of grey ringlets and she gazes out at the viewer with penetrating, dark eyes. At the base of her throat a large cameo brooch is pinned to a dark dress. It is her only visible jewellery.

While few of these images remain today, Elizabeth was proud that a professional photographer employed by the WSPU had travelled to her home in Buglawton, Cheshire for the sitting in 1907.[2] Many of the photographs were sold to raise funds for the 'suffragette' campaign, and Elizabeth was happy with the image they portrayed. She was so satisfied, in fact, that she enclosed two reproductions in a letter to her closest friend, Harriet McIlquham, together with another portrait sketch, now lost. This, 'the handiwork of a woman hostile to W[omen's] S[uffrage]' (sic), was drawn around 1867 when Elizabeth was thirty-four years old. Given the enmity of the artist to the suffrage cause it is likely that the portrait had been in some way unkind – but Elizabeth dismissed this by commenting that she 'c[ould] not see the likeness' between the figure depicted and herself.[3] Though McIlquham obviously received the cruel caricature of her friend, it was not kept with the significant cache of letters and other documents that were deposited at the British Museum after her death. It is only possible to speculate on who might have removed it and their reasons for doing so. Its loss, however, relates to more than a vanished observation on Elizabeth's political endeavours, for it would have provided an image (even if unreliable) of a much younger woman than any likeness extant. And rather than viewing the lines etched upon her face by years of struggle against misfortune and misogyny, a vision of her younger self may have enabled a better perception of the zeal that prompted the career of this great social reformer.

It is clear that this mean cartoon by a political opponent got under Elizabeth's skin, though she was not tempted to throw the image away. Getting under the skin or 'inside the mind' of a subject is also one of the skills of historical biographers, together with an ability to 'convey [their] discoveries with clarity [and] cogency'.[4] An assessment of the mind of Elizabeth Wolstenholme Elmy (who was herself an articulate biographer) would be of a determined, confident woman of formidable intellect, who possessed the mental and physical drive of a workaholic. She also had an unshakeable, almost fierce commitment to the emancipation of her sex from the patriarchal structures of Victorian society. It was this quest for humanitarian justice, an 'active' compassion for all human life, which shaped and informed everything she did. Paradoxically, though, she could be arrogant. For example, if colleagues hesitated to take her advice she often retorted that the time wasted supplying it could have been better spent.[5] None, though, was more steadfastly committed to her chosen life path and, if she had been religious, feminism would have been her faith.

Elizabeth expected every person with whom she collaborated to work to the same demanding timetable that she set for herself. She was, to a considerable degree, self-educated, but this did not prevent her emerging as an acknowledged expert on the legal position of women and the family. Famed for the clear and direct way she summarised convoluted legal judgments, the logic of her arguments was always crafted in the finest prose. Wit or light-heartedness, however, is in short supply in the documents that record her life. Only occasional flashes of humour penetrate, such as when she hopes, aged seventy-four, 'not to trouble the world for fifty years more!!!'[6] Such comments are precious for their rarity, and they give the reader a glimpse of the deeply private person that lay within the heart of the elderly suffragist who raised her voice in anguish outside the Houses of Parliament as the 'first militant' of the WSPU.[7]

Elizabeth's 'private' mind is more difficult to assess than the reformer's zeal which prompted her public labours. A pacifist, a republican and a high-profile exponent of mid-Victorian 'free thought', she was influenced by the theories of Wollstonecraft, Owen, Fourier and Saint-Simon. The right of the individual to respect, be they princess, peer or prostitute was, for her, a simple truism. Her ethical code of 'justice' overrode all other considerations, though such egalitarianism was deeply divisive in the circles in which she moved. She possessed a selfless disregard for her own comfort and security – although not, as Sylvia Pankhurst contends, for the welfare of her only son, Frank.[8] She showed a deep love for nature, literature and poetry, and although quiet and stillness were qualities she appreciated she lamented their lack in her life. The thoughts and experiences of the private woman who lived 'behind' the public activist come but rarely in Elizabeth's texts. However, she wrote that she was keen to leave a documentary record of her life because she believed it 'might be of value' to historians.[9]

There were some aspects of that life, however, that she consciously or unconsciously chose to omit from the archive. And chief among these was any detailed account of her childhood and youth. Colleagues, including Anne Jemima Clough, Emily Davies and Frances Power Cobbe left significant auto/biographical sources recording their family life and feminist motivation.[10] Elizabeth, in contrast, almost bursts upon the scene in her early thirties; information on her childhood limited to the fact that she had been the daughter of a Methodist minister and his wife (classified in one instance erroneously as a 'Lancashire cotton-spinner') and doubly orphaned by the mid-1840s.[11] Behind these bare facts, however, lay a much richer seam, and, for the young Elizabeth, a challenging familial situation.

The late Olive Banks contended that, whatever their circumstances, any Victorian woman who chose the feminist path undertook a 'deliberate act of revolt' against the cultural codes that caused her oppression.[12] It was from their place as daughters of those middle-class men who successfully claimed a stake in the citizenship of their nation following the great Reform Act of 1832 that Elizabeth and her colleagues set out to redefine what it meant to be 'ladylike' – by constructing a new conception of a genteel unmarried woman's role in society.[13] The calculated rebelliousness such women made against the prevailing doctrine of 'separate spheres' took numerous forms. For most, though, the institution of the family provided the site in which the rebellion was played out.[14] It is precisely the exclusion of her family from extant documents that have helped to make Elizabeth such an 'insubstantial' historical figure.[15] With little idea of her heritage it was difficult to 'place' precisely her within a network of friends, or to chart the actions of her own insurgency against the domestic, feminine 'sphere'. New evidence links Elizabeth to her 'hidden' past, and it places her family conclusively within the network of the Bright, Ford and Petrie circle of Quaker alliances which (centred geographically on the industrial conurbations of northern England), did so much to foster her pacifism, her humanitarianism and her feminist ideals.[16] Some among her family, perhaps surprisingly, were not so forward thinking, and she considered the sad events of childhood so private that she chose to almost obliterate any recollection of them in extant sources. She also implied that she would consider their inclusion in any future biography an 'impudent intrusion'.[17]

Childhood

Elizabeth's correspondence offers no detailed description of her parents or any indication of their mode of living. Few letters, in fact, offer clues to her history, and only one notes the name of Roe Green, an industrial village near Salford.[18] The roots of Elizabeth's maternal family lay here, for she was the third child and only daughter of the Reverend Joseph Wolstenholme and his wife Elizabeth, one of nine children of prosperous textile entrepreneur Richard Clarke of Sisley Cottage, Lumber Lane. Mrs Wolstenholme died only days after her daughter's birth, and left the infant to be placed in foster care in the nearby village of Walkden. She remained there until after her third birthday.[19]

By the time of his granddaughter's birth, Richard Clarke was approaching fifty years of age. His keen intelligence, marked by those around him, was a family trait which his granddaughter would inherit. A 'self-made' man, he had benefited from the opportunities offered by proto-industrialisation, and by working as a 'putter out' of cotton yarn to local weavers in the early years of the century, had extended both his income and his influence.[20] By the careful management of his business affairs he had elevated himself to the position of mill owner and earned the trust and respect of all. A memoir of Richard commented that, 'Finding employment first for himself, he by degrees raised his status and found employment for others, a faculty which was esteemed to be a great blessing in those days.'[21]

The family's comfortable lifestyle was not secure, however, and this situation impacted on Elizabeth's perception of herself in later years, when she became increasingly conscious of her position as 'a woman without wealth' in the circles in which she moved.[22] 'Rich women', whom she also often deemed 'idle', were particular targets for her venomous pen. Her feelings may have been formed when making a comparison of her heritage with that of colleagues. The leader of the Contagious Diseases Acts (CDA) repeal movement, Josephine Butler, for example, had grown up in comfortable circumstances as the daughter of land-owner John Grey and his 'strong-minded' wife Hannah.[23] Likewise, Jessie Boucherett was from an affluent background, her home the elegant Willingham Hall in Lincolnshire.[24] In contrast, Elizabeth's great-grandfather, Samuel Clarke, was employed as a hand-loom weaver who had moved to Roe Green in the late eighteenth century. Then, the village had an unenviable reputation owing to the extent of violence and drunkenness among its inhabitants, something which, as a devout man, Samuel worked hard to change. He issued an invitation to a group of evangelists to preach there in 1808, their sect an Independent Methodist group comprising some disaffected Manchester Wesleyans and a small number of Quakers from Bolton. One of the 'first fruits' of this mission was the conversion to faith of Samuel's future daughter-in-law, Richard's wife, Mary.[25]

Mary Clarke's faith deepened and she swiftly became a staunch follower of Independent Methodism. The small congregation rapidly expanded too and in the 1820s, as a consequence, Richard sanctioned an extension to their family home to provide a preaching room for the church. Here Mary instituted a flourishing Sunday school, which nurtured the faith of hundreds of local children. As an important and respected figure in village life, Mary was also a principal mover in fundraising efforts for the building of its chapel, which opened in 1855. To commemorate the dedication she donated the chapel's Bible. Mary died on 2 January 1857, and Independent Methodist historian, William Brimelow remarked in 1908 that she

> was most regular in her attendance at the means of grace, both public and private, and was exemplary in her character and goodness and in the beneficent influence she exercised. She warmly supported her husband in all efforts for the Church, and was kind-hearted and helpful to neighbours, especially the sick and any in trouble.[26]

The language of this tribute is, in fact, misleading, for Mary had been the one to foster the faith of her husband, who attested that she often took the lead role in family prayers.[27] However, in Brimelow's tribute she becomes the 'supportive' partner in a text which is phrased so as not to challenge conventional gender stereotypes. Her virtues are described in the traditional feminine frame of nurture, piety, generosity and exemplary moral character and the public nature of her work is subsumed beneath an account of these womanly virtues. Elizabeth's reminiscences of her grandmother are so few as to make it impossible to assess her thoughts on Mary's life – though there was fondness between them. In the mid-1850s, when Elizabeth's work as a governess called her from the area, she always returned to the house in Lumber Lane to spend her holidays with Mary.

To look back to Elizabeth's genealogy is not, therefore, to recover a heritage that places her as the social equal of many of the feminist pioneers of what came to be known as the 'Langham Place' set. She was, however, the scion of a kindly, generous family. Her character echoed her grandmother's open-handed nature and she gave away almost her last penny in the cause of her work for women. This often prompted concerned friends to insist that gifts of money were to be expressly '*spen[t] on yourself*'.[28] During Elizabeth's infancy, the large Clarke family enjoyed the fruits of Richard's labours and could afford to be generous. In addition to providing the preaching room as a source of spiritual succour to their neighbours, the family exhibited a philanthropic attitude by helping to alleviate pressing material need. Brimelow, who dedicated his account of Independent Methodism in Roe Green to Richard and Mary Clarke, noted that Richard's business, 'by finding employment' for those afflicted by dire poverty, had allowed them to obtain 'the material comforts of home and life'. The Clarke's benevolence was not simply limited to their employees, however. For when their son-in-law Joseph fell upon hard times, Richard was the one to offer a solution.[29]

THE FIRST ROE GREEN INDEPENDENT METHODIST CHAPEL.
(1855 – 1884)

Figure 2 Roe Green Independent Methodist Chapel, built 1855
Source: Reproduced with the permission of Roe Green Independent Methodist Church

The Reverend Joseph Wolstenholme, the son of a cloth weaver, remains a mysterious figure. Nothing is known of him until he arrived in Roe

Green from a ministry in Scotland during the mid-1820s, and his subsequent marriage to Elizabeth Clarke, on an unspecified date.[30] He was appointed to the parish in Cheetham Hill where Elizabeth was born, and three years after his wife's untimely death he married again. His bride, Mary Lord, was the daughter of a woollen manufacturer from Burnley.[31] The marriage provided a stable and comfortable family environment and, shortly afterwards, Elizabeth returned home from foster care. Nothing is recorded regarding the whereabouts of her elder brother Joseph Jnr during the years following their mother's death and the first mention of him recalls his time as an elementary pupil of a nonconformist academy in Sheffield.[32] Joseph had been born on 30 September 1829 and another child, a boy who succumbed to an infantile illness, preceded Elizabeth's arrival.[33] Following his remarriage, the nature of the Reverend JosephWolstenholme's work and ministry appear itinerant and from 1837 to 1841 the family removed from Cheetham Hill, via Heywood, to the coastal town of Sunderland. Here, one stormy day, the six-year-old girl watched with awe the 'devoted heroism of the life-boat crew' as they fought to rescue a stricken vessel in turbulent seas.[34]

Elizabeth named this emergency rescue as one of the 'most vivid of [her] early recollections' and the fact that it merits inclusion in a letter to McIlquham is itself a rarity. Perhaps, if she believed it would fall to Harriet to write her biography (though in 1908 when the letter was written she was hopeful of writing her own account), she thought it might serve as early evidence of her compassionate nature by recalling how she had joined the crowd of 'anxious watchers' who lined the pier.[35] While concealing so much about her childhood, she seems anxious here to play the role of 'truth teller', though in informing McIlquham of the events and concealing the personalities of those who witnessed the scene with her she tells at best only a 'half-truth' – something to tantalise rather than inform.[36] Nothing more is narrated about her life in the north-east and Joseph Wolstenholme's work there was of short-term duration. By the time of the 1841 Census he had returned to Roe Green to live in a house near his in-laws in Lumber Lane. Whether he had been unable to secure another ministerial position or whether his post had been that of a 'lay' preacher is unknown. However, an intriguing entry in his son's admissions record to St John's College, Cambridge five years later provides another view of Joseph's life.

The biographical entry for Joseph Wolstenholme Jnr on his admission as a pensioner to Cambridge University on 1 July 1846 notes that his late father held *two* occupations, those of Methodist minister and warehouseman.[37] It seems likely this employment was undertaken for his father-in-law and possible too that his home was part of a growing Clarke property base. Whether the Reverend Wolstenholme was already suffering undiagnosed symptoms of weakness while in Sunderland is unknown, but within a short while of his return to Roe Green he became seriously ill. Indeed, the family may well have returned to be cared for by the Clarkes, who had maintained close ties with their former son-in-law and grandchildren. It appears probable that this care extended into providing employment for Joseph in the family business, at least while his strength allowed. There were strong connections (both of commerce and of religion) between Richard Clarke and the textile merchants and industrialists of Manchester, and these were fellowships which his son-in-law shared. In the 1830s, for example, Joseph was the 'spiritual partner' of industrialist John Petrie, and it was in the arms of Petrie's daughter, Isabella, that Elizabeth watched Queen Victoria's coronation procession wend its way through Rochdale's streets.[38]

The fond memories of this incident, combined with the remembrance of her presence at the Manchester celebration for the repeal of the Corn Laws in 1846, could have been provided by Elizabeth as a means of legitimating her presence within these early reformist circles, with their links to the abolitionist movement. Aged twelve, she sited the birth of her political consciousness as having occurred while watching the Manchester procession. Her admiration for John Bright and Richard Cobden, the 'free traders' who saw the 'fair earth lapt in love and brotherhood' (sic) was boundless. And though she believed later exponents of laissez-faire had betrayed her faith, in 1846 she had 'drunk in' the creed of reform and viewed the whole with 'profound emotion'.[39]

As such recollections demonstrate, Elizabeth is more likely to provide memories of youth where they can be linked to her future political campaigns; but another incident illustrates an altogether more spiritual drama when the house in Lumber Lane became the setting for a memorable battle of wills between the seven-year-old and her father. It is easy to imagine Elizabeth's tiny, elfin featured, figure as she resolutely faced Joseph Wolstenholme and forced him to consider a question he had not the slightest intention of answering. Her queries 'regarding [a] childish opposition to the doctrine of eternal punishment' were considered impertinent and, worse, irreligious. She received a sound thrashing for her pains, an outcome she considered tyrannical and inappropriate. She had wished not to antagonise but to enter a dialogue with her father on the subject, and considered the actions of the one who, above all others, she 'wanted to revere' shameful.[40] The tendency always to be the one to ask the awkward question remained, though, throughout her life. One astute priest later observed that she was a 'natural sceptic [who] questioned everything'.[41]

Elizabeth called this incident her 'first little bit of martyrdom', and it was her earliest defiance of the doctrines of Christianity.[42] Religious scepticism was, however, a notable feature of Victorian feminist experience.[43] The consequences of such spiritual dilemmas could be extremely painful for all concerned; although Elizabeth's tender years had ensured she received physical chastisement rather than other, more subtle, punishments. One of her colleagues, Frances Power Cobbe, was banished from her father's house when he became unable to bear her presence and constant obstinacy in refusing to attend family prayers. This defiance was, Cobbe recalled, the site of her feminist awakening, for matters had assumed the shape of a sexual power struggle between father and daughter.[44] Elizabeth did not, seemingly, view her unjust beating in this way. She was, however, similarly banished, and placed in the first of a series of local girls' boarding schools, situated in the affluent district of Higher Broughton, Manchester.[45] She leaves no account of her time at elementary school, but it is possible to ascertain allusions to autobiographical testimony in her later disparaging remarks at the standard of education provided to the 'unhappy victims' of such regimes.[46] Her abhorrence of the 'frivolous' accomplishments which comprised the average curriculum brought about her sympathy with the works of Mary Wollstonecraft, whose bold and transforming philosophy of female education (published in *Thoughts on the Education of Daughters* [1787]) soon captivated her attention.[47]

It was a personal tragedy, however, that brought her back from a school in Leeds to Roe Green in July 1845. Upon her arrival, she found it her unpleasant task to care for her father throughout his final illness. She vividly recalled the 'long month' spent by his bedside, and the 'mournful delusions' brought on by his suffering. Hallucinating and confused, Joseph believed his wife was trying to poison him and, in consequence, accepted food only from Elizabeth's hands. The eleven-year-old girl was deeply affected, both by her father's physical symptoms and his treatment of her 'dear, good step-mother'.[48] He died on 20 August, and though obviously upset, Elizabeth appeared relieved that the trauma of her sick-room vigil was over. In the 1840s, there were no laws to grant Mary Wolstenholme any rights of guardianship to her stepchildren, and Joseph and Elizabeth were therefore removed from her care and consigned to the protection of their maternal family. They became the wards of George Clarke of 16 Spring Gardens, Worsley.[49] Mary Wolstenholme seemingly disappeared from her stepdaughter's life for almost a decade.

Elizabeth's experience of double orphanhood was unique among the leading members of the mid-Victorian feminist movement. She does not, however reflect on it deeply. In common with most of the recollections of her childhood, memories of teenage years are provided in letters to McIlquham in the wider context of contemporary events. The construction of the letters, in which the Clarke family members are always kept at a distance from Harriet provides little opportunity for 'contextualising' familial events into the wider narrative of Elizabeth's 'subsequent experiences' in the women's movement.[50] Only the most simplistic interpretation of their personalities is achievable and yet, by the application of supplementary evidence, it is possible to appraise the context in which the family lived. By understanding their role as key local figures, both in industry and religion, it is possible to see Elizabeth's sojourn within the Clarke family households as providing, in some measure, the 'crucible of subjectivity', which inspired and shaped some at least of her later actions.[51] And yet, unlike many of her colleagues, she was not to possess the leisure or the financial security which allowed them to pursue their feminist goals from the environs of privilege: something which makes her life all the more remarkable.

Young womanhood

Elizabeth's feminism was constructed through what she would later term as 'the stress of storm and strife'.[52] Her teenage years provided examples of these strong emotional feelings, not least her grief at the death of Richard Clarke on 8 August 1846. Though his mill was still a thriving business, the vibrancy associated with the family's rise to the merchant classes appeared to fade from this moment. No landed estate protected the Clarkes' wealth, and sibling rivalry ensured that Elizabeth's five uncles were not always on the best of terms. Tensions crept into Roe Green life, and the increasing precariousness of the family's finances is highlighted by the closure of the firm in the early 1860s: its fate apparently sealed by the effects of the American Civil War which brought the Lancashire textile industry to its knees.[53] It is not known precisely how such circumstances impacted upon Elizabeth's life for she 'silences' these events and distances herself from her family by the lack of detail she provides. It was, however, likely that in the more affluent 1840s a bequest from Richard Clarke's estate provided the 'happy chance' that propelled his highly intelligent and headstrong granddaughter to continue her studies at the Moravian School at Fulneck, near Leeds. She travelled there in the autumn of 1848 and remained until the summer of 1850. Her 'girlish individuality' was remembered long after her departure and her kind nature, combined with an obvious zest for life, made her a welcome friend.[54]

Recently discovered records attest to Elizabeth's academic prowess in a school which charged fees of upwards of £60 per year. In the second quarter of 1850, for example, the sum of 63 shillings was spent in relation to her pursuit of languages – the largest amount of any girl present.[55] Though clearly intended for non-conformist families of moderate means such as the Clarkes, it was not without opposition that Elizabeth took up her place at Fulneck. By the time she was fourteen, she was engaged in a battle of wills with her guardian regarding plans for her future. She was incensed at George Clarke's insistence that she confine herself to the 'useless' existence deemed socially acceptable for single, middle-class girls. And she had no compunction in allowing her outraged reaction to her uncle's comment that she 'had learned as much as any woman needed to know' to be made public.[56] To add insult to her injured feelings, her elder brother was encouraged to fit himself for a professional life. An academic career beckoned when he secured his MA in 1852 and, later, fellowships, first at St John's and then (somewhat controversially) at Christ's College, Cambridge.[57] A brilliant mathematician, Joseph enjoyed Cambridge life, but his younger sister was equally as intellectually capable and entranced by learning. She shared the frustrations of other young women who had to stand idly by as their brothers went to university, their admission justified by the issue of biological sex alone.[58] She shared with one future colleague, Emily Davies, the feeling that she 'had been sacrificed to [her] brothers' needs without compunction', and was keenly aware of the inadequacies of her own education in preparing her for a 'useful' adult life.[59]

Perhaps Richard Clarke, in bequeathing to his granddaughter the opportunity to study at Fulneck, had guessed that Elizabeth might find herself unable to submit to her guardian's will and remain happily in the domestic sphere. The two certainly had an emotional connection, and Elizabeth chose to share with Harriet McIlquham the confidence that her grandfather was 'even dearer' to her than her 'beloved' father.[60] Whatever the motives behind Richard's choice, her studies in the progressive educational environment she experienced at her secondary school equipped Elizabeth to earn her own livelihood. So limited, though, were the options available to genteel women for 'respectable employment' that a career in education seemed an obvious choice.

For the majority of single middle-class women, especially for orphans like Elizabeth, the life of a teacher or governess was not a prospect to relish, with its long hours, low remuneration and a station in life that was neither 'above nor below' stairs. Elizabeth, however, embraced this future wholeheartedly, and she returned from Fulneck in the autumn of 1850 having already formed the '*deliberate intention*' of becoming a teacher.[61] Whether she was encouraged in this ambition by interaction with a particular mentor among the teaching staff (quite a common occurrence at this time) is unclear, but her determination was unequivocal.[62] Moravian educators made a conscious attempt to provide girls with a more rigorous curriculum than was the norm elsewhere and, on her return home, Elizabeth begged her uncle to allow her to continue her studies by enrolling at the newly opened Bedford College, a request he refused.[63] In common with her criticisms regarding her chastisement by her father as a child, it appears to be the injustice of her guardians in declining a reasonable request, and what amounts to their dogmatic refusal to listen to her opinion, that most aggrieved her. Young though she was, she found their paternalism both arrogant and insulting.

Although her anger at their refusal was reported many years after the event took place, her discussion of it was conducted publicly. The extensive readership of the periodical *Westminster Review* is appraised of the circumstances in the first biographical interpretation of her life, authored in 1896 by Ellis Ethelmer (the pseudonym of Ben Elmy). Although the revelations within *A Woman Emancipator* are provided in retrospect, it is clear that Elizabeth approved of her husband's inclusion of her bruised feelings in his account. She thus tacitly sanctioned the insertion of the unhappy memories of the stultifying 'rigorous domesticity' to which she was subjected at home and which her family expected her to embrace dutifully.[64] Such was her resolve to fight her guardians' curtailment of her secondary education that between 1850 and 1852 she undertook an arduous programme of private study. The topics of political economy and law were incorporated into her self-devised syllabus – subjects which retained their place in the curriculum she would later teach as headmistress.[65] To fund the purchase of books and other essentials, the seventeen-year-old also tutored a small number of private pupils – although nothing is recorded of the identity of these young ladies. Elizabeth's desire to establish herself as a headmistress, and an 'independent' professional woman, is upheld both in public and private accounts of her life, and records one moment when an 'impudent intrusion' into the circumstances of her family life *is* permitted.[66]

In order to highlight the path she took towards entering the profession that would stimulate her public work, she obviously felt some details must be provided of the circumstances that led her to follow it. But the recollections are meagre. Even more constrained (and in this she is unlike many of her feminist counterparts) is any account of the principal reason for her 'conversion' to an overtly feminist consciousness.[67] The vital information is given in a single line in a letter that focuses almost solely on a public issue: the matter for which she became most famous, the rights of married women.

The bitter family quarrels surrounding Elizabeth's yearning for higher education occurred at precisely the same time as she acknowledged the 'iniquitous English law of sex slavery' that enforced the loss of personal identity of every wife in the land. The moment came when she was undertaking the duties of a bridesmaid. The identity of the matrimonial couple remains a mystery, but Elizabeth wrote that she had been 'so shocked' as she stood in the aisle of an Anglican church listening to the bride make her vows of 'obedience' that she swore never again to attend any similar ceremony.[68] It was a promise she kept all her life (even absenting herself from her brother's wedding in July 1869), though perhaps, as an honourable young lady of seventeen, she had an incomplete idea of what conjugal relations entailed.[69] As no contemporary memoir or diary exists to attest otherwise, we cannot know whether a youthful romance or disappointed matrimonial hopes might have coloured her impression of the married state. The prospect of spinsterhood, however, appears to have been not at all unpleasant, and the decision to seek a career is shown to be hers alone. This was not a universal situation amongst young women in her position, many of whom had been forced, by changing demographic and economic influences, to abandon comfortable homes in search of paid work. This was the state of affairs which, in part, had heralded the debates on the 'woman question': discussions in which Elizabeth would shortly take a prominent role.[70]

Governess and headmistress

In spite of George Clarke's disapproval, by late 1852 Elizabeth felt her studies had equipped her with sufficient knowledge to apply for the post of governess. She was employed by a family in Luton, Bedfordshire and remained with them until 1854. She recalls nothing of the pupils, or her employers and the only memory she offers of this time is of listening to the beauty of the call of skylarks in the surrounding countryside.[71]

Around the time of her twenty-first birthday, she returned to Roe Green where, on the advice of her guardians, she invested her small inherited capital (probably the residue of Richard Clarke's bequest) 'in a high class boarding school' under her own management and direction.[72] The ironic nature of the recommendation was not lost on Elizabeth, for now her family begged her to take up the very career which they had previously done their best to hinder. She wished, subsequently, to make public that it was her own perseverance which had fitted her for the task of equipping girls for paid employment, or, more commonly, for the world of companionate marriage and motherhood: and this at a time when more was being demanded of the conscientious wife than the ability to turn a neat stitch or play a tuneful duet.

Aided by Ellis Ethelmer's pen, Elizabeth expressed her public anger at her relatives' actions, through the auto/biographical study, *A Woman Emancipator*. Privately, however, other documents tell a contrary narrative. Ethelmer's biography gives the impression that she was left 'to struggle virtually unaided' in a 'desperately precarious' venture when she purchased her school, The Grange, in Boothstown Road, Worsley.[73] This picture of familial abandonment is misleading, however, for Worsley is situated only a short distance from Roe Green and Elizabeth was often to be found in the company her grandmother and cousins. On one memorable occasion in 1857, during a woodland walk with her uncle, she held open a park gate for Queen Victoria's carriage and received a gracious acknowledgement from the monarch as she passed through – a matter of delicious irony for the future young republican.[74] Though these memories portray a view of family relations that differs from Ethelmer's biography, it appears correct to suppose that Elizabeth was now responsible for her own livelihood and that little monetary assistance was made available to her at a time of recession in Clarke finances. The biographical narrative compares Elizabeth's economic position unfavourably with that of her brother, who was prosperous enough to spend considerable periods of relaxation in the Lake District with his closest friend, Cambridge luminary Leslie Stephen.[75] We can only speculate as to the extent of the financial support he gave his sister.

Memories of the youthful relationship between Elizabeth and her brother are few and though they shared a love of literature, and particularly poetry, they do not appear overly devoted. Only when Elizabeth recalled the events of the late 1860s does a deeper picture emerge, of shared religious and political opinions, and of personal intimacy. Nothing is told, however, of the feelings of two children united by the experiences of double orphanhood, and Ethelmer's narration of the differences in their situation acts to divide their lives rather than to imply unity. What is told appears to be a composite of 'selective' memories, recounted with either a conscious or an unconscious bias. Elizabeth is secretive about her continued fellowship with her family and chose to reveal instead their at best ambivalent, or at worst hostile, attitudes to her professional life. The image received paints her, as a pioneer feminist, in the best possible light.

While the Clarkes appear to have had little involvement in Elizabeth's professional life, one member of her family made a reappearance in the mid-1850s when Mary Wolstenholme moved to The Grange as her stepdaughter's housekeeper. It was an arrangement that worked efficiently and harmoniously, and the two ladies remained in one another's company until 1874. The Grange was, like many of its type, a small establishment, its compliment of pupils numbering a maximum of sixteen.[76] Its distinction came in the calibre and conscientiousness of its headmistress, whose opinions regarding the education of girls were far in advance of the norm. Pupils (aged between twelve and fourteen years) were drawn from the professional classes of Manchester and other northern towns. Their elementary education had, in Elizabeth's opinion, been poor, and she grew increasingly concerned at their lack of intellectual rigour.[77] Even in core subjects such as mathematics the standards were lamentable. She believed that unless something could be done nationally to improve the situation, generations of girls would remain destined for 'a sentence of lifelong pauperism and dependence': the whims and dictates of their male guardians binding them to a life of uselessness. This was something unsustainable in the present economic climate, she believed, and socially and morally unhealthy.[78] She later wrote that concern for her pupils' future struck 'fear' into her heart. And it was this emotional reaction, rather than any intellectual theorising on the subject, which prompted her to seek out the company of like-minded associates and 'to begin work . . . for the amendment of the evil laws which so cruelly oppressed womanhood'.[79] Elizabeth wrote many condemnatory words, both in public and in private texts, regarding the paucity and irresponsibility of mid-nineteenth-century female education. Yet, of all of these, it was the small postcard quoted above, and written at the request of an Edwardian autograph hunter, that offered one of the greatest insights into her motivation for taking up the mantle of a public life. Fear is a powerful motivator and Elizabeth owned it had been her own.

Reactions of parents to the education their daughters received in such establishments as The Grange may well have been mixed. Parents tended towards conservatism and some feared that girls would become devoid of feminine charms should they be educated by progressive methods. The mother of feminist Margaret Nevinson, for example, expressed the opinion that 'no one would ever marry a girl who read Greek', and Elizabeth recalled that textbooks were criticised if they were thought overly advanced.[80] Always mindful of the need to earn her living, she was forced to tread a careful path, least she find pupils withdrawn from her care. The perilous nature of self-employment must also have been a factor in May 1858 when she suffered a near-fatal illness and lay 'at the very gates of death'. It was during this time of fever-induced delirium that she experienced a prophetic vision of the world beyond the human realm, something which caused her soon to question the nature of the Christian creed of redemption – and to find it wanting. Rather than a resurrection of the body, Elizabeth's vision offered an interpretation of death which heralded a spiritual 'reunion with the constant life and force of the Universe'.[81]

Constantly appraised and re-evaluated over time it was this experience (perhaps more influential even than her quarrel with her father) that set her on the path to becoming a committed 'evolutionist'. Clearly influenced by scientific, Darwinian theories she argued later that 'the humanity of the future would as far surpass the humanity of today as we today surpass the limpet clinging to its rock'.[82] By viewing Elizabeth's life in the light of this experience it is possible to understand the forces undergirding her secular radicalism and the in-depth and scholarly way in which she approached complex questions of social reform. The nature of the human condition, and its improvement, would become a lifelong obsession and, unlike Charles Darwin, she ceased to maintain any form of religious adherence.[83] So profound was her concern and hope for the elevation of humanity that some colleagues found her 'other worldly' and idealistic.[84] This is the paradox that repeatedly confronts any deep reading of her texts and provides an image of romantic naivety which sits ill with her analytical, incisive intelligence. It helps explain, however, her deep engagement with the feminist philosophers of the Enlightenment. Though weeks later her health was restored, her faith struggles continued, in tandem with an increasing commitment to social reform.

Elizabeth was by no means isolated in her concerns regarding standards in her profession, particularly the effects of slovenly tuition on young minds, both of girls and boys. New theories of liberal education, specialising in a methodological approach, had produced calls for the professionalisation of the educational sphere. Teaching became viewed as an acceptable profession for women, but 'amateurs' were regarded critically.[85] Calls for proficiency testing were introduced, and in 1846 upwards of 300 teachers of both sexes had combined together as the College of Preceptors in order to campaign for pedagogical training. To this body, Elizabeth sent an application for membership in 1861.[86] Two strands of thought were uppermost in her mind, in addition to the practical task of raising educational standards. The first was a realisation that, as her experiences as a bridesmaid had highlighted, women's subjection (bound though it was to custom and tradition) was enshrined in law and in order to reform the situation changes at the highest level would be needed. She understood too that the issues of women's education and employment 'had to be *politically* linked' as well as being seen in the context of their social relevance.[87] Her second concern was that in upholding subjective laws by its ceremonies and statutes, she understood the Christian faith to be opposing, rather than supporting, a fair and just ordering of society – the most obvious example of this opposition being the denial of a married woman's right to the ordering of her own life and possession of her own body. The challenge to 'sex slavery' was, for Elizabeth, the taproot on which all other causes were grafted. The 'natural scepticism' noted by her parish priest in Worsley, and her increasing engagement with the theories of evolution, caused her many months of anxiety with regard to her personal faith.

She exhibited no such disquiet, though, when challenging the patriarchal notions that had bound her pupils in homes where a natural talent for learning was ignored or, worse, denied. Speaking to a distinguished audience of officials of the Crown in 1866 she noted critically that 'love of study' was too often regarded as a 'singularity in a girl'.[88] The evidence of her own life bore out that testimony, for her family viewed her as someone who held unconventional, ultra-progressive views – even though their own politics (as far as it is possible to suppose) show them firmly embedded in the radical-Liberal tradition of Bright and Cobden. Elizabeth's ambition was to ensure that every girl was educated in the values of 'sympathy . . . truth . . . [and] . . . justice'. To fail in this would, she argued, guarantee that women would be unprepared, either to educate their own children or to participate productively in the areas of public work into which poverty or necessity thrust them.[89] This required the cooperation of teachers, both with one another and with the state. Her first decade in public life was devoted to securing this laudable objective.

Notes

1 See figure 5.

2 EWE/HM, 5/6/1907, 47455, fol. 84.

3 EWE/HM, 24/6/1907, 47455, fol. 89.

4 Derek E.D. Beales, T.C.W. Blanning and David Cannadine (eds), *History and Biography: Essays in Honour of Derek Beales* (Cambridge: Cambridge University Press, 1996), p. 3.

5 EWE/HM, 27/11/1899, 47452, fol. 33.

6 EWE/HM, 31/3/1908, 47455, fol. 164.

7 Pankhurst, *My Own Story*, p. 43.

8 EWE/HM, 21/11/1901, 47452, fol. 221. Pankhurst, *TSM*, p. 32.

9 EWE/HM, 2/11/1906, 47455, fol. 1.

10 See, for example, Gillian Sutherland, *Faith, Duty and the Power of Mind: the Cloughs and their Circle 1820–1960* (Cambridge: Cambridge University Press, 2006); Daphne Bennett, *Emily Davies and the Liberation of Women* (London: André Deutsch, 1990); Lori Williamson, *Frances Power Cobbe and Victorian Society* (London, New York and Sydney: Rivers Oram, 2005).

11 Anon., 'Mrs. Wolstenholme Elmy', *The Manchester Guardian*, 13 March 1918.

12 Olive Banks, *Becoming a Feminist: The Social Origins of 'First Wave' Feminism* (Athens: University of Georgia Press, 1986), p. 9.

13 Sara Delamont, 'The Contradictions in Ladies' Education', in Sara Delamont and Lorna Duffin (eds), *The Nineteenth-Century Woman: Her Cultural and Physical World* (London: Croom Helm, 1978), p. 135.

14 Separate spheres ideology confined women to the domestic sphere by evaluating it as a haven from the turmoil of modern industrial life. It was the woman's task to create an emotionally secure environment where her husband and children would flourish, but selfless devotion to their wants and needs characterised her own existence. Kent, *Sex and Suffrage*, p. 34.

15 Holton, *Suffrage Days*, p. 1.

16 On the importance of such feminist networks see, for example, Sandra Stanley Holton, *Quaker Women: Personal Life, Memory and Radicalism in the Lives of Women Friends* (London and New York: Routledge, 2007); Wright, 'Impudent Intrusion', p. 249.

17 Anon., Report of a lecture by Mrs Wolstenholme Elmy, 'The Poet of the Nineteenth Century', Congleton Chronicle, 9 December 1893.

18 EWE/HM, 28/8/1907, 47455, fol. 104.

19 EWE/HM, 12/4/1902, 47452, fol. 283.

20 Details of Richard Clarke's business can be found in Pigot and Dean's Directory of Manchester & Salford, 1824–25.

21 William Brimelow, *Centenary Memorials of the Independent Methodist Church at Roe Green, Worsley* (Warrington and London: Mackie & Co. Ltd, 1908), p. 3.

22 Holton, 'Free Love', p. 218.

23 Jordan, *Josephine Butler*, p. 6.

24 Ellen Jordan and Anne Bridger, 'An Unexpected Recruit to Feminism: Jessie Boucherett's 'Feminist Life' and the importance of being wealthy', *Women's History Review*, 2006, Vol. 15, No. 3, pp. 385–412, p. 402.

25 Brimelow, *Memorials*, p. 8.

26 Obituary of Mary Clarke, *Independent Methodist Connexion*, August 1857, quoted in Brimelow, *Memorials*, p. 39.

27 Bert Tyldesley, *The Duke's Other Village: The Roe Green Story* (Neil Richardson, 1993), p. 15.

28 HM/EWE, 26/12/1895, 47450, fol. 239. (Emphasis in original.)

29 Brimelow, *Memorials*, p. 3.

30 Tyldesley, *Roe Green*, p. 15.

31 Marriage Certificate for 17 August 1837, Burnley Parish Church, County of Lancaster.

32 EWE /HM, 8/5/1908, 47455, fol. 172.

33 EWE/HM, 23/11/1891, 47449, fol. 197.

34 EWE/HM, 20/11/1900, 47451, fol. 137.

35 EWE/HM, 9 September 1908, 47455, fol. 205.

36 Avron Fleishmann, *Figures of Autobiography: The Language of Self-Writing in Victorian and Modern England* (London: University of California Press, 1983), pp. 9–18.

37 Biographical information on Joseph Wolstenholme Jnr. *Biographical Archive*, St John's College, Cambridge. Reproduced with permission of the Master and Fellows of St John's College.

38 EWE/HM, 20/11/1900, 47452, fol. 137.

39 EWE, 'Woman's Plea', p. 3. On feminist links to the abolitionist movement see, Barbara Caine, *English Feminism 1780–1980* (Oxford and New York: Oxford University Press, 1997), pp. 54–5.

40 EWE/HM, 12/5/1903, 47453, fol. 119.

41 EWE/HM, 8/8/1899, 47452, fol. 8.

42 EWE/HM, 12/5/1903, 47453, fol. 119.

43 Caine, 'Feminist Biography', p. 256.

44 Cobbe, *The Life of Frances Power Cobbe*, p. 100, quoted in Pauline Polkey, 'Reading History through Autobiography: politically active women of late nineteenth-century Britain and their personal narratives', *Women's History Review*, Vol. 9, No. 3, 2000, pp. 483–500, p. 489.

45 EWE to HM, 8/5/1908, 47455, fol. 172.

46 EWE, 'What Better Provision Ought to be Made for the Education of Girls of the Upper and Middle Classes?', *Transactions*, National Association for the Promotion of Social Science, 1865, pp. 287–91, p. 290. (Hereafter *Transactions*.)

47 Pankhurst, *TSM*, p. 31. Janet Todd, *Mary Wollstonecraft: A Revolutionary Life* (London: Weidenfeld & Nicolson, 2000), pp. 76–8.

48 EWE/HM, 28/8/1907, 47455, fn. 104.

49 *Biographical Dictionary*, St John's College, Cambridge.

50 Mayhall, 'Suffragette Spirit', p. 323.

51 Roper, 'Slipping Out of View', p. 67.

52 EWE, Untitled Poem, 1/1/1900, 47452, fol. 38.

53 EWE/HM, 11/9/1900, 47452, fol. 121.

54 Ethelmer, 'Woman Emancipator', p. 425.

55 Girl Boarders' Accounts, 1848–1863. D1/1. Fulneck School. Reproduced with permission of Mr T. Kernohan, Principal of Fulneck School.

56 Ethelmer, 'Woman Emancipator', p. 425.

57 Frederic W. Maitland, *The Life and Letters of Leslie Stephen* (London: Duckworth & Co., 1906), p. 48.

58 Lydia Becker wrote on the occasion of her brother Wilfred's going up to Oxford that she held the 'conviction that had the same opportunities been placed within [her] reach . . . [she] could have done as much, and might now have occupied as assured position in the world'. Joan E. Parker, 'Lydia Becker's 'School for Science': A Challenge to Domesticity', *Women's History Review*, 10 (4), 2001, pp. 629–50, p. 630.

59 Bennett, *Emily Davies*, p. 11.

60 EWE/HM, 20/8/1909, 47455, fol. 268.

61 EW, 'The Education of Girls, Its Present and Its Future', in Josephine Butler (ed.), *Woman's Work and Woman's Culture* (London: Macmillan & Co., 1869), p. 301. (My emphasis.)

62 Christina de Bellaigue, 'The Development of Teaching as a Profession for Women before 1870', *The Historical Journal*, Vol. 44, No. 4, 2001, pp. 963–88.

63 Barbara Bulmore, 'Moravian Education at Fulneck Schools, Yorkshire, in the Eighteenth and Nineteenth Centuries', unpublished PhD thesis, University of Manchester, 1992.

64 Ethelmer, 'A Woman Emancipator', p. 415.

65 Schools Inquiry Commission British Parliamentary Papers (Vols II and III) Miscellaneous Papers and Answers to Questions 1867–68. Education 18. (Shannon: Irish University Press, 1970). (Hereafter SIC); SIC, 16:244.

66 Martha Vicinus, *Independent Women: Work and Community for Single Women, 1850–1920* (London: Virago, 1985), chapter 1, especially pp. 12–20; Ethelmer, 'Woman Emancipator', p. 426.

67 Kean, 'Searching for the Past', p. 69.

68 EWE/HM (n.d.), August 1897, 47451, fol. 129.

69 Kent, *Sex and Suffrage*, p. 158.

70 Caine quotes a report by Harriet Martineau on the demographical changes affecting women. 'While the female populations ha[d] increased (between 1841 and 1851) in the ratio of 7 to 8, the number of women returned as engaged in independent industry has increased in the far greater ratio of 3 to 4', Caine, *English Feminism*, chapter 2, especially pp. 78–9.

71 EWE/HM, 17/3/1909, 47455, fol. 239.

72 Ethelmer, 'Woman Emancipator', p. 425.

73 Ethelmer, 'Woman Emancipator', p. 425.

74 EWE/HM, 28/1/1901, 47452, fol. 153.

75 Maitland, *Life and Letters*, p. 74; Ethelmer, 'Woman Emancipator', p. 425.

76 SIC, 16:190.

77 SIC, 16:200.

78 EW, 'The Education of Girls', p. 318.

79 EWE to Emily H. Smith, 24/4/1908, Paton Autograph Collection, GCRF 10/1/5, Girton College, Cambridge. Reproduced with the permission of the Mistress and Fellows, Girton College.

80 Margaret Wynne Nevinson, *Life's Fitful Fever. A Volume of Memories*, 1926, p. 17, quoted in Levine, *Feminist Lives*, p. 208: SIC, 16:219.

81 EWE/HM, 3/3/1906, 47454, fol. 221.

82 EWE/HM, 11/12/1892, 47449, fol. 310.

83 While noting that he relinquished his Christian faith when he was forty, Darwin nevertheless remained a lifelong member of his parish Church, St Mary's, Downe. William E. Phipps, *Darwin's Religious Odyssey* (Harrisburg: Trinity Press, 2002).

84 HM to Frances Rowe, 11/8/1901, 47452, fol. 195.

85 Christina De Bellaigue, *Educating Women: Schooling and Identity in England and France, 1800–1867* (Oxford and New York: Oxford University Press, 2007), pp. 108–11.

86 Elizabeth Wolstenholme was elected as an associate of this organisation in 1862. A list of the Council of the Board of Examiners, Fellows, Licentiates, Associates and other members of the College of Preceptors (London: December 1862).

87 Levine, *Feminist Lives*, p. 189.

88 SIC, 16:248.

89 EW, 'What Better Provision', pp. 288–9.

2

Headmistress: The education campaign 1862–67

Entering public life

Elizabeth's admission to the College of Preceptors marked the beginning of her public role. At the age of twenty-eight, she was now an experienced headmistress, following a profession she had consciously chosen. Her work suited both her abilities and her temperament. She believed passionately in the worthiness of her occupation and was convinced that young women shared both the rationality of their male peers *and* their aptitude for study. Mid-Victorian gendered ideology had, she argued, deliberately denied girls' intellectual needs by moulding them into preening, pious 'angels'.[1] Domesticity had left many stunted and unfulfilled and she was determined to break their shackles in the interests of human development. Her forward-thinking working practices, however, in no way mirrored the common experience of genteel education. Therefore, and in partnership with her new associates at the College of Preceptors, she set about achieving the transformation into a professional force of the shabby, decorous but amateurish mistresses who epitomised the image of female educationalists prior to the 1860s.[2]

Elizabeth found herself among kindred spirits within the College of Preceptors. Progressively minded, these men and women accepted that if women were to be emancipated then they must be educated for the consequences of that emancipation. Women's oppression had its roots in the supposition of an 'inferior' female intellect, a view Elizabeth vehemently contested. She remembered too, with horror, being given in her youth copies of the widely read conduct books by Sara Ellis. Ellis's works, aimed at a middle-class readership, insisted that the daughters, wives and mothers of England should be happy merely to perform philanthropic acts of charity and be 'content to be inferior to men – inferior in mental power, in the same proportion as [they] were inferior in bodily strength'.[3] Considering this view both erroneous and outmoded, Elizabeth was 'enraged'.[4] She saw her own experience as far from unique, and pointed out that the brains of thousands of girls had stagnated for want of intellectual exercise and too intense a concentration on 'fripperies'. A lack of academic rigour affected the wealthy and the cash-strapped alike and she argued that numerous single women (even those whose economic circumstances did not demand it) yearned to escape homes where they were viewed as mere 'substitutes for the curate, the nurse or the cook'.[5] She did not, however, see a strong world being built on philanthropy – almost the only way women could play a part in public affairs in a civil society dominated by the patriarchal, masculine, nature of the bourgeois public sphere.[6] Work, Elizabeth asserted, was the cure for 'idle hands and wasted brains' and only education, diligence and professional competence would help the unfulfilled find contentment via participation in an honourable (and remunerative) occupation. To achieve human progress, therefore, the world of work must be opened to middle-class women.[7]

Though the discourse of the 'surplus' single woman had been occupying the minds of intellectuals for some years by the early 1860s, Elizabeth was nonetheless fully aware that marriage and motherhood would form the context of most women's lives.[8] A record of a speech delivered in 1865 recalls her claim that it was 'the lot of almost *every* woman [to practice] careful fulfilment of those ... domestic duties which fall, or ought to fall' into her hands: vital obligations which a comprehensive education would ensure they performed admirably.[9] This illustrates the opinion that advances in secondary and tertiary education for bourgeois girls were achieved by feminists who took care to mount a campaign that expressed an '*adherence* to certain gendered ideologies' – even if they 'undercut' these presumptions subsequently.[10]

Elizabeth never denigrated motherhood, quite the contrary. Yet both she and her fellow reformers had at heart a more progressive agenda than merely educating girls to engage in stimulating conversation with professional husbands. This was to carve out a place for single and widowed middle-class women as respected participants in the public realm by 'professionalising' their work in education and, in addition, incorporating into the professional sphere other 'respectable' occupations including nursing and clerical work.[11] In staking a claim to a career such women were also 'aspiring to prestige', and amongst their number were those who shared with Elizabeth a clear sense of vocation to their task.[12] She felt, at last, as if she were at the heart of a fellowship network, and her membership of the College of Preceptors provided her with the contextual framework in which to test her radicalism in a public way. Nowhere, however, did she indicate that these new professional opportunities should be offered to married women or mothers.

Elizabeth's commentaries on the nature and purpose of women's education reveal an appreciation of how the instruction of middle-class girls and women impacted upon the advancement of humanity as a whole.[13] In October 1865, for example, she claimed that the true purpose of education was to prepare girls 'for a clear apprehension of the relative merits and claims of others' over the interests of self. This demonstrated her sympathy with the Liberal objects of social reform, selflessness and self-improvement – qualities advocated by one of her heroes, John Stuart Mill. Only such compassionate awareness, she pointed out, produced a human mind capable of understanding that 'justness of perception upon which . . . justice in action can be based'. And she desired that 'the utmost liberty of experiment' be applied when designing the most suitable patterns for study, for only 'under such conditions . . . [could] . . . the true process of natural selection develop that which is best' for human progress.[14] No human being, she believed, was 'incapable of rising to a worthy humanity', and the key to this happy conclusion was inclusivity, tolerance and training.[15]

Elizabeth delivered these opinions publicly, speaking personally before the Annual Congress of the NAPSS in 1865.[16] The organisation, lauded as 'an emblem' of the Victorian age, was designated by Mill as having brought 'together persons of all opinions consistent with the profession of a desire for social improvement'.[17] Elizabeth's paper, entitled 'What Better Provision Ought to be Made for the Education of Girls of the Upper and Middle Classes?', prompted robust discussion, and its later publication in the *Transactions* of the NAPSS provides one of the first documentary examples where we encounter her as a social theorist in 'real time'. From this date, the haze surrounding her life clears, and letters, reports, pamphlets and journalism provide evidence of thoughts and actions freshly experienced. The vivacity of her commitment shines through; though in no measure could the 1860s be viewed as the apogee of her achievements. They were, rather, a curtain-raiser on the whole. She shirked neither work nor responsibility and became the linchpin of a correspondence network that would become legendary. Recently, a strong case has been made, claiming that fellow campaigner Emily Davies '*was* the women's movement' during the 1860s.[18] Her labours, however, could be matched, and indeed surpassed, by Elizabeth who, of necessity, undertook a full-time teaching workload contemporaneously with her feminist commitments.

New acquaintances

Despite being brought up in a philanthropic environment, the prodigious organisational and critical skills that characterised Elizabeth's long public career were not honed by participation in her grandmother's nonconformist charitable networks, but via direct involvement in feminist endeavours.[19] While her humanitarian principles had been encouraged (for she owns they were *not* formed) by witnessing Mary Clarke's practice of religiously motivated philanthropy, her personal view was that 'religionism kill[ed] work'.[20] She believed that too focused a concentration on the trials or joys of a supposed afterlife prevented diligent toil by the human self-on-earth, and she saw little point in it. She was also unable to perceive in local acts of bourgeois largesse the means to raise the moral consciousness of a nation. In order to transform the miserable conditions of millions of women's lives this was a necessity. Elizabeth believed, therefore, that women must take the bold step of voicing their concerns themselves and act directly in the public sphere: precisely the route she had taken herself.

She was not unsympathetic, however, to the commitment that such actions required as, for some women who broke the cultural taboo surrounding female public speaking, the results could include familial and social ostracism. Reminiscing on this issue in 1907, Elizabeth recalled the cruel epithet of the 'shrieking sisterhood' that had been cast unfairly by the *Saturday Review* at the 'strong-minded ladies' (including herself) imprudent enough to practice 'stump-oratory'.[21] She was repulsed by such conservatism. In the more liberal environment of the NAPSS, however, women shared the platform at its peripatetic annual Congresses with the most notable male commentators of the age. Elizabeth, together with colleagues including Frances Buss, Emily Davies, Barbara Leigh Smith Bodichon and Jessie Boucherett took optimum benefit from the fact that the gender-inclusive policy of the society allowed for such a high-profile airing of their views – even if, at times, they differed from prevailing masculine opinions. 'Book learning for females', for example, did not meet with universal approval.[22] Remembering the courage she and fellow pioneers had shown in braving ridicule from all those who did not embrace liberal opinions towards women, Elizabeth noted she was 'glad to have lived at such a time [and] with such fellow workers'.[23]

It might have been expected that these pioneering women would have laboured in harmony, the challenging nature of their reformist agenda being contentious enough. There is clear evidence to the contrary, however, and campaigners often travelled down 'blind alleys' before settling on the kind of activism they favoured.[24] Neither was the language they employed in debate always conciliatory. Elizabeth, often with a cutting turn of phrase, regularly initiated linguistic brawls, and the sugar-coating of congeniality was sometimes extremely thin. This was especially true as the 1860s progressed. In 1862 however, though already active in spearheading Lancastrian demands for educational reform, she appeared far removed from the environment she would soon join – the affluent 'ladies of Langham Place'. This 'first centre of feminist activity' was formed in the mid-1850s and was led initially by Barbara Leigh Smith, Bessie Rayner Parkes, Adelaide Proctor and the colourful bohemian, Matilda Mary Hays.[25] The rooms taken at 19 Langham Place provided opportunities for women to seek both congenial company and employment in a sympathetic atmosphere, and Emily Davies, daughter of a Gateshead rector, became a key member of the group in 1861 on her removal to London. She quickly developed a close association with Leigh Smith's circle and shared a deep friendship with England's first accredited physician, Elizabeth Garrett (later Garrett Anderson).[26] A lack of sources makes it impossible to categorically chart the course of Elizabeth's introduction to these well-known figures in the history of mid-Victorian feminism, though it is tempting to view it as the outcome of an association with Frances Buss (Headmistress of the North London Collegiate School for Girls), who was a fellow member of the College of Preceptors. There is, however, another and hitherto unexplored possibility to explain how the acquaintance was formed, and for this it is necessary to return to the life narrative of Elizabeth's brother.

Joseph Wolstenholme's religious proclivities are only referenced once in his sister's voluminous correspondence. Its brevity, however, does not obscure the fact that, although an ordained priest in the Church of England, he shared the same scepticism about Christian doctrine which brought the career of fellow Cambridge academic Henry Sidgwick to an abrupt (if temporary) conclusion in 1869.[27] Elizabeth's own association with Sidgwick was to prove important for the women's movement but, as the 1860s dawned, she was mourning the changing direction of another friendship that had been very dear to her. This was with her brother's fiancée (Julia) whom she had known since girlhood. The couple had been betrothed since 1850 and the young women were 'as sisters' to one another. When told of Joseph's clandestine scepticism, however, the faithful Julia refused to countenance their marriage. Deeply honourable, she believed him to have been ordained against his convictions and, unable to sanction such duplicity, broke off the alliance. She became withdrawn and increasingly frail and died, still a spinster, shortly after Joseph's wedding to eighteen-year-old Swiss national Thérèse Rosalia Krauss, in July 1869. Elizabeth attributed Julia's demise to a broken heart and rarely showed warm feelings towards her sister-in-law.[28]

The lack of extant correspondence between Elizabeth and her brother makes tracing their networks difficult. Also, with few personal records remaining, Joseph's character is difficult to determine. Though his mathematical publications gained him an enviable reputation, he appeared an enigmatic man; an intellectual but incapable of sustaining a brilliant career.[29] He was close to Leslie Stephen, who had accepted a fellowship at Trinity Hall, Cambridge in 1857. Stephen (who would later find fame as an author and literary critic) was popular and his rooms were often crowded with a circle of engaging intellectuals. These included lawyers Henry and Edward Dicey (correspondents of Frances Power Cobbe) and political economist and future Postmaster-General, Henry Fawcett – who would subsequently marry Elizabeth Garrett's younger sister, Millicent. Joseph too had a place in this circle, but he was looked upon as an isolated, taciturn figure. Blessed with 'a gentle and diffident' temperament, his presence was hardly noted, and only Stephen's inclusion of him in his memoir marks out Joseph's status as a 'special friend'.[30] Stephen's sympathetic portrait below sheds light on the pain and isolation Joseph experienced in old age.

> I think especially of poor old Wolstenholme, called 'the woolly' by you irreverent children, a man whom I had first known as a brilliant mathematician at Cambridge . . . I liked him or rather was very fond of him, partly from old association and partly because feeble and faulty as he was, he was thoroughly amiable and clung to my friendship pathetically. His friends were few and his home life wretched. Julia (Stephen's wife) could not help smiling at him; but she took him under protection, encouraged him and petted him, and had him stay every summer . . . in the country.[31]

Later, one of Stephen's 'irreverent children', Virginia Woolf, made a pathetic character study of Joseph as the lonely Augustus Carmichael in her novel *To the Lighthouse*. [32] In part, this caricature resembles the 'life portrait' she made of him in her memoir *Sketch of the Past*, where he sat, an old man, 'in his beehive chair . . . watching the sea changing colour' at the Stephens' home in St Ives.[33] Joseph loved nature and isolation and developed a fascination with the wildness of the Lake District. There was even a suggestion that he would have liked nothing better than to have become a hermit at Wastdale. Stephen's ultimate assessment was that Joseph's 'heterodox opinions' made a Cambridge career 'unadvisable'. In 1871, by then a father of the first of his four sons, he relocated to the Royal Indian Engineering College in Surrey, where his twin consolations were 'mathematics and opium'.[34]

Before this sad descent into narcotic dependency, Joseph had thrived on the literary and legal discussions that ranged around Stephen's circle. This poses the question whether Elizabeth's evident interest in the law and political economy was also stimulated in conversations with this coterie. After her grandmother's death, she appeared to pass less time in Roe Green, and instead spent the long summer holidays in Cambridge with her brother, where his friends made certain her love of literature was indulged. She deeply admired the works of Tennyson, for example, and lines of his verse often punctuated her letters. So intense was her interest that she subsequently compiled a biographical lecture on the poet, which drew an audience of 300–400 enraptured listeners to Congleton in 1893.[35] In Joseph's case, a friend recalled that Stephen's 'extensive culture was most apparent when . . . discussing some question of special interest with Wolstenholme . . . whose acquaintance with the best English literature was almost encyclopaedic'. His 'brilliant' mind also loved nothing better than to grapple with the psychological complexities of Balzac's fictional characters.[36] This reminiscence provides a very different glimpse of Joseph from that of the sad, isolated man portrayed in Woolf's construction of Carmichael, and a glimpse of shared interests between brother and sister. More important, perhaps, is that it is via a consideration of her brother's life that a plausible interpretation evolves of how Elizabeth's network of friendships developed from associations with provincial reformers to include the names of Garrett, Leigh Smith, Boucherett, Cobbe and John Stuart Mill's stepdaughter, Helen Taylor – the key figures of metropolitan feminism.

Langham Place

The shape and direction of the mid-Victorian women's movement was highly influenced by the personality of Barbara Leigh Smith. Born illegitimate, but to a doting, wealthy and politically active father, the individualistic Leigh Smith was, in contrast to Elizabeth Wolstenholme, financially secure.[37] Thus she was able to approach her feminist work from the perspective of benevolence as well as conviction. After collaborative, but unsuccessful, efforts with the Law Amendment Society to secure property rights on behalf of married women prior to the passage of the 1857 Divorce Act, Leigh Smith acquired the failing *Waverley* periodical in 1858, shortly after her wedding to Eugene Bodichon, an émigré French doctor. She then lived for part of each year in Algiers, lessening her influence as de facto leader of the women's cause.[38] However, with her friends Bessie Rayner Parkes and Matilda Hays as co-editors, the *Waverley* was swiftly relaunched as the *Englishwoman's Journal* (EWJ) and published by Emily Faithfull's Victoria Press from 19 Langham Place.

Rayner Parkes considered the periodical noteworthy because she believed it 'brought the thinkers and workers of the movement together': though Emily Davies (a later editor) qualified this with the view that it had been 'very little use as a rallying point'.[39] It was perhaps more significant for the establishment of a feminist 'community' that Langham Place was also the headquarters of the Society for Promoting the Employment of Women (SPEW), founded in 1859 by Jessie Boucherett as an offshoot of the NAPSS. Emily Davies, drawn into this circle as the sister of NAPSS co-founder Reverend J. Llewelyn Davies, shared with Boucherett and with Elizabeth the view that lack of skills and intellectual ignorance determined women's dire place in the labour market. 'It is indeed no wonder', she commented, 'that people who have not learned to do anything cannot find anything to do.'[40] They determined to effect a change in these sad circumstances. Davies founded a branch of SPEW in Gateshead prior to her departure in 1861 and Elizabeth followed in her footsteps five years later, by proposing the motion (during a meeting of the NAPSS Congress) that established the Manchester office.[41] The *Daily News* of 9 October 1866 reported that the Vicar of Worsley St. Vincent Beechey, had highlighted to the gathering the crucial role local schoolmistresses would play in equipping their pupils with skills to secure productive employment.[42] Elizabeth's role in educating him in this opinion was not insubstantial.

Beechey, in addition to his clerical duties, was a keen educational theorist, and had acted for some years as examiner to pupils at The Grange. He shared Elizabeth's vision that an accredited teacher, secure in her own knowledge, could become a powerful conduit of social reform. 'Mere native kindness of heart, [or] common sense' would not suffice, she argued, and educators must take on the task of 'reform[ing] themselves' in order to tackle the particular problems of modern life.[43] The drive for pedagogical training for teachers represented part of a much wider agenda, and provided 'the key to [the] broad range of freedoms' that feminists sought.[44] Associations such as the NAPSS also provided a platform from which a united public opinion could press for legislative change. Social reform, however, depended not only on the state, but on the individuals within that state who would implement the changes – those at the 'coal-face'. Elizabeth understood herself as an 'active worker', and her association with the NAPSS offered her both an influential entrée to bourgeois public space and the chance to shape a better world. It also furnished her with introductions to some of the most prominent men the realm.[45]

The NAPSS was only one part of the complex network of associations which brought Elizabeth into fellowship with the Langham Place set. Few of these women, however, remember her fondly. Indeed, she and Bodichon were only occasional correspondents, and Elizabeth commented uncharitably that Bodichon's influence in the movement was based principally upon her ability to fund it. The self-sacrificial labours *she* prized as the most honourable service were, she declared, more evident in the case of Emily Davies than Bodichon.[46] For her part, Bodichon referred to Elizabeth simply as 'a friend of . . . Miss Davies' who worked in Manchester, something which implied that her locality diminished her significance in Bodichon's mind. No impression of friendliness is formed.[47] Parochialisation of her efforts upset Elizabeth, who later voiced her belief that an unfair privileging of the activities of London personalities had been recorded the in histories of the women's movement. She felt the actions of the northern radicals had been marginalised, and on one notable occasion claimed that bold moves could best be made at a distance from 'London intrigues'.[48] Though smarting a little from the apparent condescension of her new acquaintances, when Emily Davies wrote from London in early 1864 with a request that she raise signatures to a petition to secure the permanent extension of the examinations of the Cambridge Local Board to girls, Elizabeth was perfectly placed to aid her.

Davies had begun this campaign in a small way, thinking it prudent not 'to demand too much too quickly' and, by doing so, alienate prospective supporters.[49] In 1862, she had established a small mixed-sex committee of sympathetic associates which included (in addition to Bodichon) the Recorder of London, Russell Gurney, Lady Goldsmid and Isa Craig, the first woman to hold office as Assistant Secretary of the NAPSS.[50] No working schoolmistress, however, had been approached to serve. Bodichon's long-standing friend Frances Buss was owned to be 'too timid' to offer her support, a statement which upholds Elizabeth's terse and rather uncharitable opinion that Buss had 'little or nothing to do with the *larger* movement' for women's education.[51] Far from faint-hearted herself, Elizabeth welcomed Davies's assertive stance and the two found their ideals

compatible. Within weeks they had organised a memorial of '900 teachers of girls of the upper and middle classes' which was presented to the
Vice-Chancellor and Senate of the University of Cambridge in order to
press for girls' inclusion in the tests.[52] The University of Oxford had
dismissed the idea out of hand.

Elizabeth recalled these eventful days for her friend McIlquham in
1908. Placing herself centre-stage, she wrote that the 'education fight' had
been spurred on its way despite 'great difficult[ies] . . . as the result of a
largely signed Memorial, which Emily Davis & I got up mainly . . . [to]
persuade the Senate of Cambridge University to admit girls to the *Local
Examinations*'.[53] In fact, though not to diminish her contribution, plans
had already preceded apace beforehand, the first trial examination held
on 14 December 1863 in Suffolk Street, London. This was only six weeks
after the Cambridge Syndicate had sanctioned the girls' participation in
a one-off experiment. Despite Davies's satisfaction at the performance
of the 91 girls entered (all except for their lamentable arithmetical work),
she was well aware that the authorities had granted the experiment for
one year only.[54] Thus the hard task of lobbying and persuasion to enable
the permanent establishment of the scheme began again the following
spring. The critical reaction to a paper presented on her behalf by Sir
Joshua Fitch to the NAPSS that autumn provoked 'white-hot fury' in
Davies's heart, for she then realised the extent of the prejudice reformers
faced.[55] Not until 10 March 1865 did she learn the happy news that the
Cambridge Senate, by the narrow margin of 55 votes to 51, had agreed to
the permanency of the examination. Girls would be examined on the
same terms as boys (though in different venues) from that winter. Dining
with a tense and nervous Davies the evening before the vote had been
Joseph Wolstenholme's confidante, Leslie Stephen – who had talked
critically of her plans throughout the meal.[56]

Elizabeth, meanwhile, had been fielding similar scepticism in Manchester. Nonetheless, when the first cohort of pupils from The Grange
entered the examination room of the Royal Institution in December 1865
some, at least, of the local sceptics were converted. Elizabeth personally
chaperoned her students to the examinations, conscious that their
parents would wish her to be seen as guardian of their daughters' honour.
She was confident of their ability, but apprehensive of their reception. A
letter she received from the male Superintendent of the examination
attested, however, to a change of heart. He informed her that, although
'previously opposed to the Exam. of girls . . . [he] . . . went back home
[a] reformed spirit'.[57] All twenty-one pupils from The Grange passed
the tests.

Though she wrote with the benefit of hindsight, narrating the history of the Cambridge Local Examinations to McIlquham prompted Elizabeth to contemplate her life as she approached her seventy-fifth birthday. Looking back across almost five decades of hopes, disappointments, successes and despair triggered the recollection that she had, 'all [her] life . . . so much to do with the initiative of various movements'. She believed each campaign had, in its own way, ensured a 'glorious harvest' of reform – although she was aware that there was much still to do and many cultural suppositions to confront. Far from being a woman who deprecated her efforts in public work, Elizabeth wrote that 'errors of initiative cost so much & are so far reaching that I am very thankful, looking back, to find relatively *so few*'.[58] She had an almost excessive reserve of impeccable judgement and while it might be possible to argue that her reasoning was subjective on the matter (and her words immodest) there is little evidence to gainsay its essential message. She was, indeed, at the heart of every new initiative.

An initiator of movements

Two weeks after Emily Davies was forced to listen to Leslie Stephen's critical conversation over dinner, she met with some female friends to enjoy a more convivial evening. The participants were the guests of Mrs Charlotte Manning in Kensington and their purpose was to debate the first of a series of topical social and political subjects.[59] The gathering was a 'delightful set' of the most thoughtful and scholarly women in the land, and though Davies understood it would be impossible for Elizabeth to be present at every meeting of the newly formed Kensington Society (KS), she wished that her friend be drawn into its circle.[60] Keen to participate in the stimulating exchange of views the group promised, she contributed a written reply to the first question posed.[61]

Elizabeth's paper addressed the motion 'What is the true basis, and what are the limits, of parental authority?' and the stance she took argued that, as children grew, an 'element of respect' between the generations was essential. This allowed, not for a sweet, 'clinging fondness', but for mutual respect and affection to develop. The prime duty of parents was, she suggested, that they educate their children in the qualities of 'self-guidance & control, & to discharge rightly & worthily all the duties of life'. A child's natural 'spontaneity [and] affection' would secure their respect for a 'wise parent', who would lead by example in showing 'unselfishness, wisdom' and compassion.[62] The influence of utopian socialist views is obvious here, for her words uphold Robert Owen's premise that 'people learned through the way they lived [and] through their whole culture'.

Elizabeth praised too the merits of coeducation as a stimulus through which to encourage the 'best moral results' in pupils; as the means by which children would honour their mothers and interact more sympathetically with the wider world. And though her words do not specifically challenge, as Owen did, the power of the nuclear family unit to create a New Moral Society, she did encourage the young to interact as widely as possible with their peers to foster a spirit of inquiry and collaboration.[63] Her paper to the KS presented a very different view of the topic to that posed by Miss Heaton, who claimed simply that 'The true basis of parental authority is the Fifth Commandment.'[64] As these two examples highlight, the KS was a meeting point for discussion of severely divergent opinions. However, the group's historian, Anne Dingsdale, has pointed out that the most 'striking feature of [their] bonding was respect for the opinion of the individual [and a] shared sympathy in spite of difference.'[65] This is certainly upheld when reviewing Elizabeth's experience of the society. For her it also operated as a bureau of introduction, and as a means of helping her widen the circle of her feminist activity – even across the barriers of class.[66] And though already well aware of the work of the SPEW, it was while she was visiting Davies in the summer of 1865 for the purpose of attending a KS meeting that the introduction to the organisation's founder, Jessie Boucherett, was made. During what Elizabeth later termed as 'a time of living enthusiasm and vigorous initiative' an important new friendship was born.[67]

Though her association with Boucherett would be significant, the two women did not see eye to eye over every aspect of their work. They held diverse views, for example, on the subjects of two subsequent campaigns which were very close to Elizabeth's heart: the repeal of the Contagious Diseases Acts and married women's voting rights. Boucherett was 'honestly shocked' at her friend's deep involvement in the CDA agitation, considering the sexual subject matter as an unmentionable topic. There was, however, clear evidence of mutual sympathy in other areas, and only weeks after their first meeting, Boucherett journeyed north from her luxurious home in Leicestershire to holiday at The Grange. Though term had not ended, in the evening, when lessons were done, the women talked and their friendship matured as they 'concoct[ed] plans' for the future. Boucherett, observing closely, realised Elizabeth's potential worth to the women's movement, her clear-sighted intellect and keen knowledge of the law. And her conclusion was that the work of a headmistress was not the best use of her new friend's prodigious talents. Elizabeth recalled that, during their conversation, Jessie Boucherett had been 'desperately anxious that [she] should give up teaching and devote [herself] solely to the legal works needed in connection with the women's cause'. Neither was the request was an 'empty' plea, for with it came the offer of an annuity of £100, 'so settled that it should be independent of [Jessie's] life or any change of her views'. Putting all thoughts of financial security aside, Elizabeth refused, her reason being simply that she 'loved [her] work'. Her labours in the women's cause were vocational, teaching her profession, and she was not tempted by the money.[68]

It has been argued that Boucherett's generosity to fellow feminists simply 'transferred some of the *noblesse oblige* imperatives of her landed background into her feminist life'.[69] Her offer to Elizabeth, though, was sensitively made and just as cordially rejected – with no evidence of ruffled feathers on either side. It is tempting, with hindsight, to place the beginning of Elizabeth's later sensitivities over her financial position as a paid employee of women's organisations to this moment, but to do so would be erroneous. As Boucherett's holiday ended, the thoughts of the two friends were all of the future. Elizabeth began to write and plan her paper for the forthcoming NAPSS Congress and, in addition, to put into practice her long-cherished dream of establishing a local association for women teachers. The Manchester Board of Schoolmistresses (MBS) was inaugurated on 2 December 1865, the day following her thirty-second birthday. Elizabeth (who took the role of honorary secretary) was proud of the organisation, whose membership grew steadily, and it provided a blueprint for other female teaching professionals in Leeds, Sheffield, Edinburgh and Newcastle-upon-Tyne to follow.[70] She understood that the campaigners were only 'at the beginning' of the journey, but she held true to her belief that the best way to secure meaningful social reform was to 'offer to women as well as girls, the opportunity of real study . . . by extending the facilities of higher education available to them'.[71] Having secured the introduction of the Cambridge Local Examinations for girls, the reformers did not rest on their laurels. They turned their ambitions towards preparing young women for university entrance. In the spring of 1866, Elizabeth took her arguments in favour of this arrangement directly to the heart of the British establishment.

Schisms and factionalism

Emily Davies's correspondence offers little to suggest that her opinion of Elizabeth was overly fond. Elizabeth's letters, however, offer fulsome praise of Emily. 'Miss Davies gave her *whole life-work*' to the women's education cause, she wrote, and '[h]ers was the conception, the brain & the infinite toil of years' that blessed the work.[72] Despite the lack of reciprocal warmth on Davies's part she must, in fact, have valued Elizabeth highly. For example, when Henry Roby, Secretary to the Schools Inquiry Commission (Taunton Commission) asked Emily to supply witnesses to testify to the position of girls' education, Elizabeth's was among the names put forward. The Commission had been formed to inquire specifically into the education of *boys*, but Davies had demanded (with particular persistence) that its scope be widened to include girls.[73] Elizabeth's had been one of the signatories to a memorial Davies had forwarded to the Commissioners pleading for the girls' inclusion, and on the 19 April 1866 she presented her evidence in person before Lord Taunton and his associates. She was among the first women ever to testify before a Royal Commission.

The official transcript shows Elizabeth's answers to have been comprehensive, concise and direct.[74] She was not overawed by the occasion and expressed her opinions on the education of middle-class girls along broadly similar lines to those she had given in her paper 'What Better Provision'. Her answers, though, also provided insights into her personal experience as headmistress of an independent school. In a theme she would develop further in her 1869 essay, *The Education of Girls*, she was scathing regarding the restrictive application of educational endowments, which provided many boys with opportunities unknown in the female sector. Elizabeth noted that 'many women, and amongst them many of those who would best repay the highest culture, are prevented by poverty from getting anything like a complete education': and she poured scorn on what she considered to be the misappropriation of those endowments intended for the education of both sexes (such as that of Christ's Hospital), which had been socially engineered to boys' preference.[75] She also stated (keeping faith with her colleagues in the College of Preceptors) that she fervently believed in the implementation of a higher examination to accredit teachers, arguing that 'the basis of every such test should be the admission of the principle of a common education for men and women'.[76] It was this profession of intellectual equality which, she believed, would open the universities to her sex. It was one thing, however, for feminists to campaign for this as an ideal – quite another for them to achieve a consensus on the means of achieving it.

Elizabeth returned from London to Worsley, to a frenzy of activity, not all of it connected to women's education reform. She was soon engaged in negotiations for the relocation of her school to Congleton, the north Cheshire town where she would spend the remainder of her life. The move to Moody Hall, a late eighteenth-century house of substantial size, was made in May 1867 and Elizabeth took over the lease from a member of the local gentry. Her reasons for moving to Congleton were not recorded, but she noted the event in connection with the timing of her introduction to another indomitable figure of the women's movement: Lydia Ernestine Becker.[77] The issue that prompted their meeting was not education, but another, more controversial matter – the campaign for women's suffrage.

There is a case for arguing that, for Elizabeth, the suffrage question was a subsidiary concern during the mid-1860s. Nonetheless, and as readers of mid-Victorian feminist histories know well, the election to Parliament of John Stuart Mill in July 1865 prompted the ladies of the Kensington Society into a flurry of activity. Mill had agreed to present a petition in respect of women's parliamentary enfranchisement (under the householder franchise) – something which had been outlawed under the provisions of the Reform Act 1832. And though this earned him the soubriquet of 'the man who wants to have girls in parliament' the popular perception that he was the saviour of the women's movement was not universally held by contemporaries: Emily Davies, for example, being a fierce critic.[78] Analysis of Mill's texts has also offered a highly 'contentious' assessment of his opinions on women's subjection: one assessment being that his view was rather 'narrow, [and had] almost nothing to say about single women', the issue with which mid-Victorian feminists were, at that moment, most concerned.[79] Elizabeth witnessed Mill's speech to the Westminster electors in the company of Emily Davies, but although she claimed his influence as a 'champion' of the women's movement to have been substantial, she was not overawed by his reputation. She was quite prepared to voice an opinion of her own, even when it dissented from the eminent statesman's views. As Mill took his seat in Parliament, however, their thoughts on the enfranchisement of women were in accord.

Her biographer recalls that Barbara Bodichon began the KS's campaign to collect signatures to the ladies' petition on 11 May 1866.[80] Elizabeth, however, was ahead of her. So as to be prepared for the campaign, she had formed, the previous October, a 'small committee'. Designated the Manchester Committee for the Enfranchisement of Women (MCEW), its purpose was solely to collect signatures for the important memorial.[81] The 300 names she forwarded to the London National Society for Women's Suffrage formed one-fifth of the petition's total of 1,499. She later noted that her friends on the MBS had proved to be 'the first and the best' of suffrage workers, demonstrating that campaigners were aware that more than one cause could claim their loyalties.[82] Though Mill's tabled amendment to Disraeli's Second Reform Bill failed lamentably when it came before the House of Commons in May 1867, the act of gathering signatures in the suffrage cause proved to be of great personal benefit to Elizabeth. This was because it had brought her into contact with two women, Josephine Butler and Anne Jemima Clough, with whom she would collaborate to construct a workable solution to the problem of women's entry into higher education.[83] Clough and Butler, however, were assured of their place in history many years before Elizabeth's role was acknowledged.

Elizabeth chose to narrate to McIlquham an extremely personal account of her meeting with Josephine Butler. She did so in the light of a critique of Helen Blackburn's 1902 history of the women's suffrage movement, in which, she claims, serious errors were made – not least in the omission of much of her own labour. Keen that others whom she believed to have been the key workers in the movement were also given their 'proper place', she wished to give her friend 'the facts'.[84] She introduced, for example, the moment when Jacob and Ursula Bright joined the MCEW Committee in November 1865, and how, with such high profile new members in its ranks, discussions had centred on ways to entice more. She informed Harriet that

> We thought that our Committee would be strengthened if we made it a Lancashire Com. & I, as Hon. Sec. (& also as a private friend) wrote to Miss Davies, asking her, whether amongst the Lancashire signatures sent direct to her, there were any of persons likely to be helpful in the matter. She sent me Mrs. Butler's name & address, & also a charming little note which had accompanied the signature. I wrote to Mrs. Butler. She answered, begging me to go over to Liverpool & spend the day with her. I went, & we were friends from the moment we met.[85]

Elizabeth made the journey in May 1866 and both Josephine, who was already involved in various philanthropic projects, and her husband George, then Principal of Liverpool College, welcomed her warmly.[86] Another connection, this time between Butler and Anne Jemima Clough, soon ensured a mutual acquaintance with Elizabeth. Clough quickly formed the impression that her new colleague was 'organisationally competent', with an 'excellent network of contacts'.[87] Elizabeth's more contemplative opinion of Anne was that she was 'one of the best and most thorough workers [and the owner of] one of the truest of human souls'.[88] The three friends showed a true accord as they worked to frame their demands to further women's studies. Unfortunately, their ideas con-flicted with those of Emily Davies to such an extent that *her* close friend-ship with Elizabeth fractured completely under the strain.

Such a breach seemed inconceivable when Davies travelled north, in October 1866, to address a meeting of the MBS. She had written previ-ously to the Dean of Queen's College that it was now her firm belief that only an examination 'judged by the same standard' as the ordinary degree examinations of the University of Cambridge would truly attest to women teachers' professional competence.[89] Her speech in Manchester cemented these plans in her mind and, returning to her lodgings that evening, she concluded that only a designated women's college would provide the studious environment needed to prepare young women for the examinations. She swiftly drafted a programme of the proposed venture and sent it to Elizabeth who, with fellow members of the MBS, debated the issue on 2 February. Warm approval from both female and male teachers (who had been consulted separately on the matter) was received.[90] It was Davies's insistence, though, that the proposed women's college adhere precisely to the curriculum followed by male undergradu-ates, which proved to be the stumbling block to continuing collegiality. For even among the university community there were serious concerns as to its effectiveness in fitting young men for admirable lives. If reforms were needed, as most allowed, why were women so anxious to pursue the current mode of study?[91]

The following month, Anne Jemima Clough (by now an honorary member of the society) was invited by Elizabeth to address the MBS. Clough outlined her idea for a peripatetic lecture scheme for both pri-vately tutored and secondary school girls. She also advocated the inau-guration of a council, drawn from members of local Schoolmistresses' Associations in Leeds, Manchester and Sheffield, to coordinate a lecture series that was to herald the birth of the University Extension move-ment.[92] Clough's idea was enthusiastically supported, and the North of England Council for Promoting the Higher Education of Women was established in November 1867. Elizabeth represented the city of Manchester on the committee, which also included in its ranks Miss Lucy Wilson, her counterpart in Leeds. Clough became the organisation's Honorary Secretary and Josephine Butler (encouraged to stand for elec-tion by her husband) took office as President. It was Elizabeth, however, who drew up the rules of the organisation which were designed, as Clough put it, 'to keep [them] together'.[93] Sheila Lemoine has argued that '[t]hose present at that meeting of the Manchester Board of Schoolmistresses created an organisation which altered their lives and immeasurably increased their professional sophistication and authority', and it would be impossible to deny Elizabeth's pivotal role in proceedings.[94] She is also claimed as an 'intimate friend' by the young Cambridge academic persuaded to undertake the first series of lectures in astronomy, James Stuart. Stuart would later become an influential parliamentary figure, but as a graduate was delighted by this 'unexpected opportunity [for] starting a peripatetic university'.[95] Such was the demand for the lectures that 550 students enrolled immediately – something which caused another enthusiastic part-time tutor, F.W.H. Myers, to comment that the venture was 'a small thing accomplished, but . . . a great thing begun'.[96]

Worthy though the North of England Council's scheme appeared, it did not match Davies's idea of the future of women's higher education. Indeed, she wished it postponed on the grounds that its popularity was harming plans for the residential college she longed for, and which she and Elizabeth had discussed in April.[97] She conceded only that local lectures offered a 'little temporary stimulus' to such bookish young women as were content to dip in and out of a mismatched programme of study.[98] Davies was also particularly disappointed, and angered, at what she perceived the 'loss' of possibly her ablest lieutenant: for Elizabeth (in company with Butler and Clough) had expressed her willingness to engage with ideals which centred on the adoption of a 'separatist' curriculum, one where courses would be designed specifically to enhance women's employment prospects as teachers, governesses or nurses. This, to Davies, seemed to deny the principle upon which their actions had been based – one of wholesale equality. Given Elizabeth's heritage and previous associations, however, her leanings towards what Davies saw as a 'half loaf' of reform are understandable.

Davies recorded her distress in her diary at the close of 1867. She believed 'the beginning of the *great trouble*' had been a meeting called to 'discuss a scheme for the examn. of [women] teachers by a voluntary Board' (*sic*) of Oxford and Cambridge dons. Elizabeth had helped to organise this meeting, held on 14 December at the Society of Arts, and had been aided by George and Josephine Butler, F.W.H. Myers, and the cleric and historian, Charles Kingsley. Davies felt that Elizabeth had been duped and seduced into complying with plans to secure a specific women's examination, and she applied the stinging metaphor that her friend had been 'captured' – almost as if by an enemy.[99]

Sadly, there is nothing in Elizabeth's public or private correspondence that charts the breakdown of their friendship and though Davies later toned down her criticism, noting that she had not 'mean[t] by this that the different agencies are in the least really antagonistic', wariness remained.[100] From her diary record, written perhaps in the heat of the moment, it appears that Davies felt personally betrayed by Elizabeth, who obviously did not feel a 'captured' follower but a trendsetter. Davies maintained her cause, and with the founding of Hitchin College (later Girton) instituted, as she had wished, what she felt to be the 'superior' curriculum, based on the existing degree course.[101] Elizabeth, however, believed the 'special' examination would find favour, and also have a real chance of success in helping to cement the concept of a trained, female teaching professional. She was proved correct. At the end of 1867, in the midst of a whirlwind of activity, she travelled constantly to meetings, wrote, hosted speakers and all the while gave dedicated service to her pupils. Her work, both paid and voluntary, had opened her eyes to many things. She came to realise too that it was not enough, for her, to devote her energies merely to the one reform on which she had set her heart – the professionalisation of teachers. Important though this was, it was not the whole story. Therefore, as the New Year approached, she began the campaign by which she would become defined, the challenge to the 'slavery' of the English wife.[102]

Notes

1 Catherine Hall, 'The Early Formation of Victorian Domestic Ideology', in S. Burman (ed.), *Fit Work for Women* (London: Croom Helm, 1979), 15–32.

2 Joyce Senders Pedersen, *The Reform of Girls' Secondary and Higher Education in Victorian England: A Study of Elites and Education Change* (New York and London: Garland, 1987), pp. 62–171.

3 Sara Ellis, 'The Daughters of England', quoted in Patricia Hollis (ed.), *Women in Public: The Women's Movement 1850–1900* (London, Boston and Sydney: George Allen & Unwin, 1979), p. 15.

4 EWE/HM, 22/8/1900, 47452, fol. 115.

5 David Rubinstein, *A Different World for Women: The Life of Millicent Garret Fawcett* (Columbus: Ohio State University Press, 1991), p. 25.

6 Joan W. Scott, 'Gender: A Useful Category of Historical Analysis', in Scott, *Gender and the Politics of History*, p. 31, quoted in Catherine Hall, Keith McClelland and Jane Rendall, *Defining the Victorian Nation: Class, Race, Gender and the British Reform Act of 1867* (Cambridge: Cambridge University Press, 2000), p. 33.

7 EW, 'The Education of Girls', p. 298.

8 Vicinus, *Independent Women*, chapter 1.

9 EW, 'What better provision', p. 290. (My emphasis.)

10 Kathryn Gleadle, *British Women in the Nineteenth Century* (Basingstoke and New York: Palgrave, 2001); p. 139. Levine, *Feminist Lives*, p. 256. (My emphasis.)

11 Gleadle, *British Women*, pp. 139–53.

12 De Bellaigue, 'The Development of Teaching', pp. 963–6.

13 Eileen Janes Yeo, *The Contest for Social Science: Relations and Representations of Gender and Class* (London: Rivers Oram, 1996).

14 WE, 'What Better Provision', pp. 288–9.

15 EWE/HM, 24/1/1902, 47452, fol. 239.

16 Wolstenholme delivered her views as part of a three-person panel. The other contributors were F.D. Maurice and Dorothea Beale, Headmistress of Cheltenham Ladies College. For notes on the discussion see *Transactions*, 1865, pp. 357–62. The NAPSS was active during 1857–1886. The Association brought together leaders of both Conservative and Liberal factions under the Presidency of former Lord Chancellor Lord Brougham and developed a scientifically based critique of social issues including labour relations, public health, education and the property laws – particularly as they impacted upon women. Lawrence Goldman, *Science, Reform and Politics in Victorian Britain: The Social Science Association, 1857–1886* (Cambridge: Cambridge University Press, 2004).

17 John Stuart Mill, 17 March 1864, in F.E. Mineka and D.N. Lindley (eds), *The Later Letters of John Stuart Mill, 1849–1873* (Toronto: University of Toronto Press, 1972) quoted in Goldman, *Science*, pp. 1 and 6.

18 Caine, *Victorian Feminists*, p. 70. (My emphasis.)

19 Levine has recently qualified the extent to which participation in philanthropic work aided the expansion of feminist ideals. Levine, *Feminist Lives*, p. 256. For a positive appraisal of the links between feminism and philanthropy, see Frank K. Prochaska, *Women and Philanthropy in Nineteenth-century England* (Oxford: Clarendon, 1980).

20 EWE/HM, 12/11/1893, 47450, fol. 60; EWE/HM, 25/11/1901, 47452, fol. 221.

21 EWE/HM, 29/10/1907, 47455, fol. 125; Anon. *The Saturday Review*, 14 June 1862.

22 Bennett, *Emily Davies*, p. 45.

23 EWE/HM, 29/10/1907, 47455, fol. 125.

24 Andrew Rosen, 'Emily Davies and the Women's Movement, 1862–1867', *The Journal of British Studies*, Vol. 19, No. 1, 1979, pp. 101–21, p. 101.

25 Caine, *English Feminism*, p. 93.

26 Barbara Stephen, *Emily Davies and Girton College* (London: Constable & Co., 1927), chaps 4 and 5.

27 Joseph Wolstenholme was ordained in 1852 in Ely Cathedral. Henry Sidgwick had held the position of Professor of Moral Philosophy at Cambridge. Religious scepticism had led him to abandon his post on ethical grounds, as 'the natural, inevitable thing to do'. Henry Sidgwick to his mother, 4 June 1869, quoted in Arthur Sidgwick and Eleanor M. Sidgwick, *Henry Sidgwick: A Memoir* (London: Macmillan & Co., 1906), p. 197.

28 EWE/HM, 25/9/1899, 47452, fol. 21.

29 Joseph's most famous book, *A Book of Mathematical Problems on Subjects Included in the Cambridge Course* (1867) was reviewed as being 'a curious and almost unique monument of ability and industry, active within a restricted range of investigation'. John Peile, *Biographical Register of Christ's College 1505–1905* (Cambridge University Press, 1913).

30 Anon., Joseph Wolstenholme, Obituary. *The Eagle*, Vol. XVII, pp. 67–8; Maitland, *Leslie Stephen*, p. 74.

31 Alan Bell (ed.), *Sir Leslie Stephen's Mausoleum Book* (Oxford: Clarendon Press, 1977).

32 Virginia Woolf, *To The Lighthouse* (London: Penguin, 1992).

33 Virginia Woolf, 'Sketch of the Past', in Jeanne Schulkind (ed.), *Moments of Being: Autobiographical Writings* (London: Pimlico, 2002), p. 139.

34 Bell (ed.), *Mausoleum Book*, p. 79.

35 Anon., 'Poet'.

36 Maitland, *Life and Letters*, p. 74.

37 Bodichon's father was Benjamin Smith M P, her mother Anne Longden, daughter of a corn miller.

38 Pam Hirsch, *Barbara Leigh Smith Bodichon: Feminist, Artist and Rebel* (London: Pimlico, 1999), chapter 15.

39 Bessie Rayner Parkes, 'The Use of a Special Periodical', *Alexandra Magazine and Englishwoman's Journal*, I (September 1865), p. 258, quoted in Jane Rendall, 'A Moral Engine'? Feminism, Liberalism and the *English Woman's Journal*', in Jane Rendall (ed.), *Equal of Different: Women's Politics 1800–1914* (Oxford and New York: Basil Blackwell, 1987), p. 112; Rosen, 'Emily Davies', p. 106.

40 Emily Davies, 'Report of the Northumberland and Durham Branch of the Society for Promoting the Employment of Women', 1861, quoted in Stephen, *Emily Davies*, p. 53.

41 EWE/HM, 31/10/1905, 47454, fol. 162–3. General Committee Minutes, Society for the Promotion of the Employment of Women, 23 October 1866, GCIP/SPTW 1/1, Girton College, Cambridge. Reproduced with the permission of the Mistress and Fellows, Girton College.

42 Anon., 'The Emancipation of Women', *Daily News*, 9 October 1866.

43 EW, 'The Education of Girls', p. 312.

44 June Purvis, *A History of Women's Education* (Milton Keynes and Philadelphia: Open University Press, 1991), p. 75.

45 Joan Landes, *Women and the Public Sphere in the Age of the French Revolution* (Ithaca, NY: Cornell University Press, 1988), quoted in Hall *et al.*, *Defining*, p. 31.

46 EWE/HM, 2/2/1896, 47450, fol. 254.

47 Barbara Bodichon to Helen Taylor, 21/10/1866, Vol. 12. Papers of John Stuart Mill and Harriet Taylor, London School of Economics and Political Science. (Hereafter MTP). Reproduced with permission.

48 EWE/HM, 18/5/1892, 47449, fol. 267.

49 Bennett, *Emily Davies*, p. 45.

50 Crawford, *Women's Suffrage Movement*, pp. 148–9.

51 Bennett, *Emily Davies*, p. 48. EWE/HM, 22/1/1896, 47450, fol. 251.

52 Education Standing Committee Report, *Transactions*, 1864, p. 321. EWE/HM, 29/4/1908, 47455, fol. 170. On the collegiality of this working relationship see, Emily Davies to Barbara Bodichon, 18/3/1865, quoted in Ann B. Murphy and Deirdre Raftery (eds), *Emily Davies: Collected Letters 1861–1875* (Charlottesville and London: University of Virginia Press, 2004), pp. 152–3.

53 EWE/HM, 29/4/1908, 47455, fol. 170. (Emphasis in original.)

54 Bennett, *Emily Davies*, pp. 50–2.

55 Bennett, *Emily Davies*, pp. 56–7. Emily Davies, 'On Secondary Education relating to girls', *Transactions*, 1864, pp. 394–404.

56 Bennett, *Emily Davies*, p. 57.

57 EWE/HM, 29/4/1908, 47455, fol. 169–70.

58 EWE/HM, 29/4/1908, 47455, fol. 170. (My emphasis.)

59 Charlotte Manning was a historian and had served on the Committee of Bedford College.

60 Emily Davies to Anna Richardson, 10/5/1865, *Family Chronicle*, Part 5, fol. 421. GCPP Davies 1/1. Reproduced with the permission of the Mistress and Fellows, Girton College. (Hereafter *Family Chronicle*.)

61 Records of the Kensington Society. GCPP 10/1. Girton College. Reproduced with the permission of the Mistress and Fellows, Girton College.

62 GCPP Davies 10/6 EDIX/KEN 5, p. 16.

63 Sheila Rowbotham, *Hidden from History: 300 Years of Women's Oppression and the Fight against it*, 3rd edn (London: Pluto, 1977), p. 45.

64 GCPP Davies 10/6 EDIX/KEN 5, p. 15.

65 Ann Dingsdale, 'Generous and Lofty Sympathies': the Kensington Society, the 1866 Women's Suffrage Petition and the Development of Mid-Victorian Feminism', Unpublished PhD thesis, University of Greenwich, 1995, pp. 19–23. For a view suggesting the opposite see, Levine, *Feminist Lives*, pp. 98–9.

66 Dingsdale, *Generous and Lofty*, p. 36.

67 EWE/HM, 31/10/1905, 47454, fol. 163.

68 EWE/HM, 31/10/1905, 47454, fol .163.

69 Jordan and Bridger, 'Unexpected Recruit', p. 402.

70 Anon. [EW], Manchester Board of Schoolmistresses, Annual Report, May 1867 (Manchester: Beresford & Hanvill), p. 1. WL.

71 EWE/HM, 31/10/1905, 47454, fol. 163. Wolstenholme, 'What Better Provision', p. 288.

72 EWE/HM, 2/2/1896, 47450, fol. 255. (Emphasis in original.)

73 Emily Davies to Thomas Acland, 29/12/1864, *Family Chronicle*, Part 4, fol. 392. Stephen, *Emily Davies*, pp. 131–2.

74 Full details of Wolstenholme's evidence can be found in *British Parliamentary Papers*: Schools Inquiry Commission (Volume 5), SIC 16.182 to 16.268.

75 SIC 16:229. Christ's Hospital was at that moment educating upwards of one thousand boys. Rubinstein, *A Different World*, p. 25.

76 SIC 16:264.

77 EWE to Sylvia Pankhurst, 1/10/1907, E. Sylvia Pankhurst Papers, Institute for Social History, Amsterdam. (Hereafter ESPP.)

78 Hirsch, *Bodichon*, p. 216.

79 Caine, *English Feminism*, pp. 104–7.

80 Hirsch, *Bodichon*, p. 218.

81 EWE to Sylvia Pankhurst, 1/10/1907, ESPP.

82 EWE/HM, 10/6/1903, 47453, fol. 131.

83 Mill's amendment was defeated by 196 votes to 73 on 20 May 1867.

84 EWE/HM, 19/12/1897, 47451, fol. 172.

85 EWE/HM, 10/6/1903, 47453, fol. 132.

86 Jordan, *Josephine Butler*, pp. 87–8.

87 Sutherland, *Faith, Duty*, p. 79.

88 EWE/HM, 5/3/1892, 47449, fol. 257.

89 Emily Davies to Mr Plumptre [n.d.] September, 1866, *Family Chronicle*, Part 5, fol. 490–1.

90 MBS, Annual Report, 1867, p. 4.

91 One of a number of sceptics, history professor, J.R. Seeley absolutely refused to support Emily Davies's notion of a generic curriculum for men and women. Sheila C. Lemoine, *The North of England Council for Promoting the Higher Education of Women, 1867–1875/6*, Unpublished MEd thesis. University of Manchester, 1968, p. 324.

92 The first lecture, attended by some 160 people was given in Chorlton Town Hall, Manchester, on 9 October 1867 by James Stuart; Anon., 'Educational Lectures to Ladies', *Manchester Guardian*, 10 October 1867.

93 Anne J. Clough, *The History of the North of England Council* (handwritten testimony from Anne Clough). Newnham College, Cambridge. Published with the permission of the Mistress and Fellows of Newnham College. Wolstenholme was to attend Council meetings until 1873, even after Manchester had withdrawn formally from the organisation.

94 Lemoine, *North of England*, p. 75.

95 James Stuart, *Reminiscences* (London, New York, Toronto and Melbourne: Cassell and Co. Ltd, 1912), pp. 154–5.

96 F.W.H. Myers, 'Local Lectures for Women', *Macmillian's Magazine*, December 1868, p. 173 quoted in Jordan, *Josephine Butler*, p. 88.

97 Davies, *Family Chronicle*, Part 6, fol. 567. Also, Emily Davies to Barbara Bodichon, 6/4/1867, quoted in Murphy and Raftery, *Collected Letters*.

98 Davies, *Family Chronicle*, Part 6, fol. 535.

99 Davies, *Family Chronicle*, Part 6, fol. 543.

100 Davies, *Family Chronicle*, Part 6, fol. 567.

101 Bennett, *Emily Davies*, p. 136.

102 Ignota (EWE), 'Judicial Sex Bias', *Westminster Review*, March 1898, pp. 279–88, p. 285.

3

The 'parliamentary watchdog':
1868–Spring 1874

A 'moving spirit'

When considering Elizabeth's lifelong commitment to feminism, it is difficult to single out one period of particular endeavour. Nonetheless, the years between 1868 and 1874 were among the most demanding. She worked until January 1873 from her school at Moody Hall. By then, however, her religious scepticism had grown so pronounced that she felt unable, with a clear conscience, to teach the Christian doctrine that was central to the prescribed curriculum. Though heart-sore, she abandoned her profession, taking up, instead, an offer to become the first professional employee of the women's movement at a salary of £300 per annum.[1] As Secretary of the Vigilance Association for the Defence of Personal Rights (VADPR) her duties were to study and analyse all legislation as it affected individual privileges, and to act as a political lobbyist, with particular attention given to issues relating to women and children. Elizabeth termed her work as being that of a 'scrutiniser' of parliamentary practice and it necessitated her removal to London, where she rented a suite of rooms at 63 Finborough Road.[2]

Despite this new commitment, her voluntary contribution to the women's movement remained extensive: and by the spring of 1874 she sat like a benevolent but watchful spider at the centre of a web that reached out to enmesh a growing number of newly politicised women. Hailed by one of these, Lydia Becker, as the 'moving spirit' of British feminism, Elizabeth was energised by her labours.[3] Her resilience though, was often tested, either by the practical demands made upon her or by the indifference or hostility of some acquaintances. The deterioration of her friendship with Becker, initially so uplifting to both, was a key contributing factor to her distress.

Elizabeth made Becker's acquaintance during the winter of 1867, only weeks after the founding of the North of England Council. Becker's interests did not lie overtly in the field of women's education, however.

They centred instead on the possibility of their enfranchisement. She had only been introduced to the suffrage issue some months after Mill's petition had been presented to Parliament, her interest prompted by listening to Barbara Bodichon's lecture at the National Association for the Promotion of Social Science Congress in Manchester, in 1866.[4] Unhappy that she had been too late to make hers the 1,500th signature to the memorial, but with her enthusiasm fired, Becker wrote her own exposition of the topic. Emily Davies was impressed, but unsure how best to make use of it and sent it to Elizabeth on 7 January 1867. She pronounced it 'really *admirable*' and encouraged its publication.[5] Keen to meet the author and put a willing volunteer to work, she invited Becker to attend a meeting of the Manchester Committee for the Enfranchisement of Women.

The timing of Becker's letter was fortuitous for, while the MCEW had not (unlike its sister society in London) disbanded in disappointment following Mill's endeavours, it was undergoing a period of revision and reconstitution.[6] On 11 January, at a meeting held at the home of Prussian émigré Dr Louis Borchardt, the organisation was relaunched under the title of the Manchester National Society for Women's Suffrage (MNSWS).[7] Elizabeth retained her position as honorary secretary. Though many key MCEW associates (including Samuel A. Steinthal (Unitarian minister of Platt Chapel), Max and Philippine Kyllmann, Jacob and Ursula Bright, radical lawyer Richard Pankhurst and Mrs J.P. Thomasson) remained allied to the new society, other colleagues did not.[8] These included the ex-Owenite Robert Cooper (one of the key figures of northern secularism) and two ex-Chartists, Ernest Jones (author of the 1855 *Woman's Wrongs*) and Edward Hoosen.[9] These figures provide the first categorical evidence of Elizabeth's links with utopian-socialist ideals, although precisely how the threads of her friendship network influenced their presence on the MCEW's committee remains, to date, unknown.[10] Arguably, with their departure, aspects of the MNSWS's progressivism declined, but close interaction with the political visions of these three radicals impacted on the development of Elizabeth's own ethical and political stance. She typifies, in fact, the currents which ran between the popular politics of the mid-nineteenth century and the early twentieth-century labour movement – something which has been identified as a neglected area in feminist research.[11] Sadly, there are no direct examples of Elizabeth's feelings as MNSWS ideals became more precisely aligned to radical-Liberalism. However, she noted critically that the son of Ernest Jones, Liberal MP Llewellyn Atherley-Jones, fell far short of his father's credentials in both political steadfastness and bravery.[12]

Given these considerations, it is perhaps unsurprising that Elizabeth felt herself drawn to the 'advanced' socialist whom she encountered shortly after her removal to Moody Hall: silk-crêpe manufacturer Benjamin Elmy (known always as Ben). The son of excise officer Benjamin Elmy and his wife Jane (née Ellis), Ben was born at their home in Jermyn Street, Wardleworth on 15 March 1838. Educated in London, he was a fine scholar and, according to Elizabeth, a 'born teacher'.[13] This had been his chosen career, but he abandoned his profession in the early 1860s and entered the textile trade – although he maintained an interest in adult education almost to the end of his life as a tutor in the Workers' Educational Association. After having secured some financial capital (though its source is unknown), he purchased a small silk mill in Booth Street, Congleton in 1869.[14]

His relationship with Elizabeth most likely began when she set up the Ladies' Education Society (LES) there – a group whose lectures were open to both men and women.[15] She later noted that her husband's 'natural', as well as considered, inclination was towards feminism and his support for the women's education issue made him an instinctive ally in her new venture. Ben believed, however, that the education of women should not only be limited to their acquisition of academic skills: life-skills too were important. His talent for writing enabled him to promote his views and, taking his mother's surname as part of his pseudonym, two of his most radical publications, *The Human Flower* and *Baby Buds* were written to enable parents to impart knowledge of sexual physiology and conjugal love to young children.[16] Though there has been some debate as to the actual identity of 'Ellis Ethelmer', Elizabeth is unequivocal in stating that the pseudonym is solely Ben's.[17] For her part, she was determined to take the lessons she had learned from organising the work of the North of England Council out from the cities into the Cheshire countryside, and she followed the Council's precedent in welcoming men into the LES's governing structure. Busy as she was, channelling her energies in this direction meant that something else had to be relinquished. Though the shift proved only partial and temporary, she surrendered suffrage in favour of education.

Many practical considerations forced Elizabeth into reassessing her commitment to the MNSWS, and her decision to resign as honorary secretary was the catalyst which sparked Lydia Becker's political career. Elizabeth wrote later to Sylvia Pankhurst that:

In 1867 (May) I removed from Worsley to Congleton, & my educational work both as the head of a girls' Boarding School, & in the effort to secure University & other help for women's education, had become so serious & absorbing, that I was only too glad to resign my Hon. Secretaryship into [Miss Becker's] most capable hands.[18]

In 1908, in another letter to Pankhurst, Elizabeth recalled that she was 'getting on slowly', sorting through '*many* hundreds' of the letters she exchanged with Becker during the 'fearfully busy' years 1869–74.[19] Sadly, almost all of these are now lost, but Becker's remaining *Letter Book* (dated from 21 March to 29 November 1868) gives some indication of the deep private friendship that enriched their public labours.[20] Lydia Becker cared deeply for Elizabeth and, though she might not have fully understood the sporadic psychological fragility which surfaced when her friend was under tension, she tried to offer comfort. Becker quickly adopted the same role of trusted confidante that McIlquham was later to undertake, but the relationship did not prove so enduring. In 1874, polarised into opposing positions over the dynamics of framing the demand for women's enfranchisement, their friendship was sacrificed on an ideological technicality: namely, the terms by which (if at all) married women should be able to exercise the vote. That Becker, whose stance was always more conservative, steadfastly refused to support the proposal was, Elizabeth recalled, both a 'great grief' and a lifelong disappointment.[21]

Becker became Honorary Secretary of the MNSWS in August 1867, and for Elizabeth the joy of not having to commute the 26 miles from Congleton to Manchester on committee business quite so frequently was welcome. She was, however, still a member of the Executive during a turbulent period when tensions developed between the Manchester suffragists and their counterparts in London and Edinburgh. They worked only in loose cooperation and, when a formal union was suggested, the MNSWS (whose beliefs were far to the left of the rest) wondered blithely 'what [they should] gain' by it.[22] The campaign tactics of the three groups differed too, and by 1868 the Manchester activists were posing serious questions regarding the effectiveness of petitions as a campaign strategy – at least while there was no electoral reform bill before Parliament. Rather, boosted by the 'fortuitous clerical error' that enabled Manchester ratepayer Lily Maxwell to cast a vote for Jacob Bright in the General Election of 26 November 1867, the MNSWS sought to exploit the anomalous position this successful vote had prompted.[23] They did this by devising a new method to capture public attention – a legal challenge based on the principle of property qualification.[24] The following months saw Richard Pankhurst and his colleague Thomas Chisholm Anstey bring two cases before the courts. They proved to be futile efforts to bend the letter and spirit of the law which, after 1832, had instituted the specifically gendered concept of citizenship as the prerogative of 'male persons' only.[25]

Elizabeth's involvement in the preparation and mounting of these legal challenges was not significant, although colleagues' letters kept her informed of developments on a daily basis. The central female role was taken by Becker, who accompanied Anstey and Pankhurst on numerous visits to local electoral officials who were legally powerless, until the passage of the Municipal Corporations Act 1869, to place *any* woman's name on even the *local* government register.[26] Neither did Elizabeth comment directly (in extant sources) on the internal schism in the Manchester society, which resulted from its support of the failed legal challenge made on behalf of (the now widowed) Philippine Kyllmann to see her name placed on the electoral register. The MNSWS was financially embarrassed as a consequence. Desperate for funds, Becker had brazenly asked for money from John Stuart Mill and Helen Taylor in December 1868 to offset the costs of the case. This severely embarrassed Kyllmann and all three resigned from the organisation, Mill and Taylor having offered their support at Elizabeth's invitation.[27] The London society was also bitterly divided (thanks in no small part to the 'dictatorial' role played in its proceedings by John Stuart Mill) and, exasperated by the griping of her friends, Emily Davies turned her back on the suffrage issue, devoting all her energies in the immediate future to education.[28]

Though Elizabeth did not join Davies in abandoning suffrage, having relinquished some of her hold on the MNSWS she was likely pleased to be distanced, marginally, from the factionalism. Her energies were devoted, during the winter and spring of 1867–68 both to writing and to gathering support for the North of England Council memorial to the Cambridge Senate. This, on its passage in October, secured the professional accreditation of women educators. That their work would now (in her words) be 'tested and attested' by the award of a University diploma fulfilled of one of her dearest wishes.[29] Before this success, however, and only weeks after Becker had taken up her new post, Elizabeth took a leading role in another new initiative – that of securing for married women the ownership of their personal property.

A 'root' and 'branch' matter: the Married Women's Property Committee

Elizabeth's work for the Married Women's Property Committee (MWPC) remained for many years the only area of her life that could never be entirely subsumed by those who saw her as a marginal figure in women's politics, so great was her part within it. Nevertheless, in the late 1980s, when Mary Lyndon Shanley began her research into the ways in which feminists theorised, challenged and ultimately altered many (but *not* all) of the patriarchal laws underpinning Victorian marital relationships, she grew increasingly surprised by the tireless labours of the 'unknown' woman from Congleton.[30] The MWPC was the first organised feminist grouping to pose a legal challenge to the concept of 'separate spheres': but Shanley argues that its 'struggles against coverture kept . . . attention focused on the *legal* preconditions for spousal equality, rather than on the economic structures that created class as well as gender divisions'. The linking of socialism to feminism only became significant, in Shanley's eyes, during the 'next generation' of feminist activism.[31] Elizabeth's connection to socialists on the MCEW Executive (and particularly to Ernest Jones, as a close colleague of Karl Marx), highlights a broader vision than this assessment allows. Writing in 1871, in alliance with her Congleton neighbour Rosamond Hervey, her sympathies became clear in a strident piece of woman-centred propaganda. The authors claim:

> personal knowledge of districts where almost every married woman works in the mills, [and] where, consequently, all children are left for many hours each day in the care of those who, from age or infirmity . . . resort to nursing to eke out the scanty allowance which they receive from relatives or the parish . . . [P]ressures of want seldom leaves [fathers] the desire, and still more seldom, the power to educate [their] children.

The remedy, they suggested, was that by 'doubling, or in some cases, trebling, the rate of wages', families could be relieved from circumstances whereby their situation was best compared to that of senseless, unthinking 'brutes'.[32] In the environment of mid-nineteenth century laissez-faire capitalism, where production was driven by motives of profit over all else, these ambitions were likely to remain unfulfilled.[33]

The paper *Infant Mortality* illuminated clearly the effects of economic struggles on social relationships and the ways in which male despair led to female abuse. Indeed, despondency in men could so easily find release in vice, and drunkenness and lechery were all too often funded by the meagre income of wives who had no power to keep possession of their own earnings. Elizabeth believed that legislation to secure women's wages would not simply alleviate pressing material need. She argued that it could also succour the progress of civilisation by enabling undernourished children to thrive and thus build up the nation's fabric.

This was a theme she refined, and returned to with greater force, in the 1890s, when both she and Ellis Ethelmer engaged with the in-vogue theories of eugenics to bolster their arguments. The roots of their philosophy, however, also underpinned Elizabeth's work for the MWPC, and though there is a significant strand of thought that attributes the work of mid-Victorian feminists to the concept of the 'social mother-hood' of inferiors by middle-class women, the Elmys appear more aware than most of the need for true dialogue and understanding, rather than simply benevolence.[34] Ben Elmy, for example, while working as a manager in a textile factory in Mobberley in 1866, had faced men's wrath by 'pay[ing] the married women's wages to themselves' rather than their spouses.[35] A scandalous departure from accepted practice, it nonetheless assured him of the deep gratitude of his female staff. With such creden-tials Ben became a natural ally of the MWPC, but his existing alliance with the secularist movement cannot have helped but fuel Elizabeth's growing heterodoxy which, in turn, changed the course of her profes-sional life.

Elizabeth held a pivotal place in the MWPC from the moment of its inception. Though formally constituted in April 1868, discussions had begun the previous September when Jessie Boucherett made a short visit to Moody Hall. She wrote to Helen Taylor that the conversation had turned to

> the Memorial which is to be presented to the Social Science Council to ask them to bring forward the married women's property question. It is not decided whether we shall get up petitions on the subject this Session. Some people think as you do, that we had better wait for a reformed [Liberal] Parliament. Others think that the first session of the reformed Parliament will be so crowded with business that the married women's business would be pushed aside and that we had better go on with it this next session as it will probably be an empty one. I am in favour of going on at once . . . if Miss Wolstenholme thinks she has time for it.[36]

Clearly Elizabeth's labours were deemed essential to success. The memo-rial drafted by the two friends, assisted by Josephine Butler and Elizabeth Gloyne, was presented to the Executive Council of the NAPSS on 5 December 1867.[37] They had gathered over 300 signatures, including that of social theorist Harriet Martineau. Within weeks the Association had taken up the cause in earnest.[38] Though just the first step in a series of far more controversial challenges, Elizabeth quarrelled with John Stuart Mill on the precise angle the campaign should take. He, with almost foolhardy recklessness, had urged her to commence the fledgling MWPC's endeavours 'by seeking to overthrow the sex-dominion of the husband in marriage'. And although, privately, she shared his desire that individual bodily autonomy be enshrined in law, she believed that to adopt such a stance from the outset would kill the fledgling organisation stone dead. With hindsight, she regretted her timidity, but (clearly unafraid of Mill's almost mythic stature) held fast to her position that the moment was not 'ripe' for such a controversial challenge.[39] Her role as honorary secretary was, therefore, to steer the organisation along the lines of guaranteeing for *all* married women the legal security of their property, hitherto only available to the wealthy via the means of equitable trusts. This was a methodology already under discussion by the NAPSS and the path considered most likely to succeed.

The Liberal MP for Reading, George Shaw Lefevre, sponsored the introduction of the Married Women's Property Bill into the House of Commons on 21 April 1868.[40] Between then and the passage of the Act of 1870, Elizabeth collated 100,000 signatures to parliamentary petitions and issued over 35,000 pamphlets. In addition, she liaised with three regional sub-groupings of the MWPC, in Dublin, Belfast and Birmingham.[41] Her arduous labours were not helped by the lukewarm support she received from the Committee's Treasurer, Lydia Becker. In June 1868, Becker wrote that she believed women's suffrage to be 'the *roots* of the matter' of the woman question and warned Elizabeth against devoting too much time to the 'branch' issue of married women's property. This, she feared, would create a hornet's nest of dissenting opinions.[42] Seeking to address issues relating to single women and widows was one thing, but overturning traditional opinions and revisioning the role and status of wives quite another. Clearly, as was later proved in the schismatic debates surrounding the 'Forsyth' amendment to the 1874 Women's Suffrage Bill, the more conservative claims Becker supported were centred only on those spinsters and widows whose property qualification would entitle them to vote 'on the same terms as is or shall be granted to men'. In no respect, in her mind, was the enfranchisement of married women feasible. This placed her on a collision course with Elizabeth, who viewed their exclusion as a denial of a common humanity.

Elizabeth saw too that a grant of 'property' to wives supposed a tacit acceptance of the fact that a challenge to full citizenship could subsequently be made, as it was in the possession of 'property' that the nation sited the right of an individual to representation. This also opened the way to a fully gender-inclusive formula rather than one that relied on the possession of the civil status of a feme sole (an unmarried woman or widow). The fact that she knew the majority of working women would fall foul of the qualifying property laws was not the issue for Elizabeth at that moment: it was the matter of the concession of principle. Ultimately, Becker went so far as to beg her to keep MWPC meetings and those of the MNSWS separate, in order not to offend the sensibilities of those who might support only one measure. In practice, the organisations' membership and alliances were almost identical.[43] The dispute, though, was the thin end of the wedge in the deterioration of a fond friendship. So, although Elizabeth had avoided the worst of the factionalism in the Kyllmann affair, she was at the heart of ideological disputes within the MWPC, and she found that coping both with personality clashes and the differing demands of so many organisations (in addition to her work and the psychological trauma regarding her faith), was too much. She fell seriously ill in November 1868, and the nature of this illness casts intriguing perspectives on her psychological condition. The ice-cool political activist was also, at heart, deeply insecure.

Elizabeth's symptoms were first noted in a letter from Becker in June; when she acknowledged her friends' appeal to relinquish the MWPC Secretaryship owing to overwork – though nothing in fact came of her request to resign.[44] Five months later, shortly before her thirty-fifth birthday, she penned a distraught letter. Deeply troubled, she confided that she perceived symptoms of mental frailty allied to her physical suffering, something which forced her to recall similar events afflicting her father's last illness. The fact that she was seeking to write his biography at the time only focused her thoughts more categorically. Though Elizabeth was clearly traumatised by the memories, Becker's response was hearty and robust. She wrote that while she understood that her friend had 'much to try her', she was of the opinion that 'all diseases [were] physical'. This was probably not the reply Elizabeth had hoped for.[45] This incident provides the first recorded example of Elizabeth's fragile mental state during times of stress, and places a different complexion on the face of a woman who might otherwise be viewed as something of an automaton – the pattern of her days dictated by the next goal and the next campaign. The illness, however, was of short-term duration and her strength returned. MWPC business again took centre-stage and there was no more talk of her resignation for six years.

Playing second fiddle

It is not my intention here to provide a full assessment of the passage of the married women's property legislation. That has been ably done elsewhere, not least by Elizabeth herself in the comprehensive *Final Report* of the MWPC, written in 1882.[46] There she sought to place herself once more as an initiator of events, stating that she and her associates were 'in ignorance' of the earlier labours of Barbara Bodichon and her colleagues in 1856. The passage of the Divorce Act 1857 had, however, taken 'the wind out of the sails' of these activists, in securing certain rights for deserted wives that were thought sufficient by parliamentarians, who then refused to sanction any notion that the majority of marriages were based on other than honourable intentions. The principle of coverture remained firmly entrenched. This enabled Elizabeth to be dismissive of previous efforts, and she phrased the inauguration of the MWPC in almost messianic terms: rays of 'hope', for example, were offered to brutalised women when 'all was dark'.[47] This was far from altruistic, but she always had a deep faith in her ability to pursue the right course, and articulated her convictions clearly. She commented with regret on the loss of John Stuart Mill as a co-sponsor of the Married Women's Property Bill (on account of his defeat in the 1868 general election), and also on the obfuscatory tactics of members of the House of Lords – who had greeted the Bill's arrival in the upper house in June 1870 with a 'chorus of ridicule and disapproval'.[48] Ultimately, the Bill passed only when the meat of its egalitarian principles (that a married woman's property should be treated as if she were a feme sole) had been cut from it. If we are to look for the moment when Elizabeth's disillusionment with Liberalism began, perhaps it was here; for during the months of 1869–70 the grand vision of human equality espoused and prompted by Cobden and Bright could not help but appear a little tarnished.

The primary reason for Elizabeth's disquiet lay in the fact that the parliamentary amendments to Richard Pankhurst's (originally simply phrased) Married Women's Property Bill had clearly undercut Liberal principles of Enlightenment individualism. Wily legislators had constructed instead a new ideology of class equality – for example, by ensuring that the equity laws protecting a rich woman's property would also secure that of wage-earning women. This seemed egalitarian, on the surface. However, in practice, by classifying the working-class husband as the perpetrator of abuses against his wife, wealthy men both removed themselves from censure, and from any notion that 'separate spheres' ideology could be effectively challenged.[49] The abuses of matrimony became a working-class problem, which required the state's intervention to protect the vulnerable. There was no concession to *human* equality.

Elizabeth, perceptive in the extreme, noted the change, and in September 1870, one month after the legislation had received the Royal

Assent, she declared that, as passed, it was not the 'great measure of social reform' the MWPC had sought, 'but [instead] a measure of protection . . . applying partial remedies [to the] worst abuses' of the Common Law. It was, she concluded, 'but the compromise of conscience with selfishness'.[50] Despite the fact that the Birmingham sub-committee of the MWPC disbanded, thinking the job done, she despised Parliament's egocentric stance and began to lobby for an amendment. The selfishness of men, though, was an emotion with which she was well acquainted, for she had found herself grappling with it twelve months before in Bristol. Her central role in organising a fringe meeting of the NAPSS Congress there (the consequences of which would catapult Josephine Butler into the role of national heroine) has, however, gone completely unrecorded.

Many sources recall the telegram sent by Elizabeth to Dover to await Butler's return from a continental holiday in October 1869.[51] The message, simply, 'beg[ged] an interview' with her friend in order that Butler might be acquainted with recent and momentous events. The outcome proved to be, as she had wished, that Josephine assumed responsibility for a ladies' challenge to the Contagious Diseases Acts. The Acts had been passed in 1864, 1866 and 1869 as an attempt to address the ever increasing rates of venereal disease within Her Majesty's armed forces. They comprised, according to Elizabeth, 'sex legislation of the basest kind [and] class legislation of the cruellest character'.[52] In addition, they marked 'the high-point of sanitary interventionalism [in the] history of medico-moral regulation', and were anathema to radicals who supported extreme principles of personal liberty.[53] Opponents challenged the licentious behaviour, not only of serving soldiers and sailors, but of the male sex in general, who had 'forced women to conform to a higher standard of morality' than the values they set for themselves.[54]

In the nineteenth century, 'Masculinity and male sexuality rested on the twin pillars of motherhood and prostitution' and the poor, often illiterate, working-class prostitute acted as a conduit for what was understood to be man's innate sexual desires – desires that could not be expected to be met fully by wives.[55] Classified as somehow 'less' than women, the morally and medically 'unclean' prostitutes were perceived as a race apart and judged as a deviant group which the state had a duty to control. The CDA illustrated a principal example of how this control was instituted, as prostitutes became subject to the withdrawal of their civil liberties and the imposition of a degrading intimate medical examination. Although 'voluntary' in nature, if a woman refused to submit to the indignity she faced severe penalties. For Elizabeth, the doctors who sullied women in this way were as much responsible for their subjection as the clerics who demanded that married women (as a consequence of their part in the 'fall' of man) submit to the sexual degradation that was so often their lot. Such was her anger that she named the doctors' ministrations 'medical priestcraft'.[56]

Stephen Garton's *Histories of Sexuality* has charted the significant revisionism undertaken in the definition of Victorian sexuality. Early histories were too quick, Garton asserts, to define the era as an epoch of 'excessive sexual austerity, repression and prudery' when the true position was far more complex.[57] Feminist research, including that undertaken by Bland, Hall, Jeffreys and Marcus, has been crucial in transforming our readings, not only of heterosexual, but of same-sex relationships. It has also highlighted a series of vibrant and diverse sexual cultures – only one of which was the First-Wave feminist challenge to the sexual double standard. Radicals such as Elizabeth, however, would certainly have had sympathy with the assessment that sex was 'at the core of being'.[58] Elizabeth understood that for prostitutes, subject as they were to the severest economic, social and political subjection, the very act of sex defined their socio-cultural status. Perceived as simply 'objects' of men's desire, prostitutes were deemed unworthy of respect. Under the CDA they also became criminalised and the antithesis of those 'angel-wives' whose homes were deserted for the brothel but who could, just as swiftly, be infected with any number of noxious diseases resulting from a husband's lust. Every woman, regardless of class, was at risk. As a consequence, Elizabeth condemned the CDA as an 'immoral, unjust . . . outrage on all womanhood [and] a direct violation of the [ancient] British constitution as regards the liberty of women'.[59] Such sentiments, later named as the 'constitutionalist' construction of the 'British Free-woman', were most famously expounded by Charlotte Carmichael Stopes in the 1890s.[60] Speaking in York almost twenty years earlier, however, Elizabeth upheld an identical concept of the ancient ideal of feminine freedom. She demanded its *restitution* to *all* women via the repeal of the CDA.[61]

The government's decision in 1866 to geographically extend the influence of the CDA legislation beyond the ports and garrison towns to which it originally applied provoked a highly charged civil rights debate. Dr Charles Bell Taylor, the leader of the movement to challenge the Acts, sought Elizabeth's views after seeing her name linked to the women's education campaign. She became, he noted, 'a most valuable and efficient ally'.[62] Her brave stance was, however, not mirrored by many, for only 13 per cent of First-Wave feminists participated in the repeal campaign, which secured James Stansfeld as its parliamentary champion.[63] Those less intrepid feared a backlash against progress in other areas, such as education and employment, if bourgeois women were identified too closely with a challenge to laws that were 'the archetype of sexual harassment'. Millicent Garrett Fawcett, for example, distanced herself on the grounds of 'her aversion' to discussions on sexuality and also because of her concern for the damage it might inflict on the 'respectable' movement for women's suffrage.[64] Her sister, Elizabeth Garrett Anderson went further, and publicly condoned the extension of the Acts to the civilian population by citing its benefits to public health.[65] Elizabeth recalled that some radicals, notably Jacob and Ursula Bright, were also sceptical in the early weeks of the cause, although they soon proved extremely vocal in their support for repeal.[66] In her own case, it was Frances Power Cobbe and Jessie Boucherett who urged her to distance herself from the campaign, though she remained unmoved by their pleas.[67] Rather, boosted by the heated debates, and in another of the 'mail-shots' for which she became renowned, she campaigned on its behalf.

Among the friends drawn into the anti-CDA fold were the Bristol-based Quaker sisters, Anna Maria and Mary Priestman and their friend Mary Estlin. The Priestmans were sisters of John Bright's first wife, and their expansive networks encompassed a significant number of reforming families including, in addition to the Brights, the McLarens, the Ashworths and Katherine, Viscountess Amberley.[68] The sisters had moved to Bristol from Newcastle c.1868, and had formed the Bristol and West branch of the National Union for Women's Suffrage the same year. Inferring from statements in Elizabeth's letters, it is likely that it was one of the Priestman sisters whom she identified as the 'admirable woman' she prompted to ask Professor F.W. Newman to attend a protest meeting against the CDA organised by Bell Taylor at the Royal Hotel, Clifton during the NAPSS Congress of 1869.[69] Elizabeth was one of the promoters of that meeting and appeared closer to Bell Taylor and his associates than Josephine Butler at that time.[70] Nevertheless, Butler was married, and Elizabeth considered this an important qualification given the delicate subject matter under discussion. The idea of a spinster leading platform debates on a sexual issue was simply too contentious.

On 4 October 1869, the protestors took their challenge from hotel to conference hall and won a stirring victory. The resolution passed sought 'that the National Association for the Promotion of Social Science should protest against the Acts and take steps to resist their extension'.[71]

Elizabeth sent her telegram to Butler, which was swiftly followed by another from Bell Taylor and his associate Dr Worth to 'haste to the rescue'. Very soon, having come to understand that her decision had been sanctioned by God, Josephine Butler took up the cause by which she would become defined.[72] On 31 December 1869, the famous *Ladies' Appeal and Protest* against the Acts, signed by Elizabeth and another 125 women, was published in the *Daily News*. It began a feminist campaign which lasted for over fifteen years.

Elizabeth's personal contribution to the repeal movement was not only played out as an Executive Committee member of the Ladies' National Association (LNA), led by Butler. She also served prominently on the mixed-sex National Association, to whose Executive she was elected in 1873.[73] She travelled the length and breadth of the country to make speeches and attend rallies, often as Butler's companion and more often still in the company of Ben Elmy. Ben became Secretary of Congleton's Repeal Committee at a meeting on 9 January 1873, a gathering attended by both Elizabeth and Mrs Butler.[74] The repeal movement brought Elizabeth many new acquaintances, including Alice Cliff Scatcherd, from Morley, Leeds and Louisa Martindale, the daughter of industrialist James Spicer. Though she admired Scatcherd (and they worked collaboratively until the 1890s) she was often irritated by her. To Martindale she grew especially close, and their friendship lasted until Louisa's death in 1914.[75]

It is appropriate to reflect a little here on why Elizabeth was not tempted to press home her fruitful alliance with Bell Taylor and lead the women's challenge to the CDA herself. The answer lies in the fact that she was disinclined to limit her activities to one area, and even though she often complained about the demands placed upon her she was passionate about all the causes she supported.[76] She also believed that Josephine Butler possessed the qualities of diligence and gentility that proved so successful in overcoming opposition to the repealers' stance, and she knew her own spinsterhood to be a disadvantage. She was content, therefore, to play 'second fiddle' to Butler's lead, at least in the matter of CDA activism. Spinsterhood too, at least in its official sense, was something she had no intention of relinquishing, though her friendship with Ben Elmy blossomed into love during this time. No remembrances of the course of their courtship remain, however, to precisely date the moment when a meeting of minds transformed into a physical union. There is certainly evidence to substantiate the view that Ben, as a personal friend of Charles Bradlaugh, was already a follower of the secularist creed – something which must have impacted on Elizabeth's wavering orthodoxy. By the winter of 1871 she had formed the opinion that no belief in the 'fable' that Jesus of Nazareth was 'very God and very man ... [could ensure] justice, honour and sympathy between man and man': and though she later mourned the fact that her secularism had resulted in the abandonment of her teaching career, she set out readily enough upon a new path.[77]

The Vigilance Association for the Defence of Personal Rights

Despite making the decision to quit her school, Elizabeth was never 'lost' to the education movement. She merely channelled her energies more broadly. No historian, however, has previously recorded the conversation she had with Professor Henry Sidgwick which, in her words, marked 'the beginning of Newnham [College] and of so much else'. On holiday in Cambridge at New Year 1870, she and Sidgwick shared tea at Joseph

Figure 3   Felicia Larner, Cousin to Elizabeth Wolstenholme Elmy
Source: Reproduced with the permission of the Mistress and Fellows Newnham College, Cambridge

Wolstenholme's house in Panton Street. There they enjoyed a 'long talk ... as to ways and means of providing a home for the women students' now resident in the city; the consequence of university lectures having been opened to them the previous year. During the course of conversation, Sidgwick made a promise to her to 'pay the rent of Merton House ... until it was self-supporting'.[78] He kept his vow, and Anne Jemima Clough soon made the journey to Cambridge to become the much loved headmistress of an institution whose place in history was assured. One of her first students at Merton was Elizabeth's ex-pupil and cousin, Felicia Larner, in whose portrait we might glimpse traces of a resemblance to a young Elizabeth. The beautiful and vivacious Larner, who earned renown later as headmistress of Skipton Girls' Endowed School, had travelled to Cambridge in the autumn of 1869, at almost the same moment as her former teacher passed with Honours the Cambridge Higher Examination for Women. By doing so, she had fulfilled, on her own account, the professional accreditation for teachers for which she had long campaigned.[79]

In all likelihood, by 1871, Elizabeth believed much of what she had fought for in relation to female education had been attained. This left her free to consider other, worse, abuses. Propertied women had secured (in addition to the right to vote in municipal elections in 1869) the chance to both be elected, and to elect, representatives to local school boards under the provisions of the Education Act of 1870. It could be argued that such successes were the product of changing views about women's roles in the public realm, a relaxing of strictures and greater tolerance. Such victories also helped cement ideas that the reform of girls' education should proceed apace, for if women were to serve the state they must be fitted for the task. Elizabeth's own election campaign for the Congleton School Board stalled over her inability to designate herself a 'Church or Chapel' candidate, but on her resignation from teaching two years later it was the secular-utopian ideal of shaping a 'greater humanity' which underpinned (even more forcefully than before) her professional life.[80]

When Jessie Boucherett offered her an annuity to enable her feminist work to proceed, she had refused. Seven years later, though, she embraced the very course (that of challenging the laws upon which women's subjection was based) that Boucherett had desired. She did so because of a shift in her understanding of what 'professionalisation' meant. It appears that from around 1870 the position of her work and her vocation reversed: education became a 'vocation', feminism her 'profession', and she made a conscious decision that this would be so.[81] It was the founding of another campaign group in March 1871, the Campaign for Amending the Law in Points Wherein it is Injurious to Women (CALPIW), which presented her with the opportunity to make the change when, within months, she became its secretary. The move also set her on the path to a peripatetic life: for, while she was based in London, she travelled the length and breadth of the country on CALPIW affairs. Controversially, however, it became known that when she visited the north-west to accompany George and Josephine Butler on CDA business, Ben Elmy's home at The Low, Buglawton (where he lived with only servants for company) became her residence too. For many of her deeply religious LNA and CALPIW associates it would only be a matter of time before Elizabeth's distinctive 'personal code' of living caused them to doubt her viability as a figurehead of their movement.[82]

Elizabeth did not relinquish the lease of Moody Hall until the end of January 1873, something she notes in correspondence with Thomas and Anna Maria Haslam, strong allies on the MWPC.[83] She commented on the move during a painful reflection upon the death of a childhood friend who, worn down with constant child-bearing, was still forced to endure the attentions of a lecherous spouse. Elizabeth's distaste for the legal disability which enforced a woman's sexual submission is clearly evident here, in a letter probably written in response to Haslam's publication of *The Duties of Parents*, in which he claimed 'connubial temperance' to be the most effective method of birth control.[84] She believed the Haslams, who were resident in Ireland, were blessed with a rare companionship, their 'twin souls melted into one', and their lives selflessly devoted to work for human progress. The friends shared the idea that the elevation of humanity could be best served by limiting the size of families and his biographer considered Thomas Haslam's ideas of sexual abstinence and heredity were 'an important indicator of his growth as a feminist thinker'.[85] His philosophy also exemplified a popular strand of intellectual thought, and *The Duties of Parents* can be compared in both its sentiments and its style with Ellis Ethelmer's later works, *Life to Woman* and *Phases of Love*.

Though such books seem, as Quinlan argues, 'impossibly high-minded' today, they were a response to the fears of human degeneracy so prevalent at the time, and made a genuine attempt to link medical, moral and social discourses into an overarching, Neo-Malthusian reformist ideology.[86] That this was based on achieving both consensus of opinion and a universal willingness to reform sexual behaviour could also be argued to lie at the root of its failure. Although Elizabeth's work on behalf of the anti-CDA movement had forced her to consider the relationships of sexual power and subjection almost, perhaps, to an unnatural level, it did not preclude her from entering a sexual relationship with Ben. She was in her late thirties and knew her own mind, and though she possessed a vision of a coming world that was utopian, her character was idealistic rather than sentimental. The couple shared a clear vision of the way their relationship might proceed and, from the first, their public and private lives, and indeed their feminist lives, were seamlessly intertwined.

Ben and Elizabeth's relationship blossomed during the transformation of her working circumstances. CALPIW was formed on the understanding that its 'general objects' were 'closely identified with the special object' of the CDA campaign, but in practice it had a far broader base.[87] It provided, according to one assessment, a 'powerful analysis' of women's subjection, which 'insisted upon the close interrelationship between systems of sexual and political domination'.[88] This, as we have seen, had long been a central plank of Elizabeth's philosophy, and she was credited by W.T. Stead (whom she met in 1871, during his tenure as editor of the *Northern Echo*) as having been 'the soul' of the organisation.[89] CALPIW's title was changed in November 1871 to the only slightly less ponderous Vigilance Association for the Defence of Personal Rights, and the group remained in existence (despite various changes of name) until 1978. Very little work has been carried out into the history of this precursor of the modern-day Libertarian Alliance, but its extensive concerns ranged across such diverse subjects as public health, municipal taxation and official corruption.[90] Elizabeth was later accused of letting her involvement in other committees, for example the MWPC, slide during her time in London but, arguably, she saw the VADPR as a vehicle through which she could work on any number of fronts simultaneously.

Sometimes, though, other activists saw things differently and this led to the, by now, almost customary quarrels, such as that between herself and Josephine Butler over the services of a campaign agent in northern towns.[91] Distressed at Butler's assumption that she had falsely appropriated his services for VADPR, Elizabeth penned a note to Henry Wilson (Secretary of the Northern Counties Electoral League for Repeal) stating that she 'believed our north-country friends [always to have] understood the essential identity of the work of this Association with that of Repeal'. Work in other directions, she maintained, in no way diluted its commitment in that sphere. Her letter was aggrieved, even petulant, but it concluded with the sentiment that 'it is of no avail to expend enormous effort in the attempt to get rid of our legislative embodiment of the evil principles we are fighting [in relation to the CDA], whilst leaving untouched other equal abominations'.[92] It would have been hard to fault her argument.

In spite of her desire for a multi-pronged attack on unjust practices, Elizabeth was far from watering down her commitment to single issue causes. It was during 1873, however, that her name disappeared from the reports of the North of England Council – her move to London obviously prompting the resignation. To the work of women's suffrage and to repeal she remained deeply committed, and she was, in the words of one friend, 'an *habituée*' of the Ladies' Gallery in the House of Commons during many evening deliberations on the merits, or otherwise, of state-regulated prostitution.[93] She became the scourge of the Commons from February 1873 to October 1874, and spent much of her time there when Parliament was in session. Her small, slight figure bustling towards them struck terror into the hearts of men who, well used to her tenacious perseverance in pinning them down, wondered how best to avoid succumbing to her exquisitely reasoned requests. It was during this time that James Stansfeld helped cement her reputation as the 'parliamentary watchdog', an epithet spoken with open affection by her friends and forthright sarcasm by her opponents.[94]

The members of the VADPR were an eclectic group, many already well known in allied organisations. Its sympathisers included George and Josephine Butler, Emilie Venturi (the daughter of William Ashurst and sister of Caroline Ashurst Stansfeld), Jacob and Ursula Bright, P.A. and Clementia Taylor, Samuel Steinthal, Professor James Stuart, Alice Scatcherd and Irish suffragist, Isabella Tod. All knew Elizabeth well, and deemed her to have 'exceptional' qualities, an 'extraordinary ... knowledge of the law' and 'thoroughness' of mind.[95] Not one opposed her appointment as secretary (or indeed her high salary of £300 per annum) when the post was relinquished by Mrs Butler. Butler claimed the VADPR had been founded when it was realised that 'the idea of Liberty had been gradually undermind' (*sic*) in Britain, the consequences of which had been an 'audacious assault on the guaranteed rights and privileges' of its people.[96] It was to endeavour to prevent similar attacks that Elizabeth devoted her refashioned working life. She had, it must be stated, only limited success.

Material resources to further the VADPR's objectives were few. The organisation attracted a subscription list of approximately 180, from which an annual income resulted of between £600 and £900. Elizabeth's salary thus comprised a significant proportion of the annual expenditure.[97] With these slender funds, the hope that the fledgling group could affect much more than a skirmish to halt the 'protective' legislation eroding the attainment of 'life, liberty and the pursuit of happiness' was unrealistic. Despite the protracted and fruitless challenge they made against the Marine Mutiny Act of 1873, for example, there were instances where the group made progress, if only in raising awareness of the restrictions imposed.[98] For example, in critiques of the Infant Life Protection Bill 1871 and the Offences Against the Person Bill three years later, Elizabeth wrote forcefully of the affronts to personal freedom such legislation would sanction: although in the latter case the age of consent for young women was only raised by one year, to thirteen, as a result of VADPR diplomacy.[99]

Clearly evident in Elizabeth's reflections of this time is her anger at the insensitivity displayed by politicians towards women's needs. She wrote numerous 'flexible and politically creative' protests against legislation arguably designed to provide 'protection' for women with a fine consideration for detail. She is, however, classed by one historian as having brought a 'secularist individualist eccentricity' to the task.[100] She was certainly both secularist and idiosyncratic, but eccentric seems a misguided term to apply to the woman W.T. Stead credited with such extreme focus and clear-sightedness – unless it was these traits themselves that highlighted her unconventionality. Stead wrote that Elizabeth's brilliant mind had shaped critiques of 'many of the Bills by which a wealthy and luxurious society sought to smoothe [sic] its crumpled rose leaves by crushing the liberties of the poor in the name of philanthropy and humanity'.[101] It was an apt if florid assessment.

Elizabeth believed that the role of the state was to protect the innocent and wronged, not to interfere in the personal liberties of adult, reasoning individuals.[102] Her work for CALPIW and the VADPR had caused her to think, even more deeply than before, about where the true impediment to society's progress lay. By the spring of 1874 she had concluded that the general acceptance of the inborn nature of the male sex drive lay at the root of every evil to which women (and their children) were subject. It formed the core of the canker that blighted millions of lives. She often returned, in her texts on behalf of the VADPR, to the interlinking themes of poverty, social tension and sexual voraciousness as being the catalysts of human despair. Partnerships (whether, or not sanctioned by religious or statutory rites), were still far from conforming to the 'companionate' ideal, the yin and yang of separate spheres ideology. Many judges too dismissed domestic abuse as a justifiable crime on the quasi-scientific grounds of man's natural passion being impossible to control.[103]

Elizabeth's powerful critique of marriage (and especially those unions contracted in poverty) encouraged the VADPR to consider the implications of the proposed new Factory Acts in 1874, and she determined to lead a vigorous opposition to these new restrictions on women's labour, which would add, she understood, to their poverty and wretchedness. However, she discovered that, at the age of forty, she was pregnant. Rumours abounded as to the couple's intentions, but if we consider Elizabeth and Ben as champions of the virtues of prudence and sexual restraint, it appears safe to infer that the baby was planned.[104]

That year was a traumatic one for Elizabeth, both personally and professionally. The Liberal administration lost power in the January general election and Benjamin Disraeli led a new Conservative administration. This had a significant impact on all who fought the campaign for women's suffrage, a matter influenced further when Jacob Bright, the movement's parliamentary leader, lost his seat. The endless round of petitioning in relation to the women's vote had continued strenuously, spurred on by the defeat of Bright's suffrage bill of 1870 – brought about by the personal intervention of W.E. Gladstone after the bill had passed its second reading. Deflated, the regional societies sought cohesion, and on 6 November 1871 united under the title of the Central Committee of the National Society for Women's Suffrage (CCNSWS), with Elizabeth's friend Sheldon Amos as one of three honorary secretaries.[105] Their sole objective was the 'removal of the political disabilities of women', and on the 26 June 1873 both Elizabeth and Ben Elmy were elected to the Executive Committee, with Ben as a delegate member.[106] The 'more central mode of action' the CCNSWS desired, though, was not easily attained: the chief impediment to it being the involvement by some members in the morally 'unsavoury' anti-CDA campaigns. As Elizabeth took such a prominent part in this work, her ideals set one extreme of a bipolar debate.

William Forsyth, Conservative MP for Marylebone, was persuaded to take charge of suffragists' interests. Forsyth, however, refused point blank to proceed with the introduction of any bill that did not *explicitly* exclude women under coverture from its provisions. Forsyth's stance 'separated the realists from the extremists' and Lydia Becker, though at first angry that he wished 'to introduce the matter of marriage into the electoral law' was, reluctantly, won over.[107] Though her decision might have been taken from the most pragmatic of perspectives, Elizabeth, the arch-egalitarian, was both angry and distressed. She was supported in her protests by her erstwhile allies Richard Pankhurst and Jacob and Ursula Bright. Their complaints were based on the principle that to accede to the exclusion of married women would be to accept that it was not humanity alone upon which premise of citizenship should rest, but civil status.[108] This they refused to concede. In a hard-hearted attack, Elizabeth declared Becker 'weak-kneed', but Becker (now perceiving married women's issues as an irritant) advised her she that would do best to wind up the affairs of the MWPC, 'rest on [her] oars' and campaign hard for the vote.[109] Predictably, perhaps, Elizabeth was incensed, and the following months would see their fractured friendship collapse completely as Becker deserted the radicals to travel a more conservative course.

This unhappy episode brought to an end an era of turbulence for Elizabeth. She had relinquished one cherished career in favour of another which, though well remunerated, left her little time for relaxation. Her conception of professionalism had changed too, as her feminist work became her core goal. She had found love and was contemplating motherhood, but she had lost treasured friendships with Emily Davies and Lydia Becker, which had been sacrificed to the unyielding demands of her ethical stance and the uncompromising conviction that she knew the best course to take in public affairs. The episode of mental fragility, such a feature of her life in 1868, sat ill with the picture of a woman who held such forthright opinions, but if we contend that her whole being was reaching for the altruistic 'greater good' perhaps this is more understandable. Studying the episode certainly aids understanding of her complex, paradoxical character. In one matter she would remain obdurate: the right to individuality of married women. She believed no one could, or should, be owned, and the next months of her life show how she fought, with great resilience, the forces that conspired to see her wed.

Notes

1 Mary Priestman to Anna Maria Priestman, 15/9/1872, Millfield Papers. Clark Archive, C & J Clarke Ltd, Street, Somerset. My thanks to the Trustees and staff of the Clarke Archive for permission to quote from this material. (Hereafter MP.)

2 EWE/HM, 18/12/1901, 47452, fol. 226.

3 Lydia Becker to EW, 26/4/1868. Lydia Becker's Letter Book, M50/1/3. Manchester Women's Suffrage Collection. Reproduced with permission. (Hereafter LBLB and MWSC.)

4 EWE/HM, 10/6/1903, 47453, fol. 132.

5 Emily Davies to Lydia Becker, 7/1/1867, M50/1/2/2. MWSC. EWE to Sylvia Pankhurst, 11/10/1907, ESPP. (Emphasis in original.)

6 EWE to Sylvia Pankhurst, 20/5/1908, ESPP.

7   For Borchardt's career see, 'Louis Borchardt MD', *British Medical Journal*, 24 November 1883, p. 1047.

8   Report of the Manchester National Society for Women's Suffrage, 1867–68, p. 13. 2MNS. WL.

9   List of members, 'Manchester Committee for the Enfranchisement of Women' ([n.d.), M/50/1/9/1. MWSC. Ian Haywood (ed.) *Chartist Fiction: Ernest Jones, Woman's Wrongs* (Aldershot: Ashgate, 2001).

10 Kathryn Gleadle has noted the 'highly diffuse' nature of feminist support in the Chartist movement. This suggests Hoosen and Jones held views to the political left of the Chartist spectrum. Kathryn Gleadle, *Radical Writing on Women, 1800–1850* (Basingstoke: Palgrave, 2002), p. 2.

11 Biagini and Reid (eds), *Currents of Radicalism*, p. 1. Jane Rendall, 'The citizenship of women and the Reform Act of 1867' in Hall *et al.*, *Defining the Victorian Nation*, p. 135.

12 EWE/HM, 21/6/1905, 47454, fol. 123.

13 Ignota, 'Pioneers', p. 415.

14 Lyndon Murgatroyd, *Mill Walks and Industrial Yarns: a History of the Mills and Businesses of the Congleton District* (privately published, 2003).

15 W.B. Stevens (ed.), *History of Congleton* (Manchester: Manchester University Press, 1970), p. 291.

16 Ethelmer, *The Human Flower*; Ethelmer, *Baby Buds*.

17 See Introduction, p. 36, n. 79.

18 EWE to Sylvia Pankhurst, 11/10/1907, ESPP.

19 EWE to Sylvia Pankhurst, 3/7/1908, ESPP.

20 For example, Lydia Becker to ECW, 21/6 (1868). LBLB.

21 EWE to Sylvia Pankhurst, 7/7/1910. ESPP.

22 Lydia Becker to Helen Taylor, 12/10/1867, Vol. 12, MTP.

23 Jane Rendall, 'Who was Lily Maxwell? Women's Suffrage and Manchester Politics, 1866–1867', in June Purvis and Sandra Stanley Holton (eds), *Votes for Women* (London and New York: Routledge, 2002).

24 Jane Rendall, 'The Citizenship of Women' and the Reform Act of 1867', in Catherine Hall, Keith McClelland and Jane Rendall (eds), *Defining the Victorian Nation: Class, Race, Gender and the Reform Act of 1867* (Cambridge: Cambridge University Press, 2000), pp. 141–2.

25 Holton, *Suffrage Days*, p. 25.

26 Women had been specifically excluded on the grounds of sex from voting in municipal boroughs after the Municipal Corporations Act of 1835. The amendment to the 1869 bill, proposed by Jacob Bright, passed without discussion. Rendall, 'The Citizenship of Women', pp. 152–3.

27 J.S. Mill to Philippine Kyllman 4/12/1868. Vol. 13. MTP.

28 Caine has classified Mill's behaviour at this time as 'arbitrary, underhand and dictatorial'. Barbara Caine, 'John Stuart Mill and the English Women's Movement', *Historical Studies*, Vol. 18, 1978, pp. 52–67, p. 57.

29 Copy of the Memorial to the Vice-Chancellor and the Senate of the University of Cambridge (1868). North of England Council Box. Reproduced with the permission of the Mistress and Fellows, Newnham College.

30 Shanley, *Feminism*, p. ix.

31 Shanley, *Feminism*, pp. 12–13. Coverture should be understood as the legal sublimation of a wife's person to that of her husband.

32 Anon. [EWE and Rosamond Hervey], *Infant Mortality: Its Causes and Remedies* (Manchester: A. Ireland & Co., 1871), pp. 15–16 and 39.

33 For a critique of capitalist economics see, Expertus to the Editor of the *Daily Mail*, 'Why Cotton Lords oppose Corn Laws' [n. d.], 47452, fol. 305.

34 Goldman, *Science, Reform*, chapter 4; Yeo, *The Contest*, chapters 5 and 6.

35 EWE/HM, 19/9/1901, 47452, fol. 203–204.

36 Jessie Boucherett to Helen Taylor, 25/9/1867, Vol. 12. MTP.

37 NAPSS, *Transactions*, 1867, p. 292.

38 Anon. [EWE], Report of the Married Women's Property Committee: Presented at the Final Meeting of their Friends and Subscribers, held at Willis's Rooms, on Saturday, 18 November 1882 (Manchester, 1882), p. 12. BL.

39 EWE, 'The Marriage Law of England', p. 115.

40 Drafted by Richard Pankhurst, the central premise of the Bill was to 'prevent marriage operating any longer as a gift to the husband of the property and earning of the wife' and to 'makes a wife solely liable for her own debts'. Undated leaflet, 'The Property of Married Women' an enclosure in a letter from EW to Helen Taylor. Vol. 14, fn. 112. MTP.

41 Anon. [EWE] Married Women's Property Committee, Final Report, 1882, p. 13.

42 Lydia Becker to EW, 8/6 (1868), LBLB.

43 Only one member of the MWPC, Professor Tyndall, did not wish his name linked with the suffragist cause. EWE/HM, 17/3/1909, 47455, fol. 240.

44 Wolstenholme also declared her intention of resigning in 1871, though again it did not materialise. Anon., 'Report of the Married Women's Property Committee Annual Meeting', *Women's Suffrage Journal*, 2 October 1871, p. 103.

45 Lydia Becker to EW, 4/11 (1868), LBLB.

46 Shanley, *Feminism*, chapters 2 and 4. Holcombe, *Wives and Property*, chapters 8 and 9.

47 MWPC, Final Report, pp. 7–11.

48 MWPC, Final Report, p. 17.

49 Ben Griffin, 'Class, Gender and Liberalism in Parliament, 1868–1882: The Case of the Married Women's Property Acts', *The Historical Journal*, Vol. 46, No. 1, 2003, pp. 59–87, p. 75.

50 Report of EW's speech before the Ladies' Conference. NAPSS, *Transactions*, 1870, pp. 549–52.

51 Paul McHugh, *Prostitution and Victorian Social Reform* (London: Croom Helm, 1980), pp. 55–6. McHugh claims that it was Wolstenholme's telegram that urged Butler to 'haste to the rescue', but Josephine remembers of the two pleas addressed to her, Elizabeth's letter only 'beg[s] an interview'. Josephine E. Butler, *Personal Reminiscences of a Great Crusade* (London: Horace Marshall & Son, 1896), p. 14.

52 EWE, 'The Moral Crusade of the Nineteenth Century', *Shafts*, March 1897, pp. 85–8, p. 87.

53 Frank Mort, *Dangerous Sexualities: Medico-Moral Politics in England since 1830*, 2nd edn (London and New York: Routledge, 2000), p. 54.

54 Strauss, *Traitors to the Masculine Cause*, p. xix.

55 Kent, *Sex and Suffrage*, p. 62.

56 EWE/HM, 20/5/1897, 47451, fol. 99.

57 Stephen Garton, *Histories of Sexuality: Antiquity to Sexual Revolution* (London: Equinox, 2004), p. 101.

58 Jeffreys, *The Spinster*; Bland, *Banishing*; Hall, *Outspoken Women*; Sharon Marcus, *Between Women: Friendship, Desire, and Marriage in Victorian England* (Princeton and Oxford: Princeton University Press, 2007); Horowitz, *Rereading Sex*, quoted in Garton, *Histories*, p. 157.

59 Anon., 'Public Meeting of Women at York', *The Shield*, 7 January 1871, p. 347.

60 Sandra Stanley Holton, 'British Freewomen: National Identity, Constitutionalism and Languages of Race in early Suffragist Histories', in Eileen Janes Yeo (ed.), *Radical Femininity: Women's Self-representation in the Public Sphere* (Manchester and New York: Manchester University Press, 1998), pp. 158–63.

61 Anon., 'Campaigning against the Acts', p. 347.

62 Benjamin Scott, *A State Iniquity: Its Rise Extension and Overthrow* (New York: Augustus M. Kelley, 1968), p. 89.

63 Banks, *Becoming a Feminist*, p. 64.

64 Spender, *Women of Ideas*, p. 343.

65 Rappaport, *Encyclopaedia*, p. 14.

66 EWE/HM, 2/2/1896, 47450, fol. 255; Crawford, *WSM*, p. 80.

67 EWE/HM, 22/12/1902, 47453, fol. 86.

68 Holton, *Suffrage Days*, p. 24.

69 Scott, *State Iniquity*, p. 89.

70 Account of the meeting from the *Bristol Times and Mirror*, 11 October 1869, quoted in Judith Walkowitz, *Prostitution and Victorian Society: Women, Class and the State* (Cambridge: Cambridge University Press, 1980), p. 92.

71 EWE/HM, 22/12/1902, 47453, fol. 85; NAPSS, *Transactions*, 1869, pp. 428–51. Walkowitz, *Prostitution*, pp. 91–2.

72 Jordan, *Josephine Butler*, p. 109.

73 Full a full list of committee members see *The Shield*, 17 September 1870, pp. 222–3. On Wolstenholme's election to the Executive see *The Shield*, 17 January 1873, p. 20.

74 Anon., 'Congleton', *The Shield*, 25 January 1873, p. 28.

75 Hilda Martindale, *From One Generation to Another, 1839–1944* (London: George Allen & Unwin, 1944), p. 23.

76 EWE/HM, 27/11/1906, 47455, fol. 14–15.

77 EWE/HM, 17/1/1900, 47452, fol. 42–43.

78 EWE/HM, 29/4/1908, 47455, fol. 170. See also, Sidgwick, *Henry Sidgwick*, p. 209.

79 For biographical details of Larner see, Mary Paley Marshall, *Newnham College Roll* 'Letter', January 1933 (Cambridge: Fabb & Tyler, 1933); p. 40.

80 EWE/HM, 18/1/1889, 47449, fol. 12.

81 On the issue of constructing an awareness of feminist professionalism see Barbara Caine, 'A Feminist Family: the Stracheys and Feminism, *c.*1860–1950', *Women's History Review*, Vol. 14, No. 3–4, 2005, pp. 385–404, p. 393.

82 Walkowitz, *Prostitution*, p. 123.

83 EW to Thomas and Anna-Maria Haslam, 28/1/1873, Haslam Collection, DX/66/1, University of Hull Library.

84 Carmel Quinlan, *Genteel Revolutionaries: Anna and Thomas Haslam and the Irish Women's Movement* (Cork: Cork University Press, 2004), chapter 3.

85 Quinlan, *Genteel Revolutionaries*, p. 73.
86 Quinlan, *Genteel Revolutionaries*, p. 73.
87 Editorial, *The Shield*, 18 January 1873, p. 19.
88 Shanley, *Feminism*, p. 93.
89 William T. Stead, *Josephine Butler: A Life Sketch* (London: Morgan and Scott, 1887), p. 55.
90 See, for example, VADPR, Annual Report, 1873. Bishopsgate Library. Quoted with permission.
91 Josephine Butler to Henry Wilson, 28/5/1873, 3JBL/07/63. JBP. (Emphasis in original.)
92 EW to Henry Wilson, 19/6/1873, 3JBL/07/76. JBP.
93 Montefiore, *From a Victorian to a Modern*, p. 43.
94 Ethelmer, *A Woman Emancipator*, p. 427. EWE/HM, 14/8/1903, 47453, fol. 155.
95 VADPR, Annual Report, 1875, p. 11.
96 Anon., *The Choice Between Personal Freedom and State Protection* (Vigilance Association for the Defence of Personal Rights, 1880), p. 13.
97 VADPR Reports, 1872–75. Appendices.
98 VADPR, Annual Report, 1874.
99 EW and Hervey, *Infant Mortality*. VADPR, *Annual Report*, 1875.
100 M.J.D. Roberts, 'Feminism and the State in later Victorian England', *The Historical Journal*, Vol. 38, No. 1, 1995, pp. 85–110, pp. 85 and 107.
101 Stead, *Josephine Butler*, p. 55.
102 Anon. [EW and Hervey], *Infant Mortality*, pp. 39–40.
103 Bland, *Banishing*, p. 130.
104 Jeffreys, *Spinster*, chapter 2.
105 The London Society refused to join this coalition. Sheldon Amos was educated at Clare College, Cambridge at the same time as Joseph Wolstenholme was resident at Christ's.
106 CCNSWS, *Second Annual Report*, 1873, pp. 15–17. WL.
107 Holton, *Suffrage Days*, pp. 40–1.
108 Shanley, *Feminism*, p. 113.
109 EWE/HM, 17/9/1904, 47454, fol. 8. Lydia Becker to EWE, 1/3/1874, quoted in Pankhurst, *TSM*, pp. 48–9.

4

Calvary to resurrection: Summer 1874–82

An immoral promise?

The circumstances of Elizabeth's pregnancy could not help but cause comment once the matter came to public attention. However, the exact moment when the furore began is open to debate – though many surviving sources attest to the salacious gossip which flourished as her pregnancy advanced. The reason for these spicy exchanges was obvious, as prevailing bourgeois ideology insisted that any 'woman freed [from legal] "restraints" on her sexuality [had] crossed the threshold into vice' – the sordid, lawless and godless domain of the prostitute.[1] For a key spokeswoman of the women's movement to be regarded in this way was both divisive and distressing for its members, and many now considered Elizabeth a liability. They worked actively, therefore, to secure her resignation, both from her paid work and her high-profile voluntary labours.

The code of 'free love' radicalism which Ben and Elizabeth advocated was not new. On the contrary, it had a long-established tradition and was grounded in Enlightenment ideals. French philosopher Charles Fourier, for instance, argued that sexual slavery was the price women paid for monogamy.[2] Degraded as they were by conventional alliances, Fourier claimed that women had an equal right with men to determine the terms of their sexual gratification. Likewise, the early nineteenth-century followers of Robert Owen promoted the value of 'free unions', though this led to accusations that it was an accepted trait among male utopians to 'cast off all restraints of society and ma[ke] free with [a] neighbour's wife'.[3] Such censorious attitudes had not changed significantly by mid-century; the promiscuous and potentially temporary nature of free alliances were a serious concern for moral purists. However, in no respect was Ben and Elizabeth's liaison casual. Nor was it, in their eyes, immoral, as they were committed to raising a child in an atmosphere of sexual equality, mutual fidelity and trust. Ultimately, they fought and failed to defy the entreaties of friends (and particularly of Ursula Bright) that they marry. And as this chapter highlights, their formal exchange of vows in Kensington Registry Office, London on 12 October 1874 was arranged only to silence detractors. It had the opposite effect. Neither did the couple yield to decorous conventions of wedding etiquette, for they chose the flamboyant, cigar-smoking divorcée, Emilie Ashurst Venturi, as one of their two witnesses.

Making the personal political was an accepted part of Elizabeth's feminist practice and she both wrote, and spoke, autobiographically to illustrate topics of relevance. For example, she reflected orally on the patriarchal nature of Christian matrimony in 1877, before a large audience at the NAPSS Brighton Congress. Illustrating a point by making an example of her own wedding she said that

> Much as we disliked the most solemn promises of our lives to be given & taken in the . . . surroundings of a Registrar's office & with so little outward fitness of things, we preferred that distasteful condition to the acceptance of an *immoral* obligation [of ownership] which ought never to be imposed on any human soul.[4]

Ben (who early in their marriage coupled his wife's surname with his own) shared and respected her views on the power of individual autonomy, both in thought and action.[5] He was opposed to any law or custom which gave him 'rights' over her person, and had no desire that she feel constrained in their relationship by anything other than a moral conviction to remain in his company. It is, though, through Josephine Butler's correspondence that we learn that the shabby rite in Kensington was not the principal way the Wolstenholme Elmys celebrated their union. The fact that they did not choose to share the details of this private event more widely, however, was an important factor in how their actions were understood.

In the autumn of 1875, Butler (much against her inclination) was forced to explain the circumstances to one fierce critic, Isabella Tod. Her letter told of an unpretentious, but 'most solemn' ceremony of commitment, arranged before witnesses, in the previous spring. Possibly influenced by her Roe Green heritage, Elizabeth had chosen a ceremony based on Quaker tenets – a 'simple, equal and mutual' pledge of fidelity. This, Butler assured Tod, would have been legal had it taken place in Scotland, and, as far as Josephine was concerned, it also constituted a 'true marriage before God, [undertaken] from grave and pure motives'.[6] The unconventional ceremony (about which no further details are known) left Elizabeth legally unencumbered and as able as before to continue her independent life. Her sexual freedom was likewise guaranteed, and she was able (had she desired it) to enter into whatever liaison she chose. She quickly became aware, however, as her pregnancy progressed, that her 'free-thinking' actions could result in practical difficulties. She continued her labours at the VADPR, but grew increasingly anxious as scurrilous comments began to circulate. Psychologically affected by the criticism, by the summer she was again in the grip of an exhaustive illness.[7] Mary Priestman made the journey from the west country to care for her, and found her demanding. Priestman wrote to Mary Estlin on the difficulties of the situation and received the reply that, 'Poor dear Elizabeth draws out one's sympathy and one's vitality in no ordinary measure.'[8]

All though these summer weeks, it appears, Ursula Bright led the movement to persuade the couple to consent to a formal marriage and, if the recollections of Sylvia Pankhurst are correct, and the Elmys *were* forced into taking the step, Elizabeth's illness indicated the high psychological price she paid for abandoning her 'free-love' principles.[9] She was equally concerned, however, about practicalities and in August wrote to Anna Maria Priestman that both she and Ben were 'constantly pained by the assumption of our friends that our marriage must needs involve the cessation of interest and activity in our work'(*sic*). The letter begs for empathy, but is also written in a style which indicates that the Priestman sisters were aware of the spring commitment ceremony and understood the binding nature of the pledges made.[10] This may have been true. Yet Elizabeth's critical intelligence apparently deserted her at this point; for she failed comprehensively to grasp the depth of concern that other colleagues expressed with regard to the informal nature of the vows she had made. Though clearly not impervious to the criticism itself, she refused, for a while at least, to give ground. Blithely, she expressed a clear desire to continue the work of the VADPR until her child was born. While her wish was understandable, it was not to be fulfilled.

Elizabeth worked hard to shield Ben Elmy from the censure of their friends and wrote as if she wished to take the blame for their predicament upon herself. Sylvia Pankhurst believed that Ben 'intensely resented and never forgave' the high-handed 'interference' of others in his private affairs and it is pertinent to assess the precise reason for his reaction.[11] Activists had obviously known of the advanced views of the couple for some years, and some were probably acquainted with their decision to cohabit, even before the step was taken. It appears, therefore, that it was the matter of Elizabeth's pregnancy which induced the censure, though in fact this is too simplistic. Though critics of the liaison may have been in some measure hypocritical, their reactions also implied, as Barbara Taylor suggests, that acceptance of the broadest principles of 'free-thought' ideology by the middle classes was waning – the victim of a conservative assault.[12] The roots of Ben's hostility, as a high-profile follower of Charles Bradlaugh's ethical secularist creed, likely lay here. Attempts to ostracise the Elmys were *not*, however, immediate. For example, they graced the platform at the Annual Conference of the Northern Counties League for Repeal only two months before the end of Elizabeth's pregnancy, and no hint of disharmony at their presence was recorded.[13] While this, and other occasions, passed in an atmosphere of cordiality, during the following year, a concerted drive was mounted to oust the couple from their public role.

All too quickly the principles of moral 'justice' and freedom of expression long held by Elizabeth and Ben (and which their friends had hitherto accepted) were pushed aside, and the 'flutterings in the suffrage dovecotes' which had forced them before the registrar in Kensington escalated.[14] As she had submitted to the subjective institution of legal marriage she despised, this was a bitter pill for Elizabeth to swallow. Neither, ultimately, did it prevent a temporary withdrawal from political life. She resigned from the secretaryship (although not from member-ship) of the VADPR in January 1875 but, as she had feared, the volume of its work slumped in the wake of her departure. Josephine Butler's tart comment that it would be difficult to find someone with Elizabeth's 'brains' to fill her place was pertinently made.[15] Personal events took precedence, however, when she became a mother. Frank Wolstenholme Elmy was born on 25 January at Buxton House, Buglawton, the modest detached dwelling Ben had bought near the site of his growing textile business, Eaton and Albion mills. Elizabeth suffered a difficult and protracted confinement and a doctor was called. Ben is alleged to have taunted his wife in the throes of labour that she had believed medical aid unnecessary for a healthy woman enduring a 'natural' birth, and that he had only relented to the doctor's attendance at the 'last minute'. This slur in Sylvia Pankhurst's autobiography is damning, and it is followed by comments that Ben gave his infant son gin in order to antagonise his wife, who then neglected her 'puny' child in favour of her feminist commitments.[16] Pankhurst's auto/biographical stance in *The Suffragette Movement* has been analysed elsewhere, but the subjective construction of this influential book can be held in part to be illustrated by the nature of these harsh comments about the Elmys. Though Elizabeth aided Sylvia all she could latterly by the loan of documentary evidence to assist her journalism, Ben quarrelled seriously with Richard Pankhurst in the 1890s. His daughter's bias in favour of an adored parent's memory perhaps overrode much of her objectivity.[17]

Though Elizabeth's work for women continued throughout Frank's infancy, as one who considered motherhood to be 'the highest function of woman' it would be difficult to doubt her devotion to her baby.[18] Always conscious of the best emotional and physical environment in which to raise other people's children, she would not have wished for anything less for her own son. She was personally, unsurprisingly, not wholly contented by domesticity, and by September 1875 her work for the MWPC had resumed (Russell Gurney MP having announced his intention of introducing a bill to extend the provisions of the Married Women's Property Act 1870).[19] Her role within the organisation was not, however, wholeheartedly endorsed by its membership, and events a few weeks earlier in Cheshire provided further fuel for critics to fan the flames of condemnation.

On 2 May 1875 a friend of the Priestman sisters, Agnes Henry, wrote warmly of the delightful impression Ben had made upon her when they were introduced by Mary Estlin. Ben had visited Estlin on business for Emma Patterson's newly formed National Union of Women's Workers and, clearly smitten, Henry wrote that she had returned 'home feeling that life was richer and more worth having, for meeting with such a . . . noble minded . . . man'.[20] This eulogy sits ill with the opinion that Ben's reputation amongst feminists 'was as black as though he had been the Devil himself'.[21] The allusion is not entirely misleading, however, for the mention of his name regularly provoked extreme reactions of either criticism or commendation. Certainly Ben does not, in his wife's letters, present an overly warm personality, though Henry's assessment of him as 'noble-minded' is upheld. He had, however, abandoned the high church Anglicanism of his youth and, by so doing, cast himself beyond the pale for many who held a strong religious affiliation. Not least among these were the devout inhabitants of Congleton, who engaged him in a 'battle royal' for the right to free speech. Only days after Henry's tribute, both the town's mayor and town clerk had levied a charge of sedition against him.

Congleton did, in fact, have historical ties to secularism from the Chartist era. Ben built on these connections and formalised them by inaugurating the Congleton and Buglawton Progressive Club. As a member of the General Council of the National Secular Society, Ben was also a close acquaintance of the leaders of British atheism, Charles Bradlaugh and Annie Besant.[22] Besant was a relatively new convert to the secularist cause, but a zealous advocate of its principles. A fine speaker, she had willingly accepted Ben's invitation to visit Congleton and he had tried, in the spring of 1875, to hire the town hall for her lectures. The topics proposed were 'Republicanism' and the 'Value of Christianity'. Stunned by the nature of the material, Congleton's Mayor revoked his permission, for he had, he said, no 'wish to let the hall in order to discuss the propriety of abolishing the form of Government under which [he held] authority'.[23] Ben, however, refused to concede Besant's right to free speech, and after some forceful discussion with the town clerk, Mr Wilson, the lectures *were* held. When the evening came, Wilson's was a lone voice of protest, but his solitary rendering of the National Anthem before a packed and 'uproarious' audience faded into an insignificant murmur. With obvious relish, the *National Reformer*, Bradlaugh's secularist publication, reported that, 'Loyalty to the Brunswicks is apparently not very flourishing in Congleton [*sic*].'[24]

The fracas surrounding Besant's lecture tour brought the Elmys' secular and republican sympathies into the public spotlight. The *National Reformer* recounted the events of June 1875 in considerable detail in Besant's column, written under her pseudonym of 'Ajax'.[25] Such publicity only added to the condemnation aimed at the couple from those who could not tolerate such flagrant radicalism, especially as more details of their premarital circumstances became known. Evidence for this is given in a letter written by CDA repeal activist, I. Whitwell Wilson. Writing to a colleague, he condemned the Elmys as being part of a general trend of 'lawlessness and disrespect for recognised authority . . . not in accordance with God's word'. If left unchecked, Whitwell Wilson argued, such views would result in Armageddon. Success could, therefore, only be secured by restricting campaigning to the labour of 'religious people'.[26] It was a venomous judgement but, placed in the context of the evangelical sentiments of the majority of Repeal activists, understandable.

Ben and Elizabeth, though, did find some support and when, in October, Emilie Venturi indicated her wish to retire as editor of the CDA journal *The Shield*, Ben's name was put forward as her replacement. Josephine Butler recommended him on the grounds that he had her 'trust' but, despite this affirmation, the reservations of others ensured the move was blocked.[27] Ben, it seems, made a tactical retreat, and within a few short weeks Elizabeth had also, nominally, resigned from her role as Secretary of the MWPC, the organisation she had fought so hard to initiate. The forces of opposition to the unconventional couple gathered strength.

False friends?

The autumn of 1875 was a painful period for Elizabeth, both personally and professionally. There was little apparent willingness on the part of colleagues to try to accept her lifestyle choices, and this despite the compromise the Elmys had made in formalising their marriage. No pressure, though, however strident, convinced Elizabeth to renounce secularism; though many outside free-thinking circles perceived 'the dividing line between liberty and libertarianism' as indistinct.[28] Where she had been admired for a tenacious commitment to reform, democracy and personal rights, she was now tainted with the whiff of hedonism. Only a core group of close allies remained loyal to her, conscious of her immense capacity for diligence and hard work. That they accepted her situation, however, threatened to undermine their own status in the organisations they served, where the feminist presence was uniformly circumscribed by cultural perceptions of unimpeachable morality. Some, it is clear, dreaded the thought that they would be tainted by association.

Josephine Butler was among the first to voice her worries, and wrote from her sickbed of how 'the Elmy affair' had impacted upon her. Though she had tried, at first, to adopt a benevolent attitude, 'the coldness of letters' received from colleagues who had mistaken her sympathy for unequivocal support hurt Butler deeply as time passed.[29] Keen to secure her own position, she began to distance herself from Elizabeth and Ben, taking pains, for example, to correct Isabella Tod's mistaken impression that Elizabeth would resume her work on the VADPR Executive.[30] Matters came to a head between October and December, in the context of the annual general meetings of both the VADPR and the MWPC. The hue and cry was such that, by Christmas, Butler wished to forget that she had ever known 'such people as the Elmys'.[31]

Isabella Tod masterminded the hostile vendetta against Elizabeth, believing her to have wilfully countered every law of moral decency.[32] Determined to oust her from the VADPR at the AGM on 25 November 1875, Tod set her trap. Elizabeth knew, however, that the topic of her marriage would be played out centre-stage in Liverpool that day, as Tod suggested she be told.[33] How the Elmys *felt*, however, both individually and as a couple, it is impossible to substantiate. Elizabeth had a strong personal relationship with her detractors, built upon shared beliefs of personal rights and human equality. And yet *her* personal rights to choose her own belief systems and lifestyle were brought under a critical spotlight that even the strongest character would have found hard to endure. She appeared to react with grace and charity. She resigned from the Executive, and offered even the resignation from the General Committee Tod demanded. This was refused, on the grounds that Josephine Butler felt it would be 'cowardly' of the organisation to enforce it, and Butler's casting vote secured Elizabeth's place. Afterwards, Butler feared the consequences of her actions. And a letter to Millicent Garrett Fawcett, written two weeks after the stormy meeting, confirmed this. Struck down by illness, Butler wrote in a shaky, erratic hand and against medical advice from doctors who had urged rest. So anxious was she, however, to put forward a version of events which distanced her from her support of the Elmys, that she defied her doctor's advice.[34]

Butler's letter does, however, contain an element of grace towards Ben and Elizabeth, and she endeavours to portray them as honourable. But much of its tone is tempered by a self-preserving pragmatism. In order to maintain her own position, Butler was only too willing to accept Elizabeth's retirement from the VADPR, and wished the whole sorry business away with alacrity. This is almost pitiful when the depth of their friendship is considered. In Isabella Tod's case, *her* opinion of the Elmys appeared to have shifted substantially in twelve months, for it was she who proposed Elizabeth to the VADPR Executive in 1874, when Wolstenholme Elmy was three days married and already six months pregnant. Tod later claimed ignorance of these circumstances, to which she was only later made privy to by Mary Estlin. Tod, unlike Agnes Henry, remained immune to Ben Elmy's personal charm. Indeed, she classed Elizabeth as a 'victim' of her lover's lust and, ironically, as being overpowered by the sexual discussions which formed such a major part of her work for the VAPDR's executive – on which they both served. Tod considered the couple both selfish and immoral, and possessed of scant 'knowledge of human nature, or of the effect which events and actions have upon other people'.[35]

How the Elmys endured such ire is not recorded, but unless they were willing to go against the dictates of their own consciousness they could not do other than bear it. Their Kensington wedding clearly had not been enough to appease their detractors and they would go no further down the road of reconciliation. Whether this can be viewed as mulish intransience or honourable stoicism is a matter for debate. When the bitter scenario of the VADPR Executive was played out again the following day, at the MWPC meeting in Manchester, Jacob and Ursula Bright took on the role of Elizabeth's champions. Though it was Isabella Tod, who, once again, sought Elizabeth's exclusion from her place on the Executive, it was Lydia Becker who bore the brunt of the Brights' anger

– for daring to suggest a search of the registers to check the marriage. Raised voices ensued, and Tod wrote afterwards of the 'most awful scene' to Helen Priestman Bright Clark (niece of the Brights and the Priestman sisters). Incredulous at the events she had witnessed, Tod complained to Helen of her uncle's 'indefensible' support for an immoral situation.[36] Becker, deeply offended, tendered her resignation as the MWPC's treasurer. The office was not long vacant – it was swiftly appropriated by Mrs Bright.

Everyone at this fateful AGM (which resulted in a schismatic split between the English and Irish factions of the MWPC as Tod and her committee summarily resigned) appeared to have an opinion on the matter of the Elmys' marriage. Elizabeth would have been particularly pained at the judgement of another long-standing colleague, Samuel Steinthal, who supported Tod. The strength of Ursula Bright's anger against Becker is, perhaps, more surprising than Becker's own vindictiveness, if the bitter quarrel over the Forsyth proviso is remembered. Becker, drawn during 1875 into a London-based alliance against the northern suffragists' stipulation that married women be expressly included within the franchise demand, would have found Ursula Bright more than willing to upbraid her for matters other than her lack of charity towards Elizabeth. That Elizabeth maintained her place on the Executive, and the secretaryship of the MWPC was, in large part, due to the radical outlook of a (small) majority of sympathetic colleagues. Clearly, though, and as Sandra Stanley Holton has persuasively claimed, contextual issues of politics and personality carried as much weight in the matter as mere indignation at the Elmys' seemingly reprehensible behaviour.[37]

Whether or not Elizabeth looked on the retention of the secretaryship of the MWPC with triumph or satisfaction is unknown. It is clear, however, that the ripples caused by the fall-out of the Manchester meeting were significant – something which only highlights the complex and contentious nature of women's emancipation politics. There was to be one final and distressing denouement for Elizabeth, however, in the form of a letter she received from Millicent Garrett Fawcett on the morning of 11 December – a letter whose composition Josephine Butler had tried to prevent.[38] In happier times, Elizabeth had cradled Millicent's daughter, Philippa at gatherings around the Fawcetts' Cambridge fireside. Now she read her associate's harsh condemnation that her actions during the previous year had 'dealt a heavy blow at the very movement you had previously done so much for'.[39] Fawcett repeated Tod's demand that Elizabeth could best redeem the situation by tabling her resignation from the MWPC, but strong though her words were, her letter must not be taken out of context for it only added to the general calumny. Faced with this barrage of abuse, it is little wonder that Ben and Elizabeth wrote jointly to Josephine Butler informing her of their wish to remain 'out of sight' in Congleton 'and cease to be spoken of'.[40] Their absence from public affairs would, however, be temporary and Elizabeth's steadfastness to her political ideals would weather the storms of personal censure. It is something which only confirms Butler's later testament that she had 'the hardest head and the greatest power of work of any woman [she had] ever met'.[41]

New challenges

During her pregnancy, Elizabeth had informed Anna Maria Priestman that, should her work at the VADPR 'be given up', it would not mean a life of 'idleness and apathy' but the beginning of 'a varied form of action'.[42] With her labours in London abandoned, from 1875, Buxton House became the hub of an emerging feminist communication network on an international scale. The politicisation of the domestic environment was not an unusual situation among feminist couples. Thomas and Anna Maria Haslam and Richard and Emmeline Pankhurst, for example, also inhabited homes which doubled as the focus for political endeavour.[43] The Elmys were not wealthy, but at the time of their marriage could afford to live in modest comfort. They did not, however, enjoy the attentions of a retinue of servants, the services of Ben's former housekeeper and manservant having been dispensed with. Over the years, various local women were employed to undertake the roughest household tasks but, for the most part, housekeeping and childcare were undertaken by Elizabeth alone.

Her working day (domestic and administrative) could be as long as fourteen hours and, as their friendship deepened, she often told McIlquham of her labours in the kitchen and laundry.[44] She had little free time, but favoured walking, nature study or reading poetry for relaxation; a treat being a day excursion to the 'Manifold Valley' in Staffordshire. She appeared, though, to shield Ben from mundane domestic concerns, which left him free to indulge his leisure hours in the literary pursuits he loved. Ben's feminism was expressed in far more abstruse and esoteric prose than his wife's incisive style, evidence that again sits ill with the rather boorish portrait of him sketched in *The Suffragette Movement*. Elizabeth commented after his death that it was 'a manifest truth that the truest and noblest manhood possesses somewhat of the feminine fibre', a reflection which substantiates Tosh's view that 'men [did] not decide to work for a major change in the position of women without experiencing a modification in their own gender identity'.[45] For Ben, this 'modification' ensured that he viewed a companionate marriage as one in which men did not 'struggle helplessly to thread the labyrinth of human truth [using but] one masculine eye, [but] accept[ed] and encourage[d] the scope of the feminine eye also': this being the surest way to improve the moral and mental fibre of the young.[46] Baby Frank was brought up to honour the strengths of character of both sexes and his fond mother attested to the presence of both within his adult personality.[47]

The absence of any extant correspondence between Ben and Elizabeth denies the deep appreciation of their relationship which a reading of public texts alone obscures; yet there is little direct evidence to suggest any of the violence and cruelty from husband to wife alluded to by Sylvia Pankhurst.[48] McIlquham, when pressed, expressed a private, delicately phrased criticism of Ben, in which she noted that he 'possessed a mixed character akin to [Samuel Taylor] Coleridge'. This inferred that Elizabeth, in order to make a success of her marriage, had had to display the 'loyal unselfishness which [was] so conspicuous in her public work'.[49] For her part, Elizabeth claimed that 'true of soul . . . fervent in spirit . . . [and] earnest in action', Ben had been a valiant servant of the nineteenth-century feminist cause.[50] Her reminiscence of him also attested to the fact that he had 'overflowed with love and tenderness for the dear ones with him [especially] his two dearest on earth' – herself and their son.[51] The men who aided the emancipation of women have been likened to 'traitors to the masculine cause . . . who made no distinction between public and private morality' in their advocacy of a just, humanitarian construction of society.[52] Elizabeth, by electing to praise her husband in this way, linked his public support for exemplary standards of male moral behaviour to likewise claim his private fidelity to her – precisely the topic which had been the subject of such sensational gossip.

As Frank Elmy approached his first birthday, his mother faced the challenge of resurrecting the MWPC from the doldrums. McIlquham attests that while the Executive had actively ceased to campaign in 1875, Elizabeth had worked alone, obviously endeavouring to justify her £100 per annum salary.[53] The issue of married women's property, though, appeared no longer to be uppermost in feminists' minds; for the differences of opinion over Forsyth's suffrage bill had polarised conflicting opinions so effectively that it had negated the possibility of harmonious work in other directions. In addition, the Married Women's Property

Amendment Act 1874 had closed the most serious loophole in the provisions of the Act of 1870 and, given that a Conservative administration was now in power, prospects for further reforms appeared unpromising.[54] However, in the light of Lydia Becker's resignation as treasurer, together with those of Frances Power Cobbe and the Ashworth sisters after the fiery meeting of 26 November, the way was clear for galvanising the cause around the progressive views of the 'ultras', or northern radicals. The lacklustre committee would soon find itself revitalised under the dynamic leadership of Elizabeth and Ursula Bright.[55]

By mid-1876, the effects of their cooperation were evident and, at the meeting of the Executive held in July, Jacob Bright began Elizabeth's 'rehabilitation' into public life. Bright, in his role as chairman, had commented that 'whatever progress of opinion has taken place on this question, and whatever improvements have been made in the law, are more due to the influence which Mrs Elmy has brought to bear upon the subject, than to any other cause'.[56] Praise indeed, but perhaps still sensitive to the heated atmosphere six months earlier, Elizabeth elected to absent herself from the meeting. Her secretary's report had been read by Emilie Venturi, but Bright's praise indicates that Elizabeth's name was no longer taboo, only to be uttered sotto voce (if at all) in public. Jacob Bright was not the only speaker to attest to her worth on this occasion, and this despite Isabella Tod's continued determination to blacken her reputation in the eyes of influential figures.[57] Tod had sought, for example, to apprise George Shaw Lefevre (as sponsor of the Married Women's Property Bill) of the circumstances of Elizabeth's pregnancy, apparently with the hope of securing her removal from the MWPC.[58] Lefevre's opinion of Elizabeth would not be proclaimed publicly for some while, but it proved to be the opposite of anything Tod might have yearned for.

Of more practical importance for the MWPC's future were the lucrative benefits of Ursula Bright's passion for fund-raising. In a few short months as treasurer, she turned around its financial fortunes and increased the subscription list by one-third, to ninety members.[59] Mrs Bright's sterling efforts, combined with Elizabeth's obvious talents as secretary, can be credited with bringing the issue back to the forefront of political life. Despite these positive developments, one intriguing anomaly remains: and it illustrates just how carefully Elizabeth had to tread the path towards public restitution. While obviously working for the MWPC between 1876 and 1880 and openly acknowledged as its secretary in the *Englishwoman's Review* and the *Women's Suffrage Journal*, her name was not noted in the formal reports of the organisation until after February 1880 – the same year that Emmeline Pankhurst, newly married to Richard, was elected to its Executive.[60] This can only indicate the prevalence of a duplicitous attitude on the part of some colleagues; for they sought to utilise Elizabeth's keen knowledge of parliamentary procedure (and her influence among a wide circle of acquaintances) without a public acknowledgement of her position, endeavours or authority. Thus, whether openly vilified by critics of her ultra-radical views, or more subtly condemned by her friends to the unacknowledged fringes of public actions, she almost vanished from much of the women's emancipation narrative during the late 1870s.[61] The picture this presents is erroneous, but events during the autumn of 1876 also questioned the truthfulness of Ben and Elizabeth's desire to live a quiet life.

'Congleton Christian civilisation'[62]

Congleton residents did not hesitate to express their pleasure, or indeed displeasure, regarding topical matters of political or social interest. The mixture of vociferous support for, and opposition to, Annie Besant's lecture tour indicated this vividly. Despite the existence of the Progressive Club in the town, hostility towards secular belief prevailed. The population remained 'far from apathetic about religious matters' and when Mrs Besant announced a further lecture series in the autumn of 1876, this time accompanied by a talk from Charles Bradlaugh, confrontation loomed.[63] Bradlaugh wrote a first-hand account of the demonstrations that attended their visit and (such was the significance of the event) Hypatia Bradlaugh Bonner included a summary of it in her father's biography.[64] This time the civic authorities of Congleton had been swift to refuse Ben Elmy permission to hold the lectures in the Town Hall. Thus rebuffed, Ben, Elizabeth and their guests repaired to Salford Mill on the evening of the 25 September. A crowd had gathered intent on causing mayhem, and as Bradlaugh began his lecture (ironically entitled 'The Right to Think and the Right to Speak'), the windows of the old mill became the targets of stone throwers. One well-aimed missile struck Annie Besant on the back of the head.[65] At the conclusion of the meeting, and escorted by some stalwart members of the Progressive Club, Elizabeth and her house guests fought their way through a baying, hostile, mud-throwing throng in an agonising one and a half mile walk to Buglawton.[66] Even inside the house the noise continued, the protesters raising a strident chorus of 'Safe in the Arms of Jesus'.

The situation, rather than improving, became worse the following day, as Mrs Besant prepared to speak on the subject of 'Progress only

Possible through Heresy'. The 'rough music' of Monday evening was reprised outside Buxton House for a full two hours before the lecture began.[67] As the quartet emerged from the house, a volley of stones assailed them as they climbed into a cab. Bonner wrote that

> During the lecture eight persons came in together, and it was soon evident that a thorough disturbance was planned. One of the newcomers shouted, 'Put her out,' and as this seemed the signal for a fight, [Bradlaugh] said sternly that the next one who interrupted should be put out. A man named Burberry, a local tradesman and well-known wrestler who boasted his prize cups, invited Mr. Bradlaugh to make the attempt upon him. [Bradlaugh] saw that if the lecture was to go on something must be done, and that quickly, so he descended from the platform, and laying hands upon the champion, after a short struggle ejected him, and handed him over to the charge of the police outside. The audience cheered and hooted; the crowd outside yelled and threw stones – one of which, striking Mrs. Elmy, cut her severely over the right eye. The excitement subsided in a few minutes, however, and the lecture concluded, and discussion was held in perfect quiet and order. An attempt was made at Mr. Elmy's house to repeat the scene of the night before, but [Bradlaugh] and his host went out, and at length succeeded in frightening the disturbers away. [68]

The effect of the incessant noise upon the innocent slumbers of twenty-month-old Frank can only be imagined, though his mother carried the memory of the secularists' visit always, even after her wound had healed.

While the mutual endurance of such harsh treatment suggests that a strong friendship might exist between Elizabeth and Annie Besant, this was not the case. The acquaintance is not recorded in detail in Elizabeth's correspondence and the scant reflections that remain indicate a coolness in their relationship. Though Elizabeth approved Besant's 'gift of ready speech', she also charged her with the crime of seeking to take credit for the ideas of others.[69] Despite such tensions, the two remained occasional correspondents until 1889, but after Besant's conversion to Theosophy they became separated by issues of faith.[70] Elizabeth had no time for what she regarded as the pretensions of Theosophy – also a matter of division between her and another former pupil, Frances Swiney in later years.[71] And when Theosophist Susan E. Gay wrote advising her to 'sit at Annie Besant's feet and learn' she was clearly less than pleased.[72]

The controversies that surrounded Besant in the mid-1870s were not, however, only those of her loss of religious faith and her adoption of secularism. They centred, more practically and painfully, on the irretrievable breakdown of her marriage. Besant never wrote graphically of the physical abuse she suffered at her husband's hands. However, she claimed that her subsequent conversion to secularism was the result, not of 'a desire for moral licence . . . [but of a] . . . sense of outraged justice and insulted right' at the cultural systems that vested complete power in a husband over the actions and body of his wife.[73] These views are clearly in accord with Elizabeth's, who understood the vows she had made to Ben on the day of their commitment ceremony to be completely binding, given with mutual consent and not to be upheld by coercion. Annie Besant's sorrows (which also included acute financial hardship and the judicially sanctioned removal of her daughter from her care), only added to Elizabeth's determination to secure the legislative amendments to secure for wives the right to both personal property and to the company of their children.[74] These two campaigns would occupy her life for the next ten years, together with another even more sensitive topic – the issue of marital rape.

Return to centre-stage

As Congleton sought calm after the excitement of the Bradlaugh visit, the winter of 1876–77 provided a period of reflection for the Elmys. Ben developed his literary talents and ambitions, and published (through Bradlaugh's Freethought Publishing Company) a translation of the Italian feminist work, *The Cause of Woman*. The book was favourably reviewed and did much to enhance his status as a feminist author.[75] Elizabeth, meanwhile, prepared to cement her return to public debating circles by submitting a paper to the Aberdeen meeting of the NAPSS. Her robust defence to the 'insolent attack' of one who dared to comment that those wed by a registrar were only 'half married' was recalled autobiographically. She owned later that her words were spoken with some passion, and she could not have been more pleased that the session chairman, the Reverend Dr Phillimore, 'supported [her] plea most earnestly & thanked [her] for having had the "glorious courage" to protest'.[76] Phillimore confided to her afterwards that he had never expected to hear *any* woman speak so.

Such events certainly made a stimulating aside to the workmanlike endeavours that filled her days as MWPC secretary. The strategy of the organisation was to seek first to generate, and then to harness, public opinion to their cause, in order to place pressure on parliamentarians to revise the law. Provoking such shifts in public consciousness was, however, no straightforward task. The issue had to be 'kept alive' at a time when parliamentary attitudes were not amenable to change and it is a testament to the abilities of Ursula Bright that donations to the cause increased year on year to enable such 'educational' work to continue.[77] Elizabeth's workload comprised the distribution of the organisation's literature and the drafting, circulation and collation of upwards of 1,600 petitions: these in support of annual private members' bills that had only the slimmest chance of reaching the statute book.[78] She mourned the indifference or censure that existed in the legislature towards the issue, but recalled her delight when she had been able to exact revenge on one contemptuous peer, Lord James of Hertford. Her letter notes that His Lordship,

> In 1877 . . . told Mr. Hibbert . . . that he should oppose the MWP Bill tooth & nail as it was more mischievous even than Suffrage. In 1882 I had him move the Second Reading of that Bill in his capacity as Attorney General – the Bill having been sent down from the Lords, where Lord Selborne, then Lord Chancellor, had taken it in charge as a *Government measure.*[79]

How she must have delighted in this volte-face. John Tomlinson Hibbert (with Charles Dilke and Osborne Morgan as co-sponsors) had introduced the Married Women's Property Bill into the House of Commons in 1878, after the implacable opposition of the Conservative Lord Chancellor, Lord Cairns, had effectively blocked its passage in the upper chamber the previous year. The second reading was scheduled for 24 July, but much to Elizabeth's consternation (and negating her efforts in organising a 'whip' of MPs in the Bill's support) it was withdrawn in favour of the Army Discipline Bill.[80] She wrote later of her frustration at the 'arduous and at times depressing work' of these years, in pursuit of what must have seemed at times a fruitless cause.[81]

Soon, however, positive developments lightened her mood. First, the General Election of 1880 returned a Liberal government to office and, with it, hopes of a reformist agenda. Second, and perhaps more crucially, after a visit from an influential group of lobbyists of the MWPC in January 1881, Gladstone's Lord Chancellor, Lord Selborne, was converted to the cause.[82] Swiftly the matter was adopted as a government measure. Keen to capitalise on this important development Elizabeth travelled to the capital in March to address the London Dialectical Society, keeping up the relentless pressure in raising the MWPC's profile among London's keenest intellectuals.[83] Selborne's influence in furthering the fortunes of married women's property legislation was extremely significant, and he knew Elizabeth well. As Sir Roundell Palmer, he had grown so familiar with her VADPR labours that he referred to her 'the little Lord

Chancellor', and though the soubriquet was light hearted it indicated the depth of her legal knowledge.[84] Shanley has contended that as 'the wife of a hard pressed silk manufacturer' Elizabeth lacked the 'ease and grace' possessed by Ursula Bright when moving in parliamentary circles. Such playful interactions as this between Elizabeth and Selborne point to a greater familiarity and confidence than this assessment allows and from this moment he was her chief ally. Her contacts with the Palmer family were maintained indefinitely, and although the pragmatic Selborne's change of stance may well have been the result of rational rather than emotive thinking, his yearning for 'logical consistency' in legal affairs was swiftly allied to Elizabeth's passionate desire for reform.[85]

After an unremarkable passage, the Married Women's Property Bill for Scotland received the Royal Assent on 18 July 1881 and Elizabeth wrote to the *Englishwoman's Review* expressing her delight. She also urged that, as the new legislation 'place[d] Scotch wives in a far better position with regard to their property than English wives', it was time to redouble efforts to petition Parliament on the issue.[86] Parliamentary consideration of Irish affairs stalled matters, however, and it was to be another seven months before the Bill was considered at Westminster.[87] In the interim, Elizabeth contributed a paper to the Dublin NAPSS Congress, which highlighted her joy at the positive settlement in Scotland. She tempered her elation on the platform, however, with a practical request that her audience refocus their efforts on behalf of English and Irish women.[88] One swallow (or successful campaign) did not, in her opinion, make a summer.

Though the fight had arguably been won from the moment the Married Women's Property Bill had been adopted by the government, it is possible only to guess at Elizabeth's joy when Lord Selborne, his health restored after a stroke, introduced the English and Irish measure into the House of Lords on 14 February 1882.[89] While its passage into law 'lacked drama and suspense', Elizabeth nevertheless watched the passing of each successive stage with a keen eye.[90] Others on the MWPC were less optimistic and as the summer holidays called them from home, she worked on in isolation.[91] Her fears of last minute obstructions were, to some extent, justified when Mr Warton and Sir George Campbell both rose in the House of Commons to 'condemn the bill as fostering "social revolution" within the English family'.[92] And yet, as Lee Holcombe has claimed, the 'revolutionary principles' of the Bill 'were not set forth in revolutionary terms', but 'couched in the familiar terms of the rules of equity relating to the "separate" property' of a married woman. The consequence was that married women were to hold property 'as if [they] were a feme sole, without the intervention of any trustee', precisely the object of campaigners' desires, as was the fact that married women could be held accountable for their antenuptial debts.[93] Reformers were not seeking privilege, merely equality.

The Married Women's Property Act 1882 passed its final stages on the last day of the summer session and became law on 1 January 1883. It marked, in the words of Elizabeth's friend Zona Vallance, an 'ethical epoch'.[94] Elizabeth, though she claimed the victory as a 'bloodless and beneficent revolution', knew it still did not dispense with the ultimate element of the doctrine of coverture, sexual subjection.[95] While a wife could rightly claim her possessions as her own, her body still belonged to her husband.

The *Englishwoman's Review* for September 1882 carried Caroline Ashurst Biggs's editorial on the Married Women's Property Act together with a detailed article by Elizabeth on its provisions.[96] Biggs attested that to Ursula Bright and Elizabeth Wolstenholme Elmy, above all other supporters of the MWPC, must go 'the honour of sustaining the gallant fight through years of discouragement and delay'.[97] It was only the first of such tributes that would be heaped on Elizabeth's shoulders.[98] The greatest ovation of all was given at the final meeting of the friends and subscribers of the MWPC, held at Willis's Rooms, London, on 18 November. With something approaching a delicious irony, the chairman of this meeting was George Shaw Lefevre – the very person to whom Isabella Tod had threatened to expose Elizabeth as a moral renegade seven years earlier. Elizabeth thanked him on the Committee's behalf for his efforts (and those of all the prominent colleagues who had assisted him in securing the Bill's passage) in a short, graceful speech.[99] Then, amid a tumult of applause, she received from the hands of Alice Scatcherd (on behalf of the National Society for Women's Suffrage) a 'handsomely bound and decorated' testimonial volume, given 'in token of gratitude for the great services which [she] had rendered' to the campaign.[100] Understanding Elizabeth well, the testimonial concluded with the words that her well-wishers hoped that for many years to come she could enjoy 'the reward [she] most prize[d], the consciousness that women's lives ha[d] been made freer, happier, and nobler, by [her] courageous and ... faithful work'.[101] Elizabeth took the opportunity, in her written reply, not only to thank her colleagues for their 'touching address', but to put forward the case for those further reforms 'needed for the final perfecting of the great social revolution'.[102] Sardonically, her phrasing echoed precisely the fears of Mr Warton MP, chief detractor of the Married Women's Property Bill.

From these fond testimonies it would be tempting to believe that Elizabeth's painful exclusion from the company of some in the women's emancipation movement would now be a thing of the past. Yet though the scenes in Willis's Rooms attest to respect and honour for her work, detractors still hovered. The autobiography of American suffragist Elizabeth Cady Stanton, for example, gave the full credit for the passage of the 1882 Act to the 'tact and persistence of Ursula Bright', and carefully relegated Elizabeth's role to the sidelines.[103] An intimate of the Priestman sisters since 1840 (when she had first visited Britain to attend the World Anti-Slavery Convention), Cady Stanton was predisposed to become a natural ally of the radicals, her views on the subjection of married women much in accord with Elizabeth's circle. In Britain on this occasion to witness the marriage of her daughter Harriot to William Blatch, Cady Stanton travelled to Willis's Rooms in the company of Priscilla Bright McLaren.[104] She knew Elizabeth well, but while it would have been extremely difficult to record the passing of the Married Women's Property Act with no mention of the MWPC's secretary, Stanton does so with as little grace as possible, using one perfunctory reference.[105] On reading *Eighty Years and More*, Elizabeth was obviously piqued, and she took care to inform McIlquham that her opinion of the American was 'less favourable and friendly' than before.[106] Clearly, by the time of the memoir's publication in 1898, the cooperative relationship that had existed between Cady Stanton and Elizabeth had cooled by several degrees from its previous warm admiration.

While Elizabeth's efforts to improve the lives of the married women of Britain received commendation by at least some of her peers, her attempts to change attitudes to encompass a perception of wives as possessing a moral right to determine their own actions were less successful. That English Common Law denied a wife the right of consent to sexual intercourse, a right that even prostitutes enjoyed, was to Elizabeth an infamy.[107] And much of her subsequent writing underlined her agreement with John Stuart Mill's denunciation of a married man's right to subject his wife to the ordeal of becoming 'the instrument of an animal function contrary to her inclinations'.[108] Where previously Elizabeth had committed herself to the harrowing work of opposing the CDA to free 'the unhappy female prostitute [from] the virtual slave[ery] of the State', in the 1880s she began to publicly address the legislative curbs preventing wives' sexual freedom.[109] And while she valued the 'energy and sympathy' of Frances Power Cobbe, which had driven forward the Matrimonial Causes Act 1878 (the provisions of which negated the perceived 'natural' authority of husbands to physically chastise their spouse) her personal endeavours concentrated directly on the issue of marital rape.[110]

On 3 March 1880, at the London Dialectical Society, she addressed the matter in public, in a speech considering the cumbersome provisions of the Criminal Code Bill, then before Parliament.[111] She was the first woman ever to speak on this most delicate of subjects, and while she gave no indication of nervousness she begged the indulgence of her audience. 'It is difficult for a woman to speak [on this matter] without giving offence', she told them, and 'impossible . . . to speak at all without expressing strong feeling.'[112] Had the Criminal Code Bill passed through Parliament, it would have enshrined in law the premise that 'Rape is the act of a man, not under the age of 14 years, having carnal knowledge of a woman, *who is not his wife*, without her consent.' This would, in effect, have degraded 'every English wife to the legal position of the purchased slave of the harem'.[113] Elizabeth's contention was that this was an issue not merely for the middle classes to ponder as *all* women were affected, and this speech marked a significant moment in the creation of a 'gender-inclusive' rather than 'class-exclusive' approach to new campaigns – as equitable trusts had, in fact, largely protected the property of elite women from misappropriation. Elizabeth's speech opened up an important new avenue for the development of her feminism, and her exploration of conjugal 'rights' would have important consequences for the future of feminist ideology in the next decade.

The Criminal Code Bill did not, in fact, pass into law, much to Elizabeth's satisfaction. But it was another of the many measures included in its provisions which prompted her next campaign. This was the proposed change in the provisions for charging women with the crime of infanticide, whereby if a woman could not prove she had obtained 'reasonable assistance' in childbirth, perhaps with the intent that her baby might die (or where she had wilfully concealed her maternity), she could be subject to a capital offence. Elizabeth claimed that such actions, being impossible to prove, would lead to 'many groundless accusations of wholly innocent persons' and a poor mother, possibly deserted by her partner, might ultimately have to suffer the injustice of the gallows when her intentions had been honourable. The answer to these dilemmas was not coercive legislation aimed at women only, but a clear and true accep-tance of 'the principle of full and equal parental responsibility'.[114] Any government which refused to acknowledge such a basic concept as that of a mother's claim upon her child was, she argued, guilty of a 'crowning infamy'.[115] The campaign she launched to amend this injustice was begun only weeks after the triumph of the Married Women's Property Act.

Conducted almost solely on her own initiative, and on the conviction of the fitness of her ethical stance, she was supported throughout by the man for whom she had endured such overt public censure, her husband Ben.

Notes

1 Bland, *Banishing the Beast*, p. 155.
2 Kathryn Gleadle, *Radical Writing*, p. 4; Charles Fourier, 'Degradation of Women in Civilization', *Theorie des Quatre Mouvements et des Destinees Generales* (Paris: [n.p.] 1841–48), pp. 131–3.
3 Thomas Frost, *Forty Years Recollections: Literary and Political* (1880), p. 19, quoted in Barbara Taylor, *Eve and the New Jerusalem: Socialism and Feminism in the Nineteenth Century* (London: Virago, 1983) p. 185.
4 EWE/HM, 6/3/1904, 47454, fol. 251. (Emphasis in original.)
5 Ben Wolstenholme Elmy to the Editor, 'Prerogative and Republicanism', *The Examiner*, 13 March 1875, p. 298.
6 Enclosure by Josephine Butler in a letter from Isabella Tod to Helen Priestman Bright Clark, 16/11/1875, MP.
7 A curious and possibly misdated letter was written from Josephine Butler to Anna-Maria Priestman, in which Butler notes that Elizabeth Wolstenholme was 'compelled to retire from the Secretaryship of that Committee on the 12th October', although Butler considered, owing to Elizabeth's over-wrought condition that she 'ought to be released at once'. The letter is catalogued as 5 September [1875], but Wolstenholme Elmy had married the previous year, on 12 October, and Butler refers to her here as 'Miss Wolstenholme'. If Wolstenholme resigned her Secretaryship of the VA on the date of her marriage, as this letter indicates, Butler's letter was written in 1874. Josephine Butler to Miss Priestman, 5/9 [1875], 3/JBL/12/65. WL.
8 Mary Estlin to Mary Priestman, 12/3 [1874], MP.
9 Pankhurst, *TSM*, p. 31.
10 EWE to Anna Maria Priestman, 14/8/1874, MP.
11 Pankhurst, *TSM*, p. 31.
12 Taylor, *Eve and the New Jerusalem*, p. 276.
13 Anon., 'The Northern Counties League', *The Shield*, 25 November 1874, p. 241.
14 Pankhurst, *TSM*, p. 31.
15 Josephine Butler to Miss Priestman, 5/9[1875], 3/JBL/12/65. WL.
16 Pankhurst, *TSM*, p. 32.
17 June Purvis and Maureen Wright, 'Writing Suffragette History: The Contending Autobiographical Narratives of the Pankhursts', *Women's History Review*, Vol.12, Vol. 3 & 4, 2005; pp. 405–33 416ff. Also Kathryn Dodd, 'Introduction' to her edited *Sylvia Pankhurst Reader* (Manchester: Manchester University Press, 1993), pp. 1–30.
18 EWE, 'Women and the Law', p. 6.
19 Anon., 'Renewal of the Married Women's Property Legislation', *Women's Suffrage Journal*, 24 September 1875, p. 140.
20 This intriguing letter also includes the information that a group of friends, including the Priestman sisters, had been 'sent to Coventry' as a result of some unacknowledged

misdemeanour. There is no direct link to the Elmy situation, but Agnes Henry immediately goes on to praise Ben Elmy, whom she has recently met. Agnes Henry to Anna Maria Priestman, 2/5/1875, MP.

21 Pankhurst, TSM, p. 31.

22 Anon., 'Congleton and Buglawton Progressive Club', *National Reformer*, 19 December 1875, p. 399. On Ben Elmy's membership of the General Council see, 'National Council', *National Reformer*, 3 December 1876, pp. 355–6. On secularism in Congleton see, Edward Royle, *Victorian Infidels: The Origins of the British Secularist Movement 1791–1866* (Manchester: Manchester University Press, 1974), p. 142. Annie Besant was a recent convert to secularism, prompted by her meeting with Charles Bradlaugh on 2 August 1874. Annie Besant, *An Autobiography*, 2nd edn (London: T. Fisher Unwin, 1893), p. 134.

23 Ajax [Annie Besant], quoting from a letter from Mr Wilson, Congleton Town Clerk to Ben Elmy, 27/5/1875, 'Daybreak', *National Reformer*, 20 June 1875, pp. 389–90.

24 Ajax, 'Daybreak', p. 390; Holton, 'Free love . . .', p. 210.

25 Ajax, 'Daybreak', pp. 389–90.

26 I. Whitwell Wilson to Henry Wilson, 20/12/1875, 3/JBL/14/11. WL.

27 Mr Llewellyn to Mrs Wilson, 7/10/1875, 3/JBL/13/09. WL.

28 Edward Royle, *Radicals, Secularists and Republicans: Popular freethought in Britain, 1866–1915* (Manchester and New Jersey: Manchester University Press and Rowman and Littlefield, 1980), p. 250.

29 Josephine Butler to Millicent Garrett Fawcett, 8/12 [1875], 3/JBL/14/04. WL.

30 Copy of card from Josephine Butler to Isabella Tod. Enclosed in Isabella Tod to Helen Priestman Bright Clark, 16/11/1875, MP. (Emphasis in original.)

31 Josephine Butler to Millicent Garrett Fawcett, 8/12 [1875], 3/JBL/14/04. WL.

32 Holton, *Suffrage Days*, p. 43.

33 Isabella Tod to Helen Priestman Bright Clarke, 16/11/1875, MP.

34 Josephine Butler to Millicent Garrett Fawcett, 8/12 [1875], 3/JBL/14/04. WL.

35 Isabella Tod to Helen Priestman Bright Clarke, 16/11/1875, MP.

36 Isabella Tod to Helen Priestman Bright Clarke, 30/11/1875, MP.

37 Holton, 'Free Love', p. 211.

38 Millicent Garrett Fawcett to EWE, 10/12 [1875]. Autograph Letter Collection, Strand /09. WL. Rubinstein, *A Different World*, p. 57, fn. 55.

39 EWE/HM, [n.d., but possibly late June 1899], 47451, fol. 325.

40 Josephine Butler to Millicent Garrett Fawcett, 8/12 [1875], 3/JBL/14/04. WL.

41 Stead, *Josephine Butler*, p. 55. EWE is listed in reports of the MWPC only months after these events; Anon., 'Further Report of the Married Women's Property Committee', *Englishwoman's Review*, August 1876, pp. 375–82; Anon, 'Married Women's Property', *Englishwoman's Review*, July 1878, pp. 312–13.

42 EWE to Anna Maria Priestman, 14/8/1874, MP.

43 Quinlan, *Genteel Revolutionaries*, chapter 1; Purvis, *Emmeline Pankhurst*, Chapter 3.

44 EWE/HM, 25/4/1902, 47452, fol. 292.

45 John Tosh, 'The Making of Masculinities: The Middle Class in Late Nineteenth-Century Britain' in Angela V. John and Claire Eustance (eds), *The Men's Share?: Masculinities, Male Support and Women's Suffrage in Britain 1890–1920* (London: Routledge, 1997), p. 39; Ignota, 'Pioneers', p. 416.

46 Elmy, 'The Individuality of Woman', p. 507.

47 EWE/HM, 3/3/1906, 47453, fol. 221.
48 Pankhurst contends that Ben Elmy had been a 'violently cruel and unfaithful' husband, something unsubstantiated in any of Wolstenholme Elmy's texts. Pankhurst, *TSM*, p. 32.
49 HM to Frances Rowe, 11/8/1901, 47452, fol. 195.
50 Ignota, 'Pioneers', p. 415.
51 Ignota, 'Pioneers', p. 417. (My emphasis.)
52 Sylvia Strauss, *'Traitors to the Masculine Cause': The Men's Campaigns for Women's Rights* (Westport and London: Greenwood Press, 1982), p. xviii.
53 HM, biographical notes on EWE (n.d.), but possibly late September 1901, 47452, fol. 209. (Emphasis in original.)
54 The Married Women's Property Amendment Act 1874 earned the soubriquet of the 'creditors' bill', its purpose being to ensure that husbands were liable for their wives 'prenuptial debts to the extent of the assets he had received from her upon their marriage'. Shanley, *Feminism*, pp. 104–9, p. 107.
55 Holton, *Suffrage Days*, pp. 46–7.
56 Anon., 'Further Report of the Married Women's Property Committee', *Englishwoman's Review*, August 1876, pp. 375–82, p. 376.
57 John Hinde Palmer echoed Bright's fulsome praise, not shy to inform the MWPC of the assistance Elizabeth had given him while in Parliament. Anon., 'Further Report', p. 376.
58 Isabella Tod to Helen Priestman Bright Clarke, 30/11/1875, MP.
59 When Bright took office the debts of the MWPC were £158. By the time of the AGM the organisation had a £300 surplus. MWPC, Annual Report, 1876, pp. 9–12.
60 See, for example, Anon., 'The Property of Married Women', *Women's Suffrage Journal*, November 1876, p. 155; Anon., 'Married Women's Property Committee', *Women's Suffrage Journal*, April 1877, p. 61. Sylvia Pankhurst argues that her mother Emmeline was accepted on to the MWPC 'as a compliment to her husband' and not for any political skills she, at that stage, possessed. Pankhurst, *TSM*, p. 57.
61 Holton, 'Free Love', p. 214.
62 Charles Bradlaugh, 'Congleton Christian Civilisation', *National Reformer*, 8 October 1876, pp. 225–6.
63 Stephens, *History of Congleton*, pp. 205–6.
64 Bradlaugh, 'Christian Civilisation', pp. 225–6; Hypatia Bradlaugh Bonner, *Charles Bradlaugh*, Vol. II (London and Leipzig: T. Fisher Unwin, 1908), pp. 54–5.
65 Bradlaugh, 'Christian Civilisation', p. 225.
66 Bradlaugh, 'Christian Civilisation', p. 225.
67 Holton, 'Free Love', p. 211.
68 Bradlaugh, 'Christian Civilisation', p. 226.
69 EWE/HM, 17/1/1900, 47452, fol. 43; EWE/HM, 8/9/1904, 47454, fol. 2.
70 For a discussion of the relationship between women theosophists and the women's suffrage movement see Joy Dixon, *Divine Feminine: Theosophy and Feminism in England* (Baltimore and London: The Johns Hopkins University Press, 2001), chapter 7.
71 EWE wrote an appreciative review of Swiney's book *The Awakening of Woman* in 1899, but at the same time noted privately that its author had little critical faculty and was

'dreadfully hampered by her religion'. EWE (Ignota), 'The Awakening of Woman', *Westminster Review*, July 1899, pp. 69–72; EWE/HM, 11/12/1899, 47452, fol. 34.

72 EWE/HM, 28/1/1893, 47440, fol. 316.

73 Besant, *An Autobiography*, p. 100.

74 Besant wrote on the nature of marriage under the Common Law of England in a key paper published in 1882. Annie Besant, *Marriage, As It Was, As It Is, and As It Should Be: A Plea for Reform*, 2nd edn (London: Freethought Publishing Company, 1882).

75 Luisa To-Sko (translated by Ben Elmy), *The Cause of Woman* (London: Freethought Publishing Company, 1877); Anon., 'Review of The Cause of Woman', *Englishwoman's Review*, September 1877, pp. 406–7.

76 EWE/HM, 6/3/1904, 47453, fol. 251.

77 Shanley, *Feminism*, p. 117.

78 Over 500,000 leaflets passed through Wolstenholme Elmy's hands prior to the passage of the Married Women's Property Act 1882.

79 EWE/HM, 3/11/1908, 47455, fol. 215.

80 Anon., 'Married Women's Property', *Englishwoman's Review*, August 1879, pp. 369–71.

81 MWPC, Annual Report, 1879, p. 3.

82 The members of the deputation had included John Hinde Palmer, Jacob Bright and Sir Arthur Hobhouse.

83 'The Property and Status of Married Women', *Englishwoman's Review*, 15 March 1881, p. 133.

84 EWE/HM, 18/12/1901, 47452, fol. 226; EWE/HM, 14/8/1903, 47453, fol. 155.

85 Shanley, *Feminism*, pp. 118–23.

86 EWE to the Editor, *Englishwoman's Review*, 15 July 1881, pp. 311–12.

87 Wolstenholme Elmy notes that such was her frustration at the 'block' which Irish affairs were placing on the married women's property legislation that she wrote her 'only' letter to Charles Stuart Parnell. She did not receive a reply but noted that the 'whip' of the Irish MP's was withdrawn. EWE/HM, 15/11/1898, 47451, fol. 266. Holcombe, *Wives and Property*, p. 200.

88 NAPSS, *Transactions*, 1881, p. 248.

89 3 Hansard 266 (14 February 1882), p. 626, quoted in Shanley, *Feminism*, p. 124.

90 Shanley, *Feminism*, p. 124.

91 EWE/HM, 30/7/1904, 47453, fol. 314.

92 3 Hansard 270 (8 June 1882), 615–67, quoted in Shanley, *Feminism*, p. 124.

93 Holcombe, *Wives and Property*, pp. 201–2.

94 Zona Vallance, 'Women as Moral Beings', *International Journal of Ethics*, Vol. 12, No. 2, 1902, pp. 173–95, pp. 186–7.

95 MWPC, Final Report, p. 53; Holcombe, *Wives and Property*, Chapter 9.

96 EWE and Caroline Ashurst Biggs, 'The Married Women's Property Act 1882', *Englishwoman's Review*, September 1882, pp. 385–93.

97 Biggs, 'Married Women's Property', p. 393.

98 George Hastings, for example, gave Wolstenholme Elmy the sole credit for introducing the issue of married women's property reform to the Social Science Association in 1867. Editorial, 'The Social Science Congress', *Englishwoman's Review*, 14 October 1882, pp. 433–50, p. 434.

99 Elizabeth Cady Stanton, *Eighty Years and More* (London: T. Fisher Unwin, 1898), p. 358.

100 Anon., 'Record of Events: Married Women's Property Final Meeting', *Englishwoman's Review*, December 1882, pp. 549–53.

101 Anon., 'Record of Events', *Englishwoman's Review*, p. 553.

102 EWE Circular Letter, 1/1/1883, Guardianship of Infants papers, BL.

103 Stanton, *Eighty Years and More*, p. 358.

104 Holton, *Suffrage Days*, pp. 61–2.

105 Stanton, *Eighty Years and More*, p. 358.

106 EWE/HM, 6/4/1898, 47451, fol. 199.

107 The words of Judge Hale regarding the consent given by women at marriage, and upon which the Common Law rested, were that 'The husband cannot be guilty of a rape committed by himself upon his lawful wife, for by *their matrimonial consent and contract* the wife hath given herself up in this kind unto her husband, which she *cannot* retract.' EWE, 'The Marriage Law of England', pp. 115–16.

108 John Stuart Mill, *The Subjection of Women*, quoted in Ignota (EWE), 'The Present Legal Position of Women in the United Kingdom', *Westminster Review*, May 1905, pp. 513–29, p. 522.

109 Ignota, 'The Present Legal Position', p. 524.

110 Personal notes by Harriet McIlquham [n.d.], 47452, fol. 209. On the effect of Power Cobbe's campaign, begun with the publication of her article 'Wife Torture in England', in the *Contemporary Review* of April 1878, see Shanley, *Feminism*, pp. 164–70. See also, Constance Rover, *Love, Morals and the Feminists* (London: Routledge & Kegan Paul, 1970), p. 25.

111 Abrams, *Freedom's Cause*, p. 4.

112 EWE, *The Criminal Code in its Relation to Women* (Manchester: A. Ireland, 1880), p. 8.

113 EWE, *Criminal Code*, pp. 9–10.

114 EWE, *Criminal Code*, p. 8.

115 EWE, Circular Letter, New Year's Day 1883.

5

The 'great mole' of the women's movement: 1883–90[1]

An instrument of progress

Elizabeth rejoiced that the bells of the New Year of 1883 had rung in a new era of justice for her sex. 'The legal position of every wife in England', she wrote, 'had change[d] from that of her husband's chattel to that of a responsible human being.'[2] She did not, however, rest on the laurels of the MWPC's success. Rather, buoyed by its achievements, she turned her attention to the persistence of the sexual double standard in matters of divorce and the guardianship of children. While her work was pursued with as much enthusiasm as before, the latter 1880s were a period of increasing financial hardship for the Elmys. The economic boom which had made industrialised Britain the powerhouse of the world had shattered and the impact was wide ranging. The silk-crêpe trade could not remain insulated from the effects of the fiscal crisis and this, combined with the impact of a fire at Eaton Mill in 1886, straitened the family's circumstances.

Young Frank, a quiet, reflective child, was unable to benefit from the expensive residential education his mother had (albeit briefly) enjoyed, and he seemed content to be often in Elizabeth's company. She wrote in May 1889 of the sad spectacle they viewed on walks together through the cheerless streets of Congleton. Boom times had passed and the silk mills along the banks of the Dane turned idle, along with their machinery. Many redundant textile workers emigrated in search of a better life. The spectre of hunger hung over those who remained, and Ben Elmy acted as foreman of the jury in cases where former mill hands had died of starvation.[3] Elizabeth mourned the loss of the 'beautiful industry'; indeed, she wrote that it made her 'heart ache'. However, she was keenly aware that although there was hardship at Buxton House, for her working-class neighbours (and especially their threadbare children) things were far worse. [4] On one cold autumn morning, for example, four labouring men fought one another for the chance to bring in the family's coal.

Elizabeth's recollection of winter conditions in Cheshire was harsh. She looked towards the season of fog and frost 'with terror' and only gained 'life and strength' with the coming of spring.[5] Though feeling low and troubled by rheumatism, she was cheered one day in December 1882 to find an unexpected bequest of £500 in her, always capacious, post-bag. The donation was the gift of Hampshire philanthropist Richard Barlow Kennett, and his letter gave instructions that Elizabeth apply the money freely, to any cause she considered worthy. Perhaps tired after the conclusion of the long MWPC campaign she declined the gift, which was passed to the Vigilance Association as a 'Special Fund'.[6] The money was given with the caveat that it supported campaigns in three specific areas; first, to challenge the laws of intestacy; second, to work for the implementation of measures to abolish all suits for the restitution of conjugal rights; and finally, to seek an amendment of the law in relation to the guardianship of children. The VADPR doubled the donation using a 'matched funding' technique, but the group did not labour with sufficient swiftness for Elizabeth's satisfaction. She wrote to McIlquham later that she regretted her decision, for with Kennett's money she could have started her own campaign for changes to the child custody laws 'a year earlier'.[7]

The earliest public notice of the guardianship of infants' agitation is found in the *Journal* of the VADPR in September 1883, but the topic had long occupied Elizabeth's thoughts. In 1872, for example, she had voiced her disapproval at the palliative and inadequate provisions inherent in what would become the Infant Custody Act of 1873. This was itself a piece of revisionist legislation designed to extend the provisions of the Infant Custody Act of 1839, in which a mother was granted custody of her children only until their seventh birthday.[8] In 1877, she raised the matter again, speaking before the Jurisprudence Department of the NAPSS Congress on the desirability of making the rearing and nurturing of children the co-equal right (and obligation) of both parents.[9] Three years later she returned to the theme, this time in Edinburgh, where she intervened in the discussion following advocate John Boyd Kinnear's paper regarding the Scottish married women's property legislation. Her objective was to challenge his proposal that married women, once granted property rights, should be liable to contribute to the support of the household on an equal basis with their husbands. Why should they be thus constrained, she argued, when they had no rights whatever over the lives of their children?[10] Only the boldest of claims adopted and pursued with the highest ethical motives would ever satisfy her and in the summer of 1883 she professed her intention to pursue legislation which sought *'nothing less than the entire re-adjustment of the legal position of the mother in the family'.*[11]

The way Elizabeth elected to describe the inauguration of the infants' campaign provides a different insight into her character from that 'loyal unselfishness' with which she was often credited by her friends.[12] She recalled that the agitation was commenced purely on her own initiative and that she 'carried [it] into law without a single meeting'.[13] Within this brief aside it is possible to view the personality of a determined workaholic, who did not always toil with devoted collegiality. Her unhappy experiences of committee work helped to alienate her from working in this way, believing that large committees hindered, rather than helped, push objectives forward. She also liked to direct operations and policy, and while she accepted the need for dedicated colleagues, there was nothing she hated more than apathy. She insisted that all should labour as arduously as she did herself and believed that the *real* worth to the cause lay in the hearts of individual workers who would, if necessary, work on when all hope seemed lost.[14] Her approach could, and did, encourage mutual criticism, as few could match her exacting standards. Care must therefore be taken when reading her correspondence to retain an awareness that those she denigrates may have been far more active in their chosen work than she chooses to assume.

Elizabeth could be acerbic and cutting in her comments but, ironically, she was horrified if accused of being divisive. Sylvia Pankhurst believed her formidable, but classified her as 'an instrument in the grasp of progress', an image which conjures up a picture of a piece of human flotsam tossed by the winds of change.[15] She possessed, rather, an adventurous spirit, and the 'optimistic imagining' of a radical reformer who intended to make her mark on the future. Given this dynamism, it is little wonder that she had a number of rivals, if not outright enemies. However, 'the pot pourri' of activists of who formed her circle had each been influenced by a multitude of contrasting assumptions on the nature of the perfect society, and few shared precisely her construction of a just world.[16] She had sacrificed her friendships with Emily Davies and Lydia Becker on ideological grounds; and Florence Fenwick Miller, a member of the London School Board, who had come into Elizabeth's orbit as a sympathiser of the VADPR, was another with whom she would come to disagree. Eager to capitalise on the younger woman's evident talents and enthusiasm, the two worked well during the child custody battle, especially when Elizabeth requested that Florence interrupt the parliamentary election campaign of a prominent lawyer in order to highlight the prejudicial terms of existing legislation.[17] The ruse succeeded, but despite this promising beginning, by the turn of the decade, Fenwick Miller had earned herself a reputation as her former mentor's 'nemesis'.[18] The destruction of this friendship was a crucial part of Elizabeth's history during the 1880s.

The sacred trust of parenthood

Chief among the work Elizabeth asked of colleagues such as Fenwick Miller was the distribution of 'educational' literature throughout the many organisations with which they were associated. She was anxious that, while she could not personally fully adhere to the sentiments of some groups (for example, the Conservatives' Primrose League) the space in which they met, and their audiences, were utilised to provide opportunities for feminist conversion.[19] A frequent theme of MWPC propaganda, for instance, had been the publication of numerous and widely circulated pamphlets detailing (often with lurid clarity) the 'wrongs' that wives had suffered under Common Law. In 1884 she adopted the tactic again and drew together a series of articles under the title of *Opinions of the Press*, which narrated the heart wrenching experiences of mothers deprived of the companionship of their children by absolutist fathers.[20] This pamphlet was only one of the many methods she adopted in order to bring the matter to public attention. For instance, the pages of the *Englishwoman's Review* and the VADPR's *Journal* were also frequently used for disseminating propaganda.[21] Elizabeth was later accused by the *Women's Penny Paper* of not making best use of the 'mass appeal of the press', but she cleverly countered such criticism by noting in the meticulous record of the passage of the Guardianship of Infants Act she compiled in 1886 (subtitled *Three Years Effort*) the 'valuable aid' given to the movement by journalists.[22]

If the help of the press and of influential figures such as James Bryce (who brought in the Guardianship of Infants Bill to the House of Commons on 6 February 1884) was significant to Elizabeth so, equally, was the support she received from Ben Elmy. She deliberately highlighted their close bond in *Three Years Effort,* as a sign that their marriage had both a public and a private significance.[23] They bore together, she noted, the 'entire responsibility . . . the active direction . . . [and] . . . the greater share of the actual labour' involved from the inception of the agitation until the measure received the Royal Assent on 25 June 1886. The share of the financial burden carried by the couple is unknown, but it was likely to have been significant, with considerable sums expended in publishing and distributing over 40,000 pamphlets and 500,000 leaflets to a correspondence network of approximately 10,000 persons. Somehow, too, Elizabeth found time to write 6,000 personal letters on the issue – an exacting task which contributed to the £238.14s.10d spent on postage.[24] None of this labour was begrudged by the couple, who viewed it as a humanitarian service.

Ben also collaborated with his wife in the delivery of lectures on the arguments of the Bill. For example, he read Augustus Baker's paper *The Custody and Guardianship of Children* at the NAPSS Huddersfield Congress in 1883, and replied to questions on Elizabeth's behalf at the Birmingham meeting the following year after her lecture, 'The Infants' Bill' had provoked a contentious discussion. He also accompanied her to London on 15 October 1884, when she presented her arguments to the London Dialectical Society.[25] Her key line of reasoning was that the guardianship of children was the *natural* right of both parents, and that present legislation was 'opposed to natural law, common sense, right feeling and justice [and] can be [no] longer maintained. It [was] a degradation of the noblest fatherhood, an insult to all motherhood, and an absolute denial of justice and right to children.'[26] In this view she was supported Dr Frances Hoggan, who had presented a companion paper in Birmingham entitled the *Position of Women in the Family*. Hoggan went so far as to castigate even the radicals of the VADPR for not offering sufficient support to the campaign. Their comments during the first twelve months, had, she said, suffered from 'excessive timidity'![27]

Parliamentarians too, as we have seen in the case of the married women's property campaign, were adept at sidestepping the issue of women's 'natural' rights. Cruel and dissolute behaviour towards wives had cleverly been manipulated into a representative 'social model' of the poor, and thus as something remote from the civilised morals of elite liberal, male reformers.[28] Matters affecting the well-being of children, however, could not be so easily theorised and manoeuvred to advantage, for rich men as well as poor abused the powers that patriarchal fatherhood bestowed. W.E. Forster (who served Gladstone as Chief Secretary for Ireland during 1880–82) noted precisely this point when he commented that serious abuses occurred 'often enough among persons in the position of life of Members of the House' of Commons.[29] At the heart of the matter lay the deeply contentious issue of familial government and Elizabeth was at pains to point out that parental 'dual control' of children's lives would only increase harmonious domestic relations. In a paper for the *Englishwoman's Review* she asserted that dual control was *natural*, because

> nature herself established [it], when she gave to every human child two parents . . . [W]e have to consider whether we will continue, by unnatural devices, to defeat the great purposes of nature, or whether we will humbly and reverently accept her teachings, consonant as these are with reason, justice and the highest interests of humanity.[30]

Nailing her radical colours firmly to the mast Elizabeth expounded her belief that society had developed and was acclimatising itself to new forces, something which rendered the concept of children being their father's *property* outmoded. In this, as in so much else, she questioned assumed behaviour, this time by asserting the rights of the child over those of its parent. 'The dignity and worth of even the youngest child, as an independent human being, is becoming . . . recognized', she wrote, and as a consequence fathers had no need to be 'exalted by a selfish and stupid prerogative into a mimic deity' whose dictates were, both in practice and in custom, law.[31] While this gradual, revisionist shift in family organisation may have been apparent in private life, its effects were not so obvious when disputes came to court.[32] And public support was stimulated for the campaign late in 1883 by the highly publicised and ultimately fruitless court battle of Harriet Agar-Ellis to secure visiting rights to her sixteen-year-old daughter. The judiciary declared that, 'The limit and scope of paternal authority' was absolute, and custom ensured that fathers remained their children's guardian 'by nature and nurture . . . whatever age they may be'. Mothers, for their part, had 'no legal status, no choice, voice, lot or part in the matter.'[33]

Framed with the principal of dual control at its heart and the interests of the child to the fore, the Guardianship of Infants Bill commenced a two-and-a-half-year passage through Parliament in the spring of 1884.[34] To Elizabeth's intense displeasure, however, the egalitarian standards upon which it had been based were consistently eroded as the months passed. The key tenet of the Bill was enshrined in Clause 2, and provided that 'The parents of any infant shall during the continuance of their marriage be its joint guardians.'[35] This sweeping change, which vested the rights of 'nature and nurture' in both husband and wife, as opposed to the father alone, was sacrificed on 14 July when the Bill came before the House of Commons Committee – lost on division, by 43 votes to 19. In its place, a new Clause 5 was inserted. This swept away the ideals upon which the legislation had been based and introduced instead increased 'protection' for mothers against the law's worst abuses. Elizabeth viewed the trouncing of Clause 2 as nothing less than a 'mutilation' and roundly criticised her parliamentary colleagues for sacrificing their conscience for expediency's sake.[36]

On 25 July, when Bryce informed his colleagues that Clause 5 of the Bill would not 'extinguish the permanent Common Law right of the father' in an ongoing marriage, but merely institute measures for the 'protection' of mothers' interests in cases of separation or widowhood, Elizabeth knew her ambitions had been betrayed.[37] She argued that to frame the measure in such terms ensured that fathers would remain in a position of domestic omnipresence and cast wives into the role of unpaid nursemaids responsible for the care of their husbands' children. The principal of coverture remained intact, and while parliamentarians in both Houses had again proved themselves amenable to legislating against 'abuse' they remained, ideologically, rooted in the past. Elizabeth mourned, more than ever before, women's lack of the parliamentary vote. 'The lack of a political voice, action, or influence', she wrote, constantly resulted in legislation which 'interferes with women's freedom . . . whilst affecting to protect them'.[38] Nonetheless, she persevered, knowing that even in its reduced form the Bill retained some merits.

The Guardianship of Infants Bill completed its Commons stages at 2.40 am on 1 August 1884, after 280 petitions containing 28,272 signatures were received by Parliament.[39] As these had all passed across Elizabeth's writing table it was with some justification that Alice Scatcherd noted 'How that woman works!'[40] It would take a further nine months, however, for the measure to negotiate the prickly terrain of the House of Lords. Introduced there by Lord Fitzgerald, it had been helped on its path under the statesmanlike hand of Lord Selborne, who spoke in its support only days after the death of his beloved wife.[41] Though progress stalled in 1885, after the institution of Gladstone's third ministry in February 1886, the Bill was adopted as a government measure. This ensured its swift implementation and, despite her earlier anger, Elizabeth was disposed to be magnanimous to the government. She wrote that in some respects (as in the removal of the authority of a father's 'dead hand') the legislation had been 'solid and comprehensive', and she claimed that Gladstone had earned 'lasting honour' as a consequence of its passage.[42]

These were the last kind words she ever wrote about the Liberal premier and his increasingly beleaguered party, embroiled again in the matter of Irish Home Rule. Ultimately, her opinion that the conscience of the nation was changing was upheld by the mention of the Infants Act in the Queen's speech, which ended the parliamentary session of June

1886 – the topic of familial reorganisation not now thought too scandalous to merit inclusion. Personally, Elizabeth's lifelong interest in the affairs of children remained, and she was approached during the summer of 1902 by Lady Laura Ridding (Selborne's daughter) to serve as English delegate to the International Law Committee.[43] Then in her sixty-ninth year, Elizabeth declined to be nominated, but the level of esteem in which Ridding held her opinion was clear. The presence at the table of the 'greatest living authority' on family issues would, she argued, have added significantly to the committee's knowledge.[44]

Issues of individuality

Elizabeth's hope was that the Guardianship of Infants Act, albeit a restrictive legal acknowledgement of wives as equal guardians of their children's welfare, would alter public perceptions of them as 'mere instruments for replenishing the earth with heroes [or] clodhoppers'.[45] Her sentiments claimed a dignity for married women beyond any bestowed by cultural and legal precedent and gave them, by implication, an active voice in shaping their destiny. This was because the acknowledgement of legal guardianship attested to mothers' rationality and independence in being responsible for the care of the young and, as such, implied a means through which they could secure their citizenship. To this end, Elizabeth published 'a separate and personal appeal' as an appendix to *Three Years Effort*. It was a call to arms to fight for the ultimate prize, and it claimed for women, in an assertion that would become increasingly significant for Elizabeth's articulation of democratic citizenship, 'that personal freedom . . . and equal birthright . . . which is the most sacred right of humanity'.[46]

The 'appeal' for the vote was written at a moment when the women's suffrage movement had lost a little of its momentum, for despite a move to incorporate an amendment to the Liberal Reform Bill of 1884, the attempt had failed. Although she urged Parliament to ratify the amendment while some 'element of grace' remained, Elizabeth had nonetheless criticised its terms, as it had been phrased restrictively, to include only qualified single women and widows.[47] This she considered 'absurd, illogical, unjust and indefensible'.[48] The amendment was lost on 10 June after the dramatic personal intervention of Gladstone, who spoke in opposition.[49] The premier's comments, it has been suggested, were 'largely bluff', the truth being that he was deeply concerned that the House of Lords might reject the Bill altogether if any move to include women had passed the lower chamber.[50] Naturally enough, such a threat had incensed

Gladstone's most radical colleagues, and as he needed their support over the matter of Home Rule, the Prime Minister sought a passage for the Reform Bill that would not cause controversy. The result of its provisions was that some 60 per cent of the male population became eligible to vote. Personally, Elizabeth saw Gladstone's actions as misogynist, though he ultimately failed in his game of bluff. Home Rule was lost and the bitterly divided Liberal Party fractured. The effect was to polarise opinion in the women's suffrage movement in the latter 1880s as feminists sought, and failed, to adopt a cohesive strategy at a time when methods of campaign and ideals of personal allegiance only encouraged inconsistency and division.

The crucial issue of the married women's vote continued to be at the core of suffragists' heated debates, much as it had when Elizabeth and Lydia Becker had first quarrelled over the issue in 1874. An acknowledgement of individual worth and personal autonomy had always been crucial to Elizabeth's interpretation of a 'just' society, and she understood the rights of human individuals to be inviolable. There was never any doubt that she would continue to adhere to the most radical and wide-ranging conception of citizenship, and though the bitter quarrels surrounding her marriage had necessitated a tactical withdrawal from the Executive of suffrage societies, the late 1880s saw her return to the heart of the debates. Before she did so, however, she courted further controversy in two matters with a wider agenda. One was her alliance to the Fair Trade movement and the second, more contentious, was her response to the publication in W.T. Stead's *Pall Mall Gazette* of a sensationalist exposé of the sexual trafficking of young girls.[51]

Stead, who by now had known Elizabeth for almost fifteen years, had been Editor of the *Gazette* since 1883. He possessed an enviable reputation as a social reformer. He was an excellent propagandist, and to highlight the dark underworld of child prostitution in London he worked with former brothel-mistress Rebecca Jowett, Josephine Butler and others to secure the unlawful abduction and detention of thirteen-year-old Eliza Armstrong, the daughter of a chimney sweep. Armstrong, a virgin, had been 'bought' by Jowett from her parents for the sum of £5, removed to a brothel and drugged. She was kept confined until Stead (posing as her would-be seducer) arrived to set her at liberty.

On 6 July, the first in a series of spicy articles recounting these events was published in the *Gazette* under the title *The Maiden Tribute of Modern Babylon*. It caused uproar. It also instituted a style of journalism previously unknown in Victorian Britain – sensationalism.[52] Stead did have a supplementary motive though, and this was something in addition to merely exposing the moral depravity that lay like a miasma over mid-1880s urban life. His aim had been to secure support for the Salvation Army's campaign against 'white slavery' at a moment when the Criminal Law Amendment (CLA) Bill was before Parliament. The legislature had had little time for this Bill in the past. Indeed, it had often been talked out or quietly put away. After the *Maiden Tribute*, however, it passed into law 'in a sort of hurricane,' swept along by the resulting tide of moral fury.[53] At the heart of the CLA Act lay a contradictory premise, in that while the age of consent for girls rose from thirteen to sixteen, both homosexuality and prostitution were criminalised. An issue of 'protection' for women had, once again, been manipulated to result in a loss of liberties – chiefly for those poor women whose economic livelihoods depended on vice.

Scholars have interpreted the CLA Act as a conscious move on the part of legislators to implement a 'more coercive system of state intervention in the realm of sexual politics' and, in more nuanced terms, have illustrated how the terms of the new laws were received by those who subsequently took up the mantle of social purity reform.[54] The humanitarianism of the social purists was *not* the same as that of many others (including Elizabeth) who campaigned for moral health and well-being, being as it was located firmly 'within the hierarchical and patriarchal world of Victorian . . . England' and thus more harsh and oppressive.[55] Based on the principles of redemption and, in some measure, statist coercion, this 'new' Liberal approach was not to be confused in any way with the institution of a moral code based on 'justice' between the sexes, an ideal which looked beyond the boundaries of gender or class to seek the health and happiness of all.[56] Elizabeth made precisely this point when she argued that state-sponsored protectionism was an outrage against the personal rights of prostitutes. She considered that her friend Stead had not only blundered, but that he (and those other colleagues in the VADPR who supported him), had gone against the organisation's founding principles.

Stead, Bramwell Booth of the Salvation Army and Rebecca Jowett were prosecuted under the CLA Act following Armstrong's abduction.[57] Subsequently, in October, the VADPR's *Journal* noted that Stead had showed 'rare courage', both in his willingness to take part in the experiment and for having endured a three-month gaol term as a consequence.[58] Elizabeth distanced herself from Stead at this point, for it had become clear during the trial that he had fabricated evidence. Her integrity would not countenance such duplicity, and she issued a warning through the pages of the *Journal* that 'no purity of motive [excused] the shameful outrages' to which Miss Armstrong had been subjected.[59] Her letter was published in February 1886, but it was not the last public protest she made. On the contrary, it was just the beginning, and the consequences of her determined pursuit of individual rights would fracture the VADPR itself.

The Armstrong case attracted international attention when radical French politician Yves Guyot wrote of the issues it raised in a pamphlet, *English and French Morality*. Elizabeth reviewed the work sympathetically for the *Journal*.[60] Both she and Guyot argued that by imposing penalties of arrest and detention for suspected prostitutes, the CLA Act was constructed along the same draconian lines as the Contagious Diseases Acts – which at that moment were on the verge of being repealed.[61] This was deeply ironic, especially as the provisions of the CLA Act would be effective nationwide, as opposed to the (originally) regional character of the CDA legislation. Other activists, such as Josephine Butler, sanctioned these increasingly regulatory approaches to the 'oldest profession', and seemed less concerned by the paradox – although in no measure was the issue clear cut.

Elizabeth remained firmly wedded to the individualist ideal, and her weighty reviews of Guyot's work catapulted her back into the heart of the VADPR at a time when it was undergoing a cataclysmic transformation. Bitter words were aired, both in public and in private. Lucy Wilson, editor of the *Journal* (and Elizabeth's friend since north of England Council days), argued that Guyot's book was little more 'than a prolonged sneer at Mr Stead and some members of the Salvation Army' and had 'nothing to do with English morality'.[62] The forceful rebuttal of this assessment by Elizabeth and others drove Wilson from her post. As Guyot himself had predicted, the VADPR 'took sides' over the issue as ultra-radicals refused to countenance legislation which 'augment[ed] the arbitrary powers' of the state.[63] Heated debates raged for some months. Elizabeth noted that, painful though it was 'to differ so profoundly from . . . fellow-workers', she could not 'keep silence . . . when the difference [was] so vital and momentous' that the very principles of the VADPR were at stake.[64]

With many sympathetic to her views, she resumed her place on the organisation's Executive by late 1886, when disillusioned colleagues deserted the organisation for the newly formed, and confusingly named, National Vigilance Association (NVA) – led by Stead. Josephine Butler was one of those who resigned (though her biographer has shown that her support for the NVA was, at best, tentative), with others including Millicent Garrett Fawcett and Mrs Sheldon Amos.[65] One unlooked-for consequence of the schism was that the VADPR, unwilling to be tainted by association with the vigilante approach of the NVA, elected (grudgingly) to change its name to the Personal Rights Association (PRA). It maintained this title until its demise in 1978.

As these events illustrate, when Elizabeth chose to lead an assault on the philosophies upon which legislation was based, conflict often lay close at hand. Her commentaries on *English and French Morality*, written openly in a manner which privileged the rights of working-class sex workers to provide for their maintenance, also provide evidence of her growing distrust of party politics. Henceforth, she placed the ability to transform society not within those party-political mechanisms with which she was so well acquainted, but in the hands of individuals. A person's duty, she insisted, was not to acquiesce to coercion by legislation but to promote instead a 'nobler ideal of life and action' through the example of lives well lived.[66] This was a route to a humane, progressive society which lay open to all, not merely an elect who had earned their citizenship by prudence, privilege and diligence. Such an opinion looked, ultimately, towards universal adult suffrage and socialism but, as Karen Hunt has shown, 'sectional demands' such as the woman question were hampered by being classified as subservient to 'the key issue of class' in socialist circles.[67] This made for uneasy alliances and, as Elizabeth's particular commitments made her a feminist above all, she was unable to fully reconcile herself to the dictates of socialism. Her conscience, rather, demanded that she endeavour to 'educate' socialists to support women's freedom *before* the proletarian revolution.

Her hopes for success would bring as many frustrations and disappointments as that of her loss of faith in the power of the Liberal party to dramatically change society. But while, by 1886, she believed that it was the drive for 'justice', not party-political alliances, which would bring change for women, many of her colleagues felt differently. An atmosphere of mistrust and caution deepened between Elizabeth and those she termed the 'party women'.[68] The next few years would prove to be among the hardest of her life, more especially as the events following a mill fire at Elmy & Co. caused drastic alterations in her family circumstances.

Personal catastrophe and public schism

One evening at the end of September 1886, a fire raged throughout the four storeys of Eaton Mill, one of Ben Elmy's three premises in Congleton. Only the quick thinking of some employees saved most of the stored raw silk from the flames.[69] Though one local newspaper informed its readers that Ben was fully insured for his losses, a glance at Elizabeth's record of the events reveals a less palatable truth – ruin caused by commercial recession. Writing almost three years later, Elizabeth blamed the fire for being only the first in a series of 'catastrophes' which befell her husband's business, something which culminated in her giving hours of unpaid manual labour at the mill's cutting bench. For some months her labour was intense, and she took some pride in her technical skill.[70] Often she worked for fifty hours per week in the company of her husband and two employees (seemingly, all that remained of their work-force) and was 'half-dead' at each day's end.[71] She was not, however, depoliticised by these events. On the contrary, they helped galvanise her activism in a new direction – as a member of the Fair Trade movement, a campaign which sought to institute protectionism to mercantile affairs and overturn decades of laissez-faire capitalism.

Elizabeth was convinced that free trade had wrecked the British textile industry. She wrote extensively on the subject, and from an auto-biographical perspective, arguing that imports of cheap silk from north-ern Italy had ruined her home town. She did not, however, blame the Italians for the crisis. Instead, she levelled her criticism towards a group of wealthy textile magnates in Manchester – free traders, who utilised their capital to buy into the continental industry and, by applying econo-mies of scale, were able to undercut British prices.[72] Her views were shared by those who, concerned for the apparent stagnation in the key industries of the British economy (including cotton, wool, steel and ship-building), had founded the Fair Trade League on 17 May 1881. Fair Traders argued that international tariffs placed on imports ensured the market for British goods was reduced, while imports continued to flow without hindrance. They claimed that, in response, British tariffs should be imposed to redress the balance.[73] With his textile business severely affected by the slump, Ben Elmy found this philosophy appealing, and only weeks before the Eaton Mill fire he had been elected as Master of the Congleton Lodge of the Fair Trade League.[74]

His public partnership with Elizabeth continued on issues beyond women's rights, for both were popular speakers at League gatherings. Some of her lectures were collated and published as the pamphlet *Foreign Investments and British Industry* in 1888. One of the most significant speeches, *A Woman's Plea to Women*, begged housewives to think before buying those cheap imports which denied workers across the world a fair living.[75] Every woman, Elizabeth argued, was a 'domestic chancellor of the exchequer', and the way they elected to spend their 'pence, their shillings and their pounds' had significant implications for humanitarian justice world-wide.[76] The Fair Trade views she expressed were, however, to have broader consequences, as her comments on the inhumane consequences of free-market capitalism distanced her from some in the women's movement who supported it. Not least among these was Jacob Bright, who had borne the brunt of a direct and personal attack in one of her commentaries, *The Sugar Bounties*.[77]

Though it has been claimed that the economic situation was not, in fact, as catastrophic as Fair Traders believed, the silk industry was one of the worst causalities of the global downturn.[78] Elmy & Co. ceased trading in the autumn of 1888, Eaton Mill was advertised for sale and Ben's partnership in Albion Mill dissolved. In Congleton, the fraught economic circumstances had driven many desperate ex-silk workers to emigrate, and Ben and Elizabeth too considered the possibility in the face of their dwindling fortunes. Their plans were certainly serious, and either the United States or Germany were considered as possible destinations.[79] The trip, though, was never made as negotiations for the sale of the business were protracted and the exhaustion of it all seemed to diminish the couple's desire to relocate. Where diminishing fortunes were an element in the argument, it might be suggested that the couple's loyalties to fair rather than free trade was a reaction to their circumstances. A more sympathetic interpretation would be to acknowledge that the Elmys' steadfast commitment to universal human rights would have made the Fair Trade alliance a natural one and their personal losses merely coincidental. Perhaps the most surprising element of Elizabeth's life at this moment, when little in her world was constant or stable, was her continued and dedicated support for the women's suffrage campaign.

The Guardianship of Infants Act had provided a catalyst to rejuvenate the campaign for the parliamentary vote. Suffragists, however, proved unable to agree on the best way to proceed. Elizabeth had an ambivalent relationship with the Central Committee of the National Society for Women's Suffrage, which had instituted a 'gendered censorship' of the Elmys following their marriage. Ben's name is listed as a member of the General Committee after 1877. Elizabeth's name is not recorded, and although she worked arduously and continuously for the cause, in the NSWS literature, her part in events is almost completely obscured.[80] During the 1880s, just as she had begun to forcefully criticise Liberal parliamentarians for (seemingly) abandoning those principles on which they had been elected, key groups of suffragists were embracing the party political system as their best hope of securing the vote. The most significant and highly organised of the party-allied women's organisations was the Women's Liberal Federation (WLF), established in 1887.

The Priestman sisters and Louisa Martindale were leading figures in the WLF, but while Elizabeth sought to harness their mutual friendship networks to ensure her publications were widely distributed, she never personally believed a fracturing of women's claims along party lines would bring the issue of the franchise to a swift conclusion. She looked upon the Conservative ladies' association, the Primrose League, in a similar light; its members' allegiances understood as being first to party and then to women.[81] 'It is very disheartening', she wrote, 'to be met with people, both of the Liberal side and on the Conservative side, who seem perfectly willing to acquiesce in any amount of delay.'[82] There was, however, a strong body of opinion that understood party-political women's associations to offer a new, collaborative way forward and Elizabeth's stubborn intransigence on the issue could not have helped her achieve collegiality with fellow workers. For colleagues who perceived her as a divisive presence in suffrage circles, her actions during the winter of 1888–89 provided some support for their views.

Discussions on how to plan the next phase of the suffrage campaign came to a head during a meeting of the NSWS on 12 December 1888. It had been called by the Executive to amend the rules of the society to allow for the admission of women's social *and* political organisations. Heated words were exchanged, conciliation proved impossible and Elizabeth joined those who exited the hall in protest at the plans. Their actions prompted a deep rift in the movement, which would not be repaired for a decade and the NSWS had no option but to break up and form two new groupings in order to embrace the diversity of opinion. Their names were so confusingly similar that they became known instead by the location of their London headquarters, Great College Street and Parliament Street. The Parliament Street group (Central National Society for Women's Suffrage) was the more progressive of the two, and had voted to allow the admission of party-political organisations to their membership. While some radicals criticised this move they were, nonetheless, forced into alliance with Parliament Street because of their willingness to pursue the inclusion of married women within the parameters of the suffrage demand. This was something which the Great College Street group (Central Committee of the National Society for Women's Suffrage) refused to do, for they held to the position taken by its leading personalities, Lydia Becker, Millicent Garrett Fawcett and Lilias Ashworth

Hallett, of fighting for the vote on the exclusive 'spinsters and widows' premise.[83]

Elizabeth, ultimately, was unable to support the ethics of either organisation, both having offered support to the 'restrictive' suffrage bill which the MP for Stoke-on-Trent, William Woodall had been prevailed upon to introduce. For the ultra-radicals, who were determined to effect a specific inclusion of married women in future suffrage bills, there seemed only one viable option. Therefore, a mere four months after the schismatic events of December, Elizabeth wrote to McIlquham of her intention to drive forward the induction of a new society, the Women's Franchise League (WFrL). She was supported by a nucleus of thirty workers, including Richard and Emmeline Pankhurst, Alice Scatcherd, Agnes Sunley (the wife of a Leeds asbestos worker), 'the P.A. Taylor's, [the] Jacob Bright's and Madame Venturi'. The Brights were initially sceptical, not joining the group until February 1890, but Ursula Bright's role in the organisation would prove extremely significant to Elizabeth's own future within it.[84] The WFrL was formed with Elizabeth's personal ideological principals of ethical and moral justice and individual freedom at its heart and, as so often before, she took on the labours of secretary. The WFrL's campaign strategy was built on a manifesto that sought the removal of the effects of inequality of opportunity for women, be these inequalities related to sex, marriage, work, the law or politics. Its ideology comprised, as has been argued, the 'conscience' of radical suffragism; but the consciousness which shaped it was Elizabeth's own.[85]

'The young giant' – the Women's Franchise League[86]

Elizabeth was at pains to point out the distinctive nature of the WFrL's programme from the first, in that members campaigned not merely to secure the vote, but for *any* issue that confined women in positions of weakness and subjection.[87] The first meeting was held at the London home of Mr and Mrs William Tebb (he was also the Chair of the London Society for the Abolition of Vaccination) on 25 July 1889. The contemporary historiographical accounts of the group's formation, however, provide a conflicting narrative.[88] In her autobiography, Sylvia Pankhurst elected to place the figure of her mother Emmeline centre-stage, and she claimed the WFrL had been formed when 'a little circle of ladies' gathered in Mrs Pankhurst's bedroom following the birth of her youngest son, Harry.[89] This cosy image is easily refuted by Elizabeth's letter of 12 July to Alice Scatcherd, in which she sites Emmeline's confinement as the reason for relocating the meeting.[90] In *The Cause*, Ray Strachey fails even to mention the existence of the WFrL, principally because its ideology influenced the later militant movement she derided. Militancy, to Strachey, was based on the shifting sands of 'drama, hero-worship and self-surrender' (rather than stolid but effective diplomacy) and she erroneously classed 'the small group of people' initially connected with it as having no influential friends.[91] This is clearly both incorrect and subjective, but logical, given Strachey's sympathies.

At the time, the small cohort of WFrL radicals were determined to make a strong beginning and Elizabeth, who saw a 'grand future [for] the young giant' on the horizon, provided much of the stimulus and theoretical perspective.[92] Her exertions 'astound[ed] and impressed' even those male colleagues experienced in civic service. With her legal expertise squarely to the fore she drafted the WFrL's first piece of legislation, the fully inclusive Women's Disabilities Removal Bill. Introduced in the House of Commons by Mr (later Viscount) R. B. Haldane MP, its straightforward egalitarian framework helped the fledgling organisation attract support, and within weeks some 140 members had joined its ranks. Encouraged by this warm response, the inaugural meeting passed off in an atmosphere of goodwill, and also had the honour of receiving a testimonial address from William Lloyd Garrison Jnr, who had been the escort of Harriot Stanton Blatch.[93] The relationship flourished between Elizabeth and Stanton Blatch, and the importance of such transatlantic friendships was deeply significant for the development of British radicalism. The 'uncompromising and confrontational activism' favoured by American radicals such as Cady Stanton and her daughter influenced the work of the WFrL, most particularly in its mandate 'to establish for *all* women equal civil and political rights with men'.[94]

The particular challenge to contemporary methods of the suffragist campaign lay within this egalitarian objective, for it established an ideology that privileged gender equality over class disparity in the campaign for citizenship. Elizabeth had built on a rhetorical shift first evident in the *English and French Morality* papers to couch the WFrL's programme in a language of social inclusivity, something which reconceptualised feminist ideology along gender, rather than class, lines. And though the important texts that were later published as having promoted the ideals of the WFrL were issued under the names of Harriet McIlquham and Florence Fenwick Miller, they were, Elizabeth recalled privately, chiefly the product of her own thoughts.[95] She was the group's idealist, and first among her priorities was that the WFrL maintain its wholly non-party-political status. She was thwarted in this desire, however, for the group was later classified as having possessed an 'unwavering loyalty to Gladstone and to [the] Liberal Party'.[96]

A souring of relationships

In August 1889, an article written by Florence Fenwick Miller for the *Illustrated London News* noted the WFrL's formation and praised Elizabeth's work.[97] By that date, Fenwick Miller had accepted an invitation to join the Executive Committee, Elizabeth having been assured that her young colleague was no longer a member of the Parliament Street group and thus not subject to a conflict of interest.[98] A vibrant speaker and articulate journalist, Fenwick Miller had experienced a meteoric rise to prominence in women's emancipation circles. The daughter of a humble sea-captain, she was no 'shrinking violet' and had participated in Sophia Jex-Blake's abortive efforts to secure medical degrees for women at the University of Edinburgh.[99] Thwarted in these ambitions, she had stood successfully for the Hackney division of the London School Board at the age of twenty-two and had been a contributor to the deliberations of the London Dialectical Society. After their successful collaboration during the Infants' Act campaign, Elizabeth and Fenwick Miller came together again. This time, however, the liaison would prove neither productive nor happy, and Elizabeth's letters chart a relationship deteriorating into crisis. The correspondence, however, tells only part of the history and for a fuller picture it is necessary to contextualise events as Elizabeth faced both loss of position and financial ruin. The business of Elmy & Co. went under the auctioneer's hammer on 12 February 1890 and with it Elizabeth's financial security.

The schism in the women's suffrage movement had occurred contemporaneously with these disruptive events in Elizabeth's private life. And despite her paid post as secretary of the WFrL, after the settlement of Ben's affairs the family were '*far poorer* than [they] expected . . . ever to be', their liquid capital a figure of around £500.[100] Alice Scatcherd, the WFrL's treasurer, mirrored Jessie Boucherett's generous offer of twenty years before and offered Elizabeth an annuity in order that her worries might be eased. Once again, fiercely proud, she declined. Nonetheless, she wrote to McIlquham of the 'incessant mental worry' regarding the situation and her sense of powerlessness as the family's grip on a comfortable, middle-class existence slipped away.[101] Her determined refusal of Scatcherd's help shows both pride and stubbornness, especially when, only a week after the mill auction, she received a summons for non-payment of a debt.

Figure 4 Bill of sale for Eaton Mill, 1890
Source: Reproduced with the permission of Lyndon Murgatroyd

The writ was served by 'Helena Beatrice Temple', the pseudonym of Henrietta Müller, editor of the *Women's Penny Paper* (WPP) and a former colleague on the VADPR. Müller claimed that Elizabeth had refused to pay for a bulk order of reprints of a WPP report of a Franchise League meeting held at the Westminster Palace Hotel the previous November. Far from being pleased with the report, Elizabeth had declared it errone-ous and poorly edited.[102] She promptly cancelled the order and published instead her own account in the PRA's *Journal*, under the pseudonym of 'One Who Was There'.[103] Clearly the matter of the writ touched a raw nerve and highlighted a particular sensitivity to her financial situation. She wrote to McIlquham that 'every wall' in Congleton was 'placarded with the sale of our mills' (*sic*) and to be faced with a legal claim at such a time, when she had done 'no wrong' to the plaintiff, was more than she could bear.[104] She instructed her lawyer to settle the bill (whatever the actual rights and wrongs of the issue) to bring the matter to a swift conclusion.[105]

The stresses of this time, both physical and mental, conspired in another period of exhaustive illness similar to that Elizabeth had suffered both in 1868 and 1874, though on this occasion she did not take time out from her busy schedule to rest. Only if 'this thing could go on without [her]', she told Harriet, would she take holiday, but clearly believed her work for the WFrL to be essential.[106] Two matters conspired against her, and the first, for which she believed Fenwick Miller responsible, was a charge of mismanagement of the WFrL and an ostensible misappr-opriation of its (desperately needed) funds. Incensed, Elizabeth accused Fenwick Miller of casting aspersions on the one thing she prized above all other – her moral integrity. This, more than any other reason would have prompted the authorship of the defamatory 'Miller' letters, although she was also pained and not a little fractious that Fenwick Miller appeared to be seeking 'the whole credit [for] creating' the WFrL and devising its programme.[107]

The correspondence certainly appears both irrationally and inten-tionally critical of Fenwick Miller, but it is perhaps better understood in the context of Elizabeth's tense domestic situation, rather than as merely the stream of 'bile and vitriol' that Fenwick Miller's biographer contends.[108] Harriet McIlquham believed Elizabeth saw threats where perhaps they had never existed but, when hurts she believed long forgot-ten resurfaced to taunt her during 1890, her deep friendship with Harriet appeared her one consolation. In letters often written late at night, after her domestic labours were concluded, Elizabeth poured out her objections to her friend in a litany of grief and grievance. If the correspondence is painful to read, then the emotions that prompted it were no less so. While at any other moment in her life Elizabeth might have been able to weather criticism of her actions, her mental resilience was then at its lowest ebb.

Thus the warm relationship between Elizabeth and Fenwick Miller quickly disintegrated, and only two months after the younger woman had proclaimed her venerable colleague as the 'great mole' of the women's movement, barbed comments and mutual criticism peppered WFrL Executive meetings.[109] In her *Illustrated London News* article, Fenwick Miller had praised Elizabeth's 'self-abnegation' in public work: but if Florence believed this would allow *her* to take centre-stage in WFrL matters she was mistaken.[110] Elizabeth, though, was gracious at first, and rather than taking the platform herself, acquiesced to Fenwick Miller's wish to be the League's representative at the National Liberal Club on 25 February 1890. Despite the obvious pressures at home, Elizabeth made the trip to London to witness this forceful articulation of the WFrL's working programme. She also took the opportunity to shop with McIlquham for clothes; for she had not wished to be 'the scarecrow of the League' at such an eminent gathering.[111]

This is a rare and telling comment, for it shows a degree of vulnerability as Elizabeth wonders whether her public 'worth' would be negated if she arrived at the meeting unfashionably dressed. She was more upset, however, by Fenwick Miller's desire, to 'hurry through the press' (*sic*) a verbatim report of the evening's speech.[112] The WFrL encapsulated Elizabeth's feminist vision and she wanted the credit for it. She believed this would be denied if the speech were published under Miller's name (as indeed it was) and the acrimony between the pair stemmed from this moment. Two months later, Fenwick Miller grew increasingly petulant and irritable during a period of shared work in London, where in Elizabeth's opinion, she 'found fault with everybody and everything.'[113] Pressures of work, however, forced her to acknowledge a similar irritability in herself. Overburdened with plans for an international conference to be hosted by the WFrL during the London Universal Peace Congress in July, Elizabeth apologised to Harriet for writing of 'nothing but grumble[s]'.[114]

Irritation turned to schism during a series of WFrL council meetings in May when, Elizabeth claimed, 'the miserable personal and political intrigue' finally took its toll on her patience.[115] Prior to the meetings, she had written somewhat incoherently that she has been 'hurt beyond expression' by Fenwick Miller's attitude and behaviour.[116] The letter of 27 April is markedly different from her usual incisive style and veers from topic to topic without focus or structure. It also clearly indicates her psychological stress. She criticised Fenwick Miller openly for seeking to make the WFrL a 'stalking-horse of personal ambition' – and clearly believed that Florence intended to usurp her position as chief spokesperson of the League, in addition to appropriating the secretary's salary.[117] There is venom and bitterness in her words. She writes,

> Mrs. Miller ... had far too early in life, as a nice girl of 18 or 19, personal successes which turned her head, and that for the rest she lives on and by rich people, mixes with them whilst poor and is corrupted thereby. She *longs* to be rich, whilst I feel that *every rich man* in spite of himself, by the mere fact of being rich, does more harm to the world than all his efforts for good can neutralize.[118]

Elizabeth's splenetic phrases are, as this extract shows, directed at a broader target than the person of Fenwick Miller, towards those whose economic circumstances offer security and comfort. Her words, therefore, can only be truly appreciated in the context of her private circumstances, where financial loss haunted both her past and present. Clearly overwrought she, perhaps somewhat unfairly, made Fenwick Miller the scapegoat for her embittered feelings. Thus, on 22 May 1890, when the WFrL Executive met to consider the results of fund-raising activities it did so in an atmosphere of crisis.

One contentious issue was the financing of two fund-raising recitals, planned by Elizabeth's assistant, Romola Tynte. The first had been a successful occasion in London, the second, destined to be a conspicuous failure, was scheduled to be held the following month in Oxford. Fenwick Miller questioned the value of recitals as a means of raising funds and there is also an indication that she felt the level of pre-event expenditure to have been a wanton squandering of resources on Elizabeth's part.[119] A bitter exchange ensued, and Elizabeth was cut to the quick by the 'moral vivisection and torture' of her adversary.[120] The charge that she had undertaken expenditure counter to the best interests of the WFrL was anathema to her. Her anger was so great she resigned her position as secretary on the spot.

The second contentious issue between Elizabeth and the WFrL was far more serious in ideological terms and had little or nothing to do with Fenwick Miller, who did not attend meetings herself after the summer of 1890. One possible reason for this absence was that Ursula Bright, who did not to find Fenwick Miller an agreeable personality, had become the organisation's directing force and public voice. Elizabeth was deeply disturbed by the prospect that Jacob and Ursula Bright, once welcomed into the highest echelons of the organisation, would align it directly to the Liberal Party (in opposition to its constitution) and she was frustrated by the continual attempts of Richard and Emmeline Pankhurst to 'force Mrs Bright on the Committee against [her] persistently expressed wish'.[121] Prior to the heated exchanges at the 22 May Executive, a new, London-based sub-committee of the WFrL had been formed. This Elizabeth had initially welcomed, as a way to relieve at least some of her administrative burdens.[122] She grew increasingly concerned, however, as to the part played in the work of the sub-committee by Mrs Bright, who had secured the votes to be admitted to the Executive only on 20 May, in the company of Mona Caird, Emilie Venturi and Harriot Stanton Blatch.[123]

Elizabeth also grew alarmed at the idea that Liberal MP Sir Charles Dilke, whom she distrusted, would use an alliance with the League to resurrect a political career damaged by a notorious divorce scandal in 1886. Dilke was a close ally of Jacob Bright, but Elizabeth considered his behaviour morally reprehensible. Though donations he sent to WFrL funds were accepted, she was keen to point out that in no measure did this make him a member of the society.[124] Elizabeth refused point-blank to align the group to his (and by implication the Liberal Party's) cause – something which set her on a collision course with Ursula Bright and her supporters. In a letter written to Bright on the day of her resignation, Elizabeth noted passionately that it was the organisation's 'one great object'

> 'to establish for all women equal civil and political rights with men,' and this the League must pursue irrespective of all party consider-ations, subordinating to it all other questions. This is and must be the attitude of the League, as a League, the claims of women are to it para-mount, and neither hope, nor fear, favour nor affection must sway it from its steadily balanced course . . . *Better far that it should cease to be, than that it should be degraded to the position of a party tool.*[125]

These words confirm that Elizabeth was out of step with the actions of the majority of the WFrL, which has suffered historiographically from an assessment that it was 'simply a women's auxiliary of the Gladstonian Liberals'.[126] This, as recent work has shown, is to denigrate a forward-looking organisation and one in whose ideals the seeds of the Edwardian militant movement can be found. The WFrL continued until the late 1890s, and under the leadership of Bright, Pankhurst and Scatcherd pro-moted 'a communion of middle-class and working-class women in their shared labour, both productive and reproductive'. This, combined with its unwavering demand for the explicit inclusion of married women in the suffrage demand, influenced a new interpretation of what citizenship would mean for women. The juxtaposition of economics and sexual subjection had long been evident in Elizabeth's writing and, as Chapter 6 shows, she took the analysis to new lengths in the work of her next society, the Women's Emancipation Union.[127] Before this, however, there were two more catastrophes to overcome.

Elizabeth continued to work for the WFrL for two months, but the final severance came at the Annual Meeting held on 25 July 1890. Prior to the meeting she had stayed in Basingstoke at the home of Harriot Stanton Blatch and the pair (in the company of Elizabeth Cady Stanton) travelled to London together. Elizabeth's desire to move two amendments to the existing WFrL constitution to mitigate the powers of the London-based Executive failed and, deeply distressed, she resigned from member-ship of the organisation she had founded.[128] Such was her anguish that she vowed 'never again to take any part whatever in political action on behalf of women', and Richard Pankhurst's handwritten corrections to the WFrL Annual Report of 1890 (including the crossing out of her name from the list of those who had attended a deputation to Mr H.H. Howorth, MP) attest to the League's desire to erase, as far as was practi-cable, her primary place in the organisation.[129]

Sadly, however, that was not the end of the matter, for Elizabeth then discovered, to her horror, that she had been portrayed as 'greedy and self-seeking' in an anonymously authored leaflet, ostensibly written on behalf of the entire Executive Council of the WFrL. This was an impos-sible assertion, given that some of the members had been out of the country at the time and knew nothing of its production.[130] Accompany-ing the leaflet were extracts of (allegedly) personal letters denigrating Elizabeth's character and private life. It is difficult and harrowing to believe that her acquaintances were so offended by her behaviour that they could slight her in such a cruel way, particularly knowing the distress that the Elmys suffered when they lost their business. And the question remains unanswered as to how Elizabeth's words or actions might have prompted such a reaction? A reader of her letters is left bewildered and yearning for a fuller explanation. To resurrect events of fifteen years past, when the Elmy marriage had caused such a stir, was malicious, no matter how much Elizabeth's forcefulness in trying to hold the reins of power in the WFrL had irritated her colleagues. If Fenwick Miller did circulate this damning literature (as has often been assumed) no evidence remains to conclusively convict her. And there is just a suggestion that the culprit was Alice Scatcherd, for in a letter of 14 November Elizabeth wrote that she 'will not again, with [her] own consent be brought into contact with' the WFrL's treasurer; this after she had directly asked McIlquham to name the miscreant.[131] Desperate to leave the 1880s behind, Elizabeth expressed her intention to resign from feminist campaigns, or, in her words, to 'shake the yoke'.[132] Her resolve, however, lasted no longer than the following winter.

Notes

1 Florence Fenwick Miller, 'The Ladies Column', *The Illustrated London News*, 31 August 1899, p. 288.

2 'E' [EWE], 'The Property and Status of Married Women', *Journal*, January 1883, p. 6.

3 'Buglawton Inquest', *Congleton Chronicle*, 14 April 1894, p. 8.

4 EWE/HM, undated (probably May 1889), 477449, fol. 29.

5 EWE/HM, 8/8/1899, 47452, fol. 4.

6 EWE, Untitled pamphlet issued to supporters of the Married Women's Property Campaign, February 1883, 47451, fol. 119–20. 'The Special Fund', *Journal*, January 1883, p. 5.

7 EWE/HM, postscript to leaflet February 1883, written February 1898, 47451, fol. 191.

8 EW to the Editor, *The Women's Suffrage Journal*, May 1872, p. 64.

9 NAPSS, *Transactions*, 1877, p. 309.

10 NAPSS, *Transactions*, 1880, p. 191; Shanley, *Feminism*, pp. 143–4.

11 EWE, *TYE*, p. 3. (My emphasis.)

12 HM to Frances Rowe, 11/8/1901, 47452, fol. 195.

13 EWE/HM, 15/9/1896, 47450, fol. 317.

14 EWE/HM, 26/2/1896, 47450, fol. 270.

15 Pankhurst, *TSM*, pp. 30–2.

16 Sheila Rowbotham, *Dreamers of a New Day: Women Who Invented the Twentieth Century* (London and New York: Verso, 2010), pp. 1–3.

17 Fenwick Miller, 'The Ladies' Column', p. 288; Anon., 'Mr Ince MP and the Infants Bill', *Journal*, December 1885, p. 82.

18 Crawford, *WSM*, p. 194.

19 Hannam and Hunt, *Socialist Women*, p. 8.

20 Opinions of the Press on the law relating to the Custody and Guardianship of Children and on the Infants Bill 1884. (Manchester: A. Ireland & Co., 1884).

21 EWE, 'The Custody and Guardianship of Children', *Englishwoman's Review*, 15 November 1884, pp. 491–503; J.H. Levy, 'Parental Rights', *Journal*, 15 November 1884, pp. 93–4; 'The Infants' Act, *Journal*, 15 June 1886, pp. 57–60.

22 Anon., 'Leaderettes', *Women's Penny Paper*, 23 November 1889, p. 4; EWE, *TYE*, pp. 42–3.

23 Levine, *Feminist Lives*, p. 258.

24 EWE, *TYE*, p. 12.

25 EWE, 'The Custody and Guardianship of Children', *Englishwoman's Review*, 15 November 1884, pp. 491–503; EWE, *TYE*, p. 2.

26 EWE, 'Custody and Guardianship', p. 499.

27 'Annual Meeting', *Journal*, 15 March 1884, p. 22.

28 Griffin, 'Class, Gender', pp. 73 and 83.

29 *The Times*, 27 March 1884, p. 7, quoted in Griffin, 'Class, Gender', p. 85.

30 EWE, 'Custody and Guardianship', p. 502.

31 EWE, 'Custody and Guardianship', p. 499.

32 Leonore Davidoff, Megan Doolittle, Janet Fink and Katherine Holden, *The Family Story: Blood, Contract and Intimacy, 1830–1960* (London and New York: Longman, 1999), pp. 145–6.

33 EWE, 'Custody and Guardianship', p. 493. The dispute between Mr and Mrs Agar-Ellis was centred on the religious upbringing of their children. The children were made wards of the Court of Chancery in 1878, and ordered to be raised as their father desired. When the eldest daughter applied to the Court in 1883 for permission to spend her holiday in her mother's company she was denied, the Court claiming it has no power to interfere. Shanley, *Feminism*, pp. 142–3; EWE/HM, 7/1/1892, 47449, fol. 227.

34 EWE, *TYE*, p. 3.

35 EWE, *TYE*, p. 14.

36 EWE, *TYE*, p. 22.

37 EWE, *TYE*, p. 21. Hansard Parliamentary Debates, Series 3 (25 July 1884), p. 606, quoted in Shanley, *Feminism*, pp. 148–9. The provisions of the Infants' Act conferred the guardianship of children upon the surviving parent of either sex. It also allowed a mother to appoint a testamentary guardian in case of her death who would serve jointly with the father if the court was 'satisfied that such appointment is necessary or desirable for the welfare of such infant . . . [the father being] . . . unfitted to be the sole guardian of his children' *Hansard*, Series 3 (30 April 1885), p. 1088, quoted in Shanley, *Feminism*, p. 149.

38 EWE, 'The Parliamentary Franchise for Women: To the Editor of *The Times*, 24 May 1884', in Jane Lewis (ed.), *Before the Vote was Won*, pp. 404–8, p. 406.

39 EWE, *TYE*, pp. 18–19.

40 Alice Scatcherd to Anna Maria and Mary Priestman, 26/2/1886, MP.

41 EWE/HM, 25/12/1898, 47451, fol. 282; EWE, *TYE*, pp. 42–3.

42 EWE, *TYE*, pp. 52–3.

43 EWE/HM, 20/6/1902, 47453, fol. 13.

44 Anon., 'Leaderettes', *Women's Penny Paper*, 23 November 1889, p. 4.

45 EWE, *TYE*, p. 8.

46 EWE, *The Emancipation of Women* (1884), Preamble and p. 3.

47 EWE, 'The Parliamentary Franchise for Women', p. 404.

48 EWE, 'The Parliamentary Franchise for Women', p. 407. See also, EWE, 'Married Women and the Electoral Franchise', *Journal*, March 1886, pp. 21–2.

49 'Ignota' [EWE], 'Women's Suffrage', reprinted from the *Westminster Review*, October 1897. (Normansfield Press, [n.d.]), p. 4.

50 Martin Pugh, *The March of the Women: A Revisionist Analysis of the Campaign for Women's Suffrage, 1866–1914* (Oxford and New York: Oxford University Press, 2000), p. 67.

51 Judith R. Walkowitz, *City of Dreadful Delight: Narratives of Sexual Danger in Late-Victorian London* (London: Virago, 1992), chapters 3 and 4; Jordan, *Josephine Butler*, pp. 223–35.

52 Paula Bartley, *Prostitution: Prevention and Reform in England 1860–1914* (London and New York: Routledge, 2000), p. 88.

53 Yves Guyot to the Editor, *Journal*, February 1886, p. 12.

54 Bland, *Banishing*, pp. 99–101; Frank Mort, 'Purity, Feminism and the State: Sexuality and Moral Politics, 1880–1914', in M. Langan and B. Schwartz (eds), *Crisis in the British State, 1880–1930* (London: Hutchinson, 1985), p. 209.

55 Bartley, *Prostitution*, p. 89.

56 Roberts has argued that the 'paternalist' nature of the NVA ultimately resulted in the organisation becoming 'a machine for the surveillance and oppression of working-class women' staffed by 'evangelical volunteers'. Roberts, 'Feminism and the State', pp. 103–4.

57 For an examination of the trial see, Walkowitz, *City of Dreadful Delight*, pp. 107–20.

58 Anon., 'The "Pall Mall Gazette"', *Journal*, October 1885, p. 70.

59 EWE to the Editor, *Journal*, February 1886; p. 13.

60 EWE, 'English and French Morality', *Journal*, March 1886, pp. 25–6. Also, April 1886, pp. 38–9. Also, May 1886, pp. 49–50.

61 Roberts, 'Feminism and the State', p. 102, fn.64.

62 Editorial (Lucy Wilson), *Journal*, January 1886, p. 5.

63 Yves Guyot to the Editor, *Journal*, February 1886, p. 12.

64 EWE, 'English and French Morality', *Journal*, May 1886, p. 50.

65 Jordan, *Josephine Butler*, pp. 229 and p. 336.

66 EWE, 'English and French Morality', *Journal*, May 1885, p. 50.

67 Hunt, *Equivocal Feminists*, p. 39.

68 EWE/HM, 18/5/1892, 47449, fol. 267.

69 Anon., 'Fire at Eaton Mill,' *Macclesfield Courier*, 2 October 1886, p. 8.

70 EWE/HM, 1/4/1889, 47449, fol. 19.

71 EWE/HM, 10/6/1889, 47449, fol. 36.

72 EWE/HM, 11/5/1889, 47449, fol. 27; EWE, 'A Woman's Plea', p. 3.

73 Euan Green, *The Crisis of Conservatism: The Politics, Economics and Ideology of the British Conservative Party 1880–1914* (London and New York: Routledge, 1996), pp. 30–1.

74 'Fair Trade', *Macclesfield Courier*, 31 July 1886.

75 EWE, *Foreign Investments and British Industry* (London: Wyman and Son, 1888).

76 EWE, 'A Woman's Plea', p. 3.

77 EWE, 'The Sugar Bounties', *Foreign Investments*, p. A2.

78 Green, *The Crisis of Conservatism*, p. 29.

79 EWE/HM, 11/3/1890, 47449, fol. 97.

80 List of General Committee of the Central Committee of the National Society for Women's Suffrage, *Women's Suffrage Journal*, March 1877, p. 47. Also, Annual Reports of the CCNSWS, 1878 and 1879, WL.

81 The Primrose League had been founded in 1883 and while it never attempted to exert pressure on male Conservatives into endorsing a women's suffrage policy its influence was significant, many members contributing in various ways to the successful election campaigns of 1892, 1895 and 1900. Pugh, *March of the Women*, p. 71.

82 EWE/HM, 11/12/1896, 47451, fol. 34.

83 Holton, *Suffrage Days*, p. 75.

84 EWE/HM, 1/4/1889, 47449, fol. 19; EWE/HM, 9/5/1889, 47449, fol. 25.

85 Holton, 'Now you see It', p. 25.

86 EWE/HM, 3/5/1890, 47449, fol. 115.

87 'On the Programme of the Women's Franchise League' – an address given by Mrs Florence Fenwick Miller at the National Liberal Club, 25 February 1890, p. 1. BL.

88 Holton, 'Now you see It', pp. 20–2.

89 Pankhurst, TSM, p. 95.

90 EWE to Alice Scatcherd, 12 /7/1889, 47449, fol. 41.

91 Strachey, The Cause, p. 311, and pp. 292–3.

92 EWE/HM, 31/8/1889, 47449, fol. 55.

93 Proceedings at the Inaugural Meeting of the Women's Franchise League, 25th July 1889 (The Hansard Publishing Union Ltd. London), pp. 1 and 25–6.

94 Sandra Stanley Holton, '"To Educate Women into Rebellion": Elizabeth Cady Stanton and the Creation of a Transatlantic Network of Radical Suffragists', American Historical Review, October 1994, pp. 1112–36, p. 1132. Speech of Harriet McIlquham, Proceedings, p. 2.

95 EWE/HM, 5 June 1890, 47449, fol. 125.

96 Holton, 'To Educate', p. 1132.

97 Fenwick Miller, 'The Ladies' Column', p. 288.

98 EWE/HM, 9/5/1889, 47449, fol. 25.

99 Van Arsdel, FFM, p. 142 and chapter 1, especially pp. 6–8.

100 EWE/HM, 10/9/1891, 47449, fol. 168.

101 EWE/HM, 27/10/1889, 47449, fol. 64.

102 Anon., 'Women's Franchise League: Meeting at Westminster Palace Hotel', Women's Penny Paper, 9 November 1899, p. 27.

103 'One Who Was There' (EWE), 'Women's Franchise League', Journal, December 1889, pp. 93–4.

104 EWE/HM, 22/2/1890, 47449, fol. 90–91.

105 EWE/HM, 11/4/1890, 47449, fol. 107.

106 EWE/HM, 24/4/1890, 47449, fol. 109

107 EWE/HM, 5/6/1890, 47449, fol. 125.

108 Van Arsdel, FFM, p. 142.

109 Fenwick Miller, 'Ladies' Column', p. 288. EWE/HM, 4/9/1889, 47449, fol. 57.

110 Fenwick Miller, 'Ladies' Column', p. 288.

111 EWE/HM, 20/2/1890, 47449, fol. 88.

112 EWE/HM, 5/6/1890, 47449, fol. 125.

113 EWE/HM, 6/1/1906, 47454, fol. 192.

114 EWE/HM, 11/4/1890, 47449, fol. 102–104. The International Conference was held at Westminster Town Hall on 16 and 17 July 1890. The programme, issued under the signatories of Emmeline Pankhurst and Countess Schack, does not indicate Wolstenholme Elmy's presence or absence at the event. In a letter to Harriet, however, Elizabeth appears very excited at the prospect of attending, and 'hope[s] to have present [there] representatives of each of these nationalities [Switzerland, Italy, Spain and Germany], as well as of Russia, Armenia, India, North and South America.' EWE/HM, 25/6/1890, 47449, fol. 132. Women's Franchise League, Programme of International Conference (London [1890]). ESPP.

115 EWE/HM, 5/6/1890, 47449, fol. 127.

116 EWE/HM, 27/4/1890, 47449, fol. 110–111.

117 Holton, 'Now you see It', p. 21.

118 EWE/HM, 5/6/1890, 47449, fol. 110. (Emphasis in original.)

119 EWE/HM, 9/10/1890, 47449, fol. 137. Wolstenholme Elmy gives clear indication that members of the Executive Committee agreed with Fenwick Miller's criticisms, doing little or nothing to help promote the events.

120 EWE/HM, 26/5/1890, 47449, fol. 122.

121 EWE/HM, 5/6/1890, 47449, fol. 127. Holton, *Suffrage Days*, p. 77.

122 EWE/HM, 11/4/1890, 47449, fol. 102.

123 Women's Franchise League, Annual Report, 1890, p. 6. ESPP.

124 EWE/HM, 11/4/1890, 47449, fol. 102.

125 EWE to Ursula Bright, 22/5/1890, 47449, fol. 120–121. (My emphasis.)

126 Holton, *Suffrage Days*, p. 80.

127 Holton, 'To Educate Women', p. 1116.

128 EWE/HM, 23/7/1890, 47449, fol. 133.

129 Women's Franchise League, Annual Report 1890, pp. 3–4. ESPP.

130 EWE/HM, 9/10/1890, 47449, fol. 135.

131 EWE/HM, 14/11/1890, 47449, fol. 141.

132 EWE/HM, 25/6/1890, 47449, fol. 132–133.

6

The Women's Emancipation Union, 1891–July 1899: 'no mere suffrage society'

The catalyst for a new vision

In the aftermath of her resignation from the Women's Franchise League, Elizabeth joined her husband in working for the Fair Trade alliance. By this time, Ben had been elected to the General Council of the Fair Trade League and his literary battles with free trader rivals often featured in both the national and regional press.[1] Although asked to take a more prominent role in the national movement, he refused, and elected to work principally in the Macclesfield district. His health was no longer robust and, following his retirement from business, he appreciated having more time to write. He hoped, indeed, to profit by it. While this expectation was dashed more often than was desirable, for the sake of his family's finances, some works did find a market. His poetry, for instance, frequently appeared in the *Fair Trade Journal*, where one series of verse, the *Lays of Federation*, extolled the benefits of imperial, as opposed to global trade. A renewal of old 'Cambridge friendships' was prompted when both F.W.H. Myers and Henry Sidgwick corresponded following publication.[2] While the Elmys were delighted that these acquaintances had been resumed, it was not long before Fair Trade work had to compete once more with feminist issues for Elizabeth's attention. Her anger following the hurts experienced at the helm of the WFrL cooled, and the events of the 1890s, perhaps more than at any other time of her life, underlined her significance as an important feminist theorist.

Ben's *Lays of Federation* poems were published in April 1891. At exactly the same moment, Britain's national newspapers carried detailed commentaries on the notorious case of Regina *v.* Jackson (known colloquially as the Clitheroe judgment on account of the location of events). The controversial case was brought to court on 16 March 1891 by Edmund

Jackson, in an attempt to secure restitution of conjugal rights following his abduction and imprisonment of his wife Emily against her will.[3] Though initially successful, his endeavours ultimately failed when the Court of Appeal set Mrs Jackson at liberty under a writ of habeas corpus.[4] While traditionalists (among them the journalist Eliza Lynn Linton) declared the ruling would shatter the foundations of society by proclaiming the destruction of the married state, Elizabeth saw both progress and justice in the judgment. This was because she understood it to have implicitly ended the doctrine of coverture and, with it, the rules which bound wives in conditions of sex slavery. Elated at the turn events had taken, she declared in print that 'the servitude of the English wife [had] become a nightmare of the past, never . . . to be recalled to life again' – strong words, although her assessment of the true situation was woefully naive.[5]

The impact of the public debate surrounding the case was great. The series of five letters Elizabeth swiftly penned to the editor of the *Manchester Guardian* following its conclusion prompted her postbag to fill with 'many expressions of urgent desire' that a new campaign group be formed in order to capitalise on the shift in women's legal status.[6] In consequence, she made plans to institute the Women's Emancipation Union, the last organisation for which she undertook the labours of honorary secretary. Only three months after the Clitheroe judgment, and obviously energised by the 'pleasurable sensation of participating in [a] controversy', she circulated the draft programme of the WEU to her colleagues.[7]

As the veteran of many successful feminist campaigns, Elizabeth was confident that the broadly based, four-point agenda of the new organisation would attract support.[8] She was confident too that 'the means and the mechanism for [the WEU's] great work' would be provided, thanks to the labours of existing friends and the promises of new sympathisers gathered after the Clitheroe case.[9] With ideals similar to those of the WFrL at its inception, it might be expected that Elizabeth would declare the new organisation outside of formal, party-political structures and ties. The Council, the WEU's governing body would, she noted, extend the 'hand of fellowship' to any sympathiser.[10] Its members (though numerically never numbering more than 200 formal subscribers), therefore held a kaleidoscopic series of political allegiances, and shared an advanced interpretation of feminist ideals.[11] Declared forcefully from the outset, their mission was to demand for women 'equality of right and duty with men in *all* matters affecting the service of the community and the State', and it was a principle embodied in the broadest manifesto of any nineteenth-century suffragist group.[12] It is likely, though, that members would have challenged even that definition, for Elizabeth claimed that the organisation was 'no mere suffrage society' but rather a pioneer 'feminist' forum, as its members gave equal weight to discussions regarding employment, education, parental rights, divorce and sexuality.[13] Eliza Lynn Linton metaphorically shuddered at these 'wild women' and 'free lovers' who supported the 'grimmer designs of the women's rights movement'.[14] In other circles, however, their message was seen to constitute a refreshing change from what, after a quarter of a century of suffragist campaigning, now appeared to be the 'dull [and] humdrum' arguments of contemporaries. A reporter from the *Glasgow Herald*, for example, commented that being present at a WEU meeting was something akin to 'passing from a fog into a cold, clear biting atmosphere' of reform.[15]

Elizabeth gathered into the circle of WEU activists those who yearned for progress; those who saw feminist successes to date as being only piecemeal accomplishments – 'mere scraps and shreds of liberty', which left the core values of patriarchal society unchallenged.[16] Writing in 1885, she had claimed that, 'The emancipation of women is a . . . question [which] strikes down to the roots of social, political and religious life', and had argued that to secure true freedom, women of all classes needed to actively acknowledge the necessity of '*unit[ing] themselves in one great federation* [to] *fight*' against male tyranny.[17] During the 1890s, the WEU sought to encourage this collaboration; and to pursue it the middle-class, mixed-sex membership adopted the identity and labours of those progressive thinkers that Theodore Roosevelt would later name as 'muckrakers' – those who, by their investigative techniques, speeches and journalism sought to shame the legislature into instituting reforms.[18]

Elizabeth's transatlantic connections proved significant in this area, Harriot Stanton Blatch having met one of the leaders of American progressivism, Charlotte Perkins Gilman (then Stetson) in London in 1896. Elizabeth and Gilman corresponded through the Edwardian years and were to meet often during the latter's visits to England, in 1899 and 1905. The two were natural allies, for when Gilman wrote in 1898 of the 'heavy pressure [of the] small gold ring' felt by the millions of women obliged to bestow conjugal rights upon their husbands, she was writing directly to Elizabeth's sympathies.[19]

The central place played by the Clitheroe judgment in the WEU's formation was mirrored in the prominence given to the issue of women's sexual subjection in WEU endeavours. The organisation's unique contribution to the citizenship debate was that it was the only suffragist group to link the political disabilities of women directly to the campaign to end the doctrine of coverture. By seeking a legislative amendment to release married women from judicial 'non-personhood', the WEU claimed the legal right for every woman to determine her 'person's sacred plan' by making 'enforced maternity' a criminal act.[20] Elizabeth's place as head of the WEU highlights the significant contribution she made in the construction of this rhetoric of resistance to sexual subjection, which was then placed in direct correlation to women's consent to remain passive under the man-made laws by which they were governed. The issue of women's obligation to live by the laws of a state which governed without their active participation became an obvious feature of suffragist debate during the second Anglo-Boer War (1899–1902).[21] The seeds of this discourse of rebellion, however, were clearly evident in the earlier dialogues of the WEU: and it was a rhetoric that overrode considerations of social class to focus on disenfranchisement from a perspective which privileged gender. Though the organisation advocated an 'open, democratic, egalitarian and pioneering society' freed from the ugliness of urbanisation's social ills, the organisation's first months, however, were far from a utopian idyll.[22]

Two disputes

Despite their fruitful relationship, Harriot Stanton Blatch had not been an initial member of the twenty-strong WEU Council that Elizabeth gathered together on 21 September 1891. Indeed, Blatch had written accusing her of 'want of principle' for making it known that she would support a franchise measure which only implicitly included married women in its terms.[23] Blatch had, in fact, misread Elizabeth's meaning regarding a comment that the WEU would follow 'the line of least resistance' towards its goals: something the younger woman believed would include support for restrictive legislation.[24] Blatch considered Elizabeth to have qualified her stance by this comment, and to have moved the WEU away from the uncompromising approach to the question adopted by the rump of the WFrL – to which Harriot was still allied.[25] This was not, in fact, the case, but worn down by twenty-six years of fruitless campaigning for the parliamentary vote, Elizabeth now sought *any* chink in the armour, and the concession of the principle of equality which would open the way to more far-reaching reforms. She had not abandoned the ideals of a lifetime, but was merely being pragmatic. The issue, though, would have unfortunate consequences for radical feminist collegiality, and matters came to a head in April 1892 in the context of the debates surrounding Sir Albert Rollit's Parliamentary Suffrage (Extension to Women) Bill. It was these events which, to Elizabeth's great joy, prompted Blatch's volte face.

Elizabeth had undertaken an extensive speaking tour of northern towns in mid-April as a precursor to the forthcoming General Election (which was won by Gladstone with what she termed as a 'pitiable paper majority').[26] Though desperately tired at the end of her last engagement, she proceeded directly to London where, on the evening of 25 April, she came late to a WEU committee meeting. She found there an assembly 'in anxious session'.[27] The reason for their concern was the threatened disruption to a women's suffrage meeting organised for the following evening at St James's Hall, which was to be addressed by Millicent Garrett Fawcett. Rollit's Bill, by claiming the parliamentary vote for all women already included on the local government register *implicitly* enfranchised married as well as single women, and Elizabeth declared that it 'deserved the earnest support of every honest suffragist'.[28] Ursula Bright and her WFrL colleagues thought differently, however, and desired a more explicit phrasing of the married woman's qualification. They issued, through the press, an invitation to 'working men and women' to attend the gathering and to take part in a protest, both of the class-ridden nature of the legislation (in that it would enfranchise only women of property) and the fact that the hated 'coverture' proviso would be left, at least *explicitly*, intact.[29] In response to this plea, somewhere in the region of two hundred protesters gatecrashed the event, where they made, Elizabeth recalled, as much noise as an equal number of stampeding bulls.[30]

The Elmys (as principal coordinators of the gathering) found themselves under siege as the meeting, under the chairmanship of J.H. Levy of the Personal Rights Association, descended into chaos. The presence of women had failed to mitigate the worst excesses of 'partisan masculinity' so often exhibited at public political gatherings, and groups of young men drove forward to facilitate the capture of the platform by Herbert Burrows of the Social Democratic Federation (SDF).[31] Standing by the press table as the surge of protesters passed, Elizabeth was decidedly angry and outwardly fearless. She stood shoulder to shoulder with her husband as a 'superintending steward'.[32] Ben's conduct at this meeting, however, has long been the subject of speculation. Emmeline Pankhurst, still in the front rank of the WFrL, told of how he shredded her platform ticket and denounced it a 'forgery'. And Burrows (a man who, unlike other members of the SDF, was opposed to the women's vote unless it be placed in the context of 'adult' suffrage) claimed that in trying to prevent his charge upon the stage Ben had been the one to initiate violence – to which he and his supporters had been 'forced' to respond.[33] Stung, Ben denounced the actions of the 'ruffians' and, with spousal partisanship, Elizabeth made no criticism of his actions.[34]

The fracas over, Rollit's bill was lost on 27 April after Gladstone's personal intervention assured its defeat. As the House of Commons voted the Elmys were hosting a lively gathering of friends at their lodgings, where, putting unpleasantness behind them, they made plans for the future. Such scenes of bonhomie were not evident elsewhere, however. The events at St James's Hall had caused such an atmosphere of dispute and condemnation amongt the WFrL Committee that Blatch resigned from its ranks and swiftly accepted Elizabeth's invitation to join the WEU's Executive.[35] Shortly afterwards, and in another blow for the beleaguered WFrL, Emmeline Pankhurst also resigned, and in company with her husband Richard, joined the newly formed Independent Labour Party.[36] While these events might also indicate a further rupture in the relationship between Elizabeth and Emmeline, the break proved to be for a limited period only. The two retained the bedrock of shared beliefs, and Elizabeth was to approach Emmeline successfully to produce a paper for the WEU's London conference in 1896.

Following a short few weeks of calm, Elizabeth spent the summer of 1892 engaged in preparations for the WEU's inaugural conference. The gathering took place in Birmingham in late October, organised locally by Julia Smith, the daughter of the group's treasurer. One speech in particular caused a public outcry, when WEU activist Mary Cozens declared from the platform that: 'If they had a regiment of women who could shoot, they would have the franchise in a week.'[37] These strident words catapulted the WEU into the pages of the popular press. An editorial in *The Times* was vicious in its condemnation, and claimed that the 'anti-human sentiments of [this] Brummagem [Birmingham] *pétroleuse*' would unleash 'the worst passions of the human animal' and bring forth bloody revolution.[38] It was not only the press that derided Cozens, however. Many feminists were equally disparaging. Among the most vehement was Frances Power Cobbe, whose verdict on Cozens was derisory. She later commented that the hothead should have been 'scraped to death with oyster shells' as a punishment for her extremism.[39] The effect of such criticism was to cement, rather than mitigate Cozens's radicalism, and the majority of her WEU associates rallied to her defence. Elizabeth also appeared unperturbed, and simply recorded that only three letters of complaint from people 'in any way connected' to the organisation were received in the days following the speech.[40] Although the *Leeds Mercury* summed up the event as having done the greatest injustice to the otherwise 'fair minded' discussions at Birmingham, the publicity generated could only help to spread the WEU's message to a wider audience.[41]

Little is known of Hampshire-born Mary Cozens before her association with radical feminist politics in the 1880s, and there is no way of identifying whether she designed the speech to be deliberately inflammatory.[42] She spoke, however, in an environment which she expected might be at least sympathetic to, if not wholeheartedly supportive of, her opinions; for many workers who had shared the radical-feminist ethos of the WFrL had followed Elizabeth into the ranks of the WEU. Among these were adventurer and travel writer Lady Florence Dixie, Mona Caird (the woman credited with sparking the *fin-de-siècle* debate to refashion the married state upon the ideals of companionship and equality), Agnes Sunley and Edinburgh suffragist Charlotte Carmichael Stopes. Stopes's book, *British Freewomen*, which advocated the restitution of 'lost' citizenship rights to women, was published in 1894 while she was closely associated with the WEU.[43] Though neither Caird's nor Stopes's reactions to Mary Cozens's speech is known, the latter would have been encouraged by the published comments of another member of her audience, Caroline Holyoake Smith, who took up the role of WEU Honorary Treasurer after her husband's death. Responding to a critique of Cozens in the *Birmingham Daily Post*, Smith argued that the actions of those now termed the '"wild", new women' would soon have a greater effect on the cause of reform than any of the 'smiles and bland indifference to real injustices' meted out by those less radical.[44] She had no way of knowing, of course, how prophetic her words would be.

Caroline Smith's own radical credentials were impeccable, for she was the sister of veteran 'free thinker' George Jacob Holyoake, and a personal friend of William Ashurst. Connected to the organisation via Elizabeth's friendships with both Emilie Ashurst Venturi and his sister, Holyoake himself became a WEU subscriber. The roots of the organisation's governing body, therefore, lay deep in the soil of the political left and, as its policy statement showed, members subscribed with alacrity to what Holton has termed 'the distinctive nature of the Radical suffragist conception' of women's citizenship – namely the holistic approach to their subjection, which placed an equal stress on civil as well as political disabilities.[45] If Elizabeth had by this time grown weary of the increasingly statist practices of 'New' Liberalism it is perhaps hardly surprising that the 1890s saw her engage more deeply than ever before with socialist ideals, particularly through discussions with such friends as Isabella

Ford and Isabella Bream Pearce, who, as 'Lily Bell', wrote the women's column of the ILP journal the *Labour Leader*.

Both women worked on behalf of the WEU in addition to their socialist labours: Ford spoke on the WEU's behalf at a series of outdoor rallies in the East End of London in 1895, and Pearce contributed important papers to WEU conferences.[46] Elizabeth shared with these friends a view increasingly common among the majority of suffragists, namely that the loss of Rollit's women's suffrage bill had marked a watershed in the campaign. Women were looking for new methods and approaches, and cross-class collaboration (on the fringes of suffragist ideology hitherto) was hailed as a means whereby a new dynamism could be injected into the struggle. Perhaps the most well-known example of its effectiveness was the Special Appeal petition, organised by seven of the principal societies and signed by over a quarter-of-a-million 'women of all parties and classes'. Over three thousand people helped to collect signatures for the mammoth memorial which, though it was displayed in Westminster Hall on 19 May 1896, was never formally presented to Parliament.[47] While Elizabeth worked hard to furnish the secretary of this campaign, Julia Cameron with names for the petition, the collaborative approach adopted by the WEU was a distinctive one: and in many important aspects it paved the way for the ideology and actions of the twentieth century.[48]

The rhetoric of collaboration

Elizabeth and the sympathisers of the WEU were increasingly conscious that as partnerships across class divides facilitated a mass protest force of potentially hundreds of thousands of newly politicised women, feminism gained a new dissenting voice. This oratory was built, in part, on the influences of the 'politics of disruption' – the forms of popular protest which had been so influential in securing successive extensions of the franchise for men throughout the nineteenth century.[49] The editors of the *Glasgow Herald*, for example, considered that Mary Cozens had spoken in the manner of Tom Paine, and it was just such a forceful tone which now overlaid traditional, altruistic, liberal rhetoric as working-class women, 'restless with convulsive energy', took up the cause in earnest.[50] Drawing on a correspondence network that now numbered over 7,000 international activists, Elizabeth ensured that the WEU's place in the new direction suffragism was taking was known around the globe.

Feminist engagement with the theories of citizenship and democracy underwent a significant shift in the 1890s, but it has recently been argued that the voice of Progressivism has been given but 'short shrift' in the era's historiography.[51] Nonetheless, to view the WEU in this light is to mine a rich seam. Elizabeth, as the organisation's life-force, was viewed as 'prophetic' and a visionary by Margaret Sibthorp, editor of the radical-feminist journal *Shafts* – a publication often utilised to disseminate WEU ideals.[52] Sylvia Pankhurst's less laudatory view was that WEU policies were only a 'fine shade of distinction' apart from other contemporary societies.[53] This is a misleading assessment which, in common with some other areas of Pankhurst's text discussed above, is somewhat economical with the truth. However, as Laura Nym Mayhall has recently pointed out, the role of those she terms as 'Radical independent' campaigners was extremely significant in bringing about a shift in exploring the relationship between the nature of citizenship and democracy; for it was these campaigners who adopted 'a model encouraging women's resistance to authority as long as their right to vote' remained unacknowledged.[54] The concept of 'engaged citizenship' was crucial in this regard; and it was precisely this active involvement in political life which Elizabeth deemed essential in *any* associate of the WEU.[55] Every member must, she asserted, be an active 'worker' for women's liberty, and she designated their labours as having contributed to the 'uplifting of humanity'.[56] Paying mere lip-service to the cause was not enough, and although the society welcomed men into its ranks (three eminent lawyers, Charles Beaumont, John Boyd Kinnear and John Bayley served on its Council) a woman-centred ethos was adopted as the cornerstone of its ideals.

The members of the radical independent coalition in Britain can be classified as Progressives who 'agreed on issues across party lines . . . [exhibited] hostility towards aristocratic privilege and corruption . . . [and] sought collectivist solutions' to the problems of the age in the belief that 'justice would prevail' – 'justice' in this context being the acknowledgement that women be legally designated as man's human equal.[57] This definition clearly highlights key characteristics within the WEU's membership, which at its height (in 1897) comprised a loose grouping of radicals, individualists, socialists, anti-alienists, pacifists and jingoists. They had, however, one overriding objective and, as accurate as Mayhall and Holton have been in placing both the WFrL and the WEU as the leaders of the British Progressive faction, their texts fail to explore in depth the link between the latter's formation and its key objective: the politicisation of motherhood and its meaning for militancy. When she framed the organisation's ideology, Elizabeth understood that the concept of motherhood was universal and, as the vast majority of women's lives were still touched by the maternal function, it was a rhetoric to which all could subscribe.

As head of the WEU, Elizabeth advocated partnerships which placed 'the moral regeneration of mankind' at their heart. And she had applauded the Clitheroe decision on the grounds that it was 'epoch-making in its immediate consequences', its precepts supplanting 'the old worn-out code of master and slave' with the ethics of justice and equality.[58] This comment, coming from the woman who had been the first to speak from a public platform on the topic of marital rape, was decisive in supporting the view that it was a married woman's lot to act as the moral rejuvenator of a world plagued by the 'fantasies of decay and degeneration' that permeated modern, urbanised society.[59] She was also not shy of advocating that this struggle would be 'a revolt' against patriarchy and a battle based on the 'legal right of a wife to her personal freedom'.[60] In her last public address as head of the WEU, before the International Congress of Women in June 1899, she spoke autobiographically when she declared that, 'Only those who are constantly called to help and advise suffering wives can know what unspeakable infamies are sometimes hidden by the veil of legal marriage.'[61] And she declared that enforced maternity was a 'crime . . . against . . . the mother . . . the child . . . the race and humanity' and should be punished accordingly.[62] She concluded that although considered a natural impulse, man's unbridled lust debased the *whole* of society, and that the sad consequences of judicially sanctioned lasciviousness – disease, economic suffering and moral degeneracy – could only be remedied by the Parliament whose laws upheld the iniquities.[63] Here, though, perhaps Elizabeth's language is less fiery, she was supporting both her friend Mona Caird's insistence that the right of a woman to control her 'maternal instinct [was] the red-hot heart of the battle' and the claim of Charlotte Perkins Gilman for the imposition of 'an erotically altered new manhood' as a means to triumph over the world's ills.[64]

Mona Caird had accepted Elizabeth's invitation of a seat on the WEU Executive, and she also worked collaboratively with Ben Elmy who, under his pseudonym of Ellis Ethelmer, penned a series of polemical works on sex education and women's sexual physiology which were published privately, under the auspices of the WEU, from 1893 to 1897.[65] They offered the first 'explicitly feminist' literature on the subject, and presented 'a coherent analysis of why and in what manner women were subordinated'.[66] To lay stress upon these texts, however (and particularly Ethelmer's misconstrued beliefs surrounding menstruation, which he considered to be the result of the pathological abuse by men of women's bodies), obscures the true significance of the WEU's wider voice as an agent of Progressive politics. Such discussions also place the organisation too firmly as a discursive hub for high profile, middle-class intellectuals. This is something which negates the considerable contribution made to its ideals and its practical work by the wider membership – for example Amy Hurlston, the daughter of a Coventry watchmaker.

Hurlston, aged just twenty-eight, presented a paper on *The Factory Work of Women in the Midlands* to the WEU conference of March 1893. She informed the audience that personal association with the working women of her home town had highlighted not only their depressing economic plight, but also a new awareness that collaborative association with middle-class feminists could release them from their 'continual fear of starvation and the gutter of the workhouse'.[67] Hurlston's survey, which was subsequently published by the WEU, ensured her designation as one of Roosevelt's 'muckrakers', for she brought the plight of the women of her area before the public and demanded change. Hurlston was pleased that her actions had communicated to labouring women that they need no longer lie crushed under the 'relentless heel' of patriarchal despotism. They would fight their way free, in order to establish the conditions in which they could thrive as mothers.[68] Elizabeth, who welcomed the earnest commitment of young workers such as Hurlston, Julia Smith and Katharine Reid (who, alongside Isabella Ford took the WEU's message to the factories of London's East End) likewise placed the path to redemption into women's own hands.[69] 'Women must win their final victory by their own efforts [and] open the gates of freedom by their own exertions', she argued, and urged '*every women* [to] *help* . . . by [application of] individual personal influence and effort'.[70] Such words clearly subscribe to the Byronic notion that those who wished for freedom 'must themselves strike the blow', a precept which lay at the heart of the subsequent philosophy of the militants.[71] While Elizabeth's sentiments do not, perhaps, express the same explicitly violent connotations as those of Mary Cozens, it is clear that her message contained an equally forceful undertone of resistance, and a rhetorical (rather than an explicit) call to arms.

While Cozens' outspokenness proved effective in catapulting the WEU into the public sphere, the relationship between Elizabeth and the younger woman suffered. Elizabeth had been enthusiastic when, its membership broadened by new supporters of Charles McLaren's Women's Suffrage Bill, the WEU instituted a parliamentary sub-committee in London during the last weeks of 1893.[72] Mary Cozens took a leading role in its organisation, but that winter proved to be a period of increasing tension and lack of cohesion between members overall. The actions of Liberal MP Llewellyn Atherley-Jones were also unhelpful. Elizabeth believed him to have entertained serious thoughts about staking a claim to the leadership of the WEU – something she firmly rebuffed on the grounds that it needed 'no master'.[73] She was spectacularly angry, and wrote to McIlquham that Atherley-Jones showed none of the political bravery and staunchness exhibited by his father, Ernest Jones. The 'falling away' of the son from the path lit by the father was heartbreaking, she noted, and she cast Atherley-Jones as a turncoat who put party-political concerns before humanitarian ideals in ways the staunch Chartist would have considered shameful.[74] Matters reached breaking point in February 1894, when Mary Cozens, now classified by Elizabeth as '*ineffably* silly' and 'not fully reliable', retreated from the WEU and formed, in company with Atherley-Jones, the Parliamentary Committee for Women's Suffrage (PCWS).[75] The PCWS archive makes no mention of the society's WEU heritage, and it is difficult to conclude that Elizabeth felt any real regret at Cozens's departure.[76] By this time '[w]orn out with illness, overwork and worry' she had equally pressing domestic difficulties to contend with.[77]

The Elmys' finances, never robust following Ben's retirement, were perilous by Christmas 1893. Even his widely reviewed sex education books *The Human Flower* and *Baby Buds* arguably cost more to publish than they ever earned in royalties. And this would certainly have been true for the late 1890s feminist polemics *Life to Woman* and *Phases of Love*. The heavily annotated poem *Woman Free* sold only moderately, within the niche 'feminist' market.[78] To save costs, therefore, the administration of the WEU was undertaken by Elizabeth and her son, and she was adamant that the organisation's funds should not be raided to provide them with an income.[79] Such was the concern of her friends that McIlquham, Louisa Martindale and others contributed to a New Year's gift of £9. Outside of such kind gestures, though, financial disaster was looming. The family's sacrifice of their personal security was made in February 1894, when Ben arranged a £200 mortgage on Buxton House to enable WEU work to continue.[80] Worse was to follow, only weeks later, when he lay desperately ill as the result of a bronchial infection. In a moment of semi-consciousness delirium, he experienced a vision of the life beyond the grave, something which brought him even closer to his wife, who now believed both had been granted a revelation of the divine future. Harriet McIlquham, deeply concerned, offered her services as Ben's nurse. Touched by the gesture, Elizabeth refused, but noted that of 'no other friend still living [would she have asked] such a sisterly service'.[81]

Ben's recovery was slow and he never truly emerged from a semi-invalid life. Gifts of produce from McIlquham's Staverton estate and of wine from the cellars of C.W. Pearce and Co. in Glasgow were gratefully received. He often kept to his room, wrote when able and, perhaps surprisingly given his weakness, found the energy to institute the Male Electors' League for Women's Suffrage in early 1897 – the first men-only society to specifically campaign for the parliamentary vote.[82] Charles Pearce was swiftly co-opted onto its Executive, alongside Alan Greenwell, who became chairman. Always deeply caring of Ben, Elizabeth was now permanently fearful for his health and, for some while, far less willing to travel extensively. In consequence, Buxton House became not only the centre of the Elmys' domestic world, but also the hub of their public life, especially when the WEU international mailing was posted from Congleton, twice a year. Letters crossed the globe, their contents as eagerly awaited in America as in New Zealand, Scandinavia, South Africa and Switzerland.

Though confined more to home, Elizabeth utilised the period of Ben's convalescence productively. She wrote widely for *Shafts* and the *Westminster Review* (among other outlets), and built on elements of previous activism to campaign for a legislative barrier against the final, and most stubborn, element of the doctrine of coverture, marital rape in perhaps her most important paper ever published, *Woman and the Law*. While under no illusions as to the difficulties the WEU faced in securing the support of those who had the power to push through reform, her commendable efforts to secure it were based on a strong adherence to John Stuart Mill's assertion in his seminal *The Subjection of Women*: namely that it was 'barbarous . . . that one individual could, under any circumstances, have a *right* to the person of another'.[83] Writing that to continue to uphold the double standard of sexual morality was to make wives 'the abject slave[s] of the lowest appetites of the mere male animal', and that opposition to this tyrannical position was '*the true meaning of women's suffrage*', Elizabeth reappraised Mill's arguments for contemporary readers.[84]

Elizabeth Wolstenholme Elmy's engagement with Mill's ideology was both extensive and critical.[85] It is, therefore, only to be expected that she noted the 'double analogy' implicit in his treatise, namely that his 'use of slavery as analogous to women's condition [was] overlaid with an older political imagery of tyranny and despotism' – characteristics which could be legitimately challenged by the politically marginalised to achieve redress.[86] The ideals and campaigns of the WEU, however, implied a greater rebellion than Mill envisaged, for they incorporated within the 'politics of disruption' not only those middle-class women who would gain the parliamentary vote under existing electoral qualifications (and who were, therefore, in direct relationship with their tyrannical 'oppressors') but all womanhood.[87] Thus, when Charlotte Carmichael Stopes chose the WEU's 1896 conference to declare that the modern women's movement should rightly be aligned to Francis Bacon's *Novum Organum* in its call for the overthrow of existing customs and traditions, it was into the hands of those termed the 'voteless toilers' – the mothers of the labouring classes – that the torch of reform was passed.[88]

The extent to which wives, even armed with a legislative sanction against marital rape, would have taken to law their right to refuse a husband's demands for sex remains questionable. Nevertheless, it was around the premise that they *would* do so that Elizabeth refashioned the discourse surrounding female bodily autonomy in order to link the issue of 'consent' to maternity to 'consent' in matters of government. To do it she built on earlier article, published in 1885, in which she had argued that 'not even war' should compromise the vision of a truly egalitarian construction of citizenship. 'War is a hideous and unnatural thing,' she asserted, 'but if it has to exist there is no reason why women should not take part in it as men take part in it,' facing the same risks and dangers in acknowledgement of their common humanity.[89] At the head of the WEU, she extended the argument. She applied the language of combat to highlight the fact that since the Third Reform Act seven million working-class men had been granted the privilege of voting for the representatives of a government that might send them to die for their country; the ability to defend the nation in war the bedrock of the traditional construction of citizenship. In her 1895 pamphlet, *Women and the Law*, Elizabeth argued that if consenting to offer one's life for the nation was the main constituent of determining the electoral qualification, then women possessed the superior claim, having risked their lives daily in childbed for the 'perpetuation and progress of the race' from which the nation drew its armies.[90] She demanded independence for women, first, to bear only those children whose health and well-being they could ensure, and second, in order to insert women's voices into the rhetoric of warfare (via the speeches of their elected representatives) as an effective counter to the aggressive bellicosity of state directives that sent so many to their deaths. The 'special dignity and worthiness' possessed by mothers was '*superior* to that of the mere male faculty of fighting', and it was for this reason that women now demanded the opportunities for self-development afforded by the possession of the rights and duties of national citizenship.[91] War affected all mothers, and thus this discourse transcended the divisions of class.

The diverse allegiances of the WEU

To argue, as Elizabeth had done, for national citizenship on the grounds of a woman's right to choose the direction her maternity would take was a significant matter, and it was a demand made by the WEU on behalf 'not [of] this generation only, but for all men, for all women, and for all time'.[92] Penned by Mrs E.O. Fordham, the WEU's local organiser in Bedford, this personal plea for social regeneration contained sentiments which were echoed again and again by its wider membership. They sought not a sop to public opinion (which was becoming increasingly amenable to the notion of a middle-class feminine civic role) but rather the 'awakening of woman', the title of a polemical treatise by theosophist Frances Swiney. Swiney, herself a member of the WEU, affirmed that 'woman's patient endurance of pain is a psychic quality, and not a merely physical one', and as the age of the 'new woman' dawned, a new spirit was being forged among ultra-Radicals, which understood feminism to be a conscious creed – something to be experienced from within as well as without.[93]

Though this 'introspective turn' within feminism is understood to have reached its apogee during the 1910s and 1920s, from the earliest days of the WEU, its local organisers recorded an embryonic shift in this direction.[94] Although it is doubtful that even a handful of those involved would have acknowledged their feelings as 'feminist' per se, Amy Hurlston noted that she had witnessed in the working-class women of the Midlands an awareness of their oppression not previously evident, their consciences awakened by an acknowledgment that (both individually and as a collective) they were deeply affected by patriarchal systems. What they yearned for was 'emancipation from the tyranny of custom' and a right to bargain for a fair day's wage to feed and clothe the wretched children that the laws of coverture required they bear without limit.[95] WEU local organisers (and by 1895 there were ten local offices in cities from Glasgow to Bristol) understood it to be their duty, both to personally awaken a feminist mindset in the hearts and minds of the poor and to bring before the public accounts of the true effects of socio-economic deprivation. These literary exposés nestle precisely within the boundaries of the approach to journalism defined as 'muckraking', the attributes of the successful author being 'personal investigative exploration, sympathy with the working-class and an abiding interest in understanding the social, economic and political forces shaping society'.[96] Articles were written both to highlight the author's moral indignation and to demand legislative change. To view the WEU's ideology through the lens of Progressivism and to understand its activists as being 'social housekeepers' (rather than simply moral purists) can transform our understanding of these pre-militant suffragists.[97]

The highs and lows of WEU campaigning were recorded purely because Elizabeth believed its activities historically significant and wished to secure its archive. She catalogued and forwarded many of its publications, reports and accounts to the British Museum within months of its demise, believing the 'amount of work done under constant difficulties' to be noteworthy.[98] Within the collection, it is obvious that Hurlston's paper was not an isolated example of 'muckraking'. Another author who had gathered first-hand evidence of the lives of the labouring poor was William Henry Wilkins, a somewhat paradoxical figure who is best known for his work as literary assistant to Lady Isabel, widow of anthropologist Sir Richard Francis Burton.[99] A notorious anti-Semite and anti-alienist (affiliations not uncommon among Progressives), Wilkins acted as private secretary to Lord Dunraven, the chairman of the House of Lords Commission into the Sweated Trades.[100] In the course of his labours for the Commission, Wilkins had conducted personal research into the lives of the needlewomen of the East End of London, and presented a summary of his work to the WEU's 1893 conference. His paper, *The Bitter Cry of the Voteless Toilers*, put forward an appeal not only for the enfranchisement of the middle-classes but of the 'weak, disorganised, underpaid and overworked' mothers of the masses.[101] Only with the vote, Wilkins concluded, would these 'feeble . . . crushed' women be freed to fight the 'physical evil[s]' of ill-health and moral laxity that impaired the 'tender delights' they might experience as mothers who were full citizens of their country. For only with the vote could they work to rejuvenate the nation's health through the birth of healthy children.[102] This ideal, when combined with Elizabeth's insistence that women, once enfranchised, would influence the passage of legislation against marital rape, squared the circle linking regeneration, bodily autonomy and consent to government. It also highlighted the complicated nature of Progressive suffragist politics, for Wilkins' desire that the government actively intervene to promote social and industrial reform (even if the personal rights of some members of the community would be affected), was not shared or advocated by all WEU members – or even by Elizabeth herself.

Writing for *Shafts* in 1897, Elizabeth claimed that direct state involvement had 'cripple[d] the weak and strong alike', and by 'its restrictive laws . . . had identified itself with caucus, coercion, cloture and compulsion'.[103] And given these strident opinions, it might be wondered how such views could mingle so seamlessly in WEU circles with those of socialists such as Isabella Ford, Isabella Bream Pearce, and the many other working-class women attracted to socialist politics. These included the many labouring women that Elizabeth addressed in Manchester as the guest speaker of the dynamic new secretary of the North of England Society for Women's Suffrage (formally the MNSWS), Esther Roper – the woman who had taken 'the Special Appeal [to] the factory women of Lancashire and Cheshire'.[104] Given Elizabeth's pride in her association with the Chartist leadership, however, her sympathies with the cause of labour are more easily understood. As a humanitarian seeking the perfect world, she desired that all might benefit from the 'new', just society. She saw in feminist agency the path towards that society, and later wrote that while she 'regard[ed] *the Enfranchisement of women as of more urgent importance* than the establishment of Socialism' she did so only because she felt '*manmade Socialism would be little, if at all better* – than a manmade Liberalism, or Toryism'.[105] Elizabeth was above all else a feminist; but for socialists whose world-view looked beyond the 'theoretical ambiguities', which ensured that 'women's oppression was recognised but immediately buried within the larger . . . question' of the oppression of class, she had the utmost respect.[106]

Elizabeth invited Isabella Bream Pearce, then President of the Glasgow Women's Labour Party, to speak from the platform at the WEU's 1896 conference where, unsurprisingly, she upheld the power of socialism as a transforming force. An intellectual and securely middle class, Pearce suffered no difficulty in reconciling the demands of allegiance to both feminism and socialism, unlike many working-class women who had to traverse a complex minefield of divided loyalties in the process of feminist activism.[107] Pearce adroitly linked the themes of socialist politics, feminist consciousness, bodily autonomy and the rejuvenation of society in a paper entitled *Women and Factory Legislation*. Women, she argued, were 'beginning to awake' to the challenges posed by modern living – challenges that needed a new approach to governance. Pearce was convinced that the people, when awakened to the fact that the power and the 'duty to prevent the possibility of social misery' lay with them, would 'recognise . . . their responsibilities . . . [and] devise a new system' which would make it impossible in the future for any individual to oppress a fellow human being. 'Call it Socialism or call it what you will', she concluded, this was the means by which humanity would thrive.[108]

While her political proclivities are obvious in her analysis of the destructive power of the capitalist economy, Pearce praised the fact that it was these very conditions that had awakened the spirit of battle in women – admiring especially the resistance labouring women had made against protective legislation that had effected (even when seeking to 'confer a benefit') to discriminate against them.[109] Directly linking the analogy of the working woman as her employer's chattel to a wife's 'complete surrender of her bodily person' to her husband's pleasure, Pearce contended that women were no longer content to 'sell [their] birthright . . . for "a mess of pottage"' either in labouring or domestic life. The time of slavery was now at an end. In concluding her comprehensive appraisal of the position, Pearce argued that 'For the race to progress we cannot go back, [but only] forward to a new and better life.'[110] And for Pearce, and many like her, that better life was envisioned through socialism or via the trade union movement. 'The rational aspirations of the labour movement' gave both direction and 'organisational strength' to radical suffragists, but while the tide of suffragism was moving afresh in this area, the influence of the WEU on its actions was waning.[111]

The end of an era

The work of the Radical-independent Progressives of the WEU had therefore, under Elizabeth's direction, defined the tone of the debates, which transformed the campaign for the parliamentary franchise after Queen Victoria's death. As the organisation's work drew to a close, however, no suffragist could have foretold the events to come. The important part the organisation played in shaping the future was also, largely, ignored by those whose histories shaped scholars' understanding of 'the cause'. In her lifetime, only the work of Ethel Hill and Olga Fenton Shafter gave Elizabeth a prominent place in its narrative, the authors seeing no reason to denigrate the 'cool courage' of those whose campaign methods were more radical. 'Great suffragists', they argued, came in many guises, and their inclusion of Elizabeth in the volume of 'prominent leaders, and writers, and thinkers' of the movement, published in 1909, went some way to mitigating both her personal, and by implication the WEU's, exclusion elsewhere.[112]

However, it is clear that Elizabeth did not always aid the interests of the WEU as ably as she might. She certainly did not always seek the conciliatory path. For example, when the wider suffrage movement united under the leadership of Millicent Garrett Fawcett as the National Union of Women's Suffrage Societies (NUWSS) in 1897, Elizabeth kept the WEU aloof from its circle. This was despite the fact that Fawcett had declared the NUWSS, in common with WEU aims, independent of party politics. Elizabeth's reasons were that she understood the 'suffrage only' objectives of the NUWSS to be too narrowly focused, its organisation inefficient, and many of its members mired in the 'slough' of partisan allegiances.[113] She also had a horror, under the NUWSS's plan to work regionally, that her labours would be confined to the Macclesfield area. Clearly, she felt herself a figurehead rather than a 'drone'. The fact that she felt sidelined by the new organisation's leadership might well have influenced her harsh assessment, but she nonetheless felt an alliance would ensure her 'hands [were] tied'.[114]

Likewise, her interaction with other party-political groups was often either lukewarm or querulous – although both she and the regional WEU workers accepted many engagements to speak and distribute the organisation's literature at meetings of the Women's Co-operative Guild, the Women's Liberal Federation (WLF), the Manchester National Society for Women's Suffrage and the Union of Practical Suffragists (UPS) – a ginger group of the WLF established in 1896 under the leadership of her two close friends, Anna-Maria Priestman and Louisa Martindale.[115] The relationship of any party-political society with the WEU was, however, always that of associate rather than partner – for, in her heart, Elizabeth believed that those she termed 'party women' would always put women's suffrage 'in second place'.[116] She did, however, share the sentiments of her UPS friends, such as Dora Montefiore, on the matter of making women's suffrage a 'test question' in the selection of potential parliamentary candidates: something this group of Liberal ladies had advocated since 1893.[117] In a letter to the editor of the *Woman's Herald*, in July 1895, Elizabeth stated clearly that sympathisers should 'strive earnestly to secure the selection of a favourable candidate to the women's cause and . . . refuse to work, or to vote, for any[one] hostile or indifferent'.[118] The significance of her evaluation of the 'test question' is discussed later, but, following the Local Government Act of 1894, she put parliamentary concerns aside to worked tirelessly with the others of the WEU to encourage women to vote, and to stand for election to the bodies of local administration to which they had recently been enfranchised. As a consequence, many WEU organisers offered themselves for service and Elizabeth noted that in the December elections, 'Over 100 of our women . . . were elected . . . as Poor Law Guardians or Parish Councillor's.'[119] Her informants were the successful candidates themselves, and though her personal campaign to secure election to Buglawton Urban District Council failed, she saw, and welcomed, the great progress overall.[120] So significant did she believe the contribution women could offer to local administrative bodies to be that she wrote four detailed articles on the topic for the *Westminster Review*.[121]

Despite the significance of its practical and ideological labours, sheer practicalities contributed as much to the WEU's demise as collegiate disagreements or theoretical differences between workers. Though she was to push its forces into one last supreme effort in support of the Parliamentary Franchise (Extension to Women) Bill of 1897, Elizabeth's personal financial resources could no longer propel the work of the Union as much as they had sustained her labours hitherto. Indeed, she was now personally dependent on the support of others, including Louisa Martindale and Carolyn Holyoake Smith who, in addition to its principal benefactress, Harriet McIlquham, had instituted the 'Grateful Fund', both to pay tribute to Elizabeth's feminist labours and to cloak a charitable bequest to the Elmy family with the gloss of honour.[122] From this source she received a sum which varied between £1 and £1 10s 0d each week, paid between 1896 and 1910. She grew so reliant upon it that letters abound regarding its prompt payment: this to ensure that she might do her 'marketing' and leave things 'cosy' at Buxton House before making trips to Manchester or London on WEU business.[123] In addition, the loss of the women's suffrage bill of 1897, in which so many hopes had been vested, almost halved the WEU's subscription list, and its financial situation grew increasingly desperate after the death of its principal benefactress, Mrs. Russell Carpenter, in the spring of 1898.[124] As a non-party-political group, the WEU was unable to associate formally with socialist or Liberal organisations, which might have secured its financial future, and the loose nature of the Progressive coalition and the disparate allegiances of its members ensured few, if any, put the needs of the group before other considerations.

Nonetheless, and in the context of future action, few could dispute Elizabeth's willingness to partake personally in those 'politics of disruption' that she would continually advocate as the right course for suffragists in the new century. Indeed, it could be argued she set the trend. Putting aside, for once, her scepticism regarding the NUWSS, Elizabeth had travelled to London to work with them prior to the suffrage debate

in the House of Commons on 7 July 1897. There the Parliamentary Franchise (Extension to Women) Bill (introduced that year by Emily Faithfull's nephew Ferdinand Faithfull Begg) was ignominiously talked out,
as time-wasting opponents occupied the entire afternoon in discussion
of the tabled amendments to the Verminous Persons Bill. In a furious
temper, but controlled, Elizabeth led the angry contingent of suffrage
protestors into Broad Sanctuary, where, raising her voice, she declared
that 'no lower depth of coarseness, levity and vulgarity' could have been
reached during the deliberations.[125] This moment of high drama was,
however, soon forgotten – and though Elizabeth recalled later that
authority had 'complained', her disruptive actions had not earned her
arrest. Even at sixty-three years of age she appeared to relish the prospect.
By 1899, having seen a great opportunity pass by, Elizabeth made the
prophetic comment that she 'feared W[omen's] S[uffrage] would never
be won in England till women were willing to go to prison for its sake'.[126]
For the moment, however, with the organisation facing financial ruin,
she had no recourse but to post the notice of the WEU's final meeting,
sending a card to supporters emblazoned with Arthur Hugh Clough's
poem *The Struggle*. Held on 1 July 1899 in London, speakers included
Charlotte Stopes, Dr Alletta Jacobs, Louisa Martindale and Harriot
Stanton Blatch.[127] The principal guest, however, was Charlotte Perkins
Gilman, visiting Britain as a delegate to the International Congress of
Women. Never were the WEU's links to American Progressivism more
manifest.

Margaret Sibthorp recorded in *Shafts* that those assembled at the 1
July meeting gathered in an atmosphere of 'respect [and] love' for the
WEU's founder. They had found it, indeed, almost 'too hard to part with'
her. Their view of her was as a prophet, and they credited her with setting
in motion a new 'great work . . . consolidat[ing] stone by stone, the great
edifice of the future power and strength of the human being' via an
unshakeable determination to continue to campaign for the 'struggle of
women for freedom and opportunity'.[128] If history is to look for the legacy
of the WEU, though, it must do so by following Elizabeth's actions in the
years after its demise. Now acting individually, but at the centre of her
famed network of contacts, she began labouring in earnest to secure that
which she had long sought – that 'great federation' of workers who were
prepared to risk everything for the women's cause.[129] To her delight, her
part in the events that achieved this was not insignificant, and she was
aided throughout by a revitalised relationship with 'Britain's most
notorious muckraker', W.T. Stead.[130]

Notes

1 Anon., 'Report of Annual Meeting', *Fair Trade Journal*, 8 June 1888, p. 505. For a discussion of further issues raised by the work of the WEU see, Wright, 'The Women's Emancipation Union'.

2 Ben Elmy, 'The Lays of Federation', *Fair Trade Journal*, 2 January 1891, p. 149. See also 6 March 1891, p. 256 and 17 April 1891, p. 329. Bernard Porter notes the 'quasi-imperialist' agenda of the Fair Trade League, one of a number of organisations working for a defined objective, but from a clear imperialist standpoint. Bernard Porter, *The Absent-Minded Imperialists: Empire, Society and Culture in Britain* (Oxford: Oxford University Press, 2004), p. 175. EWE/HM, 23/7/1891, 47449, fol. 166.

3 For a full account of the proceedings in *Regina* v. *Jackson* see Ginger Frost, 'A Shock to Marriage?: The Clitheroe Case and the Victorians', in George Robb (ed.) *Disorder in the Court: Trials and Sexual Conflict at the Turn of the Century* (New York: Palgrave, 1999), pp. 100–18. Also Rubinstein, *Before the Suffragettes*, Chapter 5.

4 Anon. 'High Court Proceedings', *The Times*, 17 March 1891.

5 Elizabeth Wolstenholme Elmy, *The Decision in the Clitheroe Case, and its Consequences. A Series of Five Letters* (Manchester: Guardian Printing, 1891), p. 1. Over 100,000 copies of this pamphlet were eventually circulated. WEU, *Final Report*, 1899, p. 1. *Regina* v. *Jackson* did not categorise the act of rape in marriage as a crime per se, something that was not affected until the case of *Regina* v. *R.* on 23 October 1991, when a husband's immunity from prosecution in this regard was abolished. Bland, *Banishing the Beast*, p. 138, and p. 338, fn. 38.

6 WEU, *Inaugural Report*, 1892, pp. 1–2.

7 Frost, 'A Shock to Marriage', p. 114.

8 The four key principles of the WEU's ideology were; equality of right and duty with men in all matters affecting the service of the community and the state; equality of opportunity for self-development by the education of the schools and of life; equality in industry by equal freedom of choice of career and equality in marriage and in parental rights.

9 EWE/HM, 23/7/1891, 47449, fol. 163.

10 WEU leaflet, November 1891, p. 1. Papers of the Women's Emancipation Union, British Library. (Hereafter WEUP.)

11 Mayhall, *Citizenship and Resistance*, chapter 1.

12 WEU, *Final Report*, 1899, pp. 1–2.

13 WEU, *Inaugural Report*, 1892, p. 2.

14 Eliza Lynn Linton, 'The Judicial Shock to Marriage', *Nineteenth Century*, Vol. 29, May 1891, pp. 691–700, quoted in Shanley, *Feminism*, p. 182.

15 Anon. [Editorial], *Glasgow Herald*, 27 October 1892.

16 Anon. [EWE], 'The Emancipation of Women', leaflet reprinted from an article published in the *Cambrian News*, 2 October 1885, p. 4. WEUP.

17 Anon. [EWE], *Emancipation of Women*, p. 4. Emphasis in original.

18 David W. Gutzke, 'Britain's "Social Housekeepers"', in Gutzke (ed.), *Britain and Transnational Progressivism*, pp. 149–83, p. 149.

19 Charlotte Perkins Stetson, *Women and Economics* (1898), p. 71, quoted in Allen, *The Feminism of Charlotte Perkins Gilman*, p. 107.

20 Ethelmer, *Woman Free*, Stanza XL.

21 Laura E. Nym Mayhall, 'The South African War and the origins of suffrage militancy in Britain, 1899–1902', in Ian C. Fletcher, Laura E. Nym Mayhall and Philippa Levine (eds), *Women's Suffrage in the British Empire: Citizenship, Nation and Race* (London and New York: Routledge, 2000), pp. 3–17.

22 WEU, *Final Report*, 1899, p. 32. F.M.L. Thompson, 'Introduction' in Gutzke (ed.), *Britain and Transnational Progressivism*, p. 9.

23 EWE/HM, 14/1/1892, 47449, fol. 233. (My emphasis.)

24 WEU, *Final Report*, 1899, p. 2.

25 Holton, 'Now you see it', pp. 23–4.

26 EWE/HM, 18/7/1892, 47449, fol. 282.

27 EWE/HM, 25/3/1892, 47449, fol. 261; Anon. 'Central National Society for Women's Suffrage', *The Woman's Herald*, 16 April 1892, p. 7.

28 WEU, *Final Report*, 1899, p. 2; WEU, *Inaugural Report*, 1892, p. 3.

29 Holton, *Suffrage Days*, p. 85. The Women's Franchise League had issued their bulletin in the *Daily News* of 25 April 1892.

30 EWE/HM, 18/5/1892, 47449, fol. 270. For an eyewitness report of the meeting see that of Mr J.M. Robertson quoted in J.H. Levy, 'The Political Enfranchisement of Women', *Personal Rights Journal*, May 1892, pp. 152–4.

31 Jon Lawrence, 'Contesting the Male Polity: The Suffragettes and the Politics of Disruption in Edwardian Britain', in Vickery (ed.), *Women, Privilege and Power*, p. 203.

32 EWE/HM, 18/5/1892, 47449, fol. 269.

33 Women's Franchise League Minute Book, 2 May 1892 and 23 May 1892. Thanks to Harriet Lightman for permission to work from a microfilm copy of this source. Original manuscript held at McCormick Library of Special Collections, Northwestern University, USA. Purvis, *Emmeline Pankhurst*, pp. 36–7. On Burrows see Karen Hunt, *Equivocal Feminists: The Social Democratic Federation and the Woman Question 1884–1911* (Cambridge: Cambridge University Press, 1996), pp. 15–16.

34 EWE/HM, 18/5/1892, 47449, fol. 269–270.

35 Women's Franchise League Minute Book, 23 May 1892.

36 Purvis, *Emmeline Pankhurst*, p. 41.

37 Anon., 'Report of the WEU Conference', *Personal Rights Journal*, November 1892.

38 Anon., *The Times*, 12 November 1892. Cozens is being compared here to the 'Communardes', working women of Paris who were alleged to have set fire to much of the city during the final days of the Paris Commune in May 1871.

39 Frances Power Cobbe to Millicent Garrett Fawcett, quoted in Ray Strachey, *Millicent Garrett Fawcett* (London: John Murray, 1931), p. 158.

40 EWE/HM, 11/12/1892, 47449, fol. 310.

41 Anon. [Editorial], 'Women's Emancipation Union', *Leeds Mercury*, 28 October 1892.

42 Crawford, *WSM*, pp. 145–6.

43 Holton, 'British Freewomen', pp. 158–63.

44 Caroline Holyoake Smith to the Editor, *Birmingham Daily Post*, 4 November 1892.

45 Holton, *Suffrage Days*, p. 2.

46 WEU, *Third Report*, 1896, p. 10. Mrs C.W. Pearce, *Women and Factory Legislation*, 1896, WEUP.

47 Crawford, *WSM*, pp. 648–9.

48 EWE/HM, 30/10/1893, 47450, fol. 54.

49 Jon Lawrence, *Speaking for the People*, p. 190.

50 Anon. [Editorial], *Glasgow Herald*, 27 October 1892. Amy Hurlston, *The Factory Work of Women in the Midlands*, 1893, p. 8. WEUP.

51 Ian Tyrrell, 'Transatlantic Progressivism in Women's Temperance and Suffrage,' in Gutzke (ed.), *Britain and Transnational Progressivism*, pp. 133–48, p. 133; Holton, 'To Educate Women', pp. 1132–3.

52 Anon. (Margaret Sibthorp), 'Women's Emancipation Union', *Shafts*, July–September 1899, p. 47.

53 Pankhurst, *TSM*, p. 96.

54 Mayhall, *Citizenship and Resistance*, p. 9.

55 Mayhall, *Citizenship and Resistance*, p. 11.

56 WEU, *Final Report*, 1899, pp. 1–2.

57 Mayhall, *Citizenship and Resistance*, p. 23.

58 EWE, *The Decision in the Clitheroe Case*, pp. 3–4.

59 Sally Ledger and Roger Luckhurst, 'Introduction', in Sally Ledger and Roger Luckhurst (eds), *The Fin de Siecle: A Reader in Cultural History c.1880–1900* (Oxford: Oxford University Press, 2000), p. 1; EWE, *The Criminal Code in its Relation to Women*.

60 EWE, *The Decision in the Clitheroe Case,* pp. 7 and 10.

61 EWE, 'The Marriage Law of England', pp. 118.

62 EWE, 'The Marriage Law of England', pp. 118–19.

63 EWE, *The Decision in the Clitheroe Case*, p. 13.

64 Mona Caird, *The Daughters of Danus* (London, 1894), quoted in Kent, *Sex and Suffrage*, p. 112; Allen, *The Feminism of Charlotte Perkins Gilman*, p. 237.

65 Ethelmer, *Life to Woman*; Ethelmer, *The Human Flower*; Ethelmer, *Baby Buds*; Ethelmer, *Phases of Love*.

66 Bland, *Banishing the Beast*, p. 141.

67 Hurlston, *Factory Work*, p. 8.

68 Hurlston, *Factory Work*, p. 9.

69 WEU, *Third Report* (1896), p. 10.

70 Elizabeth Wolstenholme Elmy, 'Women's Suffrage', *Shafts*, July and August 1897, p. 209.

71 Maroula Joannou, 'She who would be Free', pp. 31–44.

72 EWE/HM, 'Christmas Eve' 1893, 47450, fol. 78.

73 EWE/HM, 25/2/1894, fol. 86.

74 EWE/HM, 21/6/1905, fol. 123.

75 EWE/HM, 22/2/1894, 47450, fol. 83. Emphasis in original.

76 Minutes of the Parliamentary Committee for Women's Suffrage, PCWS/2/1, 1893–4 and PCWS/2/2, 1894–5, John Rylands University Library, Manchester.

77 EWE/HM, 22/2/1894, 47450, fol. 83.

78 Between August 1895 and May 1895, 2,600 copies of *The Human Flower* had been sold. This is in comparison to 160 copies of *Woman Free*. EWE/HM, 15/5/1895, 47452, fol. 193.

79 EWE/HM, 3/7/1898, 47451, fol. 224.

80 HM to Frances Rowe, 11/8/1901, 47452, fol. 195.

81 EWE/HM, 23/3/1895, 47450, fol. 187.

82 EWE/HM, 1/9/1897, 47450, fol. 134.

83 John Stuart Mill, *The Subjection of Women* (1869) quoted in Wolstenholme Elmy, 'The Marriage Law of England', p. 117.

84 EWE, 'The Marriage Law of England', pp. 117–18; EWE, 'Women's Suffrage', *Shafts*, March 1897, p. 84. (Emphasis in original.)

85 The extent of Wolstenholme Elmy's interaction with Mill's ideals is illustrated when, in 1904, she collaborated with Dr Stanton Coit, émigré minister of South Place Chapel, to prepare an Introduction to a new edition of *The Subjection of Women*. EWE/HM, 22/3/1890, fol. 99; EWE/HM 12/10/1904, fol. 19; John Stuart Mill, *The Subjection of Women*, ed. Stanton Coit, (Longmans, Green & Co., 1906).

86 Laura E. Nym Mayhall, 'The Rhetorics of Slavery and Citizenship: Suffragist Discourse and Canonical Texts in Britain, 1880–1914', *Gender and History*, 13 (3), 2001, pp. 481–97, p. 485.

87 Mayhall, 'Rhetorics', pp. 487–8.

88 Charlotte Carmichael Stopes, *The Woman's Protest*, 1896, p. 1; Mayhall, *Citizenship and Resistance*, p. 23. William H. Wilkins, *The Bitter Cry of the Voteless Toilers* (WEU: Manchester, 1893), p. 15. WEUP.

89 Anon. (Elizabeth Wolstenholme Elmy), *The Emancipation of Women*, 1885, p. 5. WEUP.

90 Elizabeth Wolstenholme Elmy, *Women and the Law*. A series of four letters from *The Western Daily Press* (Women's Emancipation Union, 1895), p. 6.

91 Wolstenholme Elmy, 'Women and the Law', p. 6.

92 E.O. Fordham, *The Duty of Woman: Towards Humanity and our Country: Towards Our Family: Towards Ourselves*, 1894, pp. 1–2. WEUP.

93 Ignota (Elizabeth Wolstenholme Elmy), 'The Awakening of Woman', *Westminster Review*, July 1899, pp. 69–72.

94 Lucy Delap, *The Feminist Avant-Garde: Transatlantic Encounters of the Early Twentieth Century* (Cambridge: Cambridge University Press, 2007), pp. 19–21 and 315–16.

95 Hurlston, *Factory Work*, pp. 6–7 and 9.

96 Gutzke, 'Social Housekeepers', p. 161.

97 Gutzke, 'Social Housekeepers', p. 161.

98 EWE/HM, 16/8/1900, 47452, fol. 113.

99 Geoffrey Alderman and Colin Holmes, 'The Burton Book', *Journal of the Royal Asiatic Society*, 2008, 18, pp. 1–13, p. 7.

100 David W. Gutzke, 'Progressivism in Britain and Abroad' in, Gutzke (ed.), *Britain and Transnational Progressivism*, p. 45.

101 Wilkins, *Bitter Cry*, p. 15.

102 Wilkins, *Bitter Cry*, pp. 12–14.

103 Elizabeth Wolstenholme Elmy, 'The New Priestcraft', *Shafts*, September 1897, pp. 245–9, p. 245.

104 Gifford Lewis, *Eva Gore Booth and Esther Roper: A Biography* (London: Pandora, 1988), p. 85.

105 EWE/HM, 5/2/1907, 47455, fol. 49. Emphasis in original.

106 Hunt, *Equivocal Feminists*, p. 55.

107 Hannam and Hunt, *Socialist Women*, p. 105.

108 Mrs C.W. Pearce, *Women and Factory Legislation*, 1896, pp. 3–4. WEUP.

109 Pearce, *Women*, p. 4.

110 Pearce, *Women*, p. 3.

111 Lawrence, *Speaking for the People*, p. 195.

112 Hill and Olga Shafter (eds), *Great Suffragists and Why*, pp. 11–13 and 66–70.

113 EWE/HM, 18/12/1898, 47451, fol. 276. EWE to HM, 31/10/1896, 47450, fol. 330.

114 EWE/HM, 15/9/1896, 47450, fol. 316.

115 WEU, *Second Report*, 1894, Appendices.

116 EWE to HM, 1/9/1897, 47451, fol. 134.

117 Crawford, *WSM*, p. 693.

118 EWE to the Editor, *Women's Herald*, 4 July 1895.

119 EWE/HM, 9/5/1895, 47450, fol. 191.

120 For the report of the elections see EWE/HM, 20/12/1894, 47450, fol. 162. Also, *Congleton Chronicle*, 15 December 1894 and 22 December 1894.

121 Ignota [EWE], 'The Part of Women in Local Administration: England and Wales', *Westminster Review*, July 1898, pp. 32–46. Also, September 1898, pp. 246–60. October 1898, pp. 377–89; and February 1899, pp. 159–71.

122 Julia Smith to HM, 20/7/1896, 47450, fol. 307.

123 EWE/HM, 1/5/1903, 47453, fol. 117.

124 EWE/HM, 13/4/1898, 47451, fol. 202.

125 WEU, *Final Report*, 1899, p. 26.

126 EWE/HM, 23/10/1905, 47454, fol. 154.

127 EWE/HM (undated card, but June 1899), 47451, fol. 326.

128 Sibthorp, 'Women's Emancipation Union', p. 47.

129 Anon. [EWE] 'The Emancipation of Women', p. 4.

130 Gutske, 'Historians and Progressivism', in *Britain and Transnational Progressivism*, p. 27.

7

'The cold dark night is past':
August 1899–May 1906[1]

Our 'outlanders at home' – a pacifist's struggle

The winding up of the WEU, the organisation to which Elizabeth had given her time as a 'labour of love', did not signal a period of rest. Within three weeks, she had written a topical polemic on the suffrage question for the *Manchester Guardian*, entitled 'Our "outlanders" at home', castigating the government for preparing to defend the rights of disenfranchised male settlers in the Boer Republics of South Africa while every British woman remained without a political voice.[2] Cleverly, 'Outlanders' turned the tables on those who considered weakness a consideration in the matter, for Elizabeth pointed out that if matters 'of personal security' and 'protection' were the key factors in determining who should exercise the privileges of enfranchisement, then women had an 'equal if . . . not greater' claim to the security it afforded.[3] Though perhaps morally justified in her criticism of the 'warmongers' she was naive, for there were more pragmatic considerations on the government's side than the mere adoption of the moral high ground – not least geographical imperial dominion and the vast wealth of the Rand goldfields.

Nonetheless, Elizabeth was foremost among those radical suffragists (many, like herself, pacifist) who built upon the government's willingness to fight for Uitlander ('outlander') rights in order to justify the use of force in the political arena.[4] The Uitlanders had provoked armed conflict on the grounds that they had not consented to be governed by the Boers. Elizabeth took this supposition, and built on the narrative of resistance and 'disruption' she had composed in the 1890s to argue that women should never be forced to passively sanction laws which *they* had no voice in shaping – especially when their government had taken issue with such high-handedness elsewhere.

As we have seen, Elizabeth argued in *Women and the Law* that motherhood, not militarism, should be the foundation for the granting of citizenship, and that the chief precondition to pregnancy should be a woman's consent to it. In 'Outlanders' she explored the issue of consent from a wider perspective, claiming that:

> Our legislators are but human, very human, and naturally give their attention first to those interests which can make themselves felt and to those persons who can punish their negligence . . . [W]omen, being 'Outlanders' in their native land, can only sue as a favour for that which they are by law prevented from claiming as a right.

She argued that all the while women could not 'punish . . . negligence' their power was paltry, their only recourse 'passive resistance'.[5] If the government's military action legitimated force as a method of resolving citizenship disputations then, equally, force was available to those excluded from citizenship as a means of claiming it. Her logic, as always, was cutting. Her words were among the first written by Radical-independents on this theme, but her 'humble pupil', Dora Montefiore, took up the mantle forcefully as the war progressed.[6] A mere two months later in the *Ethical World*, Montefiore argued that 'if nothing but war will meet the situation then war must be declared by women at all parliamentary elections' by a refusal to support any candidate who did not admit the moral benefits that would result from the women's franchise.[7] Thus the ex-activists of the WEU declared war on the British government. They underlined their militancy by an 'insistence on being treated as full participants in the theatre of public politics', and threatened to invade, in the maelstrom of electioneering fervour, the citadel of patriarchal privilege which for so long had ensured their voice remained unheard. Elizabeth's personal construction of militancy, however, was never one that would envisage the loss of human life. A lifelong pacifist, she had adopted the rhetoric of combat only to construct a vision of women's citizenship based on their right to corporal individuality, not to envision the moment when women would actually take their place on the battlefield. Paradoxically, when considering that the basis for female militancy had been penned from an engagement with the military ideal of citizenship, she argued that 'peaceful evolution' rather than 'violent revolution' was the true way to secure the world's progress.[8]

The herald of peace

'Our "outlanders" at home' was written shortly after the International Peace Conference held at The Hague in July 1899, during which the Permanent Court of Arbitration was founded. W.T. Stead had attended, and had played an important part in convening this gathering. He told of his adventures at a 'grand Peace meeting' in Leek, attended by Frank Elmy in early October.[9] On 20 October, Stead launched the journal *War Against War in South Africa* in an attempt to popularise the pacifist perspective.[10] All animosity between Stead and Elizabeth regarding the *Maiden Tribute* scandal was put to one side and, from this point, she lobbied her colleagues, McIlquham among them, into support for Stead's campaign. '[M]ilitarism', she told them, was 'the worst of the many existing foes of justice to women.'[11] When Harriet, a more strident patriot perhaps, refused to bend to her pleas Elizabeth commented pragmatically that 'it [was] surely better to dwell on the thousand points [on] which we agree than on the one upon which we differ.'[12]

Elizabeth's own sympathies were so profoundly proclaimed that it is important here to ground their formation. Her views align clearly with the definition of 'pacifist feminism' put forward by Heloise Brown, and the Quaker influences that interlinked with Independent Methodism can be argued to have influenced these opinions from the days of Elizabeth's youth.[13] As long ago as July 1872, she had met American pacifist Julia Ward Howe at the home of Isabella Ford, when both were en route to the Ladies' Peace Meeting held at St George's Hall in London.[14] The *Herald of Peace*, journal of the British Peace Society, reported that Howe (who had planned her visit during the Franco-Prussian conflict of 1870–71), informed her audience that the 'mere absence of hostilities' did not constitute her concept of peace – which she construed to mean adherence to the principles of justice, freedom and religion. Anything else, she contended, was mere 'surface peace' and would never be sustained.[15] Though Elizabeth's own Christian orthodoxy had, by 1872, altogether dissipated (and she would henceforth substitute in her texts the word 'love' where others used 'faith') she shared Howe's wider objectives, as did another intimate friend, Josephine Butler.[16]

In the autumn of 1870, Butler had initiated the collection of signatures to an international protest against the Franco-Prussian War, but her commitment to the pacifist movement waned in the light of her all-consuming involvement with the international campaigns against the state regulation of vice during the 1880s and 1890s.[17] Elizabeth, similarly, was not formally allied to the Peace Society; the vast scope of her many concerns making her little more than a sympathiser of its aims and objectives. The declaration of the war against the Boer Republics of the Orange Free State and the Transvaal, however, galvanised her into making her opposition public. She had studied South Africa's history closely (inspired by her admiration for Olive Schreiner and through her communication with close friends who had settled in Cape Colony), and she believed forcefully that if the Liberal government had acted justly in 1880 and restored the independence of the Transvaal as had been promised, 'there would have been no "Majuba" to revenge'.[18] For this political deception, Elizabeth laid the blame squarely at the feet of her chief adversary, W.E. Gladstone, and she would also follow Stead in strongly criticising Joseph Chamberlain's conduct during the course of the Anglo-Boer conflict.[19] Four months after war was declared, in a letter to McIlquham, she criticised both the militarism which caused such grief and hardship to women and children and the fiscal policies of British politicians and financiers. The 'helots of Park Lane', as she named them, had sought to conceal their true objective (the acquisition of mining rights) beneath the rhetoric of legitimate redress of Uitlander franchise grievances.[20] The war, she declared, was one waged by a band of 'thieves and liars', and it would 'shake the British Empire to its foundations'.[21]

Elizabeth's sympathies allied her to the small but significant minority of activists who adopted a 'pro-Boer' stance, and she took issue with colleagues who argued that 'British moral superiority, like its racial counterpart, justified the imposition of Britishness on others.'[22] She espoused a racially inclusive view and viewed the indigenous populace of Southern Africa as capable of 'rising to a worthy humanity'. They were, she considered, 'our equals in intelligence [and] our superiors in many points of morals'.[23] While she had, earlier in the 1890s, adopted the rhetoric of imperialism to claim that the enfranchisement of British women would 'lead to the development of a higher social and political morality all over the world', it is clear that by the conclusion of the war in 1902 her views on the value of imperial munificence to the native populations of the Empire had been revised.[24] Such was her distress at what she perceived to be the moral degradation jingoism had brought upon her country, that she declared herself ashamed of being English.[25]

One rare surviving published poem (see pp. 242) illustrates her position clearly, and though it has been argued that early twentieth-century 'pacifist verse was often shrill and hardly peaceful', Elizabeth's poem combines elements of both observations.[26] Writing as Ignota, she contends that the 'wild pomp of War's made revelry' brings only 'a message of despair', and while this might be termed 'shrill' her following lines foretell a hope that peace would reign when those 'who seek, and hope and strive for good', call the world '[t]o nobler life'. Her deep sadness at the progress of the war, the waste of human life and the 'wild pomp [and] revelry' of the jingoism that swept the nation with the fever of vengeance is evident in her poem. Congleton, too, was swept up in the glory of war as the townsfolk 'rejoic[ed] in the "send-off" of five reservists' on 27 December 1899, the town band giving an uplifting performance of the National Anthem as the train steamed away.[27] For the Elmy family, such celebrations were abhorrent and the war lay 'like a constant nightmare' upon their daily lives. Elizabeth noted that victory would not 'be the holiday walk-over' the jingoes believed, belying the editorial in the *Macclesfield Courier*, wherein a 'short and sharp' conflict was predicted – 'the headstrong Boer' having learnt a lesson he would long remember.[28] Her own belief in the power of imperialism to bring about justice swiftly declined during these turbulent months and brought her into conflict once more with some among her suffragist colleagues.

Elizabeth, in common with Dora Montefiore, Emmeline Pankhurst and J.A. Hobson (co-editor with Stanton Coit of the journal *Ethical World*) strongly supported the 'pro-Boer' stance on ethical grounds. This brought Elizabeth back into closer sympathy with Mrs Pankhurst, but placed the group as a whole at odds with fellow suffragists, including Josephine Butler and Millicent Garrett Fawcett who both supported the British imperialist position. Though it has been suggested that women's suffrage activity 'had to be virtually suspended during the war', such a view is not upheld when reading Elizabeth's correspondence.[29] Despite the obviously disappointing absence of any formal progression on the franchise issue in the House of Commons, literally thousands of letters winged their way to and from Buxton House in an unsuccessful effort to remedy the frustrating situation. However, it was Emily Hobhouse, a woman not directly allied to any formal suffrage organisation, who was to divide suffragist imperialist and 'pro-Boer' factions most forcefully, after the publication in 1901 of her *Report of a visit to the Camps of Women and Children in the Cape and Orange River Colonies*.[30] Hobhouse, as Honorary Secretary of the women's branch of the South African Conciliation Committee, had become critical of the increasingly severe conditions suffered by the Afrikaner women and children after a 'scorched earth' policy was adopted by British forces in the autumn of 1900. She had set off on an individual humanitarian crusade and had distributed aid in the concentration camps of Bloemfontein and Springfontein. Her *Report* was published on her return to Britain, but her compassionate kindness to the Afrikaner foe was not looked upon with favour by the British government, or indeed by the majority of the British population.[31] Elizabeth, however, sympathised with Hobhouse's criticisms, and wrote in the spring of 1902 that if *she* 'were a Boer woman [she] would die in a "concentration" camp before . . . ask[ing] "my man" to yield to dastardly Britain'.[32]

Elizabeth's pride in her nation suffered a crippling blow during the Anglo-Boer War. She informed McIlquham that never again, '[u]ntil this wicked land repents' of its deeds, would her family 'float a British . . . flag – or take part in any national rejoicing' and, true to their vow, the Elmys played no part in the great celebrations Congleton staged on the declaration of peace.[33] A commentary made on the cessation of hostilities in her local newspaper would have incensed her. The *Chronicle* noted that it was as well the conflict had been fought 'out to the end' in order to establish that 'there is not a Boer household in South Africa where it is not understood that the British Empire is united and invincible'. Paradoxically, though, while such comments highlighted a nationalistic premise that understood challenges to British imperial rule must *always* fail and that British superiority was unassailable, the same newspaper also encouraged a racially exclusive Teutonism. Now peace had been declared the *Chronicle* advocated that the British and the Boer should cooperate, for they were both of Teutonic stock. The view adopted was that Afrikaners had 'pluck' and 'common sense', as did the British, and now was the time to settle down together – as long as the British took precedence.[34] Elizabeth could not concur with this view, her Cape Colony correspondents having furnished her with the information that the indigenous labourers in the Rand goldmines were subject to harsher conditions under British rule even than under Afrikaner administration. She believed, prophetically, that the inhumanity of the war had highlighted a situation whereby Britain's 'children w[ould one day] have to bear the penalty of our national wrong-doing'.[35] A scant thirteen years later, with no little debt owed to the jingoism that went hand in hand with European imperial ambitions, Britain would find herself embroiled in the cataclysm of the First World War.[36]

Advent of the 'insurgent women'

Elizabeth yearned for a new injection of forcefulness among suffragists at the turn of the century and, while she worked diligently to support the work of the NUWSS, she grew increasingly exasperated with what she perceived as their lacklustre attitude. Despite her actions in keeping the WEU outside of NUWSS dominion she appeared unaware that this had contributed to her marginalisation. She felt excluded by some of the leading figures, and owned she sometimes felt this isolation 'resentfully'.[37] Despite all she had achieved, the taints of irreligion and sexual impropriety still clung to her name among middle-class colleagues who had distanced themselves from such advanced opinions. Acceptance of sexual radicalism was now also losing favour among the labouring class, where the concept of 'monogamous marriage' was increasingly promoted 'as a haven . . . from the economic ravages of . . . capitalism'.[38] In addition to these ideological shifts, Elizabeth's resolute non-partisan stance had not aided her efforts to keep women's suffrage centre-stage after the demise of the WEU. And she certainly did not, for example, share the view of Eva McLaren (daughter-in-law of her long-time friend Priscilla Bright McLaren) that 'if women were to obtain the franchise there must be a means, and the party was that means'.[39] Elizabeth held to her ideals and to her independence, and perhaps surprisingly, it helped her, from 1900 to 1903, to become a force for unity among her disparate colleagues.

To examine Elizabeth's closest friendships at this time is to trace allegiances across the political spectrum. Harriet McIlquham adhered to Liberal Unionism and Anna Maria Priestman and Louisa Martindale were also firmly in the Liberal camp. Dora Montefiore was allied to the SDF (in addition to her labours for the Union of Practical Suffragists and the Women's Local Government Society), and Emmeline Pankhurst (now widowed), Isabella Ford and Isabella Bream Pearce were important female figures in the Independent Labour Party (ILP).[40] Bream Pearce had been significant, in 1895, in securing an 'explicit commitment' from the ILP's Annual Conference in respect of women's suffrage, her aim being to promote the view of a common 'workers' identity' built on the representation of labour. However, after an unsuccessful campaign in the General Election that year, the ILP's closer ties to the trade union move-ment conspired to help solidify the cultural perception that waged work (so important in helping women achieve their freedom) was 'unsuitable' for women. The pre-1895 elements of socialism that had aided a feminist ideal, for example, the sympathetic reception given to 'New Woman' fiction in labour publications, was lost latterly. And even the ILP's leader, J. Keir Hardie claimed in 1898 that 'people [were] beginning to use their vote to assert their *manhood*'.[41] Hardie's is just one example of how, among the men of the ILP, support for the women's vote was more ambivalent than early histories suggest – something which offered strong reasons for socialist women to seek cooperation where it was offered by middle-class suffragists.

Among the members of the SDF, historically cited as misogynist, the position was also unclear. Karen Hunt offers a significant corpus of evi-dence to show its supporters were far more than 'equivocal feminists' and the views expressed in the journal, *Justice*, were much broader than the 'bitter, tactless and narrow minded' opinions of its founder, H.M. Hyndman.[42] Elizabeth's direct engagement with the propaganda of the

Labour movement is often not obvious. She was, for example, only an occasional correspondent of the *Labour Leader*, her view being that any-thing she needed 'said' could be inserted in the writing of Bream Pearce or, latterly, after 'Lily Bell's column ended in 1898, Mrs Pankhurst.[43] She did, however, write for *Justice*, where she expressed the opinion that the 'all but universal failure of male Socialists to recognise *practically* in women the other half of humanity, with rights absolutely equal to' their own had had an adverse effect on securing women's support for socialism as a whole.[44] If the attitudes of socialist men towards women's emancipa-tion had many shades at the turn of the century, however, the attitudes of socialist women were equally as diverse.

The key issue that divided socialist women suffragists in the early 1900s was whether or not to support the campaign for a limited franchise based on the property qualification, or to press forward with claims for full, adult suffrage – the better to fulfil the ultimate aims of socialism. Disputes raged, but Elizabeth, her feminism to the fore (and still with more than a trace of liberal sympathies evident) had criticised in 'Outlanders' those socialist 'progressives' who sought to pressurise for 'manhood' suffrage before a qualified women's vote had been achieved. To do so would, she believed, be 'a decisive blow [to] the onward progress of humanity'.[45] Though her allegiance appears somewhat curious, as she seems to be moving away from her long-held commitment to gender inclusivity, this was not the case. She had seen, for example, in the provi-sions of Mr Faithfull-Begg's Women's Suffrage Bill of 1897, that 'fifteen working women' of Congleton would have received the vote, opening up the way to a broader franchise. She did not perceive a contradiction to be evident and shared the later stance of the young ILP agnostic Teresa Billington that women's suffrage and adult suffrage were but two facets of one great cause.[46] Those socialists, including Billington, Isabella Ford and Emmeline Pankhurst, who supported the 'limited' demand, did so on the grounds that they believed it to be compatible with socialism's ultimate aims, but moves to press forward a 'manhood' fran-chise resulted in divisions between the labour and the women's move-ments upon which Elizabeth offered her own, very powerful opinions.

The National Convention

By 1903, Elizabeth had shrugged off the mental lassitude that had affected her during the trials of the Anglo-Boer War and, despite being in her seventieth year and reliant on the most meagre of domestic help at home, was determined to help mobilise the formidable force for change the politicised labour women offered. Once again, as in the earlier campaigns for women's education, it was the radical women of the north-west who were at the forefront. As Chapter 6 demonstrated, Isabella Ford's help in promoting the WEU's message to the working women of the East End had shown clear links between Elizabeth's vision for the future and that of more 'overt' socialists. Now, after the organisation's demise, she strongly supported similar direct propaganda initiatives made by the Lancashire and Cheshire Women Textile and Other Workers' Representation Committee (LCTOWRC), formed in Manchester during the summer of 1903. Headed by Esther Roper of the NESWS; her companion, the wealthy Anglo-Irish gentlewoman, Eva Gore-Booth; Sarah Reddish of the Women's Co-operative Guild and Sarah Dickinson of the Manchester and Salford Women's Trade Union Council, the organisation was instituted following Roper's disillusionment that cash raised from women trade unionists in support of David Shackleton's successful election candidacy had not been repaid by his commitment to their enfranchisement thereafter.

After a furious row with Labour Representation Committee secretary, Ramsay MacDonald, Roper begged the LCTOWRC to support the candidature of independents to Parliament in the interests of 'representing the claims of women's labour to political enfranchisement'.[47] Elizabeth approved of the non-party political stance of the women Jill Liddington and Jill Norris describe as 'radical suffragists' and wrote a strongly worded letter to the ardent Free-Trader, John Morley MP enclosing their manifesto.[48] It 'furnished', she asserted, 'abundant evidence that they are not satisfied with their industrial position', a position that could only be remedied when women, enfranchised, were no longer 'the subjects of masculine despotism, tempered only by the good feeling of their despots'. She endorsed the textile workers manifesto by noting too that only 'full enfranchisement' would negate the moral decadence, that 'seed crop of folly', sowed by a legislature which continued to deny women a voice in the nation's affairs.[49] Elizabeth had been in close touch with Roper at the time of the formation of the LCTOWRC and she later criticised the NUWSS policy of excluding from its ranks any society whose sole objective was not the women's parliamentary franchise. Many of the most 'ardent and vigorous supporters' of women's emancipation were thus debarred from its membership because of a broader emphasis to their grievances, something the founder of the WFrL and the WEU could not support.[50] Elizabeth therefore decided that the time was right to bring together women of all classes to focus public attention on the wider oppressions to which her sex was subject. Her benefactor for this enterprise was W.T. Stead.

In a letter written shortly before the outbreak of the Anglo-Boer conflict, Elizabeth had urged Stead that if he ever gave up the crusade for peace she 'should expect him to devote himself to the immediate enfranchisement of women'.[51] Stead did not disappoint his friend and after the peace of 1902 he wrote, as a supplement to the monthly *Review of Reviews*, a feminist polemic entitled *In Our Midst*. A copy, complete with a fulsome dedication, was sent to Congleton as a Christmas gift.[52] Elizabeth reviewed the book favourably for the *Westminster Review* and was convinced that, with Stead's support secured, 'the final campaign of our long war for WS [was] about to open'.[53] On 1 May 1903, she penned a letter to Harriet telling of her forthcoming plans for a visit to London, where she was to address a women's suffrage meeting at the offices of the *Review of Reviews*, Mowbray House. She was, she confessed, energised by the prospect, and travelled to the meeting in the company of her old friend (and Grateful Fund stalwart) Louisa Martindale. Such was the press of people in the room that Elizabeth was forced to hoist herself onto a chair to deliver her speech in order that her slight frame might be seen – a steadying hand placed on Margaret Sibthorp's shoulder. Reflecting on the occasion eight years later, Stead (who had listened to the lecture sitting at Elizabeth's feet) remembered it has having sounded '*the signal for the beginning of the militant [suffrage] campaign*' – five months prior to Emmeline Pankhurst's formation of the Women's Social and Political Union.[54]

Elizabeth's Mowbray House speech helped break new ground in suffrage activism. Convinced that women had the power of moral right to refuse to consent to the laws that bound them without an acknowledgement of their citizenship, her speech held the audience enraptured for over half an hour. The meeting was also addressed by American Kate Trimble Woolsey, author of *Republics Versus Woman*, whose controversial views regarding women living in a monarchical state provoked extreme criticism from the socialist sympathisers present – who considered the economic oppression suffered by women in 'advanced' republics to be just as damning. The event as a whole was a resounding success, however, and Stead took the risk of underwriting a significant amount of feminist activism on the strength of this one evening, one element being what Elizabeth described as 'a *great* Women's Suffrage Convention'.[55] Her task was to drum up support for it and in this she was assisted by another member of her Mowbray House audience, Edith Palliser, Secretary of the NUWSS.

There is no doubting the significance of the Wolstenholme Elmy/Stead liaison in convening the National Convention in Defence of the

Figure 5 Elizabeth Wolstenholme Elmy, photographed at Buxton House, Buglawton 1907
Source: Mary Evans Picture Library

Civic Rights of Women. Elizabeth was determined that the gathering, held in London on 16 and 17 October 1903, would be independent of any political affiliation and that representatives of 'all organisations' working in the interests of women would be welcome.[56] Plans for the conference were finalised on further visits to London in July and September, Elizabeth this time travelling with Esther Roper. During the first visit, she addressed an audience of sixty dinner guests including the prominent Fabians H.G. Wells and George Bernard Shaw. Wells, she remembered, 'flushed with pleasure [like] a child' at her compliments to him over dinner.[57] Invigorated by this new intense activity she proceeded to fundraise with alacrity, immensely proud of this 'new and aggressive phase' in the life of the women's movement. One of her greatest benefactors, giving a donation of £250, was John P. Thomasson, now President of her long ago employers, the Personal Rights Association.[58]

Stead and Elizabeth had been prompted into their decisive frame of mind by the possibility of an imminent general election.[59] Scanning the lists of probable Cabinet members had forced Elizabeth to conclude (prophetically) that a Liberal government would not give way on the issue of women's suffrage and she hoped, therefore, to 'get some instalment of justice' before the downfall of Balfour's Conservative administration.[60] Relieved that, with Miss Palliser's able assistance, she had 'enthused' the NUWSS (despite its 'timid and feeble' Executive) to host the Convention, Elizabeth was in buoyant mood as it began.[61] This comment shows she was not above casting derogatory aspersions upon many NUWSS members who had worked hard over the issue, but she preferred instead to tell McIlquham of the contribution of those socialists who shared her greater radicalism: Isabella Ford and Eva Gore-Booth. Both women, she wrote, had spoken convincingly of the determination of the 'organised women in Lancashire . . . to make their influence felt at the general election, by refusing to support any candidate who failed to support women's suffrage' and thus deprive such candidates of their mainstay in the arduous work of canvassing, clerical assistance and administration.[62] In its report of the Convention, praised by Elizabeth for its accuracy, the *Manchester Guardian* commented that this decisive shift in women's political strategy had, with rousing approval, been adopted 'across the board' whereas previously only the small UPS had advocated making the matter a 'test question'.[63]

Women from over twenty suffrage and labour groups had made their way to Holborn Town Hall, and Stead used his speech from the platform to declare to the hundreds assembled that by refusing support for women's suffrage a parliamentary candidate had implicitly declared that 'if women [were] not fit to vote they [were] not fit to canvass'.[64] By supporting the resolution to withdraw such labour, women took up a practical rebellion to the cultural customs which had viewed such help as commonplace. This put into practice precisely the 'politics of disruption' upon which later militant tactics were based, and the possibility of direct confrontational intervention between women and politicians drew ever nearer. Elizabeth's peerless organisational skills and her philosophy of 'consent' to government based on personal autonomy were crucial in achieving the success of the Convention, and certainly she 'was closer to the centre of this new development in suffrage organisation and strategy than most . . . accounts acknowledge'.[65]

An important new society

Delegates to the Convention had also responded enthusiastically to a resolution moved by Charlotte Carmichael Stopes, which noted the extent to which working men's grievances had been successfully addressed on their recent acquisition of the franchise.[66] Stopes begged the same consideration now be given to labouring women, who suffered grievous social and economic deprivation through their inability to force the hand of the legislature to alleviate their sufferings (though it must be remembered that very few working-class women would have been enfranchised under the 'qualified' system then in operation).[67] This resolution was especially welcomed by the members of the North of England Society for Women's Suffrage who, during the week following the Convention held a special committee meeting in Manchester. Though not present at the meeting, Elizabeth had sent Esther Roper 'a long letter of suggestions' for discussion, for, as she noted to McIlquham, 'It is a fatal mistake not actively to encourage these young, ardent souls.' Theirs was the future triumph.[68] One likely attendee, though, was twenty-one-year-old law student Christabel Pankhurst, who had joined the North of England Society in 1901 after forming a friendship with Roper and Eva Gore-Booth. Roper had encouraged Christabel, both to attend at Owen's College and to join in active work for women with herself and Eva. Such was Christabel's impact as a committee member that early the following year Elizabeth first commented upon what many would later acknowledge as Miss Pankhurst's considerable political aptitude.[69] Christabel was a dark-haired, strikingly pretty woman, and had inherited her father's keen intelligence. She grew to be cherished by Elizabeth almost as a granddaughter and the veteran campaigner delighted in resuming the close ties with the Pankhursts, which had become strained (if not altogether severed) during Christabel's childhood. Given the vehemence of Elizabeth's views on party-political allegiances, the connection ultimately brought about another, perhaps unlooked-for, development.

On 21 November 1905, at a meeting of the Manchester Central Branch of the ILP chaired by Christabel Pankhurst, Elizabeth was welcomed as a party member.[70] To say she had embraced Labour politics in toto would be to take too simplistic a stance, for her ideals were still primarily those of the utopian and the humanist: 'revolutionary', levelling socialism would *not* have found favour in her eyes.[71] Her pacifist heart, for example, would never have been able to accept the loss of human life suffered in the maelstrom of the Russian Revolution of 1917. Nonetheless, her formal alliance with the ILP does show an ever growing sympathy with socialist views. To follow Elizabeth's path, particularly from the mid-1890s to 1904, is to find evidence of a still evolving political consciousness, and a stronger desire than ever to engage at the grassroots level with politicised working-class women. She trod this path, for the next decade, in the company of the Pankhurst family.

While the National Convention has been somewhat sidelined in the women's suffrage narrative, 10 October 1903 is known world-wide as the day when Emmeline Pankhurst founded the Women's Social and Political Union at her home, 62 Nelson Street, Manchester.[72] The WSPU, whose membership was open only to women, was classed by Elizabeth as 'an active offshoot' of the ILP, but it had been brought into being by Mrs Pankhurst following her increasing doubts about the seriousness of its male membership in their support for women's claims. Many, indeed, did not consider the matter 'vital' to achieving socialism. William Anderson, for example, wrote to the *Labour Leader* that, 'It is inconsistent for a socialist to bolster up a class disability under the guise of removing a sex one.'[73] Elizabeth, though, sympathised with Emmeline's worries and would soon join the WSPU. She also encouraged other friends to join, and Dora Montefiore and Frances Rowe (among others) swiftly did so. The rank and file membership were drawn from women already active in labour politics and WSPU methods followed the tried and trusted route of petitions, lobbying, public meetings and propaganda. Some years would pass before Mrs Pankhurst coined the provocative phrase that 'Deeds, not words' should be the organisation's mantra.

Co-opted onto the fledgling group's Executive, Elizabeth often returned to Congleton by the late evening train, after time spent at Nelson Street. And after one such business dinner she noted that 'Mrs Pankhurst [was] immensely improved though she ha[d] nothing like the brain of her husband & oldest daughter.'[74] The brilliant Christabel was undoubtedly both clever and committed to the ILP's cause but, as historians have charted, shifts in socialist ideology, especially in the context of the debates surrounding the Women's Enfranchisement Bill during 1904–5, showed a cooling of socialist support for women's suffrage.[75] These debates also signalled strain in the friendship between Miss Pankhurst, Esther Roper and Eva Gore-Booth in 1904, when Christabel forced a split in the Women's Trades and Labour Council over the suffrage issue. 'For all her capacity for winning adorers', one commentator noted acidly, Christabel was also capable of creating 'the atmosphere of a dog fight'.[76] This is just one example of how tensions flared between women, but Elizabeth was not backward in showing either her admiration for Miss Pankhurst or of articulating their shared commitment to feminism over and above that given to socialism. Writing for the *Westminster Review*, she argued that the 'cruel competition' of capitalism had 'brought wages to such a point that in multitudes of cases the home and family cannot be maintained without the added labour outside the home of the wife and mother. Yet the remedy which seems to suggest itself most readily to the masculine mind is the driving of such women, either wholly or partially, from paid employment.'[77] This, she believed, they could do all the more easily now that some 60 per cent of working-class men possessed the power of the parliamentary vote.

In August 1904, Elizabeth mused on the prospect for women's suffrage should the Liberal party win the next general election. She wrote privately to McIlquham that, if the Labour movement were to capitalise on their increasing influence in national affairs to promote electoral reform, it was 'almost certain' that a Liberal administration would concede 'to give "manhood" Suffrage, calling it "adult" Suffrage, & so put us in a worse position than ever'.[78] It was not only in private that she voiced her discontent, as from 3 December 1904 until 2 September 1905 she authored a fortnightly column for Coit and Hobson's *Ethical World*. Her articles in '*Ethics*' (as she fondly termed it), clearly underlined her anti-adult suffragist stance. For example, on the 29 April 1905, she wrote with some satisfaction of the defeat of an 'adult' suffrage amendment to the women's suffrage resolution tabled at the ILP Annual Conference.[79] She believed some socialists, including Harry Quelch of the SDF and Margaret Bondfield, founder of the Adult Suffrage Society (ASS), had misjudged the position, writing that 'our adult suffrage friends refuse to see' that: 'The present Ministry has no intention of granting "adult" suffrage, in the true sense of the words.'[80] Politicians sought rather, she believed, to offer 'adult' suffrage to placate the grievances of those males still disenfranchised, while leaving all women beyond the 'high wall' of patriarchal privilege.[81] Women's course was clear, she declared, it was the *'sex disqualification'* not the class bias that was most important. Elizabeth gave up her column for *Ethics* having fallen out somewhat with Coit's editorship and, despite her reluctance to subscribe to the 'adult' suffragist position, now believed firmly in the power of the socialist press to reach wider audiences. She positively encouraged Dora Montefiore, for example, to place articles in the *New Age* 'where she ha[d] a free hand' from a sympathetic editor.[82] Montefiore would grievously disappoint her latterly, both because of her tempestuous relationship with the Pankhurst family and on account of her decision to support the 'adult' suffragist stance in 1907, but in earlier debates they were able to be conciliatory.[83]

First militant of the WSPU

Elizabeth wrote with fondness of the day in July 1904 when she was introduced to the young mill worker Annie Kenney at a meeting of the Women's Trades and Labour Council. The fragile-looking Kenney, as a close confidant of Christabel Pankhurst, would later become a heroine of the militant suffrage movement, but on that summer's day she excitedly plied Elizabeth with questions after her lecture was over.[84] During the following years, Kenney often took tea with the Elmys at Buglawton, seeking guidance and gathering information. Delicately pretty, Annie Kenney was to gain a special place in public affection for her charming and sprightly manner. Elizabeth thought her capable of 'rising to any height [she] chose', her 'true heart' allowing her to do so as a benefactress of others and not on her own account.[85] Kenney later represented the WSPU at the Frankfurt conference arranged by the German Women's Suffrage Society in 1907, but in 1904 it was Dora Montefiore who was its rather less charismatic representative at the Berlin conference of the International Council of Women.[86] Of this great gathering Elizabeth wrote to Harriet that it was a '[s]ign of the times, & prophesy of the future'.[87] She was excited, and not only at the positive impact the Berlin conference had had upon the worldwide feminist movement. Of even greater moment was the fact that the woman she endowed more than any other with the attributes of a heroine, American Susan B. Anthony, was to break her homeward journey with a visit to Britain.

Elizabeth and Anthony had first met during the American's visit to England in 1882, and Elizabeth's regard is expressed in another rare surviving example of her poetry.[88] The stanzas are penned from a humanitarian perspective, and Anthony is hailed as a citizen of the world rather than America: a woman whose 'Great soul, . . . toilest through the darkest hour' in ceaseless pursuit of women's freedom.[89] During the visit, Elizabeth was a principal speaker at a Manchester garden party in the last week of July 1904, hosted by the now venerable Samuel Steinthal. Memories of the trip were soured for her, however, when Anthony acquired the unfavourable impression that she was 'impractical', obstructive, and unable to 'work in harmony with others'.[90] Few extant sources deal directly with the issue, but it appears likely that Anthony had written to Elizabeth personally on the matter, which had caused her great distress. She hastened to correct the impression, which she believed had been given by the widowed Ursula Bright, whom Anthony had visited. There is no way to corroborate her assumption but, following McIlquham's prosaic advice, she sent Anthony copies of her published work relating to the Infants Act and WEU activities as evidence of her collaborative labours.[91]

Before this sad episode had soured her memories, the sweet delight of Anthony's visit had gladdened Elizabeth's heart. She had introduced Christabel Pankhurst to Anthony in Manchester and, though possibly a little awed, Christabel had published in the *Daily Dispatch* of 25 July an appreciation of the visitor which had 'delighted' the American.[92] Though the events of October 1905 would soon prove Christabel's commitment to the women's cause, it is to her mother that Elizabeth owes her own title of the 'first militant' of the WSPU, in recognition of her courageous actions outside the House of Commons in May.[93] Anthony's visit was now a memory, but it had contributed to the 'fast, furious & almost cruel' pace of women's suffrage issues in Manchester prior to the introduction of the Women's Enfranchisement Bill by Mr Bamford Slack. Taking a full part in the activities, Elizabeth had organised a 'whip' of over three hundred MPs in April.[94] She travelled to London on 12 May to lobby MPs prior to the debate, and there she joined with the crowds of 'suffragists of all grades' who descended on the House of Commons.[95] Rather than the glorious triumph the suffragists had longed for, however, the bill was once again subject to the 'delaying tactics' of experienced opponents when the clauses of the Vehicles' Lighting Bill were debated to the point of absurdity.

When she recalled the events of the afternoon of 12 May 1905, Elizabeth claimed that a 'future historian of the Woman's Suffrage movement' would note it 'as one of the red-letter days of that cause'.[96] The reason for her words was that she believed it had marked the 'the fusion of classes . . . for women who had left the wash-tub to come to the House [had] walked hand in hand, side by side with fashionably dressed ladies'.[97]

She omits, however, any description of the moment after the bill's failure when, outside the Strangers' Entrance and in a melee of angry and disappointed suffragists, she began to give an account of the formation of the women's suffrage movement in 1865. Shielded from the press of people by Keir Hardie, Elizabeth moved from the shelter of the statue of Richard I and out into Broad Sanctuary where a resolution of 'indignation against the Government' was passed.[98] It has been suggested that Emmeline Pankhurst's autobiography, in recalling this event, 'added a new dimension to militancy, one which associated this new current within the suffrage movement with a readiness to disrupt public order'.[99] It must be remembered, however, that Elizabeth had made a similar protest in Broad Sanctuary after the loss of the 1897 bill, and therefore *her* willingness to suffer any consequences resulting from her disruption of public order pre-dates the formation of the WSPU by six years. She had no fear that her bones might be crushed in the road leading to women's freedom, as she had publicly proclaimed.[100] However, whilst in 1897 she had held to the hope that Lord Salisbury's government might be sympathetic to the suffragists' demands, by 1905 she saw clearly that the Conservatives were as loath as the Liberal opposition to concede full citizenship to women. Therefore (with the added divisiveness within the socialist movement that rendered *any* party political assistance by men to be negligible to women's suffragists), when Christabel Pankhurst and Annie Kenney undertook their infamous protest at a Liberal Party meeting held at the Free Trade Hall in Manchester on the 13 October, Elizabeth recorded her personal exhilaration at their brave stance.[101] Both young women were imprisoned and Elizabeth commented that Christabel's 'splendid work' had been crowned 'by [an] even more splendid self-sacrifice'.[102]

On 20 October, a reception was organised by the ILP's Sam Robinson at the Free Trade Hall to hail the released prisoners, and Elizabeth recalled how the large crowd gathered outside had 'raise[d] a ringing cheer' as the WSPU motor car, in which she, Esther Roper and Eva Gore-Booth were passengers, was driven away by Sarah Dickinson. She compared the scene to that of Peterloo, where, on the same site in 1819, the people of Manchester had gathered to solicit the power of the vote for men – and had been charged by mounted militia for their pains. Glad that their evening had been more tranquil, she nevertheless believed, almost a century later, that there was an equally profound popular support for the women's franchise. With public opinion on their side they would succeed. It was, she believed, 'the beginning of the end'.[103] Sadly, the friendship between Roper, Gore-Booth and Christabel

Pankhurst was tested and at the AGM all three resigned from the NESWS. Roper's leadership role was adopted by Margaret Ashton, the unofficial Treasurer of the local Women's Local Government Society.

Bereavement and honour

Elizabeth undertook the arduous work following the National Convention at a time of extreme anxiousness in her private life. As the Liberal Party, under the leadership of Henry Campbell-Bannerman, swept into office at the General Election of 1906, Ben Elmy lay valiantly fighting the effects of terminal cancer. He worked to the last, his final project being a translation into Esperanto of Tennyson's *The Princess*. In the small hours of 3 March 1906, Ben's life slipped away. Elizabeth, his diligent nurse, had snatched a few hours' rest, but was woken by Frank as the end approached. She returned to the sickroom where she shared a last earthly embrace with her husband. Writing to Harriet that same evening, she noted that Ben, who no longer had the strength to speak, had recognised her with a 'bright gleam of the eye' and died with her 'warm kiss on his lips'. She was consoled, however, by the belief that her husband had, through death, been reunited with the 'constant life and force of the Universe' – something the couple had discussed after the near-death experiences they had both endured.[104] Elizabeth spent the first day of her widowhood grieving quietly at home, but for Frank Elmy it was a day crammed with activity. The funeral arrangements were set in motion, and a secular ceremony arranged three days later at Manchester crematorium. The coffin was borne by four stalwart working-class men, known to Ben through the adult educational work he had undertaken in Congleton.[105] His widow received, within six weeks, over two hundred letters of condolence.

The day after the funeral, Elizabeth recounted the event in detail to McIlquham, who had not attended. Mourners, though doubtless soberly dressed, had not been swathed in black crêpe and neither was there a hearse or 'funeral trappings' – in accordance with Ben's wishes.[106] The Congleton party were met at the crematorium by WSPU members Christabel Pankhurst, Esther Roper, Mrs Morrissey and Mrs Horsfall, and Christabel and Esther shared with Elizabeth the task of giving the funeral oration. Afterwards, at tea, the talk turned to women's suffrage and Miss Pankhurst, in particular, sparked discussion among the Congleton mourners to whom she was introduced. The 'sweet, disarming girl' quite fascinated them and they could scarcely believe her to be 'the terrible Miss Pankhurst', now notorious following her imprisonment. Such was the impression made by the WSPU ladies upon Elizabeth's neighbours that they declared 'that if these were the "wild" women then it would be well that all women should become "wild".'[107] Elizabeth heartily concurred with the sentiment.

The new widow's innermost feelings are not immediately articulated, though she authored (under her pseudonym) a public tribute to her husband, 'Pioneers, O Pioneers', which appeared in the April issue of the *Westminster Review*. It is possible only to speculate on her emotional state when reading a letter of two months later, in which she writes that a visit to London on suffrage work would provide a desperately needed change for her, lest she 'break down utterly & hopelessly'.[108] Whatever Ben Elmy's personal failings as a husband might have been, it is clear Elizabeth admired him greatly. He was also her 'darling' and greatly beloved. Surprisingly, however, Ben's much evidenced championing of women's emancipation was not upheld in one crucial way. His final Will and Testament – brief both in form and content – granted all his worldly possessions to his son.[109] A profound change seems to have been wrought in Frank Elmy after his father's death. While journalism had hitherto provided him with only a sporadic income, it appears he was now determined to give up the veneer of 'gentlemanly' status and seek paid employment.

Frank's administrative aid was, and would continue to be, invaluable to his mother, but it in no way provided for their subsistence. He appears an intelligent though somewhat meek man with few friends, yet he was thirty-one years old in 1906 and it might have been expected that he would have attained a good position in a profession. His mother noted that he had the abilities of an excellent civil servant, but the impetus to succeed in the professional world seems to have eluded him.[110] He clearly had a profound social conscience, and had been elected to the Buglawton Urban District Council in March 1904, at a second attempt.[111] He continued to undertake the work of the Male Electors' League, under the chairmanship of Alan Greenwell and, though the small society did not have a lasting impact on the suffrage issue, its literature was distributed on many occasions at Women's Trade and Labour Council and WSPU meetings. Elizabeth, as most mothers might, offered a subjective assessment of her son. He had, she believed, 'the resonance and energy of a man [coupled with the] tenderness and deftness of a girl' and was destined to do 'good and real work in the world'.[112] She attributed to him the best traits of both sexes, but her portrait is idealistic, as might be expected.

Two months after her bereavement, Elizabeth travelled to London, in Frank's company, to take part in the women's suffrage demonstration scheduled for 19 May 1906. She believed the visit would provide an anti-dote to the pain of her bereavement although, politically, she had little faith in the power of the suffragist deputation to Henry Campbell-Bannerman to move him – or indeed his government – to action. The Prime Minister would, she prophetically declared, 'give a few twaddly words, binding to nothing'.[113] Residing with Dora Montefiore in Ham-mersmith, she attended the meeting of over three hundred suffragists held at the Foreign Office as a delegate of both the Lancashire and Cheshire Women's Suffrage Society and the ILP, and walked between Montefiore and Frances Rowe at the head of a procession of twelve hundred people. Ray Strachey argued that Campbell-Bannerman had consented to receive the deputation as a direct result of the dedicated perseverance of the constitutional campaign of the NUWSS, and claimed further that its disappointing outcome promulgated the irrevocable establishment of the militant suffrage movement.[114] Sylvia Pankhurst agrees with the latter premise. She notes, rather, that the prime minis-terial audience was granted as a consequence of militant endeavours during the previous weeks, culminating in the WSPU action of 19 April, when protests had erupted from the Ladies' Gallery at the House of Commons as the proposed women's suffrage Resolution, to be moved by Keir Hardie, was threatened with being 'talked out'. The ensuing furore led to the ejection of the protestors – and to a hostile greeting of 'cold looks and bitter reproaches' from more modest suffragists when they reached the lobby.[115] Elizabeth, although not present herself on this occasion, had no doubt where her sympathies lay – she supported the 'insurgents heart and soul' and bitterly refuted any criticism of their actions.[116]

One month later, and after listening respectfully to her old friend and colleague Emily Davies, who opened the proceedings of the deputa-tion (at which forty MPs were present), Elizabeth interjected forcefully.[117] Sylvia Pankhurst recalled how 'in her frail old voice' she had interrupted the Prime Minister when he exhorted the women to be patient, to remind him that she had been a suffragist since 1865.[118] Was that not evidence of patience enough? It has recently been suggested that Campbell-Bannerman 'frankly accepted that the case for the vote had been estab-lished' but, while this may have been so on a personal level, it is likely that the Prime Minister believed himself unable to exert any practical influence over his Cabinet and party colleagues.[119] Campbell-Bannerman therefore urged the women to 'go on pestering people' – a comment that inflamed the more radical among the delegates into a condition of righteous anger. Elizabeth castigated the Prime Minister roundly in an interview given that afternoon to the *Daily Mirror*, when she claimed his words to be empty platitudes and his 'sympathy' false.[120] Indignant at their reception, the deputation members left the Foreign Office to lead a procession which, headed by a vibrantly coloured sea of banners, made its way to Trafalgar Square. Once there, Elizabeth took Keir Hardie's arm to mount the platform in front of the National Gallery. Sharing the stage with them were Emmeline Pankhurst, Australian suffragist Nellie Martel and Councillor Frank Smith, who read the short speech Elizabeth had prepared. Looking down at the crowd, she became intensely emotional and wiped her eyes continually. She was now aged almost seventy-three, but her speech proclaimed that, 'When you have enthusiasm for a great cause you know you have discovered eternal youth. I have been fighting . . . half my life, and yet I am as enthusiastic as when I started.' Concluding, she vowed to 'go on fighting still. Even an old woman can do something when she is in earnest'.[121]

Such humility touched many of her colleagues, and some were in tears as they sought to comfort her. And the evidence of the *Daily Mirror* interview and front page photograph indicate the increasing level of esteem and reverence now given to Elizabeth as a national suffragist leader. Her local newspaper too gave its own laudatory account of the Trafalgar Square proceedings, on 25 May. Revered in the town in which she had so often been reviled, the *Chronicle's* editor concluded with the words that: 'Those who have worked with [Mrs Wolstenholme Elmy] have been constantly indebted to her knowledge of all that has gone before, and to her readiness to grasp what was essential to the immediate work in hand; and, most of all, to her courtesy and generous appreciation of the part taken in the work by her colleagues.'[122] Such sentiments were far removed from the literal mud-slinging of Congleton residents in the 1870s. Shortly after the demonstration, Elizabeth authored the poem which acknowledged most openly her admiration for the newest of her colleagues, and in the '*Song of the Insurgent Women*' she passed the mantle of all those 'sisters who have waited long' in the shadows to those she felt promised a new age for women's politics – the militant suffragettes. 'The cold, dark night is past', she foretold and the clear, strong light of day shone on the horizon.[123]

As Elizabeth's life moved to its conclusion, there were still battles to fight. Her engagement with socialist ideals took a final and possibly surprising turn and her total commitment to the style of militancy advocated by the WSPU was revised. The pacifist adherence which had made her such a strong advocate of pro-Boer sentiments during 1899–1902 took centre-stage once more in 1912, when she declared the extreme militant tactics of some suffragettes to be 'criminal folly' and careless of human life. Elizabeth still had much to do as 'an old woman', and her role was not merely that of a 'mascot' to those who took up the causes to which she had devoted her life. On the contrary, she remained to the last one of Edwardian feminism's most adept philosophers.

Notes

1 EWE/HM, 14/11/1906, 47455, fol. 11.
2 EWE, 'Our "Outlanders" at Home', *Manchester Guardian*, 22 August 1899.
3 EWE, 'Outlanders'.
4 Mayhall, 'South African War', pp. 9–13. Mayhall, 'The Rhetorics of Slavery and Citizenship', pp. 487–8; Montefiore, *From a Victorian*, p. 77. See also Heloise Brown, *'The Truest Form of Patriotism': Pacifist Feminism in Britain, 1870–1902* (Manchester: Manchester University Press, 2003), esp. pp. 164–78.
5 EWE, 'Outlanders'; Mayhall, 'South African War', p. 11.
6 Montefiore, *From a Victorian to a Modern*, p. 77.
7 Dora B. Montefiore, 'Women Uitlanders', *Ethical World*, 14 October 1899, pp. 642–3, quoted in Mayhall, 'South African War', p. 11.
8 EWE, printed enclosure in a letter to HM, 31 May 1895, EWEP, fol. 197.
9 EWE/HM, 8/10/1899, 47452, fol. 23.
10 Anon. [W.T. Stead], 'Why We Are Now At War', *War Against War*, 20 October 1899, p. 2.
11 EWE/HM, 30/8/1898, 47451, fol. 248.
12 EWE/HM, 10/2/1900, 47452, fol. 49.
13 Brown notes that during the late nineteenth century, 'pacifist analyses of power relations between nations and the effects of military force were combined with feminist understanding of the ways in which women were oppressed. Ideas evolved which encompassed both the claim that women had the right to define their own place in society, and also the desire to renounce war and establish alternative models of conflict resolution. As a result, specifically "pacifist feminist" standpoints can be identified which denote a politics where the two modes of analysis are applied together to an understanding of the social and political order.' Brown, *Pacifist Feminism*, p. 4.
14 Anon., 'Ladies' Peace Meeting', *Herald of Peace*, 1 August 1872, p. 107. Wolstenholme Elmy's recollection of these events is inaccurate. She dates the peace meeting as 1871 and gives Ford's age as ten years, rather than seventeen. EWE/HM, 12/5/1903, 47453, fol. 121.
15 'Ladies' Peace Meeting', p. 107.
16 Antoinette Burton, 'Josephine Butler on slavery, citizenship and the Boer War', in Christopher Fletcher, Laura E. Nym Mayhall and Philippa Levine (eds), *Women's Suffrage in the British Empire*, pp. 18–32; Mayhall, 'South African War', pp. 6–7.

17 Josephine Butler to the Editor, *Herald of Peace*, 1 September 1870, p. 112; Brown, *Pacifist Feminism*, p. 166.

18 EWE/HM, 10/2/1900, 47452, fol. 48.

19 Gladstone had, in opposition, condemned the annexation of the Transvaal in 1877, stating publicly that they were 'obtained by means dishonourable to the character of the country', and would be repudiated should the Liberals be returned to office. However, on their successful election, he failed to honour his pledge. Edgar Holt, *The Boer War* (London: Putnam, 1958), p. 20. On Stead and Chamberlain see, M. van Wyk Smith, *Drummer Hodge: The Poetry of the Anglo-Boer War (1899–1902)* (Oxford: Clarendon Press, 1978), pp. 127–8.

20 Mayhall, 'The South African War'; p. 5; EWE/HM, 10/2/1900, 47452, fol. 50; Anon., 'The Story of the Diamond Fields – Interview with President Steyn', *War Against War*, 5 January 1900, p. 181.

21 EWE/HM, 10/2/1900, 47452, fol. 49.

22 Antoinette Burton, *Burdens of History: British Feminists, Indian Women and Imperial Culture, 1865–1915* (Chapel Hill and London: The University of North Carolina Press, 1994), p. 39.

23 EWE/HM, 24/1/1902, 47452, fol. 239.

24 EWE, 'Women's Franchise: The Need of the Hour', *Westminster Review*, Vol. 148, 1897, pp. 357–72.

25 EWE/HM, 28/10/1899, 47452, fol. 28.

26 Smith, *Drummer Hodge*, p. 140; Ignota, 'New Year's Day, 1900', *War Against War*, 29 December 1900, p. 170.

27 EWE/HM, 27/12/1899, 47452, fol. 37; Anon., 'Congleton Men for the War', *Congleton Chronicle*, 30 December 1899, p. 4. The presence of the Congleton Town Band as the troops left for South Africa served to inculcate, as Jeffrey Richards has argued, a spirit of 'spectacle [and] patriotism' in the public mind, a patriotism that 'increasingly involved the Empire and imperialist sentiment'. Jeffrey Richards, *Imperialism and Music: Britain 1876–1953* (Manchester: Manchester University Press, 2001), pp. 412 and 16.

28 EWE/HM, 11/12/1899, 47452, fol. 35. 'Editorial', *Macclesfield Courier*, 14 October 1899.

29 Jill Liddington, *The Road to Greenham Common: Feminism and Anti-Militarism in Britain since 1820* (Syracuse University Press, 1991 [first published 1989]).

30 Liddington, *Road to Greenham*, p. 43.

31 Liddington, *Road to Greenham*, pp. 46–53; Brown, *Pacifist Feminism*, pp. 169–72.

32 EWE/HM, 25/4/1902, 47452, fol. 293. (My emphasis.)

33 EWE/HM, 25/4/1902, 47452, fol. 293. EWE/HM, 3/6/1902, 47453, fol. 1.

34 Editorial, 'Boer War Peace', 7 June 1902, *Congleton Chronicle*.

35 EWE/HM, 29/10/1901, 47452, fol. 216.

36 On the tensions between Britain and Germany, and the prevalence of a pro-Boer stance among non-elite Germans at the time of the Boer War, see Donal Lowry, '"The Boers were the Beginning of the End"?: The Wider Impact of the South African War', in Donal Lowry (ed.), *The South African War Reappraised* (Manchester and New York: Manchester University Press, 2000), pp. 215–16.

37 EWE/HM, 11/2/1902, 47452, fol. 245.

38 Holton, *Feminism and Democracy*, p. 55.

39 Crawford, *WSM*, p. 398. On EWE and Bright McLaren see EWE/HM, 27/12/1897, fol. 173.

40 Richard Marsden Pankhurst had died in 1898.

41 Laura Ugolini, '"It is Only Justice to Grant Women's Suffrage": Independent Labour Party Men and Women's Suffrage', in Eustance Ryan and Ugolini (eds) *A Suffrage Reader*, pp. 126–44, pp. 128–31.

42 C. Tsuzuki, *H.M. Hyndman and British Socialism* (Oxford: Oxford University Press, 1961), quoted in Hunt, *Equivocal Feminists*, p. 8.

43 EWE/HM, 7/9/1905, 47454, fol. 139; EWE/HM, 11/12/1895, 47450, fol. 232.

44 EWE in *Justice*, 25 October 1902, quoted in Hunt, *Equivocal Feminists*, p. 196.

45 EWE, 'Outlanders'; Holton, *Feminism and Democracy*, pp. 53–4.

46 Billington in *Clarion*, 3 February 1905, quoted in Hannam and Hunt, *Socialist Women*, p. 109.

47 Lewis, *Gore-Booth and Roper*, pp. 89–91.

48 Jill Liddington and Jill Norris, *One Hand Tied Behind Us: The Rise of the Women's Suffrage Movement* (London: Virago, 1978), see esp. p. 15.

49 EWE to John Morley, 8/11/1903, 47453, fol. 198.

50 Ignota, 'The Case for the Immediate Enfranchisement of the Women of the United Kingdom', *Westminster Review*, November 1906, pp. 508–21, p. 508.

51 EWE/HM, 11/9/1899, 47452, fol. 16.

52 W.T. Stead, In Our Midst: The Letters of Callicrates to Dione, queen of the Xanthians, concerning England and the English, Anno Domini 1902, *The Review of Reviews Annual*, 1903 (London: William Clowes and Sons, 1903). For Stead's dedication see, W.T. Stead/EWE, 20/12/1902, 47453, fol. 84.

53 EWE/HM, 9/1/1903, 47453, fol. 94. EWE/HM, 12/5/1904, 47454, fol. 120. Ignota, 'In Our Midst', *Westminster Review*, February 1903, pp. 186–192.

54 William T. Stead, 'Woman's Suffrage in the Ascendant', *Review of Reviews*, July 1911, p. 18. [My emphasis.]

55 EWE/HM, 12/5/1903, 47453, fol. 119 ff.

56 EWE/HM, 24/7/1903, 47453, fol. 145.

57 EWE to HM, 3/8/1903, 47453, fol. 149–50.

58 EWE/HM, 28/9/1903, 47453, fol. 170.

59 Editorial, 'The Plea of the Women', *Review of Reviews*, August 1903, p. 114.

60 EWE/HM, 1/5/1903, 47453, fol. 118.

61 EWE/HM, 10/10/1903, 47453, fol. 179.

62 EWE/HM, 28/9/1903, 47453, fol. 172. Anon., 'Civic Rights of Women: National Convention in London', *Manchester Guardian*, 17 October 1903.

63 Anon., 'Civic Rights of Women', p. 12.

64 Enclosure in EWE to HM, 24 May 1905, fol. 119–21.

65 Holton, *Suffrage Days*, p. 107.

66 Anon, 'Civic Rights of Women', p. 12.

67 Holton, *Feminism and Democracy*, p. 60.

68 EWE/HM, 16/12/1903, 47453, fol. 212.

69 EWE/HM, 15/4/1902, 47452, fol. 288.

70 Minute Book of the Manchester Central Branch of the ILP, 21 November 1905, M42/1/2, Manchester Central Library.

71 Holton, *Suffrage Days*, p. 86.

72 Purvis, *Emmeline Pankhurst*, p. 67.
73 William Anderson to the Editor, *Labour Leader*, 18 November 1904, quoted in Ugolini, 'ILP Men', p. 137.
74 EWE/HM, 30/3/1904, 47454, fol. 263.
75 Holton, *Feminism and Democracy*, pp. 53–4. Hannam and Hunt, *Socialist Women*, pp. 109–11; Ugolini, 'ILP Men', pp. 134–40. Among Wolstenholme Elmy's published opinions are, 'The Present Legal Position of Women in the UK', *Westminster Review*, May 1905, pp. 513–29.
76 Helena Swanwick, *I Have Been Young* (London: Gollanz, 1935) quoted in Lewis, *Gore Booth and Roper*, p. 98.
77 Ignota, 'Enfranchisement of Women', p. 520.
78 EWE/HM, 17/8/1904, 47453, fol. 324.
79 EWE, 'The Women's Movement', *Ethical World*, 29 April 1905, pp. 133–4.
80 Ignota, 'The Case for the Immediate Enfranchisement', p. 519. For Wolstenholme Elmy's opposition to the views of Harry Quelch see EWE, 'The Women's Movement', *Ethical World*, 4 February 1905, pp. 37–8.
81 Hannam and Hunt have criticised Holton's *Feminism and Democracy* for failing to consider 'adult suffrage . . . as a [long-standing] demand in its own right' and for weighting the argument too heavily with 'the perspective of women's suffragists.' Hannam and Hunt, *Socialist Women*, p. 107.
82 EWE/HM, 7/9/1905, 47454, fol. 139.
83 Hunt, 'Politics of Dora Montefiore', pp. 170–3.
84 EWE/HM, 23/10/1905, 47454, fol. 153. Also EWE to Sylvia Pankhurst, 7/10/1907, ESPP.
85 EWE/HM, 23/10/1905, 47454, fol. 154.
86 Crawford, *WSM*, p. 419. Under the auspices of this meeting the International Women's Suffrage Alliance was founded. June Hannam, Mitzi Auchterlonie and Katherine Holden (eds), *International Encyclopedia of Women's Suffrage* (Santa Barbara: ABC-Clio, 2000), pp. 145–7.
87 EWE/HM, 5/6/1904, 47453, fol. 292.
88 Ignota, 'The Grand Old Woman of To-day', *Westminster Review*, Vol. 161, No. 3, March 1904, pp. 321–6; EWE/HM, 8/2/1904, 47453, fol. 236.
89 Ignota, 'The Grand Old Woman', p. 326.
90 EWE/HM, 26/6/1904, 47453, fol. 298. EWE/HM, 17/9/1904, 47454, fol. 7.
91 EWE/HM, 27/9/1904, 47454, fol. 10.
92 EWE/HM, 28/7/1904, 47453, fol. 312. Christabel Pankhurst, 'An American Reformer in Manchester', *Daily Dispatch*, 25 July 1904.
93 Pankhurst, *My Own Story*, p. 43.
94 EWE/HM, 26/5/1905, 47454, fol. 109.
95 Pankhurst, *TSM*, p. 183.
96 EWE, 'The Women's Movement', *Ethical World*, 27 May 1905, p. 163.
97 EWE to Sylvia Pankhurst, 7/10/1907, ESPP.
98 Pankhurst, *TSM*, p. 184.
99 Holton, *Suffrage Days*, p. 110.
100 Anon. [EWE], *The Emancipation of Women*, p. 5. WEUP.
101 Christabel Pankhurst and Annie Kenney had made their determined vocal protest at the Liberal Party meeting at which Sir Edward Grey was the chief speaker. Twice Kenney asked Grey to state the intention of the Liberal government, if returned, to

give votes to women. The women were ignored, ejected roughly from the hall and, after Christabel had committed a 'technical offence of spitting at a policeman', were arrested and sentenced to one week's imprisonment. Purvis, *Emmeline Pankhurst*, pp. 74–5.

102 EWE/HM, 18/10/1905, 47454, fol. 149.

103 EWE/HM, 23/10/1905, 47454, fol. 152–153.

104 EWE/HM, 3/3/1906, 47453, fol. 221–2.

105 Ignota, 'Pioneers, O Pioneers', p. 415.

106 EWE/HM, 3/3/1906, 47454, fol. 222.

107 EWE/HM, 7/3/1906, 47454, fol. 227–228.

108 EWE/HM, 6/5/1906, 47454, fol. 253.

109 Will of Ben Elmy dated 14 February 1906. Cheshire Archives and Local Studies Centre. MF 91/55.

110 EWE/HM, 23/10/1898, 47451, fol. 260.

111 Frank Elmy had first stood for Buglawton Urban District Council in March 1901, polling 102 votes. Anon., 'Buglawton Council Elections', *Congleton Chronicle*, 30 March 1901. On his successful election see EWE/HM, 30/3/1904, 47453, fol. 262.

112 EWE/HM, 3/3/1906, 47454, fol. 223.

113 EWE/HM, 6/5/1906, 47454, fol. 253.

114 Strachey, *The Cause*, pp. 298–301.

115 Pankhurst, *TSM*, pp. 209–13.

116 EWE/HM, 6/5/1906, 47454, fol. 253.

117 Davies had not deserted the suffrage cause after the foundation of Girton College. She rejoined the London National Society in 1874, and the Central Committee of the National Society in 1888, and by 1905 was a member of the Executive Committee of the NUWSS. Crawford, *WSM*, p. 159.

118 Pankhurst, *TSM*, p. 210.

119 Pugh, *March of the Women*, p. 58; Purvis, *Emmeline Pankhurst*, p. 83.

120 Editorial, 'Women's March to Downing Street', *Daily Mirror*, 21 May 1906.

121 'Women's March to Downing Street', *Daily Mirror*, 21 May 1906.

122 Anon., 'By The Way', *Congleton Chronicle*, 25 May 1906, p. 4.

123 EWE, 'Song of the Insurgent Women', 47455, fol. 11.

8

'At eventide there will be light': June 1906–March 1918[1]

Disputes and schisms

Though Elizabeth privately lamented the loss of her husband she seldom reflected on their lives together in her correspondence after 1906. As always, she resolutely overcame distress and looked to the future. Ben's death afforded her a chance to travel more widely and to 'make holiday' – though journeys often combined work with pleasure.[2] One such trip was made to Manchester on 30 June 1906 to witness Christabel Pankhurst's graduation as a Bachelor of Law at the Whitworth Hall. She greatly enjoyed the ceremony, and noted that the crowd's cries of 'Why haven't you brought your banner?' as celebrity suffragette Christabel mounted the platform were drowned by enthusiastic cheers.[3] The day ended, however, with suffrage discussions. A fortnight later Elizabeth and Frank took a ferry to the Isle of Man to commit Ben's ashes to the tides – a key personal event noted only as an aside when informing McIlquham of the plans for a women's suffrage demonstration at Boggart Hole Clough on 15 July.[4] The events of that day saw Elizabeth once more facing an unruly Mancunian crowd, something which may have brought back memories of her seven-year-old self, caught up with her Aunt Mary in the maelstrom of the city's bread riots in 1841.

A crowd of 15,000 people gathered at Boggart Hole Clough on that summer Sunday. The Clough was an area of sixty-three acres that had been purchased by the City Council for public use, but in the preceding months a number of ILP members had been arrested and imprisoned for holding political meetings there. The suffragists were not deterred, but a small group of young men gathered in the vast crowd were determined to cause trouble. By pushing forward they caused the crowd to press into the natural hollow of ground where the speakers were attempting to be heard, instigating a fracas.[5] The *Manchester Guardian* reported that while Elizabeth had been 'in the thick of the crush' she had remained 'perfectly calm'.[6] Her own recollections of the meeting were published in the same newspaper in response to two hostile letters to the Editor from Mr Harry Kiddle, who had condemned the increasingly common practice of suffragette heckling at political meetings. In the face of such behaviour, Kiddle wrote, 'it is asking too much of human nature [to] expect no reprisals'. He went on to beg Elizabeth, as a long-standing constitutional advocate of women's suffrage, to distance herself from the dishonourable actions of her associates.[7] She responded tartly that the only offences committed at Boggart Hole Clough were those against the militants and their largely sympathetic audience, whose lives and limbs had been imperilled through the actions of the rowdies.[8]

A week later, an even larger crowd attended a demonstration in Stevenson Square, and on 25 July Emmeline Pankhurst told Elizabeth about it during a delightful stroll around the Botanical Gardens. During their walk, Emmeline talked of her eldest daughter's campaign (with Teresa Billington and Marion Coates Hansen) at the recent by-election in Cockermouth.[9] The women, though all ILP members, had refused to campaign for Robert Smillie, the Labour candidate, and Christabel also declared, for the first time, the militants' anti-government policy – something which confirmed the WSPU's intention of remaining 'entirely and scrupulously independent' of party politics. Suffragettes, Miss Pankhurst said, would no longer be 'a frill on the sleeve' of the Conservative, Labour or Liberal male politicians who denied them their citizenship, a comment that surely echoed the resolution passed at the National Convention some three years earlier when the issue of women's role as political canvassers had been debated.[10] Elizabeth strongly supported Christabel's stance, although the policy of opposing Labour party candidates (as well as those of their contenders) would have unhappy consequences for the women's suffragists of the Manchester branches of the ILP.[11] Elizabeth's emotions veered between sadness and anger as friendships built on a shared commitment to socialism and suffrage began to fracture.

It was some weeks later when Elizabeth told McIlquham of her horror on hearing the news that the North Manchester Branch of the ILP had demanded the expulsion of Billington and Pankhurst after the Cumbrian campaign. She gave the reason as being the fact that the women had 'put W[omen's] S[uffrage] before the personal interest of Robert Smillie, the "adult" Suffragist'.[12] While it may not have been an 'unreasonable expectation of the ILP' that the WSPU activists would campaign for Smillie, socialist moves to make reprisals were swift

– although Elizabeth declared North Manchester's censure to be an 'impertinence [and] babyishly silly'.[13] Julia Dawson, editor of the socialist newspaper *The Clarion*, felt differently, commenting that 'the mighty' force of the WSPU 'had fallen' by the wayside by its actions in Cockermouth.[14] Elizabeth was suffering from an undisclosed illness at this juncture and Frances Rowe had offered to fund a doctor. Nonetheless, and despite pain and fatigue, she tabled an amendment at the Manchester Central ILP meeting of 4 September 1906 'committing the Branch to the unreserved support of the demand for the enfranchisement of women *during the autumn Session*'. Her sympathies obviously lay with the militants. Delighted that wherever and whenever women's suffrage was discussed on a public platform 'thousands can be brought together for a . . . meeting at a few hours' notice', Elizabeth believed that 'we can better afford to dispense with the ILP than they to dispense with us!'[15] On a personal note she commented that the 'quarrel', though it might adversely affect publication of her recently authored women's suffrage pamphlet by the ILP, was not unduly serious – the article would simply be issued instead by the WSPU. Ultimately, the federated council of the Manchester and Salford ILP *did* vote to expel Billington and Christabel Pankhurst from the party, but the local, Manchester Central branch, refused to impose the sanction.[16]

In October 1906, Elizabeth travelled to London for a week of intense work, visiting colleagues in the NUWSS and the WLF, and leading meetings on behalf of the WSPU. She also took the opportunity to visit Sotheby's with a parcel of her late husband's books for auction, before returning to face the horrors of the damp days of the Cheshire winter that aggravated her painful rheumatic condition.[17] The following year, in the face of unremitting pressure, both Emmeline and Christabel Pankhurst resigned from the ILP. This occurred some months after Emmeline, a delegate to the ILP Conference held in Derby at the beginning of April, had sought to defend the WSPU's policy at Cockermouth. She had argued, in response to questions from, among others, Isabella Ford and Charlotte Despard (also a prominent SDF and ex-ASS supporter) that 'women could not wait [un]til a Labour Party was in power', and she challenged the conference to consider whether they believed her 'conduct inconsistent with [her] membership'.[18] On the same day, 2 April 1907, she wrote of her actions to Elizabeth, who, upon reading the letter, decided that Emmeline 'ha[d] been purified as by fire'.[19] Elizabeth likewise grew increasingly wary that the 'gap between socialist rhetoric and practice on the woman question' would stall the political alliance the women needed to conduct a successful campaign.[20] And therefore, when Mrs Pankhurst (after the tragic deaths of her mother, sister and elder son) resigned her employment as Registrar of Births and Deaths, sold her Manchester home and moved to London (the better to conduct national WSPU labours), she aided her in the best way she could – by fund-raising for the organisation.[21]

There is no evidence, however, to indicate that she resigned from the ILP, something which is illustrated by her inclusion as one of the 'notable men and women' honoured in Labour's *Reformers' Year Book* for 1908.[22] She appeared reluctant to abandon the idealised, socialist philosophy of 'justice' she had held on to for decades and, though never less than a woman-centred feminist, her views allied perhaps more precisely with those of Isabella Ford, who chose to emphasise 'how the vote would make women at last "fully human" and that for this, cooperation with men was necessary'.[23] Certainly, Elizabeth held that those men who had laboured in the cause of feminism had often been treated unfairly in its histories and, in the case of Manchester ILP couple Annot and Sam Robinson, considered Mr Robinson a more able advocate of justice to women than his wife.[24]

The separatists

Party-political quarrels were not the only divisive issues to hover around the militant suffragettes at this time. There were also internal divisions, and their working out often caused Elizabeth deep personal grief. Perhaps the most crucial grievance centred on the increasingly strained relationships within the Pankhurst family. Elizabeth was devoted to Christabel, but she had also aided her younger sister Sylvia in her literary work for the women's movement by lending her numerous documents – sometimes to the detriment of her own journalism.[25] Sylvia had resigned as honorary secretary of the WSPU in the spring of 1906, and during the following months was experiencing the first conscious awareness that her personal and political views diverged from those of her mother and elder sister, whom she later charged with 'incipient Toryism'.[26] It has been argued that, in moving the headquarters of the movement to London, Mrs Pankhurst and Christabel were determined to change the 'class' profile of the organisation by attracting the support (and funds) of women who might not have felt comfortable in a group allied (albeit indirectly) to the ILP.[27] If this was so, Sylvia's criticism as a deeply committed socialist is understandable. Her 'bitter personal memories of her mother and her elder sister' are especially evident when she comments on their requests to WSPU members to resign from 'men's political parties' and to concentrate solely on suffragette activities.[28] This was something Sylvia could not countenance and although she undoubtedly suffered much (even the torture of forcible feeding) in the following years endeavouring to be steadfast to the WSPU's ideals, her loyalty to the Labour movement was deeply ingrained and she felt unable to 'leave [it] behind'.[29]

Though fond of Sylvia, Elizabeth believed Mrs Pankhurst and Christabel had the drive, tenacity and ability to push forward a national campaign. Thus it is possible to view sympathetically her reasons for supporting Emmeline's decision to institute an 'autocratic' management style, when the tensions surfaced that would split the WSPU in two in 1907. Mrs Pankhurst had been concerned when the WSPU's joint honorary secretaries, Charlotte Despard and ex-mathematics lecturer Edith How Martyn, had questioned the organisational structure of the Union, wishing for greater democratic involvement – something not inconsistent with their shared socialist roots. Mrs Pankhurst's prediction that 'divided counsels would result' proved accurate on 10 September following a stormy Committee meeting (during which she cancelled the organisation's annual conference and annulled its existing constitution), when Despard, How Martyn and the newly married Teresa Billington-Greig resigned.[30] Together with a minority of the membership, they formed a new organisation, the Women's Freedom League (WFL). Elizabeth, at first outraged at the challenge to Mrs Pankhurst, labelled Despard and her associates 'the Separatists' and roundly castigated Frances Rowe for viewing their complaints sympathetically.[31]

Her anger though was short-lived, and on a visit to Glasgow in the first week of October 1908 she accompanied Billington-Greig onto the platform of a WFL meeting. The younger woman had, in fact, been married from the house of the now widowed 'Lily Bell' Pearce, where Elizabeth was a guest, and thus it is unlikely that hostilities between these friends would have continued.[32] Also, later that month, she shared a '*sisterly* greeting with Charlotte Despard' on a suffragist platform at the Albert Hall in London.[33] This softening of Elizabeth's hostility towards the WFL resulted principally from her sympathy with their broad focus on the multiple issues that conspired to cause women's subjection. As Hilary Frances has shown, the 'leading members of the WFL extended the boundaries of public debate on sexual issues' to encompass matters directly relating to the construction of twentieth-century feminism, such as 'incest, domestic violence and prostitution'.[34] Such a forward-looking approach was simply an extension of Elizabeth's personal ideals and she was thus in natural sympathy with the organisation's ethics.

All unpleasantness with the 'separatists' was now at an end and Elizabeth commented (without any hint of irony at her past astringent tone) that the WSPU and WFL were now simply 'two wings of the one great army'.[35]

This dispute was happily resolved, but Elizabeth had been faced at the same time with a good deal of anxiety regarding her relationship with Dora Montefiore. Frances Rowe had written to her early in 1907 criticising Montefiore, with whom she had quarrelled over branch policy of the Hammersmith WSPU. Rowe believed Montefiore 'unprincipled' and self-seeking, but Elizabeth rebuked her ex-student for her harshness.[36] She had, however, expressed her own concerns regarding Montefiore's increasingly erratic behaviour and was crestfallen over the growing antagonism between Dora and the central leaders of the WSPU. In 1906, Montefiore had included quotations from both Elizabeth and 'Ellis Ethelmer' in her *Woman's Calendar*, which, she claimed, was designed to 'aid women in their efforts to "self-realization".'[37] By that time, however, their friendship was already suffering the first stages of disintegration. On 7 January 1907, Elizabeth wrote to Harriet that she had 'hardly slept' the previous night after receiving letters from Montefiore castigating the Pankhursts for appearing to denigrate Dora's role in the WSPU – statements which are upheld in part by her omission or marginalisation from their autobiographies.[38] Montefiore's psychological position must be questioned too, in the light of Frank Elmy's concern about the possible effects of her excessive consumption of cocaine lozenges, taken for a persistent cough. On the Elmys' most recent visit to London, both mother and son had noticed a distinct change in Dora's character and she appeared to be suffering from physical and/or psychological symptoms of illness. Elizabeth had also complained that the visit had been punctuated by one long wail of discontent from Dora whenever the three of them were alone.[39] In order to alleviate some of the strain Montefiore was experiencing, Elizabeth tried to arrange short holidays for her prior to her journey to Copenhagen to represent the WSPU at the Congress of the International Alliance of Women Suffrage Societies.[40] Wishing only good for Dora, Elizabeth classed her 'next to Christabel . . . in the category of *active* workers', a 'brave fighter [and a] true soul' who needed support rather than censure.[41]

During the next few months things changed, and though in February 1907 Elizabeth still referred to Montefiore as 'dear', by May she felt that she could no longer 'go on receiving the cruelly unjust complaints of Mrs M & trying to reason her out of her perverted views' about the Pankhursts.[42] She had loyally supported Montefiore throughout her three-year campaign of tax resistance from 1904, but she believed that individual civil disobedience would not be effective and that 'unless the case is made public, & other women follow her example, [the] protest will be in vain'.[43] Her wish for publicity was granted in 1906 when Dora's home became known by the soubriquet 'Fort Montefiore' when, for six weeks and aided by her suffragist colleagues, she held out against the bailiffs.[44] Montefiore gained popularity and a high profile in London WSPU circles, but this contributed to the development of friction between herself and the central leadership. She subsequently left the WSPU, and debate exists as to whether she took the initiative and resigned, or whether the Pankhursts demanded her expulsion. Holton has argued that a focus on *their* displeasure denies Montefiore's own agency in initiating the schism, for Dora was indeed a feisty character who would not have taken kindly to submitting to 'autocracy'.[45] Certainly, she was deeply upset and felt slighted, but she went on to pursue a highly successful career with the ASS (becoming its secretary in 1909) and latterly with the British Dominions Women's Suffrage Union.[46]

As a close friend, Elizabeth found the episode deeply distressing, but her loyalty was ultimately to the Pankhursts and the WSPU. Her letter of 10 May 1907 is the last to mention Montefiore's name. The frequent, loving and admiring recollections of the past ten years ceased so abruptly that her despair at Dora's recriminations must have reached crisis point, although her patience was tried on account of her own, repeatedly expressed, 'exhaustion'. Montefiore's biographer notes that their 'cherished friendship' had been a life-changing one for Dora, and her autobiography, published in 1927, included loving tributes to Elizabeth's mentorship.[47] She credited her, indeed, as being the 'soul' which moved the inert mass of the women's movement forward to glory – though her style, by placing Elizabeth as an icon, denies the vibrant practical nature of her work.[48] No recollections beyond 1907, however, were included in the memoir. The split was total and Elizabeth wrote that she had 'no strength left' to bear the pain of it.[49]

'This is for you' – Nestor of the suffrage movement

Despite the differences in approaches and ideologies that had brought the suffragettes of the WSPU to the point of division, the years of 1906 and 1907 were, on balance, successful. The skills of its new Treasurer, Emmeline Pethick Lawrence and her husband Fred (introduced to Mrs Pankhurst by Keir Hardie) brought efficiency and, more importantly, financial security. Whilst monies cascaded into the central organisation's coffers, however, Elizabeth expended considerable effort into securing support for the northern WSPU branches, whose finances were often perilous.[50] Emmeline Pankhurst was certainly not oblivious to this, for she noted that 'many members . . . really can't afford to pay anything at all' to Union funds.[51] Elizabeth sent copious requests for money by post and travelled widely, addressing many local and national meetings – the trips financed in part by the recent employment of her son as assistant overseer and rate collector for Buglawton Urban District Council. A sale of books and artefacts after Ben's death had enabled a reduction in the mortgage on Buxton House and Frank's salary, combined with the weekly Grateful Fund cheque, ensured Elizabeth greater ease of mind in financial matters.[52] Before taking up his post, Frank had accompanied his mother to London for their fateful visit to Dora Montefiore. And on 23 October they had travelled from Hammersmith to the women's suffrage demonstration at the House of Commons on the occasion of the opening of Parliament. There, in the lobby, women of all classes had mixed together happily, but amid the tumult of voices crying 'Votes for Women', the police had intervened to eject the protestors. After draping a 'Votes for Women' banner around a convenient pillar and raising her voice in a cry of 'Shame!' Elizabeth was removed along with the rest. She did not, however, suffer the fate of many younger colleagues – that of arrest and detention. Aged seventy-three, and in company with fellow veteran Charlotte Despard, she escaped custody. Both felt 'aggrieved that [they] were thought unworthy of the crown they have placed on our dear sisters' heads'.[53]

Elizabeth's detailed account of that week's campaign was given to 'be of value later.'[54] She knew McIlquham had collated their correspondence and was 'writing to history' by putting forward a version of events that she hoped later to publish in auto/biographical form.[55] She placed herself at the centre of the dramatic events and noted both her importance as a speaker during the WSPU meetings held prior to the House of Commons fracas and her willingness to be a martyr for militancy by putting herself in line for arrest. She wrote to Harriet often of the 'sorting' or 'turning-out' of the room-size collection of personal papers and other artefacts at Buglawton, and sometimes enclosed items of interest; but in the spring of 1908 she was subject to a particularly debilitating bout of influenza which left her 'weak as a baby' and disinclined to labour.[56] Her recovery in April coincided with the retirement of Sir Henry Campbell-Bannerman and Herbert Asquith's assumption of the Liberal premiership. Asquith's anti-suffragist sentiments were well known, and Elizabeth noted in combative tone that his accession would 'mean a more stubborn . . . fight' – though WSPU members were 'spoiling for the fray'.[57]

This might have been so, but ex-Chancellor Asquith was to prove himself a force for cohesion for his party and a strong leader – something Elizabeth might not have foreseen when, at the end of the month, she noted with sadness the death of her long-term associate Clementia Taylor.[58] 'Mentia', she reflected, had been a 'brilliant woman' who had shared the convictions of radical-Liberalism from her earliest involvement in the women's movement.[59] Reflecting on their shared hopes, Elizabeth rejoiced that the members of the WLF were at last, and as she understood it in the light of Asquith's intransigence, bestirring themselves to action. The comment by Florence Balgarnie, an Executive member of the WLF (and Elizabeth's associate since VADPR days) that they had been 'hewers of wood and drawers of water too long' would have delighted her.[60] Asquith exerted extreme influence on his party, however, and his implacable opposition to the women's parliamentary vote ensured anything but a quick resolution to suffragists' demands.

In May, now fully recovered, Elizabeth journeyed to Manchester for two days of energetic campaigning and discussion regarding the planned 'women's month' in London, where both the NUWSS and the WSPU had organised mass public demonstrations.[61] She travelled to the capital days after the NUWSS procession, on 19 June, to join the vast national protest planned by Christabel Pankhurst to counter the claim by Home Secretary Herbert Gladstone that women would be disinclined to participate in a mass rally in respect of their political grievances. Elizabeth, once again, showed her desire to earn a martyr's crown by announcing that she would return to Congleton 'if alive & not in prison' after the WSPU demonstration.

On 21 June, 'Women's Sunday', seven columns of enthusiastic suffragists, many dressed in white to denote purity, marched from different points of the capital to converge together at Hyde Park, where a crowd of a 125,000 waited. Despite her advancing years, Elizabeth walked side by side with Emmeline Pankhurst and at the head of some 40,000 marchers. She carried before her a 'lovely ... bouquet of ferns, huge purple lilies and lilies of the valley', which artfully displayed the colours of the WSPU in an elegant piece of floral propaganda.[62] On her arrival in Hyde Park, she observed the thrilling scene from the vantage point of a platform (one of twenty erected), seated next to Charlotte Carmichael Stopes. The 80 speakers, struggling to be heard above 'good humoured' heckling, included (in addition to the famed Pankhursts) Nellie Martel, Annie Kenney, Emmeline Pethick Lawrence and the delightfully witty ex-Vice President of the Leeds ILP, Mary Gawthorpe.[63] On 26 June, still elated, Elizabeth summed up the experience with the words that as 'a mere picture it was beyond expression beautiful, & when one thought of all it expressed & signified!!! It was an hour of glorious life'.[64]

More excitement followed, at a meeting at the Queen's Hall that same evening, when Elizabeth received the accolade of her peers as 'Nestor', or 'wise one' of the suffrage movement.[65] Recounting the event for McIlquham, she wrote that having arrived a little late at the Hall she was not giving the proceedings her full concentration and had taken little notice of the applause that broke out as she sought her seat on the platform. A little confused, she had

> thought the storm of cheering, everybody rising & standing, was for some point of the lady speaking which my deafness had missed. As I walked . . . to . . . the platform, the cheering continued – & it was not till I stood by Mrs. Martel, who whispered – 'This is for you,' that I realised the position. The same scene was repeated after the few words I said to our friends during the meeting. I tell you this, because I know you will like to realise the depth of loving sympathy & fuller co-operation which this implies.[66]

Her last sentence indicates Elizabeth's deep emotional reaction to this great reception. She had worked for so long in the hope of achieving a 'sisterhood' of women who would work for their own emancipation

Figure 6 Elizabeth Wolstenholme Elmy with Emmeline Pankhurst and others, Hyde Park demonstration 1908
Source: Mary Evans Picture Library

without distinction of class or creed. She had been censured and ostra-
cised by some of those with whom she had worked, even those, such as
Lydia Becker and Ursula Bright, bound closest to her through ties of
friendship. This rapturous ovation, during which women of all classes
(many who had travelled on specially hired trains from the provinces for
the day's excursion) hailed her contribution to the cause they had all
consciously adopted as their own, healed these painful memories. She felt,
at last, fully welcomed within a loving, supportive circle and was delighted
to be honoured for both her past and her present actions. The balm to
her soul was sweet and the day one of the most significant of her life.

Sadly, the harmony was not to last, and a new departure in WSPU
strategy soon troubled Elizabeth's humanitarian conscience. The glorious demonstration of 21 June had left Asquith unmoved and the militants, responding to his obduracy, gave notice that a deputation would
wait upon him on the afternoon of 30 June, led by Emmeline Pankhurst
and twelve volunteers.[67] Unsurprisingly, they were turned away on their
arrival at the House of Commons. That evening, in a crowded Parliament
Square monitored by 2,000 police officers, the suffragettes endured
brutal treatment as policemen tried to quell their protests. Two young
women, Edith New and Mary Leigh, acting on their own initiative, ven-
tured through the crowd and took a taxi to Downing Street where they
threw stones at the windows of the Prime Minister's residence.[68] By these
actions they lost Elizabeth's sympathy and she wrote the following day
that she considered the deed a 'reckless . . . folly, for how [could] they be
secure against hurting the innocent?'[69] This simple comment, almost lost
in the copious sources that favoured the militants' stance, highlights how
the ideals of Elizabeth the pacifist would, over the following months and
years, overlay those of Elizabeth the militant.[70] The mere possibility of
loss of life was anathema to her, and even though Mrs Pankhurst had
decreed that no protest be undertaken with that direct intention, there
was no security against an accident.

'Criminal folly': militancy repudiated?

Elizabeth's heart, energies and total commitment had been given, since
its formation, to the WSPU. The 'woman-centred' policy of the organisation and the pomp and panoply of the mass marches and demonstrations warmed the soul of the now elderly woman who had once been a
member at the genteel gatherings of the Kensington Society. She had
wholeheartedly praised Mrs Pankhurst's determination to take direct,
disruptive action in seeking the adoption of a *government* women's

suffrage bill, but the escalation of the methods of militancy used during 1908–12 brought her increasing unease.

The value of WSPU militancy as a political tactic has been the subject of extensive research. In his widely reprinted *Strange Death of Liberal England*, George Dangerfield is scathingly contemptuous, writing of the inept and 'ludicrous . . . swish of long skirts [and] the violent assault of feathered hats' as being the actions of a weak and ineffectual minority.[71] Brian Harrison, writing in 1987, was also critical and trivialised the militant action, seeing it as a counter-productive force that stalled the political progress of the constitutional movement under Millicent Garrett Fawcett.[72] Purvis's revisionist biography of Emmeline Pankhurst countered this with the interpretation that she was 'a practical politician, seeking practical solutions to complex problems' in a way that challenged male dominance in public space.[73] And Paula Bartley, in a careful summary of Holton's 'provocative and sophisticated' essay, *In Sorrowful Wrath*, concludes that the bedrock to Pankhurst's militancy was her belief that 'those who were disenfranchised had every right to break the law in the fight for parliamentary reform' and that the context in which militancy was set was just as significant as the violence itself.[74] Bartley also contends that Emmeline, a long-standing advocate of the politics of disruption was, like Elizabeth, 'a radical in the old tradition' which favoured evolution above revolution; but the argument of the stone (a 'time honoured' method of protest) was to drive a wedge between them.[75] Political stalemate caused frustration, and women with hammers hidden in reticules and muffs soon wreaked vengeance upon the windows of city department stores with as much force as New and Leigh had thrown stones in Downing Street. Though Elizabeth had been clear, in *Woman and the Law* and *Outlanders*, that physical protest was both right and lawful in the pursuit of citizenship, it is only by viewing her reaction to WSPU violence through the lens of her pacifism that we can chart the reasons for her subsequent decision to sign a formal public protest against the WSPU militants and to resign her position on its Executive.[76]

Increasing dilemma

Elizabeth's schism with the WSPU was a long way distant, though, when she embarked on a strenuous round of summer cleaning at Buxton House at the end of July 1908. She was expecting a short visit from New Zealand's suffragist leader Katherine Sheppard in mid-September and wished her home to look pristine. Sheppard spent two nights with the Elmys en route to Glasgow, where she resided with her son and daughter-in-law – the daughter of and old friend from CDA days, Margaret Sievwright. Sievwright, originally from Scotland, had worked with Elizabeth during the CDA campaign, but had later emigrated to New Zealand. She worked collaboratively with Sheppard on the colony's successful campaign for women's suffrage and at the time of her death in March 1905 was President of the National Council of Women of New Zealand.[77]

The 'young Sheppards' lived only minutes away from Isabella Bream Pearce, and Elizabeth travelled north at the beginning of October to join the happy gathering. During her stay she met, and was much impressed with, University of Edinburgh graduate J. Chrystal Macmillan. Macmillan would make history that year as the first woman to plead before the House of Lords in an unsuccessful attempt to gain the parliamentary suffrage for female university graduates, and a fruitful correspondence developed between her and the veteran suffragist.[78] In 1909, the journey to Scotland was repeated and this time Elizabeth was an honoured guest at the Edinburgh women's suffrage demonstration on 9 October, where she rode 'with the three oldest Scottish suffragists in the last carriage of the procession.' She declared that the overworked Emmeline Pankhurst, who was also present in Edinburgh and whose younger son Harry was terminally ill, had looked *'fagged out'* after her speech.[79] She hoped Mrs Pankhurst's long sea voyage to America, to participate in a series of speaking engagements organised by Harriot Stanton Blatch, would grant her some respite.

The reasons for Emmeline Pankhurst's strain, in addition to her private worries in relation to her son, were obvious. The Liberal government had been caught off-balance by the introduction of WSPU hecklers at political meetings in 1905 and by the glorious demonstrations where women marching with elegance and grace had commandeered public sympathy for their cause: a support that was extended by the large-scale coverage given of the events in the press.[80] However, although perhaps wrong-footed, the government had remained steadfast in its opposition. In addition and crucially, women's suffrage (despite the high-profile publicity it attracted) was not high on the list of government priorities at this juncture, the House of Lords having rejected the 1909 Budget of Chancellor David Lloyd George 'in defiance of the Constitution'.[81] The by-election strategy introduced by Christabel Pankhurst at Cockermouth (and pursued with varying success by militants thereafter) was found to be non-productive in the face of fierce party loyalties which prevailed during the general election campaign following the Budget crisis., In an effort to break the stalemate, militants organised ever more risk-laden protests and were seemingly heedless of the fact that the government could turn this to their own advantage by portraying such moves as threats to public safety. This only stimulated public approval of the criminal charges levied against the suffragettes and undid much of the good their own propaganda had achieved.

Such was the outcry following the actions of Mary Leigh who, accompanied by Charlotte Marsh, threw an axe at the Prime Minister's car during a visit to Bingley Hall, Birmingham on 17 September 1909, that a ban was placed on women attending *any* Liberal political meeting. Commenting on the episode, Elizabeth wrote that this new turn in events had made her ill and 'terribly worried'. She had tried, she continued, 'to save the Executive of the WSPU from disgracing itself & damaging our woman's cause by adopting a policy of *violence* which must delay, not advance, our cause. If the London Executive persists in supporting [such endeavours then] I must withdraw from [it].'[82] While it has been argued that the central Executive had 'little choice but to endorse' the actions of the WSPU's most reckless adherents, Elizabeth clearly did not uphold such behaviour.[83]

Leigh and Marsh, meanwhile, confined to their cells in Winson Green gaol, followed the example of another extremist, Marion Wallace Dunlop, and adopted the tactic of the hunger strike. The government, deeply embarrassed by Wallace Dunlop's reminiscences of her starvation ordeal, determined that Leigh and Marsh should be denied the same opportunities for propaganda. Regardless of their wishes, they would be fed and by force if necessary. The brutal and humiliating process began within days.[84] Appearing to reverse her earlier censure of the women, Elizabeth sent a strongly worded letter to the *Manchester Guardian*, protesting against the 'iniquitous treatment of [the] women political prisoners'. She also took care to remind readers that 'for these atrocities the Home Secretary [was] responsible'.[85] Hers was both a political and a humanitarian protest, for she held humanity as a sacred state. Neither the authorities nor the militants should, she believed, demean the value of human life so that murder, torture or martyrdom were considered acceptable. It was to counter such barbarism sanctioned by the policies of male legislators that justified women's participation in Parliament, Elizabeth argued, and her views (though often quoted anonymously) were liberally applied by W.T. Stead in his column 'Progress' in the *Review of Reviews*. The militants, Stead wrote in October 1909, had 'awakened their own sex to the justice of their demands' but, by sanctioning violence, had removed 'the struggle from the sphere of reason, where they are supreme, to the arena of brute force, where they have not even got a fighting chance'.[86]

The words were a prophetic omen and, though written under his hand, could well have been furnished by his revered friend, Elizabeth. Their long collaboration, therefore, made it obvious that it would be Stead to whom she pledged the manuscript of her autobiography, *Some Memories of a Happy Life*, in which she promised to give 'justice to . . . the early workers – especially the men who helped' her.[87] Sadly, Stead's tragic loss on the Titanic in April 1912 might supply one reason why Elizabeth's memoir remained unpublished, and though no record exists of her feelings on learning of his death it is likely she mourned his passing bitterly, both for their friendship and for the faithfulness of his reforming zeal.

So long as I live here on earth I shall miss her

The political cataclysm surrounding the Budget of 1909 preceded two general elections, the first in January and the second in December 1910. Asquith's majority in the House of Commons was obliterated in the January poll and a hung Parliament returned.[88] The resulting uncertainty sparked a process of 'conciliation' in the women's suffrage movement, for Christabel Pankhurst, anxious for the future, believed the practices of 'mild militancy' to have been 'played out'.[89] An all-party conciliation committee was formed in February 1910 to devise a solution. Much encouraged by advance notice of this move, Elizabeth wrote briefly to McIlquham on 21 January, expressing also her 'earnest wishes for [her] quick recovery' from an undisclosed illness.[90] Sadly Harriet was not to rally, and a mere four days later Elizabeth wrote again, this time to her daughter Mary, to convey her profound love for the woman whose death had ended a friendship that had spanned 'more than half a lifetime'.[91] Elizabeth expressed her grief with the moving words that she would miss her friend's counsel and companionship 'so long as I live here on earth'.[92]

As the financial mainstay of the Grateful Fund, McIlquham's support for Elizabeth had been both temporal and spiritual. And while it might be argued that such a depth of friendship was never repeated in any of her other relationships, events that followed showed a continuing and genuine concern for her well-being. McIlquham's role as Treasurer of the Grateful Fund was immediately adopted by Louisa Martindale, who co-opted her Sussex neighbour Mrs George Holyoake as a signatory to the account. In the week after Harriet's death, Elizabeth received the money without interruption.[93] It is possible to question, without McIlquham's largesse, if the sums gifted to Elizabeth would have been indefinitely maintained. Such was the esteem in which she was held, however, that suffragists (militant and non-militant alike) came together to honour her by presenting a Testimonial fund of £500, collected during the autumn of 1910.[94] The organising committee of the fund included Louisa Martindale, Emmeline Pankhurst and Lady Constance Lytton, a WSPU militant whose grandmother had been a regular correspondent during the Infants' Bill campaign in the 1880s.[95] Stead penned a tribute article entitled 'Honour to Whom Honour is Due' to help gather support for the Testimonial and 292 suffragists contributed. The Testimonial was a document of honour and love and yet it is not mentioned in Sylvia Pankhurst's *The Suffragette Movement* – although ironically the full text forms part of her archive.[96] Elizabeth was, the Testimonial revealed, the 'first, the most zealous and the most constant' of Victorian women's emancipators and the 'greatest authority' on its history.[97] Aided by a fund that provided her with a secure annuity, she would be constant to the end.

Despite the easing of her material circumstances, this was no time for Elizabeth to relax and enjoy her colleagues' largesse. She worked on, and soon expressed grave concerns regarding the lack of progress of the Conciliation Commission. It was an unease shared by its chairman, Lord Lytton, and Elizabeth furnished W.T. Stead with evidence of His Lordship's worries that the parliamentary debate on women's suffrage promised by the Prime Minister showed no sign of taking place (although, with a general election on the horizon, the issue of the women's franchise might not have been uppermost in the his mind). Making use of the information offered Stead highlighted the fact that, rather than a specific commitment to discuss women's enfranchisement during the next session of Parliament, Asquith had only agreed to a promise 'for some Bill in some Session of the next Parliament'.[98] Determined to register their displeasure at authority's deceit, the militants 'declared war' and marched on Downing Street on 18 November 1910, when many women suffered extreme personal indignities at the hands of the police. Forever afterwards the day was marked by suffragettes as 'Black Friday'.[99] The *Review of Reviews* (in an obvious criticism of those hitherto lauded as having brought an 'effervescent element' to British politics), lamented that the women's tactics had been counter-productive for, during a parliamentary election, it seemed 'hardly reasonable to ask electors to subordinate all other questions to that of' votes for women.[100]

Elizabeth's own comments on Black Friday were scathing. She condemned the actions of both stone throwers and police on humanitarian grounds and begged for cohesion among suffragists in order to press for the reintroduction of the Conciliation Bill after the Liberals were returned to office in December. Therefore, when Teresa Billington-Greig published the first of three stinging attacks on Emmeline Pankhurst and the WSPU in the *New Age* on 12 January 1911, Elizabeth wrote to the *Manchester Guardian* that this sensitive time was 'the least fitting for an attack by one suffragist upon another or by one body of women suffragists upon another'.[101] Billington-Greig, she continued, had trivialised the movement at a time when it was imperative to press home the significant change in public opinion that demanded a formal debate on the issue. To her satisfaction, in February 1911, the WSPU declared the 'truce' re-adopted. She wrote on 14 March that

> Whatever else the Conciliation Bill may or may not do, it will put an end at once and finally to the legal disqualification of women as parliamentary voters, and will practically assure that whenever adult suffrage is conceded it *will* be adult suffrage and not mere manhood suffrage.[102]

She had reckoned, however, without Asquith's deceit, which remained well concealed until after the second reading of George Kemp's Second Conciliation Bill on 5 May 1911, when the legislation passed the House of Commons by a resounding majority of 255 votes to 88. By 1 June 1911, the truce in militant activity seemed assured when Sir Edward Grey indicated that during the 1912 parliamentary session the Bill would be given a 'real' opportunity to pass into law.[103] In the light of such progress, Elizabeth looked forward with delight to the part she would play in the 'Coronation Procession of the Women of Britain . . . the first and the longest and most original of all the processions that celebrated the King's crowning'.[104] The new monarch, George V, did not witness this demonstration of feminine patriotism but, by making public their loyalty to him, women issued a conscious challenge to any who considered that only men should have the opportunity of demonstrating nationalistic fervour.

The *Review of Reviews* commented that, to anti-suffragists, the glorious procession of 17 June 1911 which passed under the windows of the clubs of Pall Mall must have appeared to resemble 'a deadly boa constrictor stretching its coil around its fascinated victim'.[105] The procession was unique in that it was the only one in which all suffrage societies had combined together, and Lisa Tickner has argued that the complicity of the WSPU in a procession 'into [which] a set of dominant and topical representations of sovereignty' had been inserted, was 'indicative of the Pankhursts' increasingly conservative position', which would lead to them taking a patriotic stance in the First World War.[106] Elizabeth did not, however, foresee this divergence with her personal views on militarism when she gazed down on the scene from a balcony in St James's Street. Seated in a chair canopied with a large banner inscribed 'England's Oldest Militant Suffragette Greets Her Sisters' she had an uninterrupted view of the procession. Those marchers (British and international alike) who carried pennants lowered them in homage as they passed her.[107] W.T. Stead believed that for Elizabeth, 'the procession must have sounded the signal, "Lord, now lettest Thou they servant depart in peace, for mine eyes have seen Thy salvation"', as thousand upon thousand of committed women from twenty-eight suffrage societies took upon themselves the burden she had borne so constantly and for so long.[108] And while Stead's use of the biblical allegory of the ancient Simeon might seem inappropriate for the secularist Elizabeth, it was one she once had applied herself, perhaps in memory of her lost non-conformist past.[109] Whatever her emotions as she watched the procession, the woman who, in 1886, had battled 'almost single-handed . . . to win for the widowed mother the rights to the custody and guardianship of her children' might have been forgiven a moment of pride that her work had acted in many ways as a precursor to this astonishing spectacle.[110]

The Coronation procession had shown that women were prepared to stake, ever more clearly, their right to public representation and to citizenship as loyal subjects of the new monarch. However, the harmonious relationship between constitutional and militant suffragists that persisted through the summer of 1911 was soon shattered when the militants realised the duplicity of the government regarding the Conciliation Bill. On 7 November, when Asquith announced that he intended to introduce a *Manhood* Suffrage Bill, to which, if tabled, a women's suffrage amendment might be voted on by the House of Commons, the suffragettes of the WSPU were furious. On the 17 November (when her mother was once more touring the United States of America), Christabel Pankhurst declared the 'truce' concluded and Elizabeth's fervent hopes for success via the constitutional route were, for the moment, dashed. She wrote to the editor of the WSPU periodical *Votes for Women* that the tabling of the Manhood Suffrage Bill offered 'the grossest possible insult to the womanhood of these islands'.[111] Mrs Pankhurst, writing from America, urged British women to 'civil war', but Elizabeth could not ultimately, for consciousness sake, follow the policies of extreme militancy that swept through the WSPU as a result.[112] Though she urged that suffragists be committed to the cause unto death, the argument of the arsonist would, and very shortly, reduce her own militant career to ashes.[113]

A letter in *Votes for Women* on 12 January 1912 reveals a prominent shift in Elizabeth's understanding of the adult suffrage demand, and helps put into perspective her increasingly complex relationship with the tactics of the WSPU. She wrote that, 'If manhood is to be the qualification for men, womanhood must be the qualification for women, and full Adult Suffrage must take the place of any limited franchise.'[114] The premise of adult suffrage, which she had hitherto advocated only as an ideal future principle, now found favour in her eyes. Her reasoning might well have been influenced by a resolution passed at the Labour Party Conference supporting the premise that only a suffrage measure explicitly including women would be acceptable. The vision of socialism she longed for, in which an acknowledgement of justice to women was clearly made, Elizabeth could now perceive in this move by the Labour Party; and by his voluble support for the measure, Philip Snowden confirmed her opinion of him as '*the orator*' of the Labour cause.[115]

Elizabeth's continuing support for the ILP after the resignation of Mrs Pankhurst and Christabel offers interesting considerations. The party, she noted, had 'been substantially true' to the women's cause and, quite used to maintaining a multiplicity of alliances, she saw no conflict of interest in preserving her links to both it and the WSPU.[116] Though there is no direct evidence to support the claim, the shift in her stance towards adult suffrage was complimentary to that of Margaret Bondfield (now working for the ILP) and Margaret Llewelyn Davies who, in 1909, had (with others) formed the People's Suffrage Federation (PSF). William Anderson, who had been so sceptical in his support for the women's vote in the *Labour Leader* in 1904, had also revised his stance and now, as chairman of the ILP, sat on the Executive of the Federation. Having built a strong parliamentary base of 110 MP's by 1911, the PSF pursued its goal of adult suffrage from the premise that this '"democratic measure of reform" . . . would enfranchise all men and women on the grounds of "common humanity"'. [117] This humanitarian outlook would certainly have appealed to Elizabeth who had worked all her life to unite women of all classes in a mass campaign for their freedom.

Other suffragists likewise followed innovatory routes, including those members of the NUWSS whom Elizabeth had criticised as 'laggards' in the cause. Equally disgusted by the final loss of the Conciliation Bill in April 1912 (for which every Labour MP had voted), the NUWSS joined in formal alliance with the socialists. While the union was not universally welcomed in the Labour camp, sufficient goodwill prevailed, and the Election Fighting Fund was established to aid Labour by-election nominees.[118] The fund financed four successful 'anti-Liberal' campaigns in 1912 and one of its most ardent workers was Elizabeth's Manchester ILP colleague, Annot Robinson.[119] Despite what might appear to be a sharp re-focusing of Elizabeth's political beliefs towards adult suffrage, events within the wider movement provided the context in which the changes occurred. She was, however, still a member of the entirely anti-party-political WSPU Executive, and she wrote encouraging messages to members through the columns of *Votes for Women* while Emmeline Pankhurst (following a trial for conspiracy in May 1912) paced her prison cell listening to the cries of her followers as they endured forcible feeding.[120] It was the events of 13 July, however, when suffragette Helen Craggs was found in the garden of government Minister Lewis Harcourt's home carrying incendiary devices in a capacious holdall, which cut the formal ties between Elizabeth and the WSPU, the organisation that had encapsulated her strongest hopes for dramatic success.

No record remains of Elizabeth's private communications with the WSPU leadership on the matter. Her public, and very condemnatory, testimony was published under the heading of 'Criminal Folly' in the columns of the *Manchester Guardian* on 18 July, in which she unequivocally condemned 'the madness which seems to have seized a few persons . . . whose anti-social and criminal actions would seem designed to wreck the whole [suffrage] movement'.[121] She also appended her signature (the only key former militant to do so) to a jointly authored letter decrying the WSPU for being 'more attached to their own methods than to the good of the cause, and as being in effect its worst enemies.'[122] The letter, entitled 'The Militant Outrages', was simultaneously published in *The Times* and the *Manchester Guardian* on 23 July, signed, among others, by Margaret Ashton, Sir Edward Grey, Ethel Annakin Snowden and Millicent Garrett Fawcett. The letter showed, by the political spectrum the names of the signatories represented, the extent to which the extreme militancy of some suffragettes had created a new element of cohesion among constitutional suffragists.[123] Public opinion, initially so sympathetically stirred by the actions of the fearless young women of the WSPU, had undergone a significant reversal. This was noted in the 'Militant Outrages' by the comment that

> Electors who are strongly in favour of extending the franchise to the other sex are shocked and disgusted. Instead of pressing their representatives to support the cause of the women they remain silent, while those who are against the measure become more insistent and determined in their opposition.[124]

How Elizabeth must have grieved before signing this controversial public statement that condemned the actions of some of her closest associates, and, by implication, Christabel Pankhurst, whom she loved deeply. Only her belief in the sanctity of life and opposition to anything that, even accidentally, would place any human being in mortal peril could have forced her hand. She severed the connection with the WSPU Executive immediately, and her subsequent actions were, in her own words, those of a 'non-militant'.[125]

Martin Pugh has supported the view expressed in 'Militant Outrages' by arguing that, owing to the tactics of extreme militancy, 'the WSPU . . . lost its grip on public opinion'.[126] Indeed, some of its own members castigated Christabel Pankhurst for insisting that militancy continue, even when her mother's life was under threat. In 1913, weakened and emaciated by continual hunger-striking, Emmeline endured humiliating journeys to and from prison under the terms of Home Secretary McKenna's Prisoners' Temporary Discharge Act (the 'Cat and Mouse' Act).[127] Mrs Pankhurst, however, showed equal resolve and her 'resolute determination not to pander to public opinion about the arson and bombing campaign' can be viewed either as a heroic stance or, less charitably, as a sign of a zealot's commitment to a failing endeavour.[128] The WSPU certainly lost members at this time, though possibly none were sadder at the turn events had taken than eighty-year-old Elizabeth.

Into the shadows

Her resignation from the WSPU Executive was not, however, the end of Elizabeth's public life. When the Manchester section of the NUWSS suffrage pilgrimage passed through Buglawton en route from Macclesfield to London in the summer of 1913 the 'veteran suffragist' led them for a short distance, mounted on her quiet pony, Vixen. A women's suffrage resolution was passed at the Market Street Fair Ground in Congleton to the accompaniment of wild cheers.[129] Some months previously, the town had honoured its 'venerable and respected' resident by reprinting in the local newspaper an interview she had given to the *Christian Commonwealth*, and her presence at the head of the pilgrimage had set the seal on her local popularity.[130] As one obituary would later confirm, her 'interest los[t] none of its keenness as the years advanced' and through the columns of the *Manchester Guardian* she voiced another protest on the suffering of imprisoned WSPU members under the 'Cat and Mouse'

Act.[131] While she did not condone the acts of extreme militancy that many had committed, neither did she excuse the torturing of prisoners by an obdurate government. Elizabeth also continued to advocate policies of civil disobedience, and of tax resistance as a method of passive protest and she was honoured at the end of January 1913 when she was invited by the Executive Committee of the Tax Resistance League (founded under the umbrella of the WFL in 1909) to become an honorary Vice-President of the organisation.[132] By such alliances she sought to continue her campaigning for the women's franchise along constitutional and humanitarian lines and always maintained the compassionate pacifist stance so central to her character. The small minute in the archives of the Tax Resistance League gives, however, the last evidence of her executive role in any women's emancipation group.

As Elizabeth's journalism and letters to the press diminished in subsequent years, her life fades from the pages of history. It can only be imagined, for example (in the light of the agonies she endured at the time of the Boer conflict) with what horror and despair she greeted the outbreak of the 'War to End All Wars' in August 1914. It must have been with some regret that she observed that the activities of the Tax Resistance League were wound up on the declaration of hostilities, although she would have welcomed the announcement by the WSPU that militant tactics would be abandoned for the course of the war. She would not, however, have advocated Emmeline and Christabel Pankhurst's patriotic plans for encouraging women to participate in war work to support government initiatives, although Mrs Pankhurst believed that by doing so, women would hasten their enfranchisement.[133] Such opinions could have only served to cement Elizabeth's distancing from her former WSPU friends, as her own internationalist, pacifist creed found only minority support amid the patriotic fervour that swept the nation. In addition, Elizabeth would have found herself out of step with Millicent Garrett Fawcett who adopted a policy of 'gentle patriotism'.[134] She would have been, once more, courageously treading a minority path.

One significant enigma regarding Elizabeth's later life centres on the breaking up of her archives; though eye-witnesses remembered documents being removed from the house in wheelbarrows during a community collection of waste paper in 1917.[135] By this time she was both physically and psychologically debilitated. Rheumatics and deafness plagued her, and, significantly, an increasing susceptibility to short-term memory loss. Her constant repetition of information in later letters attest to the onset of this distressing condition which most likely escalated. One late addition to her letter collection, from Frances Rowe to Mary McIlquham, indicates that the combination of all Elizabeth's infirmities had caused her, in her ninth decade, to 'practically give up her life'.[136] Frank Elmy had been a devoted carer, with Elizabeth, of his father during his final illness and it would be charitable to suggest that only the severest of circumstances would have forced him to pass to others the responsibility for his mother's care. Elizabeth's last days were, however, spent not at Buxton House but at a nursing home belonging to Miss Macneary and situated at 231 Upper Brook Street, Chorlton Upon Medlock, Manchester.

Precisely when the move was made, or the exact reason, is unknown. But it is likely that Elizabeth, had she been lucid and physically able, would have strongly protested at the destruction of her archives. She believed her labours to have had historic significance and had, for example, carefully selected collections from the 'hundreds' of letters from Josephine Butler and Lydia Becker as gifts to the NUWSS and WSPU, hoping they would be seen as both useful and valuable.[137] She had also forwarded the WEU and Guardianship of Infants archives for collation by the British Museum in 1900 to ensure their preservation for scholars. These depletions of her collection had been undertaken with care and forethought, and it seems unlikely that a seemingly disorganised removal of such vast quantities of artefacts could have been accomplished in her presence – especially if the collection was made as a contribution to the war effort, as Crawford suggests.[138] Thus it is likely that she had already taken up residence in Manchester.

Frank Elmy continued to live in Buglawton and to serve on its district council during the First World War, but his name is not among those elected to office, after the election of 1919.[139] At some time, however, he became a librarian and worked for the council until his death, from heart failure on 20 April 1927.[140] It appears he never married.

If she was suffering some form of debilitating illness it is impossible to know the extent to which Elizabeth was aware of the passage of the Representation of the People Bill through the Houses of Parliament in 1918. The provisions of the Bill (the principles of which had been negotiated at an all-party Speaker's Conference in January 1917) included full adult suffrage for all males aged over twenty-one, and for women over the age of thirty who were university graduates or voters on the local government register. The final impediment on the Bill's journey into law was removed when Lord Curzon, hitherto a firm anti-suffragist, advised those of his noble colleagues not in favour of the measure to abstain when it came before the House of Lords on 10 January. The vote was

134 in favour, 74 against and the Act received the Royal Assent the following month.

Upwards of eight million women were enfranchised. Even during the final negotiations to seek a successful formula on which to base the terms of women's enfranchisement, differences between suffragists remained.[141] Eventually, however, only Sylvia Pankhurst maintained an isolated stance, supporting (as the head of the East London Federation of Suffragettes) a position of full, equal, adult suffrage. Other societies, including a NUWSS now invigorated by increased support among working women, recognised the importance of, at least outwardly, maintaining a united position to clinch success – a success they marked with a joyous celebration at the Queen's Hall on Wednesday, 13 March 1918.[142] Sadly, Elizabeth was not on the platform to rejoice with her colleagues, for her long life had drawn to its close the previous day. Aged eighty-four, she had suffered multiple injuries after slipping down a flight of stairs at the end of February, and such was her physical frailty that she did not recover. Her obituary in the *Manchester Guardian* recorded that she had 'lived just long enough to hear the good news that the vote had been granted' to her sex.[143] How great her delight must have been, perhaps mirroring that of her erstwhile critic, Millicent Fawcett, who felt as if she were 'in a dream'.[144] Elizabeth would have been proud that, despite its restrictive provisions, the principle of women's right to participate in the 'making of parliaments' had, in her life's last hours, been accepted, and her long-held belief that the concession of the principle would lead, through later amendments, to a system of full equality, was correct. The Equal Franchise Act, which received the Royal Assent on 2 July 1928, gave women the vote on the same terms as men.

Departure

The perfect rest that Elizabeth had so often longed for when working on her correspondence in the small hours of the morning was now hers; and it can only be hoped for this ardent humanitarian that the transcendent knowledge of the human condition she had yearned for was finally revealed. The *Common Cause*, in its tribute published on 22 March, noted the simplicity and gracefulness of her funeral, conducted by Dr Edward Vipont Brown on the previous Saturday.[145] Her body had been carried into the chapel at Manchester Crematorium to the strains of Handel's 'He Shall Feed His Flock' and the congregation mourned in silence in accordance with the Quaker tradition. The form of service used linked

Elizabeth once more to her roots, to those long ago Quakers who had joined with a small, dissident group of Wesleyans to bring the creed of Independent Methodism to her ancestors in Roe Green. Her life had truly come full circle.

The short funeral oration was given by Manchester's first woman councillor, Margaret Ashton, long an associate and recently elected to the position of Vice-Chairman of the Women's International League, the British Section of the International Council of Women for Permanent Peace.[146] The pacifist thread that had formed such a key part of Elizabeth's life was ably represented in the persons of Ashton, Mrs G.G. Armstrong and Annot Robinson, all of whom attended as representatives of the Women's International League. The final minutes of the funeral were spent listening to a recitation of John Masefield's *By a Bierside*, read by Dr Vipont Brown. The lines were quoted in full in the *Common Cause* and deserve inclusion here as a true example of Elizabeth's yearning for the fuller knowledge that she believed was given to souls after their work on earth was over.

> This is a sacred city built of marvellous earth,
> Life was lived nobly here to give such beauty birth,
> Beauty was in this brain and in this eager hand,
> Death is so blind and dumb; Death does not understand.
> Death makes justice a dream, and strength a traveller's story,
> Death drives the lonely soul to wander under the sky,
> Death opens unknown doors. It is most grand to die.[147]

Although Dr Vipont Brown received no mention in Elizabeth's correspondence, he clearly appreciated her character. Masefield's lines captured exactly her desire to live nobly and to form 'sacred cities' on earth built on principles of justice and cooperation. Her love of nature and her spiritual questing are also summed up in the final lines. Life was indeed a 'traveller's story' for Elizabeth and she never faltered on her journey for the freedom of her sex. She did not live to rejoice at the conclusion of the First World War on 11 November 1918. However, it can surely be argued that the granting of women's suffrage would have brought this most ardent of campaigners a deep sense of peace as it seemed in the last hours of her earthly life that the greater war, the war of the sexes, would now end harmoniously. She would not live to see the battles yet to come as women sought to re-cast their lives in a new mould – the mould of the female citizen, whose rights and duties to their nation and to humanity were as those of men. She had died, as one might have wished, at a moment of triumph.

Notes

1 EWE/HM, 13/4/1904, 47453, fol. 268. These words were written to Wolstenholme Elmy in a letter from Josephine Butler.

2 EWE/HM, 6/6/1906, 47454, fol. 263.

3 EWE/HM, 3/7/1906, 47454, fol. 275. Anon., 'Manchester University: Degree Day', *Manchester Guardian*, 2 July 1906.

4 EWE/HM, 10/7/1906, 47454, fol. 281.

5 For Keir Hardie's assessment of the meeting see, 'Boggart Hole Clough Meeting: Mr. Keir Hardie's Views', *Manchester Guardian*, 17 July 1906; Pankhurst, *TSM*, pp. 136–41.

6 Anon., 'Boggart Hole Clough Meeting', *Manchester Guardian*, 16 July 1906.

7 Harry Kiddle to the Editor, *Manchester Guardian*, 21 July 1906.

8 EWE to the Editor, *Manchester Guardian*, 19 July 1906.

9 EWE/HM, 31/7/1906, 47454, fol. 285.

10 Christabel Pankhurst, *Unshackled: The Story of How we Won the Vote*, ed F.W. Pethick Lawrence (London: Hutchinson, 1959), pp. 68–9; Krista Cowman, '"Incipient Toryism"? The Women's Social and Political Union and the Independent Labour Party, 1903–1914', *History Workshop Journal*, Vol. 53, Spring 2002, pp. 129–48, pp. 137–8.

11 Cowman, 'Incipient Toryism', pp. 137–8.

12 EWE/HM, 3/9/1906, 47454, fol. 301.

13 Cowman, 'Incipient Toryism', p. 138; EWE/HM, 28/8/1906, 47454, fol. 299.

14 *Clarion*, 24 August 1906, quoted in Hannam and Hunt, *Socialist Women*, p. 121.

15 EWE/HM, 3/9/1906, 47454, fol. 301. (Emphasis in original.)

16 Cowman, 'Incipient Toryism', p. 138. (My emphasis.)

17 EWE/HM, 15/10/1906, 47454, fol. 319.

18 Purvis, *Emmeline Pankhurst*, p. 93.

19 EWE/HM, 5/4/1907, 47455, fol. 66.

20 Hunt, 'Journeying Through Suffrage', p. 171.

21 Wolstenholme Elmy's fund-raising ability is shown in a letter written in February 1907 where she notes that she had recently written fifty 'begging letters' on behalf of the WSPU. EWE/HM, 22/2/1907, 47455, fol. 57.

22 Anon., 'Notable Men and Women', *The Reformer's Year Book* (London, 1908), p. 232.

23 Hannam and Hunt, *Socialist Women*, p. 115.

24 EWE/HM, 19/8/1908, 47455, fol. 195.

25 Many items in Wolstenholme Elmy's private collection were passed to Sylvia Pankhurst to aid her in her production of *The Suffragette*, published in 1911, and the 'History of the Women's Suffrage Movement', published in the WSPU periodical *Votes for Women*. EWE to Sylvia Pankhurst, 11/10/1907, ESPP. EWE/HM, 8/7/1908, 47455, fol. 188. For a discussion of Pankhurst's stance see, John Mercer, 'Writing and re-writing Suffrage History: Sylvia Pankhurst's *The Suffragette*', *Women's History Magazine*, Vol. 56, Summer 2007, pp. 11–18.

26 Pankhurst, *TSM*, p. 221.

27 Paula Bartley, *Emmeline Pankhurst* (London and New York: Routledge, 2002), p. 90.

28 Purvis and Wright, 'Writing Suffragette History', p. 426; Editorial (Christabel Pankhurst), *Votes for Women*, October 1907, p. 6.

29 Purvis and Wright, 'Writing Suffragette History', pp. 416–18.

30 Pankhurst, *TSM* p. 216.
31 EWE to Sylvia Pankhurst, 11/10/1907, ESPP; EWE/HM, 10/9/1907, 47455, fol. 110.
32 Crawford, *WSM*, p. 55.
33 EWE/HM, 26/10/1908, 47455, fol. 212. (Emphasis in original.)
34 Hilary Frances, 'Dare to be Free! The Women's Freedom League and its Legacy', in June Purvis and Sandra Stanley Holton (eds), *Votes for Women* (London and New York: Routledge, 2000), chapter 8, p. 181.
35 EWE/HM, 31/10/1908, 47455, fol. 213.
36 Frances Rowe to Harriet McIlquham, 9/1/1907, Vol. 13/A, Autograph Letter Collection, WL.
37 Dora B. Montefiore, *The Woman's Calendar* (London: A.C. Fifield, 1906), pp. 19 and 28.
38 EWE/HM, 7/1/1907, 47454, fol. 195; Hunt, 'Journeying Through Suffrage',p. 169. (This letter, and fol. 192 dated 6 January, are misdated as 1906 in the BL correspondence. It is clear, however, that the events refer to 1907.)
39 EWE/HM, 6/1/1907, 47454, fol. 192.
40 EWE/HM, 7/1/1907, 47454, fol. 195.
41 EWE/HM, 11/7/1906, 47454, fol. 283. (Emphasis in original.)
42 EWE/HM, 10/5/1907, 47455, fol. 76; EWE/HM, 19/5/1904, 47453, fol. 283.
43 EWE/HM, 9/12/1905, 47454, fol. 177; EWE/HM, 19/5/1904, 47453, fol. 283; EWE/HM, 12/7/1905, 47454, fol. 127.
44 Hunt, 'Journeying Through Suffrage', p. 168.
45 Sandra Stanley Holton, 'Women and the Vote', in June Purvis (ed.), *Women's History: Britain, 1850–1945: An Introduction* (London and New York: Routledge, 1995), p. 291.
46 Hunt, 'Journeying Through Suffrage', pp. 170–1.
47 Hunt, 'Journeying Through Suffrage', p. 170.
48 Montefiore, *From a Victorian to a Modern*, p. 77.
49 EWE/HM, 10/5/1907, 47455, fol. 76.
50 Purvis, *Emmeline Pankhurst*, pp. 80–1; EWE/HM, 22/2/1907, 47455, fol. 57.
51 *Votes for Women*, 14 May 1905, p. 165, quoted in Bartley, *Emmeline Pankhurst*, p. 91.
52 EWE/HM, 30/1/1907, 47455, fol. 47.
53 EWE/HM, 3/11/1906, 47455, fol. 6.
54 EWE/HM, 2/11/1906, 47455, fol. 1.
55 Pauline Polkey, 'Reading History through Autobiography: Politically Active Women of late Nineteenth-century Britain and their Personal Narratives', *Women's History Review*, Vol. 9, No. 3, 2000, pp. 483–500, p. 484.
56 EWE/HM, 31/3/1908, 47455, fol. 164.
57 EWE/HM, 8/4/1908, 47455, fol. 166.
58 Roger Fulford, *Votes for Women* (London: Faber & Faber, 1958) p. 169.
59 EWE/HM, 29/4/1908, 47455, fol. 169.
60 Pankhurst, *Unshackled*, p. 86.
61 EWE/HM, 1/6/1908, 47455, fol. 178. The NUWSS had planned a demonstration for 13 June and the WSPU for 21 June. The days had been named 'Suffrage Saturday' and 'Suffrage Sunday' by the journalists of the *Manchester Guardian*.
62 EWE/HM, 26/6/1908, 47455, fol. 185.
63 Purvis, *Emmeline Pankhurst*, p. 109.
64 EWE/HM, 26/6/1908, 47455, fol. 186.

65 Mary Gawthorpe, 'Demonstrations in the Provinces', *Votes for Women*, 23 July 1908, pp. 331–3, p. 333. Elizabeth wrote to the Editor of *Votes for Women* that she was by no means the only Victorian suffragist who was still working for the cause, and that some were older than herself 'and therefore with far stronger claims' to the title of 'veteran'. EWE to the Editor, *Votes for Women*, December 1907, p. 35.

66 EWE/HM, 26/6/1908, 47455, fol. 186.

67 Purvis, *Emmeline Pankhurst*, p. 109.

68 The actions of New and Leigh indicate a challenge to the view that all WSPU members acted only on the 'autocratic' orders of Emmeline and Christabel Pankhurst. June Purvis, 'A "Pair of . . . Infernal Queens"? A Reassessment of the Dominant Representations of Emmeline and Christabel Pankhurst, First Wave Feminists in Edwardian Britain', *Women's History Review*, Vol. 5, No. 2, 1996, pp. 259–80, pp. 270–1.

69 EWE/HM, 1/7/1908, 47455, fol. 187.

70 Jill Liddington has shown a similar perspective to have been evident in the life of Quaker Isabella Ford. The pacifist Ford could not 'condone' window smashing 'however tempting it might seem'. Jill Liddington, *Rebel Girls: Their Fight for the Vote* (London: Virago, 2006), p. 214.

71 George Dangerfield, *The Strange Death of Liberal England* (Stanford: Stanford University Press, 1997), p. 133.

72 Brian Harrison, *Prudent Revolutionaries: Portraits of British Feminists between the Wars* (Oxford: Oxford University Press, 1987), chapter 1, esp. p. 46.

73 Harrison, *Prudent Revolutionaries*, p. 35; Purvis, *Emmeline Pankhurst*, pp. 139–40.

74 Sandra Stanley Holton, 'In "Sorrowful Wrath": Suffrage Militancy and the Romantic Feminism of Emmeline Pankhurst', in H.L. Smith (ed.), *British Feminism in the Twentieth Century* (Aldershot: Edward Elgar, 1990), quoted in Bartley, *Emmeline Pankhurst*, p. 80.

75 Bartley, *Emmeline Pankhurst*, p. 80.

76 EWE *et al.* to the Editor, 'The Militant Outrages', *Manchester Guardian*, 23 July 1912.

77 EWE, 'The Women's Movement', 29 April 1905, *Ethics*, pp. 133–4.

78 See for example, EWE/HM, 16/12/1908, 47455, fol. 210.

79 EWE/HM, 21/10/1909, 47455, fol. 278–279. (Emphasis in original.) Purvis, *Emmeline Pankhurst*, p. 137.

80 Lisa Tickner, *The Spectacle of Women: Imagery of the Suffrage Campaign, 1907–1914* (London: Chatto & Windus, 1987), pp. 58–9.

81 The Budget of 1909 introduced a 'super-tax' and taxes on 'unearned increment of land value' – both measures graphically designed to provoke Conservative opposition, especially from the hereditary Upper House. Fulford, *Votes for Women*, pp. 169–70.

82 EWE/HM, 17/9/1909, 47455, fol. 270. (Emphasis in original.)

83 Purvis, *Emmeline Pankhurst*, p. 133.

84 June Purvis, 'The Prison Experiences of the Suffragettes in Edwardian Britain', *Women's History Review*, Vol. 4, No. 1, 1995, pp. 103–33.

85 EWE/Editor, *Manchester Guardian*, 28 September 1909.

86 W.T. Stead, 'In Praise of the Suffragettes', *Review of Reviews*, October 1909, pp. 318–19.

87 EWE/HM, 17/3/1909, 47455, fol. 240.

88 The Liberals polled 275 seats to the Conservative 273.

89 Purvis, *Emmeline Pankhurst*, p. 143.

90 EWE/HM, 21/1/1910, 47455, fol. 292.

91 EWE/Mary McIlquham, 25/1/1910, 47455, fol. 293.

92 EWE/Mary McIlquham, 26/1/1910, 47455, fol. 299.

93 Louisa Martindale to Mary McIlquham, 28/1/1910, 47455, fol. 300.

94 'Public Testimonial to Mrs. Wolstenholme Elmy', *Votes for Women*, 19 August 1910, p. 762.

95 EWE/HM, 17/3/1909, 47455, fol. 240.

96 Full text and list of the Wolstenholme Elmy Testimonial, ESPP, Reel 18, fol. 135, pp. 1–3.

97 'Public Testimonial', ESPP, Reel 18, fol. 129.

98 W.T. Stead, 'Women's Suffrage', *Review of Reviews*, December 1910, p. 531.

99 Stead, 'Women's Suffrage', p. 531. See also, W.T. Stead, 'Suffragettes and the Police', *Review of Reviews*, March 1911, p. 277.

100 W.T. Stead, 'The Women's Demonstration', *Review of Reviews*, July 1910, p. 11; Stead, 'Suffragettes and the Police', p. 277.

101 EWE, 'The Militant Suffrage Movement and Mrs Billington-Grieg', *Manchester Guardian*, 26 January 1911; Purvis, *Emmeline Pankhurst*, p. 156.

102 EWE, 'The Policy for Women's Suffrage', *Manchester Guardian*, 14 March 1911.

103 Purvis, *Emmeline Pankhurst*, pp. 163–4.

104 W.T. Stead, 'Women's Suffrage in the Ascendant', *Review of Reviews*, July 1911, p. 18.

105 Stead, 'Women's Suffrage in the Ascendant', p. 18.

106 Tickner, *The Spectacle of Women*, p. 124.

107 *Votes for Women*, 23 June 1911, p. 625.

108 Stead, 'Women's Suffrage in the Ascendant', p. 18.

109 EWE/HM, 30/11/1893, 47450, fol. 75.

110 Wolstenholme Elmy Testimonial, ESPP, Reel 18, fol. 135, p. 1.

111 EWE/Editor, *Votes for Women*, 17 November 1911, p. 105.

112 Purvis, *Emmeline Pankhurst*, p. 174.

113 Purvis, *Emmeline Pankhurst*, p. 179; EWE/Editor, *Votes for Women*, 17 November 1911, p. 105.

114 EWE/Editor, *Votes for Women*, 12 January 1912, p. 235.

115 EWE/HM, 30/1/1906, 47454, fol. 206. (Emphasis in original.)

116 EWE/HM, 29/1/1907, 47454, fol. 45.

117 Hannam and Hunt, *Socialist Women*, pp. 122–4; Crawford, *WSM*, p. 553.

118 H.L. Smith, *The British Women's Suffrage Campaign, 1866–1928*, 2nd edn (Harlow: Pearson, 2007), chapter 5.

119 Crawford, *WSM*, p. 603.

120 EWE/Editor, *Votes for Women*, 21 June 1912, p. 624; Purvis, *Emmeline Pankhurst*, p. 188.

121 EWE/Editor, 'Criminal Folly', *Manchester Guardian*, 18 July 1912.

122 EWE *et al.* to the Editor, 'The Militant Outrages', *Manchester Guardian*, 23 July 1912.

123 Pugh, *March of the Women*, pp. 253–6.

124 EWE *et al* to the Editor, 'The Militant Outrages'.

125 Sylvia Pankhurst notes that Wolstenholme Elmy was a Executive Committee member up until 'the autumn of' 1912. Pankhurst, *The Suffragette Movement*; p. 266. EWE/Editor of the *Manchester Guardian*, reprinted in *Votes for Women*, 27 June 1913, p. 575.

126 Pugh, *March of the Women*, pp. 204–6.

127 The Prisoners' Temporary Discharge Act (or 'Cat and Mouse' Act) allowed for the release from prison of hunger-striking suffragettes on medical grounds. When they

had recovered sufficient strength they returned to custody to serve the rest of their sentence.

128 Purvis, *Emmeline Pankhurst*, p. 236.

129 Anon., 'Modern Pilgrims Progress', 12 July 1913, *Congleton Chronicle*; Crawford, *WSM*, p. 205.

130 Anon. 'Two Octogenarian Suffragists: Early Work of Mrs. Wolstenholme Elmy and Miss Emily Davies, LL.D', *Christian Commonwealth*, 29 January 1913, p. 318.

131 EWE/Editor of the *Manchester Guardian*, quoted in *Votes for Women*, 27 June 1913, p. 575.

132 Minutes of the Committee Meeting of the Tax Resistance League held on 29 January 1913. Tax Resistance League Papers, 2/WTR. WL.

133 June Purvis, 'The Pankhursts and the Great War', in Alison Fell and Ingrid Sharp (eds), *The Women's Movement in Wartime: International Perspectives 1914–1919* (Basingstoke: Palgrave, 2007).

134 Angela K. Smith, *Suffrage Discourse in Britain during the First World War* (Aldershot and Burlington: Ashgate, 2005), p. 52.

135 'Oxymel', 'The lady who wrote with both hands', *Congleton Chronicle*, 17 August 1984; Shanley, *Feminism, Marriage and the Law*, p. 177; Crawford, *WSM*, p. 205.

136 Frances Rowe to Mary McIlquham, 22/4/1913, 47455, fol. 313.

137 See, for instance, EWE/HM, 18/9/1906, 47453, fol. 312.

138 Crawford, *The Women's Suffrage Movement*, p. 205.

139 Anon., 'Buglawton Urban District Council', *Congleton Chronicle*, 12 April 1919.

140 Certified copy of death certificate 287, for the district of Sandbach, Chester, 1927.

141 Holton, *Suffrage Days*, pp. 225–6.

142 Rubinstein, *A Different World for Women*, p. 242.

143 Anon., 'Mrs. Wolstenholme Elmy', *Manchester Guardian*, 13 March 1918.

144 Millicent Garrett Fawcett to Helen Fraser, 28/2/1918, quoted in Rubinstein, *A Different World for Women*, p. 240.

145 Anon., 'Notice of the funeral of Elizabeth Wolstenholme Elmy', *Common Cause*, 22 March 1918, p. 655.

146 Women's International League (British Section of the International Committee of Women for Permanent Peace). First Yearly Report, October 1915–October 1916, p. 5.

147 John Masefield, *By a Bierside*, quoted in *Common Cause*, 22 March 1918, p. 655. Quoted with the permission of The Society of Authors as the Literary Representative of the Estate of John Masefield.

Conclusion

Women . . . will never know how much they owe to her

After Elizabeth's death the colleagues with whom she had shared the struggles of women's emancipation remained strangely silent. She received a meagre tally of obituaries: one, anonymously authored, appeared in the NUWSS journal, the *Common Cause* and another (also anonymous) in the *Manchester Guardian* – this reprinted in her local paper, the *Congleton Chronicle*.[1] The third and most detailed was authored by Sylvia Pankhurst and published in the socialist *Workers' Dreadnought* on 23 March 1918.[2] In her 1931 autobiography, Sylvia endeavoured to portray Elizabeth as a worthy and progressive activist, but also condemned her notoriety as a scandalous, 'free-love' secularist. Also, in her construction of a pathetic, 'Jenny-wren' figure, Pankhurst took care to subsume much of Elizabeth's drive and innovative political ideology; crediting those traits instead to her own parents, Emmeline and (chiefly) Richard. This is not the case, however, in the obituary. It is a flowing, deeply moving tribute, which asserts that

> When others faltered because the cause was unpopular and the goal seemed far away Mrs. Elmy remained constant and steadfast, and accomplished an immensity of work . . . Even in her extreme old age she rose during the small hours of the morning in order that all her housework and cooking for the day might be finished before nine a.m. in order that she might devote the rest of her time to toiling for the cause of women and progress . . . The women of to-day and to-morrow will never know how much they owe to her; but those of the younger generation who have been privileged to know her and work with her will not forget the inspiration which they derived from her selfless devotion to principle and keen, vigorous, and never-pausing industry in the cause.[3]

These words offer a very different interpretation of the woman who would later be named as a poor mother to her 'puny' son, and a wife whose husband delighted in psychological cruelty and unfaithfulness. It might be wondered, therefore, how the passage of a mere thirteen years could have brought about such a strange change of tone. One answer may lie in an exploration of events in which Elizabeth played no part (having taken place ten years after her death), but which, nonetheless, illustrate the prevalent attitudes to any woman who chose a conscious path towards unmarried maternity.

Sylvia Pankhurst was deeply hurt to have been excluded from the commemorations which attended the unveiling of a statue of her late mother in Victoria Tower Gardens on 6 March 1930 – the chief reason for the veto being a rift in mother–daughter relations, unhealed at the time of Emmeline's death. Mrs Pankhurst had been both embarrassed and angst-ridden by her middle daughter's pregnancy out of wedlock in 1928 and, in her outrage, had openly castigated Sylvia for following Eliza-beth Wolstenholme Elmy's example.[4] Sylvia's estrangement from Emme-line was deeply affecting. It coloured her judgement and caused her to write The Suffragette Movement with a bitter pen; blaming the mother who 'put the women's cause before family loyalty' for her own unhappi-ness.[5] The resulting psychological trauma also likely coloured Sylvia's attitude to Elizabeth (as the subject of her mother's unkind comparison), for neglectful parenthood was precisely the criticism she levelled at her. Put simply, she slated Elizabeth, as she likewise condemned Emmeline, for having placed feminism above family.

If, as June Purvis has shown, this was an erroneous judgement in Mrs Pankhurst's case, it was similarly a poor assessment of Elizabeth, who devoted hours of care and selfless nursing to Ben and constantly pondered and worried over the fate of her only son. The obituary itself negates any idea that Elizabeth was not as focused on her domestic life as on her public work, but the portrait of 'selfless devotion' it portrays is, later, played down. Pankhurst's image of the willing but browbeaten 'Jenny-wren', inserted in a book which would become the foundation for so many histories of the women's movement in the mid-twentieth century, bequeathed to Elizabeth a poor legacy. Clearly, as Dodd has argued, it is a simple fallacy to accept the reminiscences of The Suffragette Movement as an 'uncomplicated repository' of its author's thought.[6] In Elizabeth's case, she became, via its pages, just one name of the many whose histories were encapsulated in three or four paragraphs, each and every activist subservient to Sylvia's memories of her father Richard and of herself as 'heroine' of the WSPU.[7]

Most historians of the early twentieth century, though, appeared only too willing to consign Elizabeth, the outrageous utopian secularist, to the literary shadows. Thankfully, this has now changed and this biography contributes (as the most significant study of her life to date) to this revisionism. A key element in the 're-reading' of Elizabeth's character undertaken here is the exceptional cache of letters lodged by Mary McIlquham in the British Museum. Mary had made a conscious decision not to inform Christabel Pankhurst of the whereabouts of the letters in 1914, obviously fearful of the archive's disappearance or fragmentation.[8] There is just a hint that Elizabeth herself wished for their return around this time, but we must be grateful that McIlquham relied on a possible lapse of memory to hope that a request to copy the material be forgotten.[9] Frances Rowe considered the letters 'relics' to 'reverence' and that 'true sacredness' lay in the lines, often penned so late at night that Elizabeth could barely see for exhaustion. The correspondence tells, in Rowe's words, the narrative of 'perhaps the greatest struggle for liberty that has ever been' and, as such, the letters comprise 'a most precious bundle'.[10] Rowe's assessment is correct and if I own to having a regret at the end of this book it is that they deserve further scrutiny. For researching the minutiae of individual feminist campaigns they provide an unsurpassed resource, often too comprehensive for inclusion in a broad, biographical study. Their value to historians of feminism – its formation, shape, execution and philosophy – is considerable and worthy of further investigation.

In her group biography *Suffrage Days*, Holton writes that it is her intention to 'shake the kaleidoscope . . . [to bring] . . . different aspects of the historical pattern for the fore'. To contextualise her narrative of 'lesser known' suffragist lives Holton began with the 'quaint' figure of Elizabeth Wolstenholme Elmy.[11] Though this opened the world's eyes more fully to Elizabeth, to see in her portrait merely the 'quaintness' of the grey ringlets and the lined face is to miss one crucial essential: the fathomless wisdom of her dark, sensitive eyes. In their depths, even in old age, lies the unquenched sparkle of determination, which shaped a public career of over fifty years. Her feminism, which had been consciously acknowledged in 1850, had been moulded (and re-moulded) long before the term was a household word: and she owned it as being a part of her 'natural' make-up – a trait as inherent as breathing. Joining a group of women who each (though by a myriad of different routes and opinions) shared her discontent with the binds and shackles placed upon their lives by Victorian patriarchal society, she found an outlet for both her intellectual idealism and the practical talents of organisation, journalism and administration. Exceptional as her endeavours were, however, while her colleagues (among them Josephine Butler, Emily Davies and Anne Jemima Clough), became household names, hers remained in shadow: and this despite the fact that, from a perspective which privileged above all the drive for humanity's progression, she pushed forward a succession of high-profile legislation which changed all women's lives. When Emmeline Pankhurst determined to 'put women first' above party-political loyalty she was merely adhering to Elizabeth's earlier example but, unlike some of those who swelled the ranks of the WSPU, Wolstenholme Elmy was not a 'man-hater' but a reformer who understood that the road to women's progress (initially at least) had to be smoothed and paved by the male legislature.[12] She understood too that the cultivation of sympathetic public opinion was a key factor in forcing through legislative change and this, combined with her pacifist conviction, provided the elements which forced her into naming the extreme militancy of the suffragettes as a 'criminal folly'. The 'argument of the stone' was not, she believed, the golden path to the ballot box.[13]

To focus too exclusively on Elizabeth's part in the women's suffrage movement is, though, to gloss over her true character – that of the humanist philosopher, who believed the possession of a human soul should alone guarantee to its custodian the rights of respect, honour and freedom. From this premise she campaigned for that most sacred of human rights, the right of a woman to determine when (or if) to become a mother, so that every soul born should know itself conceived in the knowledge that its mother had welcomed her baby into the world. In perhaps the most innovative interpretation of the demand for citizenship ever made, she linked the issue of maternal consent directly to the acquisition and exercise of the parliamentary franchise: women's role as mothers of potential soldiers giving them a greater right to elect those who would send their sons to possible death than any rights possessed by the soldiers themselves. Elizabeth believed in sexual abstention and moral purity but, paradoxically, she dwelt significantly on the individual right of prostitutes to earn their living as they chose. She dwelt too on the dire economic and moral circumstances that made so many women's lives a living hell under the patriarchal system, and determined to effect an amendment. More than any other Victorian feminist she can be argued to have achieved a successful assault upon women's multiple subjection: for by initiating the campaigns which resulted in the passage of the Married Women's Property Acts of 1870 and 1882, and the Guardianship of Infants Act of 1886, and via her founding role in the North of England Council in the 1860s, she was the mainstay and motivator of significant social change. That her campaign to criminalise marital rape failed was the fault of an inherently patriarchal legislature which refused to remove the last bastion of its privilege, rather than any lack of endeavour on Elizabeth's part. That the rape of wives, the ultimate perhaps of the 'rights of man', remained legally sanctioned until 1991 shows the enormity of the task she faced. Nevertheless, in acknowledgement of her multiple and exhaustive labours, Congleton Borough Council erected a blue plaque on the red brickwork of Buxton House in 1997 – although the house had by then been divided into two dwellings. After over a century, the town's feminist prophet had found honour in her own locality.

Despite Elizabeth's 'extra-ordinary' contribution to the British women's movement she also led an 'ordinary' life in Congleton, and it is in the mundane trials and troubles surrounding her own family and those of her neighbours that she found much of the motivation for her struggles on the national and international stage. She was a wife, mother, a deeply caring friend and the employer of various domestic servants, snippets of whose pitiful lives she often chronicled.[14] As both the granddaughter and wife of industrialists who worked directly alongside their staff, she was intimately connected with those whose social class was below hers, and these connections prompted and encouraged her work as a social reformer and feminist. Knowing both prosperity and poverty as Ben Elmy's wife, she nevertheless remained devoted to him – even though she had never vowed to remain by his side 'for richer [or] poorer'. Her association with him, however, tainted her character in the eyes of many whose religious scruples shunned connections with those turned apostate, and this also helped fashion the reputation she acquired in the literature of the women's movement. Her desire to pen her autobiography, and indeed her willingness (even in the depths of her own bereavement) to write an obituary of her husband, showed all too clearly her belief that both had earned a right to a public reputation.

The obituary, entitled *Pioneers! O Pioneers!*, followed the conventional biographical principles of the day in that, in common with Josephine Butler's extensive narrative of the life of her clerical husband George, it seeks to narrate the public work of a 'man of experience and weight', an accolade not afforded to Ben by some of his acquaintance.[15] Ben's earlier biography of her likewise sought to amend a narrative poorly told, and to write boldly not only of Elizabeth's feminist and political commitments but of the secularism that prompted them. Both short biographies were a rallying call for internationalism but, in parallel with continuing experience, so often the voice of the pacifist-humanitarian goes unheeded in the clamour for status, position or national grandeur. The word 'utopia', which categorises the Elmys' harmonious, socialist worldview, can be as dismissive a label today as in the jingoistic *fin-de-siècle*.

Thus, at the end of this book, we have learned something more of Elizabeth's life-narrative, even though the essence of her 'self' will always remain, at the heart, her own. The documents that detail her life have been examined in the light of the knowledge that her 'self' (in common with her narration of it), was constantly 'made and re-made, read and re-read, constructed and de-constructed' and the best judgement that can be made is that much of her life was 'imagined backwards' through the often flawed faculty of an ageing memory.[16] It is, nevertheless, and as she acknowledged, a life of worth and historical value. We have also, against her specific wishes, undertaken an 'impudent intrusion' into the nature and circumstances of her private world – something she considered an irrelevance to biographers considering the character of the lives of those who make the nation's history. For modern authors, however, such an intrusion is essential, for it contextualises a subject and helps understanding of the multiple traits and emotional subjectivities which shape the actions that affect (by the working out of new philosophies and ideals) thousands, hundreds of thousands or even millions of lives distant from their own.

Elizabeth, whose intellect supplied 'the grey matter in the brains of the women's movement', did not, however, labour alone; and it is therefore possible to question whether she is better treated, as in other recent accounts, as one element of a composite narrative of nineteenth and early twentieth-century feminism rather than as the focus of a full-length biography. This book begs to suggest otherwise, for the individual biography can illuminate not only the exceptional qualities of its subject, but also their typicality – as they sought to overcome, albeit in diverse ways, the 'gendered nature' of the ordering of society.[17] In this way, the history of the changing 'self' of the individual becomes the history of changes in society. Elizabeth shared with many contemporaries a yearning to promote changes in the human condition, in how people lived and how they understood the world they inhabited. Her labours, however, were conducted from a perspective of an orphan needing to earn her own living and away from the comfortable circumstances of those 'household names' of Victorian feminism, whose paths, first to an education and then to public life, were smoothed by both wealth and impeccable political connections. She could be argued to be a go-between, someone who, as a provincial schoolmistress, had such a keen sense of history that it led her to chronicle and archive her work from the 1860s and to chart the interactions (and the tensions) between the diverse factions of the women's emancipation cause, particularly across the divide of social class.

Determined on her path of secularism, and fearless in the promotion of the most radical reforms (such as in her support for the Contagious Diseases Acts repeal campaign) she never shrank from confrontation; although she was often cut to the heart by the hostility of those who could not share in her vision of the world, defined by the true equality of the two halves of humanity – in work, in marriage and in citizenship. Elizabeth identified the most prized characteristics of the 'Insurgent Woman' as the ability to bring 'Hope, in the place of despair, truth in everything and justice everywhere.'[18] She had lived her long life according to this creed and her labours helped transform the political, social and economic situation of many thousands of women. Though one chief objective, the criminalisation of marital rape, remained unachieved in her lifetime, and though in many nations of the world women remain far from achieving emancipation, Elizabeth's brave example can be read (and applauded) by any who seek to eradicate human inequality.

Notes

1 Anon., 'Mrs. Wolstenholme Elmy', *Common Cause*, 22 March 1918; Anon., 'Mrs Wolstenholme Elmy', *Manchester Guardian*, Wednesday, 13 March 1918.

2 E. Sylvia Pankhurst, 'A Suffrage Pioneer', *The Workers' Dreadnought*, 23 March 1918.

3 Pankhurst, 'Suffrage Pioneer'.

4 Purvis, *Emmeline Pankhurst*, p. 358.

5 Purvis, *Emmeline Pankhurst*, p. 356.

6 Dodd, 'Introduction', p. 5.

7 Jane Marcus, 'Introduction' to her edited *Suffrage and the Pankhursts* (London: Routledge, 1967), pp. 5–6, quoted in Purvis and Wright, 'Autobiographical Narratives', p. 420.

8 Handwritten note from Mary McIlquham on a letter from Christabel Pankhurst, 8/6/1914, 47455, fol. 314.

9 Frances Rowe to Mary McIlquham, 14/2/1910, 47455, fol. 307.

10 Frances Rowe to Mary McIlquham, 22/4/1913, 47455, fol. 313.

11 Holton, *Suffrage Days*, pp. 1–2.

12 Purvis, *Emmeline Pankhurst*, p. 360.

13 EWE to the Editor, *Votes for Women*, 17 November 1911, p. 105.

14 EWE/HM, 26/11/1891, 47449, fol. 199.

15 Josephine Butler, *Recollections of George Butler* (Bristol and London: J.W. Arrowsmith, Simpkin, Marshall, Hamilton, Kent & Co. Ltd, 1892), p. 175.

16 Keith Jenkins, *Why History? Ethics and Postmodernity* (London: Routledge, 1999), p. 101.

17 Barbara Caine, 'Feminist Biography and Feminist History', *Women's History Review*, Vol. 3, No. 2, 1994, pp. 249 and 252.

18 'Song of the Insurgent Woman'.

New Year's Day 1900

War Against War in South Africa,
29 December 1899

Sad last year of a dying century,
That dawnest in the stress of storm and strife,
Of witless waste of sacred human life,
And the wild pomp of War's made revelry.
Dost thou but bring a message of despair?
Have heroes wrought, have martyrs died in vain?
Is there no healing for the deadly pain
Of Greed, and Lust, and Hate and sickening Care?
Not so, this fateful hour of Destiny
Calls each who seeks, and hopes, and strives for Good
To higher effort, to a loftier mood,
To nobler life; so may the holy Three,
Love, Truth and Justice, rule from shore to shore,
And Peace make glad this earth for evermore.

'*Ignota*' [*pseudonym of E.C. Wolstenholme Elmy*]

Cast of characters

Elizabeth Garrett Anderson (1836–1917). Daughter of Newson and Louisa Garrett. Licentiate of the Society of Apothecaries, 1865. Gained MD, Paris 1870. Member of the London School Board, 1870. Spoke in support of the Contagious Diseases Acts, 1869.

Margaret Ashton (1856–1937). Daughter of Thomas Ashton. Sister-in-law of James Bryce. Founder of North of England Women Guardians Society, 1880s. Chairman Lancashire and Cheshire Women's Liberal Federation, 1903. Elected as Manchester's first women councillor, 1908. Chairman of the North of England Society for Women's Suffrage 1906–15. Vice-Chairman of the Women's International League for Peace and Freedom, 1919.

Lydia E. Becker (1827–90). Secretary of the Manchester Society of Women's Suffrage from 1867. Founding editor of the Women's Suffrage Journal. Treasurer of the Married Women's Property Committee. Parliamentary agent for the Central Committee of the National Society for Women's Suffrage 1877. Secretary of the Executive Committee of the Central Committee from 1881.

Harriot Stanton Blatch (1856–1940). Daughter of Elizabeth Cady Stanton. Resided in England 1882–1902. Member of the Central National Society for Women's Suffrage. Resigned 1890 to join the Women's Franchise League. Resigned to join the Women's Emancipation Union in 1893. Executive Committee member of the Fabian Society c.1894. Organised lecture tours of United States of American by Emmeline Pankhurst in 1907, 1909 and 1913.

Jessie Boucherett (1825–1905). Daughter of Louisa Pigou and Ayscogne Boucherett. Founder of the Society for Promoting the Employment of Women, 1859. Member of Kensington Society. Drafted 1866 women's suffrage petition, together with Bodichon and Emily Davies, presented to Parliament by John Stuart Mill in 1866. Founding editor of *The Englishwoman's Review*, 1865.

Jacob Bright (1821–99). Radical-Liberal MP for Manchester, 1867–74, 1876–85 and for the southern division, Manchester, 1886–95. Brother of

John Bright and Priscilla Bright McLaren, wife of Duncan McLaren, Lord Provost of Edinburgh. Executive Committee member Manchester National Society for Women's Suffrage from 1867. Moved Women's Suffrage Bill, 1870. Member of the Married Women's Property Committee 1868–82. Member of the Council of the Women's Franchise League, 1890.

Ursula Bright (1835–1915). Daughter of Joseph Mellor and niece of Thomas Thomasson. Married Jacob Bright, 1855. Member of the Manchester National Society for Women's Suffrage, 1867. Founder member of the Executive Committee of the Central Committee of the National Society for Women's Suffrage, 1871. Founder members of the Ladies' National Association, 1870. Treasurer of the Married Women's Property Committee, 1874–82. Founder member (1889) and Honorary Secretary of the Women's Franchise League from 1890. President of the Lancashire and Cheshire Union of Women's Liberal Associations, 1890s.

James Bryce (1838–1922). Liberal MP 1880–1907. Member of the Cabinet 1886–1907. Created Viscount Bryce 1914. Member of Girton College, Cambridge, 1872–1922.

Josephine Butler (1828–1906). Born into the influential Grey family of Northumberland. Married George Butler January 1852, and settled in Oxford. Moved to Liverpool 1866, George Butler taking up the position of Head of Liverpool College. Colleague of Wolstenholme's on the North of England Council for Promoting the Higher Education of Women from 1867. Most noted for her work to repeal the Contagious Diseases Acts, 1869–86.

Richard Clarke (1784–1846). Son of handloom weaver Samuel Clarke of Sisley Cottage, Roe Green. Textile Manufacturer. Grandfather of Elizabeth Wolstenholme Elmy.

Anne Jemima Clough (1820–92). Provided written evidence to Taunton Commission. Paper 'The Hints on the Organisation of Girls' Schools,' published *Macmillan's Magazine*, October 1866. Honorary Secretary North of England Council for the Promoting of Higher Education of Women from 1867. Inaugural Headmistress, Newnham College, Cambridge, from 1870.

Frances Power Cobbe (1822–1904). Writer and social reformer. Born in Newbridge, County Dublin. Italian correspondent for the *London Daily*

News 1856. Worked with Mary Carpenter in the 'ragged' schools in Bristol. Co-founder of the London National Society for Women's Suffrage, July 1867, but resigned in October the same year. Dame of the Primrose League, 1880s. Co-founder of the Victoria Street Society for the Protection of Animals liable to Vivisection.

Stanton Coit (1857–1944). Born in Ohio, emigrated to England in 1888. Minister of South Place Chapel, taking over the role from Moncure D. Conway. Leader of the Ethicist movement in Britain. Member of the Women's Franchise League, 1890. Treasurer of the Men's League for Women's Suffrage, 1907. Subscriber to the Election Fighting Fund, 1912.

Isabella (Isa) Craig (1831–1903). Assistant Secretary to George Hastings of the Social Science Association, 1857. Committee member Ladies' Sanitary Association, 1859. Member of the Kensington Society, 1865. Signature to Women's Suffrage petition, 1866.

Emily Davies (1830–1921). Daughter of the Rev. John Davies. Editor of *Victoria Magazine*, 1864. Hon. Sec. of the Kensington Society, 1865. Co-organiser of the women's suffrage petition, 1866. Founder of Hitchin (later Girton) College, 1869. Executive Committee member National Union of Women's Suffrage Societies, 1897.

Benjamin J. Elmy (1838–1906). Husband of Elizabeth Wolstenholme Elmy. Businessman, poet and author. Member of the Northern Counties League for the Repeal of the Contagious Diseases Acts, 1870s. Council member of the Central Committee of the National Society for Women's Suffrage, 1873. President of the Congleton and Buglawton Progressive Club, 1875. General Council Member and past Vice-President of the National Secular Society, 1876. Master of the Congleton Lodge of the Fair Trade League, 1886. Founder of the Male Electors' League *c.* 1897.

Mary Estlin (*c.*1820–1902). Leader of the Bristol and Clifton Ladie's Anti-Slavery Society, 1851. Executive Committee member of the Ladies' London Emancipation Society, 1863. Committee member of the Bristol and West of England Women's Suffrage Society, 1868, and its Treasurer, 1870. Joint secretary of the Bristol Women's Liberal Association, 1890.

Millicent Garrett Fawcett (1847–1929). Daughter of Newson and Louisa Garrett. Married Henry Fawcett, 1867. Active in women's suffrage movement from that date. Honorary Secretary of the Central Committee of the National Society for Women's Suffrage, 1888. President of the National Union of Women's Suffrage Societies, 1897.

Russell Gurney (1804–78). Recorder of London, 1857–78. Conservative MP for Southampton 1865–78. Took charge of the Married Women's Property Bill in the House of Commons, 1870.

Louisa Martindale (1839–1914). Married 1871 and moved abroad. On return, settled in Lewes, Sussex. Active in Women's Liberal Federation from 1891. Member of the Women's Emancipation Union 1895. Vice-President of the Central Society for Women's Suffrage 1906.

John Stuart Mill (1806–73). Political economist and philosopher. Published *The Subjection of Women*, 1869. Husband of Harriet Taylor-Mill, author of *The Enfranchisement of Women*, 1851. Introduced women's suffrage amendment to the Conservative Reform Bill, 1866. Subscriber to the Married Women's Property Committee, 1868. Supporter of the London National Society for Women's Suffrage, 1867. Member of the Manchester National Society for Women's Suffrage, resigned 1868. Lost parliamentary seat 17 November 1868.

Florence Fenwick Miller (1854–1935). Elected as a Liberal to the Hackney Division of the London School Board, 1876. Member of the Vigilance Association for the Defence of Personal Rights, 1880s. Joined Women's Franchise League, 1889. Editor and proprietor of the *Woman's Signal*, 1895–99. Attended the World's Congress of Representative Women in Chicago, 1893. President of the Women Writers' Suffrage League, 1915.

Harriet McIlquham (1837–1910). Member of the Bristol and West of England Society for Women's Suffrage and the Manchester National Society for Women's Suffrage, 1870s. First married woman to be elected as Poor Law Guardian, 1881. President of the Women's Franchise League, 1889–90. Council member of the Women's Emancipation Union, 1891–99.

Dora Montefiore (1851–1934). Born in Surrey. Emigrated to Australia, where she founded the Womanhood Suffrage League of New South Wales in 1891. Returned to Europe in 1892. Member of the Theosophical Society 1892–1900. Executive Committee member of the Central National Society for Women's Suffrage, 1896. Executive Committee member of the Union of Practical Suffragists, founded 1896. Member of the

Hammersmith Trades and Labour Council, 1906. Member of the Women's Social and Political Union, 1904–7. Honorary Secretary of the Adult Suffrage Society 1909–12.

Roundell Palmer (Lord Selborne) (1812–95). Called to the Bar in 1837. Served as Solicitor General for England and Wales 1861–63. Attorney General for England and Wales, 1863–66. Lord Chancellor, 1872. Created Earl of Selbourne 1882.

Christabel Pankhurst (1880–1958). Eldest daughter of Richard and Emmeline Pankhurst. Executive Committee member of the North of England Society for Women's Suffrage, 1902. Awarded LLB degree 1906. Member of the Women's Social and Political Union, suffering first imprisonment in October 1905. Fled to Paris 1912. Stood as parliamentary candidate for Smethwick 1918.

Emmeline Pankhurst (1858–1928). Member of Married Women's Property Committee, 1882. Executive Committee Member of Women's Franchise League, 1889. Executive Committee member of the Manchester National Society for Women's Suffrage, 1893. Joined Independent Labour Party, September 1894, resigned 1907. Founder of the Women's Social and Political Union, 1903.

Richard Marsden Pankhurst (1835–98). Radical lawyer called to the Bar by Lincoln's Inn in 1867. Member of the Manchester National Society for Women's Suffrage 1867. Drafted the Women's Disabilities Removal Bill, 1870. Member of the Married Women's Property Committee 1868–82. Inaugural member of the Women's Franchise League, 1889. Joined Fabian Society, 1890. Joined Independent Labour Party, 1894, elected to its Executive 1895.

[Estelle] Sylvia Pankhurst (1882–1960). Second daughter of Richard and Emmeline Pankhurst. Manchester Municipal School of Art 1900–2. Inaugural member of the Women's Social and Political Union 1903, expelled 1914. Founder of the East London Federation of Suffragettes, 1912, Honorary General Secretary 1913–18.

Anna-Maria Priestman (1828–1914) **and Mary Priestman** (1830–1914). Quakers, born in Newcastle. Sisters-in-law of John Bright. Signatories to the women's suffrage petition, 1866. Anna-Maria subscribed to the Enfranchisement of Women Committee 1866–67. Anna-Maria member of Executive Committee of the Bristol and West of England Society for Women's Suffrage, 1870–1908. Anna-Maria founded, 1881, the first Women's Liberal Association in Bristol. Mary Priestman member of the Women's Liberal Federation in 1898. Anna-Maria Priestman founded and Mary Priestman was an Executive Committee member of the Union of Practical Suffragists, 1896. Subscribers to the Women's Social and Political Union, 1907.

Esther Roper (1868–1938). Daughter of the Rev. Edward and Mrs Annie Roper. First woman to attend the Victoria University, Manchester. Graduated 1891. Secretary of the Manchester Society for Women's Suffrage 1893. Executive Committee of the Central National Society for Women's Suffrage 1896. Executive Committee member NUWSS, 1899. Formed Lancashire and Cheshire Women Textile and Other Workers' Representation Committee, 1903.

Frances Rowe (c.1855–1940s). Daughter of Isaac Hoyle. Former pupil of Elizabeth Wolstenholme Elmy. Honorary Secretary Hammersmith Branch of the Women's Social and Political Union 1905. Member of the Fabian Women's Group 1909 and supporter of the Tax Resistance League.

Alice Cliff Scatcherd (1842–1906).Wife of Oliver Scatcherd, textile manufacturer of Morley, Leeds. Secretary of the Yorkshire Society for Women's Suffrage, 1873. Speaker against the Contagious Diseases Acts, 1873. Executive Committee member of the Manchester National Society for Women's Suffrage, 1876. Founder member of the Women's Franchise League, 1889.

Henry Sidgwick (1838–1900). Fellow of Trinity College, Cambridge, 1859–69. Knightbridge Professor of Moral Philosophy, 1883–1900. Founder of Newnham College, 1870.

Barbara Leigh Smith (later Bodichon) (1827–91). Daughter of Benjamin Leigh Smith and his common-law wife Anne Longden. Sponsor of Girton College. Founder member of Langham Place group. Co-founder of the Society for Promoting the Employment of Women. Co-organiser of the Women's Suffrage petition, 1866.

Caroline Holyoake Smith (c.1821 –?) Sister of George Holyoake. Member of the Birmingham National Society for Women's Suffrage, 1872. Member of the Women's Franchise League, 1889 and the Women's Emancipation Union, 1891.

William T. Stead (1849–1912). Newspaper editor and spiritualist. Editor *Northern Echo* 1871. First entered into correspondence with Wolstenholme during this year. Assistant Editor *Pall Mall Gazette*, 1880. Author of *The Maiden Tribute of Modern Babylon*, 1885. Editor *Review of Reviews*, 1890. Died aboard the Titanic, 1912.

Leslie Stephen (1832–1904). Author and critic. Father of Virginia Woolf and Vanessa Bell. Studied at Trinity Hall, Cambridge, graduated BA, 1854. Friend of Joseph Wolstenholme Jnr.

James Stuart (1843–1913). Fellow of Trinity College, Cambridge and Professor of Mechanism and Applied Mechanics, 1875. Lecturer for the North of England Council for the Promotion of the Higher Education of Women from 1867. Member of Parliament for Hackney, 1884. Alderman of the London County Council, 1890.

[Rosa] Frances Emily Swiney (1847–1922). Born in India and former pupil of Elizabeth Wolstenholme Elmy. Theosophist and author. President of the Cheltenham Women's Suffrage Society, 1903. Subscriber to the Women's Social and Political Union, 1907 and 1908. Founder and President of the League of Isis.

Clementia (Mentia) Taylor (1810–1908). Married Peter A. Taylor (later MP for Leicester) 1842. Committee member of the Society for Promoting the Employment of Women, 1865–70. Secretary of the London National Society for Women's Suffrage, 1867–71. Executive Committee member of the Central Committee of the National Society for Women's Suffrage, 1874. Treasurer of the Vigilance Association for the Defence of Personal Rights. Member of the Council of the Women's Franchise League, 1889.

Helen Taylor (1831–1907). Stepdaughter of John Stuart Mill. Member of the Manchester National Society for Women's Suffrage, but resigned in 1868. Maiden speech on women's suffrage, 26 March 1870. Elected to Southwark School Board, 1876.

Elizabeth Wolstenholme Elmy (1833–1918). Member of the College of Preceptors, 1862. Founder of the Manchester Board of Schoolmistresses, 1865. Inaugural member of the Manchester Committee for the Enfranchisement of Women, 1865, the Manchester National Society for Women's Suffrage, 1867, the North of England Council for the Promotion of Higher Education for Women, 1867, the Married Women's Property

Committee, 1868 and the Congleton Schoolmistresses Association, 1869. Executive Committee member of the Ladies National Association for the Repeal of the Contagious Diseases Acts 1870. Member of the Council of the National Association for the Repeal of the Contagious Diseases Acts 1870 and of its Executive, 1873. Member of the Central Committee of the National Society for Women's Suffrage, 1871. Secretary of the Campaign to Amend the Law in Points wherein it is Injurious to Women, 1871 and the Vigilance Association for the Defence of Personal Rights, 1871–74. Executive Committee member of the Vigilance Association for the Defence of Personal Rights 1877–90. Member of the Congleton Branch of the Fair Trade League, 1880s. Member of the Central National Society for Women's Suffrage 1888–89. Founder and Honorary Secretary of the Women's Franchise League, 1889 and the Women's Emancipation Union, 1891. Executive Committee Member of the Women's Social and Political Union (? 1903–12). Member of the Independent Labour Party, 1905. Vice-President of the Tax Resistance League, 1913.

Frank Wolstenholme Elmy (1875–1927) Son of Ben Elmy and Elizabeth Wolstenholme Elmy. Member of Buglawton Urban District Council, 1904–18 (?). Member of the Male Electors' League for Women's Suffrage.

Joseph Wolstenholme Snr. (c.1801–45). Son of a cloth weaver. Married Elizabeth Clarke c.1828. Father of Elizabeth Wolstenholme Elmy. Methodist Minister and warehouseman.

Joseph Wolstenholme Jnr. (1829–91). Son Joseph and Elizabeth Wolstenholme. Brother of Elizabeth Wolstenholme Elmy. Married Thérèse Krauss, 1869. Fellow of St John's and Christ's College Cambridge. Professor, the Royal Indian Engineering College, from 1871.

Select bibliography

All primary sources are fully referenced within the text, but main collections include:

BRITISH LIBRARY
Elizabeth Wolstenholme Elmy Papers, Add. Mss. 47449–55
Guardianship of Infants Act Papers
Women's Emancipation Union Papers

BISHOPSGATE INSTITUTE
Papers of the Vigilance Association for the Defence of Personal Rights

CAMBRIDGE UNIVERSITY LIBRARY
Reports of the Married Women's Property Committee

HULL UNIVERSITY LIBRARY
Haslam Papers

INSTITUTE OF SOCIAL HISTORY, AMSTERDAM
E. Sylvia Pankhurst Papers

GIRTON COLLEGE, CAMBRIDGE
Papers of Emily Davies
Records of the Kensington Society

LONDON SCHOOL OF ECONOMICS AND POLITICAL SCIENCE
Papers of John Stuart Mill and Harriet Taylor
Papers of the Independent Labour Party

MANCHESTER CENTRAL LIBRARY
Manchester Central ILP Minutes
Manchester Local Studies Collection
Manchester Women's Suffrage Collection, including the papers of Lydia Becker

NEWNHAM COLLEGE, CAMBRIDGE
Papers of Anne Jemima Clough

NORTH WESTERN UNIVERSITY OF ILLINOIS
Minute book of the Executive Committee of the Women's Franchise League

WOMEN'S LIBRARY, LONDON METROPOLITAN UNIVERSITY
Josephine Butler Collection
Papers of Harriet McIlquham
Papers of the North of England Council
Papers of the Manchester Schoolmistresses Association
Papers of the Tax Resistance League
Women's Suffrage Collection, Autograph Letter Collection

Newspapers and periodicals

Bristol Times and Mirror
Christian Commonwealth
Common Cause
Congleton Chronicle
Daily Sketch
Daily Mirror
Daily Paper
Englishwoman's Review
Ethical World
Fair Trade Journal
Herald of Peace
Illustrated London News
International Journal of Ethics
Journal of the Vigilance Association for the Defence of Personal Rights
Justice
Macclesfield Courier
Manchester Guardian
National Reformer
Personal Rights Journal
Revue Internationale du Movement Feminine
Review of Reviews
Reynolds Newspaper
Saturday Review
Shafts
The Dawn
The Shield
The Times
The Woman's Herald
Transactions of the National Association for the Promotion of Social Science
Votes for Women
War Against War in South Africa
Women's Penny Paper
Women's Suffrage Journal
Workers' Dreadnought

Parliamentary papers

British Parliamentary Papers (Vols II and III), Education General 18. Schools Inquiry Commission. Miscellaneous Papers and Answers to Questions 1867–1868 (Shannon: Irish University Press, 1970).

British Parliamentary Papers, Schools Inquiry Commission, 1867–1868. Education General 20.

British Parliamentary Papers, Report from the Select Committee on the Factory and Workshop Acts, Industrial Revolution, Factories 5, Vol. XXX (Shannon: Irish University Press, 1968).

Books and articles pre 1918

A Perplexed Mother [Elizabeth Wolstenholme Elmy], 'The Medical Profession and the Public', reprinted from *The Manchester Examiner and Times*, 25 January 1882.

Anon. [Elizabeth Wolstenholme Elmy and Rosamond Hervey], *Infant Mortality: Its Causes and Remedies* (Manchester: A. Ireland & Co., 1871).

Anon. [Elizabeth Wolstenholme Elmy], *Report of the Married Women's Property Committee: Presented at the Final Meeting of their Friends and Subscribers* (Manchester, 1882).

Anon. [Elizabeth Wolstenholme Elmy], *The Infants' Act, 1886: The record of three years' effort for Legislative Reform, with its results* (London: Women's Printing Society, c.1888).

Anon., *Proceedings at the Inaugural Meeting of the Women's Franchise League*, 25 July 1889 (London: The Hansard Publishing Union Ltd, c.1889).

Anon., *On the Programme of the Women's Franchise League*, An address given by Mrs Florence Fenwick Miller at the National Liberal Club, 25 February 1890.

Anon., 'Notable Men and Women', *The Reformer's Year Book 1908* (London, 1908).

Besant, Annie, *Marriage, As It Was, As It Is, and As It Should Be: A Plea for Reform*, 2nd edn (London: Freethought Publishing Company, 1882).

Blackburn, Helen, *Women's Suffrage: A Record of the Women's Suffrage Movement in the British Isles* (London and Oxford: Williams & Norgate, 1902).

Brimelow, William, *Centenary Memorials of the Independent Methodist Church at Roe Green, Worsley* (Warrington and London: Mackie & Co. Ltd, 1908).

Butler, Josephine, 'Introduction', in Josephine Butler (ed.), *Woman's Work and Woman's Culture* (London: Macmillan & Co., 1869).

Caird, Mona, 'Marriage', *Westminster Review*, Vol. 130, No. 2, 1888, pp. 186–201.

Elmy, Ben, 'The Individuality of Woman: From a Masculine Point of View', *Westminster Review*, November 1902, pp. 506–14.

Ethelmer, Ellis [pseudonym of Benjamin Elmy], *Woman Free* (Congleton: Women's Emancipation Union, 1893).

Ethelmer, Ellis, *The Human Flower* (Congleton, 1894).

Ethelmer, Ellis, *Baby Buds* (Congleton, 1895).

Ethelmer, Ellis, 'A Woman Emancipator: A Biographical Sketch', *Westminster Review*, Vol. CXLV, 1896; pp. 424–8.

Ethelmer, Ellis, *Life to Woman* (Congleton, 1896).

Ethelmer, Ellis, *Phases of Love: As it Was, As it Is, As it may Be* (Congleton: 1897).

Gawthorpe, Mary, 'Demonstrations in the Provinces', *Votes for Women*, 23 July 1908, pp. 331–3.

Hill, Ethel, and Olga Fenton Shafter (eds), *Great Suffragists and Why: Modern Makers of Future History* (London: Henry J. Drane, 1909).

Ignota [pseudonym of Elizabeth Wolstenholme Elmy], *Women's Suffrage*, reprinted from the *Westminster Review* (Normansfield Press, *c.*1897).

Ignota, 'The Part of Women in Local Administration', Parts 1–IV, *Westminster Review*, July 1898, pp. 32–46; September 1898, pp. 246–60; October 1898, pp. 377–89; February 1899, pp. 159–71.

Ignota, 'Judicial Sex Bias', *Westminster Review*, March 1898, pp. 279–88.

Ignota, 'The Awakening of Woman', *Westminster Review*, July 1899, pp. 69–72.

Ignota, 'Republics versus Woman', *Westminster Review*, June 1903, pp. 643–51.

Ignota, 'The Grand Old Woman of To-day', *Westminster Review*, March 1904, pp. 321–6.

Ignota, 'The Present Legal Position of Women in the UK', *Westminster Review*, May 1905, pp. 513–29.

Ignota, 'The Enfranchisement of Women', *Westminster Review*, July 1905, pp. 21–5.

Ignota, 'Pioneers! O Pioneers!', *Westminster Review*, April 1906, pp. 415–17.

Ignota, 'Russia and the United Kingdom', Parts I and II, *Westminster Review*, August 1906, pp. 164–8 and September 1906, pp. 284–93.

Ignota, 'The Case for the Immediate Enfranchisement of the Women of the United Kingdom', *Westminster Review*, November 1906, pp. 508–21.

Maitland, Frederic W., *The Life and Letters of Leslie Stephen* (London: Duckworth & Co., 1906).

Mill, John Stuart, *The Subjection of Women*, ed. Stanton Coit (Longmans, Green & Co., 1906).

Montefiore, Dora, *The Woman's Calendar* (London: A.C. Fifield, 1906).

Pankhurst, E. Sylvia, *The Suffragette: The History of the Women's Militant Suffrage Movement 1905–1910* (New York: Sturgis & Walton, 1911).

Peile, John, *Biographical Register of Christ's College 1505–1905* (Cambridge University Press, 1913).

Pethick Lawrence, Frederick and Joseph Edwards (eds), *The Reformers Year Book 1908* (Brighton: Harvester, 1972).

Stead, William T., *In Our Midst: The Letters of Callicrates to Dione, Queen of the Xanthians, concerning England and the English, Anno Domini 1902* (London: William Clowes and Sons, 1903).

Stead, William T., 'In Praise of the Suffragettes', *Review of Reviews*, October 1909, pp. 318–19.

Stead, William T., 'The Women's Demonstration', *Review of Reviews*, July 1910, p. 11.

Stead, William T., 'Suffragettes and the Police', *Review of Reviews*, March 1911, p. 277.

Stead, William T., 'Honour to Whom Honour is Due', *Review of Reviews*, September 1910, p. 223.

Stead, William T., 'Women's Suffrage', *Review of Reviews*, December 1910, p. 531.

Stead, William T., 'Suffragettes and the Police', *Review of Reviews*, March 1911, p. 277.

Stead, William T., 'Women's Suffrage in the Ascendant', *Review of Reviews*, July 1911, p. 18.

Taylor, Harriet, 'The Enfranchisement of Women', *Westminster Review*, July 1851, pp. 289–311.

To-Sko, Luisa, *The Cause of Woman*, translated by Ben Elmy (London: Free-thought Publishing Company, 1877).

Wilkins, W.H. *The Bitter Cry of the Voteless Toilers* (Women's Emancipation Union, 1893).

Wolstenholme, Elizabeth, 'What Better Provision Ought to be Made for the Education of Girls of the Upper and Middle-Classes?', *Transactions of the National Association for the Promotion of Social Science*, 1865, pp. 287–91.

Wolstenholme, Elizabeth, 'The Education of Girls, Its Present and Its Future', in Josephine Butler (ed.), *Woman's Work and Woman's Culture* (London: Macmillan & Co., 1869).

Wolstenholme Elmy, Elizabeth, *The Criminal Code in its Relation to Women* (Manchester: A. Ireland & Co., 1880).

Wolstenholme Elmy, Elizabeth (ed.), *Opinions of the Press on the Law Relating to the Custody and Guardianship of Children and on the Infants Bill, 1884* (Manchester: A. Ireland & Co., 1884).

Wolstenholme Elmy, Elizabeth, 'The Parliamentary Franchise for Women: To the Editor of *The Times*', 24 May 1884, reprinted in Jane Lewis (ed.), *Before the Vote was Won: Arguments for and Against Women's Suffrage* (New York and London: Routledge & Kegan Paul, 1987), pp. 404–8.

Wolstenholme Elmy, Elizabeth, 'The Emancipation of Women', reprinted from the *Cambrian News*, 2 October 1885.

Wolstenholme Elmy, Elizabeth, 'A Woman's Plea to Women', *Macclesfield Courier*, 20 November 1886.

Wolstenholme Elmy, Elizabeth, *Foreign Investments and British Industry* (London: Wyman and Son, 1888).

Wolstenholme Elmy, Elizabeth, *The Decision in the Clitheroe Case, and its Consequences: A Series of Five Letters reprinted from the Manchester Guardian* (Manchester: Guardian Printing Works, 1891).

Wolstenholme Elmy, Elizabeth, *The Enfranchisement of Women* (Women's Emancipation Union, 1892).

Wolstenholme Elmy, Elizabeth, and John P. Thomasson, *Replies to Mr. Samuel Smith M.P. on Women's Suffrage* (Manchester: Guardian Printing Works, 1892).

Wolstenholme Elmy, Elizabeth, *Women and the Law* (Women's Emancipation Union, 1895).

Wolstenholme Elmy, Elizabeth, 'Women Suffragists and the Lash', *Humanity* (London: Bonner, 1899).

Wolstenholme Elmy, Elizabeth, 'The Marriage Law of England', in *Women in Industrial Life: The Transactions of the Industrial and Legislative Section of The International Congress of Women* (London, 1899), pp. 115–19.

Wolstenholme Elmy, Elizabeth, *Woman's Franchise: The Need of the Hour*, 2nd edn (London: Independent Labour Party, *c*.1907).

Autobiographies and biographies

Abrams, Fran, *Freedom's Cause: Lives of the Suffragettes* (London: Profile, 2003).

Bartley, Paula, *Emmeline Pankhurst* (London and New York: Routledge, 2002).

Beecher, Jonathan, *Charles Fourier: The Visionary and His World* (Berkeley, Los Angeles and London: University of California Press, 1986).

Bennett, Daphne, *Emily Davies and the Liberation of Women* (London: André Deutsch, 1990).

Besant, Annie, *An Autobiography*, 2nd edn (London: T. Fisher Unwin, 1893).

Bonner, Hypatia Bradlaugh, *Charles Bradlaugh*, Vol. II (London and Leipzig T. Fisher Unwin, 1908).

Butler, Josephine E., *Recollections of George Butler* (Bristol and London: J.W. Arrowsmith, Simpkin, Marshall, Hamilton, Kent & Co. Ltd, 1892).

Butler, Josephine E., *Personal Reminiscences of a Great Crusade* (London: Horace Marshall & Son, 1896).

Caine, Barbara, *Victorian Feminists* (Oxford and New York: Oxford University Press, 1992).

Clough, Blanche A., *A Memoir of Anne Jemima Clough* (London and New York: Edward Arnold, 1897).

Fawcett, Millicent Garrett and E.M. Turner, *Josephine Butler: Her Work and Principles and their Meaning for the Twentieth Century* (London: Association for Moral and Social Hygiene, 1927).

Hannam, June, *Isabella Ford* (Oxford and New York: Basil Blackwell, 1989).

Hirsch, Pam, *Barbara Leigh Smith Bodichon: Feminist, Artist and Rebel* (London: Pimlico, 1999).

Jordan, Jane, *Josephine Butler* (London: John Murray, 2001).

Lewis, Gifford, *Eva Gore Booth and Esther Roper: A Biography* (London: Pandora, 1988).

Martindale, Hilda, *From One Generation to Another, 1839–1944* (London: George Allen & Unwin, 1944).

Montefiore, Dora B., *From a Victorian to a Modern* (London: E. Archer, 1927).

Morley, Ann, with Liz Stanley, *The Life and Death of Emily Wilding Davison* (London: The Women's Press, 1988).

Murphy, Ann B., and Deirdre Raftery (eds), *Emily Davies: Collected Letters 1861–1875* (Charlottesville and London: University of Virginia Press, 2004), pp. 152–3.

Pankhurst, Christabel, *Unshackled: The Story of How we Won the Vote*, ed. F.W. Pethick Lawrence (London: Hutchinson, 1959).

Pankhurst, Emmeline, *My Own Story* (London: Eveleigh Nash, 1914).

Pankhurst, E. Sylvia, *The Suffragette Movement: An Intimate Account of Persons and Ideals* (London: Virago, 1978).

Phipps, William E., *Darwin's Religious Odyssey* (Harrisburg: Trinity Press, 2002).

Purvis, June, *Emmeline Pankhurst* (London and New York: Routledge, 2002).

Quinlan, Carmel, *Genteel Revolutionaries: Anna and Thomas Haslam and the Irish Women's Movement* (Cork: Cork University Press, 2004).

Romero, Patricia W., *E. Sylvia Pankhurst: Portrait of a Radical* (New Haven and London: Yale University Press, 1990).

Rubinstein, David, *A Different World for Women: The Life of Millicent Garrett Fawcett* (Columbus: Ohio State University Press, 1991).

Sidgwick, Arthur and Eleanor M. Sidgwick, *Henry Sidgwick: A Memoir* (London: Macmillan & Co., 1906).

Stanley Liz, with Ann Morley, *The Life and Death of Emily Wilding Davison* (London: The Women's Press, 1988).

Stanton, Elizabeth Cady, *Eighty Years and More* (London: T. Fisher Unwin, 1898).

Stead, William T., *Josephine Butler: A Life Sketch* (London: Morgan and Scott, 1887).

Stephen, Barbara, *Emily Davies and Girton College* (London: Constable & Co., 1927).

Strachey, Ray, *Millicent Garrett Fawcett* (London: John Murray, 1931).

Stuart, James, *Reminiscences* (London, New York, Toronto and Melbourne: Cassell and Co. Ltd, 1912).

Sutherland, Gillian, *Faith, Duty and the Power of Mind: the Cloughs and their Circle 1820–1960* (Cambridge: Cambridge University Press, 2006).

Todd, Janet, *Mary Wollstonecraft: A Revolutionary Life* (London: Weidenfeld & Nicolson, 2000), pp. 76–8.

Van Arsdel, Rosemary, *Florence Fenwick Miller: Victorian Feminist, Journalist and Educator* (Aldershot and Burlington: Ashgate, 2001).

Williamson, Lori, *Frances Power Cobbe and Victorian Society* (London, New York and Sydney: Rivers Oram, 2005).

Books and articles published after 1918

Alderman, Geoffrey and Colin Holmes, 'The Burton Book', *Journal of the Royal Asiatic Society*, 2008, 18, pp. 1–13.

Allen, Judith A, *The Feminism of Charlotte Perkins Gilman: Sexualities, Histories, Progressivism* (Chicago and London: University of Chicago Press, 2009).

Banks, Olive, *Faces of Feminism* (Oxford and New York: Basil Blackwell, 1981).

Banks, Olive, *The Biographical Dictionary of British Feminists* (Brighton: Wheatsheaf, 1985).

Banks, Olive, *Becoming a Feminist: The Social Origins of 'First Wave' Feminism* (Athens: University of Georgia Press, 1986).

Bartley, Paula, *Prostitution: Prevention and Reform in England 1860–1914* (London and New York: Routledge, 2000).

Beales, Derek E.D., T.C.W. Blanning and David Cannadine (eds), *History and Biography: Essays in Honour of Derek Beales* (Cambridge: Cambridge University Press, 1996).

Bell, Alan (ed.), *Sir Leslie Stephen's Mausoleum Book* (Oxford: Clarendon Press, 1977).

De Bellaigue, Christina, 'The Development of Teaching as a Profession for Women before 1870', *The Historical Journal*, Vol. 44, No. 4, 2001, pp. 963–88.

De Bellaigue, Christina, *Educating Women: Schooling and Identity in England and France, 1800–1867* (Oxford: Oxford and New York, 2007).

Bland, Lucy, *Banishing the Beast: English Feminism and Sexual Morality 1885–1914* (London: Penguin, 1995).

Brown, Heloise, *'The Truest Form of Patriotism: Pacifist Feminism in Britain, 1870–1902* (Manchester and New York: Manchester University Press, 2003).

Burton, Antoinette, *Burdens of History: British Feminists, Indian Women and Imperial Culture, 1865–1915* (Chapel Hill and London: The University of North Carolina Press, 1994).

Burton, Antoinette, 'Josephine Butler on slavery, citizenship and the Boer War', in Ian Christopher Fletcher, Laura E. Nym Mayhall and Philippa Levine (eds), *Women's Suffrage in the British Empire: Citizenship, nation and race* (London and New York: Routledge, 2000), pp. 18–32.

Caine, Barbara, 'John Stuart Mill and the English Women's Movement', *Historical Studies*, Vol. 18, 1978, pp. 52–67.

Caine, Barbara, 'Feminist Biography and Feminist History', *Women's History Review*, Vol. 3, No. 2, 1994, pp. 247–61.

Caine, Barbara, *English Feminism 1780–1980* (Oxford: Oxford University Press, 1997).

Caine, Barbara, 'A Feminist Family: the Stracheys and Feminism, c.1860–1950', *Women's History Review*, Vol. 13, Nos 3 & 4, 2005, pp. 385–404.

Collini, Stefan, *Public Moralists: Political Thought and Intellectual Life in Britain 1850–1930* (Oxford: Clarendon Press, 1991).

Cowman, Krista, '"Incipient Toryism"? The Women's Social and Political Union and the Independent Labour Party, 1903–1914', *History Workshop Journal*, Vol. 53, 2002, pp. 129–48.

Cowman, Krista, *Women of the Right Spirit: Paid Organisers of the Women's Social and Political Union (WSPU) 1904–18* (Manchester and New York: Manchester University Press, 2007).

Crawford, Elizabeth, *The Women's Suffrage Movement: a Reference Guide, 1866–1928* (Manchester and New York: Manchester University Press, 2001).

Dangerfield, George, *The Strange Death of Liberal England* (Stanford: Stanford University Press, 1997).

Davidoff, Leonore, Megan Doolittle, Janet Fink and Katherine Holden, *The Family Story: Blood, Contract and Intimacy, 1830–1960* (London and New York: Longman, 1999).

Delamont, Sara, 'The Contradictions in Ladies' Education', in Sara Delamont and Lorna Duffin (eds), *The Nineteenth-Century Woman: Her Cultural and Physical World* (London: Croom Helm, 1978), pp. 134–63.

Delap, Lucy, *The Feminist Avant-Garde: Transatlantic Encounters of the Early Twentieth Century* (Cambridge: Cambridge University Press, 2007).

Dixon, Joy, *Divine Feminine: Theosophy and Feminism in England* (Baltimore and London: The Johns Hopkins University Press, 2001), chapter 7.

Dodd, Kathryn, 'Introduction', in Kathryn Dodd (ed.), *A Sylvia Pankhurst Reader* (Manchester: Manchester University Press, 1993).

Fleishmann, Avron, *Figures of Autobiography: The Language of Self-Writing in Victorian and Modern England* (London: University of California Press, 1983).

Fordham, E.O., *The Duty of Woman: Towards Humanity and our Country: Towards Our Family: Towards Ourselves*, (Women's Emancipation Union, 1894).

Frances, Hilary, 'Dare to be Free! The Women's Freedom League and its legacy', in June Purvis and Sandra Stanley Holton (eds), *Votes for Women* (London and New York: Routledge, 2000).

Frost, Ginger, 'A Shock to Marriage?: The Clitheroe Case and the Victorians', in George Robb (ed.) *Disorder in the Court: Trials and Sexual Conflict at the Turn of the Century* (New York: Palgrave, 1999), pp. 100–18.

Fulford, Roger, *Votes for Women* (London: Faber & Faber, 1958).

Garton, Stephen, *Histories of Sexuality: Antiquity to Sexual Revolution* (London: Equinox, 2004).

Gates, Barbara T., *Kindred Nature: Victorian and Edwardian Women Embrace the Living World* (Chicago and London: University of Chicago Press, 1998).

Gleadle, Kathryn, *British Women in the Nineteenth Century* (Basingstoke: Palgrave, 2001).

Gleadle, Kathryn, *Radical Writing on Women, 1800–1850* (Basingstoke: Palgrave, 2002).

Goldman, Lawrence, *Science, Reform and Politics in Victorian Britain: The Social Science Association, 1857–1886* (Cambridge: Cambridge University Press, 2002).

Green, Euan, *The Crisis of Conservatism: The Politics, Economics and Ideology of the British Conservative Party 1880–1914* (London and New York: Routledge, 1996).

Griffin, Ben, 'Class, Gender and Liberalism in Parliament, 1868–1882: The Case of the Married Women's Property Acts', *The Historical Journal*, Vol. 46, No. 1, 2003, pp. 59–87.

Gutzke, David W. (ed.), *Britain and Transnational Progressivism* (Basingstoke: Palgrave Macmillan, 2008).

Hall, Catherine, 'The Early Formation of Victorian Domestic Ideology', in S. Burman (ed.), *Fit Work for Women* (London: Croom Helm, 1979), 15–32.

Hall, Lesley A., 'Suffrage, Sex and Science', in Maroula Joannou and June Purvis (eds), *The Women's Suffrage Movement: New Feminist Perspectives* (Manchester and New York: Manchester University Press, 1998), pp, 188–200.

Hall, Lesley A., *Outspoken Women: An Anthology of Women's Writing on Sex, 1870–1969* (London and New York: Routledge, 2005).

Hannam, June, with Mitzi Auchterlonie and Katherine Holden (eds), *International Encyclopedia of Women's Suffrage* (Santa Barbara: ABC-Clio, 2000).

Hannam, June, and Karen Hunt, *Socialist Women: Britain, 18802–1920s* (London and New York: Routledge, 2001).

Harrison, Brian, *Separate Spheres: The Opposition to Women's Suffrage in Britain* (London: Croom Helm, 1978).

Harrison, Brian, *Prudent Revolutionaries: Portraits of British Feminists between the wars* (Oxford: Oxford University Press, 1987).

Harrison, Patricia Greenwood, *Connecting Links: The British and American Woman Suffrage Movements, 1900–1914* (Westport, Connecticut and London: Greenwood Press, 2000).

Haywood, Ian (ed.), *Chartist Fiction: Ernest Jones, Woman's Wrongs* (Aldershot: Ashgate, 2001).

Heilmann, Ann, 'Mona Caird (1854–1932): wild woman, new woman, and early radical feminist critic of marriage and motherhood', *Women's History Review*, Vol. 5, No. 1, 1996, pp. 67–95.

Holcombe, Lee, *Wives and Property: Reform of the Married Women's Property Law in Nineteenth Century England* (Toronto and Buffalo: University of Toronto Press, 1983).

Holt, Edgar, *The Boer War* (London: Putnam, 1958), p. 20.

Holton, Sandra Stanley, *Feminism and Democracy: Women's Suffrage and Reform Politics in Britain, 1900–1918* (Cambridge: Cambridge University Press, 1986).

Holton, Sandra Stanley, 'Free Love and Victorian Feminism: The Divers Matrimonials of Elizabeth Wolstenholme and Ben Elmy', *Victorian Studies*, Vol. 36, 1994, pp. 199–222.

Holton, Sandra Stanley, 'From Anti-Slavery to Suffrage Militancy: The Bright Circle, Elizabeth Cady Stanton and the British Women's Movement', in Caroline Daley and Melanie Nolan (eds), *Suffrage and Beyond: International Feminist Perspectives* (Auckland: Auckland University Press, 1994), pp. 213–33.

Holton, Sandra Stanley, '"To Educate Women into Rebellion": Elizabeth Cady Stanton and the Creation of a Transatlantic Network of Radical Suffragists', *American Historical Review*, October 1994, pp. 1112–36.

Holton, Sandra Stanley, 'Women and the Vote', in June Purvis (ed.), *Women's History: Britain 1850–1945: An Introduction* (London and New York: Routledge, 1995), pp. 277–306.

Holton, Sandra Stanley, *Suffrage Days: Stories from the Women's Suffrage Movement* (London and New York: Routledge, 1996).

Holton, Sandra Stanley, 'Now you see it, Now you don't: The Women's Franchise League and its Place in Contending Narratives of the Women's Suffrage Movement', in Maroula Joannou and June Purvis (eds), *The Women's Suffrage Movement: New Feminist Perspectives* (Manchester and New York: Manchester University Press, 1998), pp. 15–36.

Holton, Sandra Stanley, 'The Making of Suffrage History', in June Purvis and Sandra Stanley Holton (eds), *Votes for Women* (London and New York: Routledge, 2000), pp. 13–33.

Holton, Sandra Stanley, 'Elizabeth Wolstenholme Elmy', in H.C.G. Matthew and Brian Harrison (eds), *Oxford Dictionary of National Biography: From the Earliest Times to the Year 2000* (Oxford: Oxford University Press in association with the British Academy, 2004), pp. 302–4.

Holton, Sandra Stanley, *Quaker Women: Personal Life, Memory and Radicalism in the Lives of Women Friends, 1780–1950* (London and New York: Routledge, 2007).

Hunt, Karen, *Equivocal Feminists: The Social Democratic Federation and the Woman Question 1884–1911* (Cambridge and New York: Cambridge University Press, 1996).

Hunt, Karen, 'Journeying Through Suffrage: The Politics of Dora Montefiore', in Clare Eustance, Joan Ryan and Laura Ugolini (eds), *A Suffrage Reader: Charting directions in British Suffrage History* (London: Leicester University Press, 2000), pp. 162–76.

Hunt, Karen, 'Rethinking Activism: Lessons from the History of Women's Politics', *Parliamentary Affairs*, Vol. 62, No. 2, 2009, pp. 211–26.

Jeffreys, Sheila, *The Spinster and Her Enemies: Feminism and Sexuality, 1880–1930* (London and New York: Pandora, 1985).

Jenkins, Keith, *Why History? Ethics and Postmodernity* (London: Routledge, 1999).

Joannou, Maroula, '"She Who would be Free Herself Must strike the Blow": Suffragette Autobiography and Suffragette Militancy', in Julia Swindells (ed.), *The Uses of Autobiography* (London: Taylor & Francis, 1995), pp. 31–44.

Jordan, Ellen, and Anne Bridger, 'An Unexpected Recruit to Feminism': Jessie Boucherett's "Feminist Life" and the importance of being wealthy', *Women's History Review*, Vol. 15, No. 3, 2006, pp. 385–412.

Kean, Hilda, 'Searching for the Past in Present Defeat: the construction of historical and political identity in British feminism in the 1920s and 1930s', *Women's History Review*, Vol. 3, No. 1, 1994, pp. 57–80.

Kent, Susan Kingsley, *Gender and Power in Britain, 1640–1990* (London and New York: Routledge, 1999).

Kent, Susan Kingsley, *Sex and Suffrage in Britain 1860–1914* (Princeton: Princeton University Press, 1990).

Lawrence, Jon, *Speaking for the People: Party, Language and Popular Politics in England, 1867–1914* (Cambridge: Cambridge University Press, 1998).

Lawrence, Jon, 'Contesting the Male Polity: The Suffragettes and the Politics of Disruption in Edwardian Britain', in Amanda Vickery (ed.), *Women, Privilege and Power: British Politics 1750 to the Present* (Stanford: Stanford University Press, 2001), pp. 168–200.

Ledger, Sally, and Roger Luckhurst, 'Introduction', in Sally Ledger and Roger Luckhurst (eds), *The Fin de Siecle: A Reader in Cultural History c.1880–1900* (Oxford: Oxford University Press, 2000).

Levine, Philippa, *Feminist Lives in Victorian England: Public Roles and Private Commitment* (Los Angeles: Figueroa Press, 2003).

Liddington, Jill, and Jill Norris, *One Hand Tied Behind Us: The Rise of the Women's Suffrage Movement* (London: Virago, 1978).

Liddington, Jill, *The Road to Greenham Common: Feminism and Anti-Militarism in Britain since 1820* (Syracuse University Press, 1991).

Liddington, Jill, *Rebel Girls: Their Fight for the Vote* (London: Virago, 2006).

Lowry, Donal, '"The Boers were the Beginning of the End"?: The Wider Impact of the South African War', in Donal Lowry (ed.), *The South African War reappraised* (Manchester and New York: Manchester University Press, 2000), pp. 223–39.

Marcus, Sharon, *Between Women: Friendship, Desire, and Marriage in Victorian England* (Princeton and Oxford: Princeton University Press, 2007).

McHugh, Paul, *Prostitution and Victorian Social Reform* (London: Croom Helm, 1980).

Margadant, Jo Burr, 'Introduction', in Jo Burr Margadant (ed.), *The New Biography: Performing Femininity in Nineteenth-century France* (Berkeley and London: University of California Press, 2000).

Marshall, Mary Paley, *Newnham College Roll* (Cambridge: Fabb & Tyler, 1933).

Mayhall, Laura E. Nym, 'Defining Militancy: Radical Protest, the Constitutional Idiom, and Women's Suffrage in Britain, 1908–1909', *Journal of British Studies*, Vol. 39, 1994, pp. 340–71.

Mayhall, Laura E. Nym, 'Creating the "Suffragette Spirit": British feminism and the historical imagination', *Women's History Review*, Vol. 4, No. 3, 1995, pp. 319–44.

Mayhall, Laura E. Nym, 'The South African War and the origins of suffrage militancy in Britain, 1899–1902', in Ian Christopher Fletcher, Laura E. Nym Mayhall and Philippa Levine (eds), *Women's Suffrage in the British Empire:*

Citizenship, Nation and Race (London and New York: Routledge, 2000), pp. 3–17.

Mayhall, Laura E. Nym, 'The Rhetorics of Slavery and Citizenship: Suffragist Discourse and Canonical Texts in Britain, 1880–1914', *Gender and History*, Vol. 13, No. 3, 2001, pp. 481–97.

Mayhall, Laura E. Nym, *The Militant Suffrage Movement: Citizenship and Resistance in Britain, 1860–1930* (Oxford: Oxford University Press, 2003).

Mercer, John, 'Writing and Re-writing Suffrage History: Sylvia Pankhurst's *The Suffragette*', *Women's History Magazine*, Vol. 56, Summer 2007, pp. 11–18.

Mineka, Francis E. and Dwight N. Lindley (eds), *The Later Letters of John Stuart Mill 1849–1873* (Toronto and Buffalo: University of Toronto Press and Routledge & Kegan Paul, 1972).

Morgan, Simon, *A Victorian Woman's Place: Public Culture in the Nineteenth Century* (London and New York: Tauris Academic Studies, 2007).

Mort, Frank, 'Purity, Feminism and the State: Sexuality and Moral Politics, 1880–1914', in M. Langan and B. Schwartz (eds), *Crisis in the British State, 1880–1930* (London: Hutchinson, 1985).

Mort, Frank, *Dangerous Sexualities: Medico-Moral Politics in England since 1830*, 2nd edn (London and New York: Routledge, 2000).

Murgatroyd, Lyndon, *Mill Walks and Industrial Yarns: a History of the Mills and Businesses of the Congleton District* (privately published, 2003).

Parker, Joan E., 'Lydia Becker's "School for Science": A Challenge to Domesticity', *Women's History Review*, Vol. 10, No. 4, 2001, pp. 629–50.

Pedersen, Joyce Senders, *The Reform of Girls' Secondary and Higher Education in Victorian England: A Study of Elites and Education Change* (New York and London: Garland, 1987).

Phillips, Melanie, *The Ascent of Woman: A History of the Suffragette Movement and the Ideals Behind it* (London: Little Brown, 2003).

Polkey, Pauline, 'Reading History through Autobiography: Politically Active Women of Late Nineteenth-century Britain and their Personal Narratives', *Women's History Review*, Vol. 9, No. 3, 2000, pp. 483–500.

Porter, Bernard, *The Absent-Minded Imperialists: Empire, Society and Culture in Britain* (Oxford: Oxford University Press, 2004).

Prochaska, Frank K., *Women and Philanthropy in Nineteenth-century England* (Oxford: Clarendon, 1980).

Pugh, Martin, *The March of the Women: A Revisionist Analysis of the Campaign for Women's Suffrage, 1866–1914* (Oxford and New York: Oxford University Press, 2000).

Purvis, June, *A History of Women's Education in England* (Milton Keynes and Philadelphia: Open University Press, 1991).

Purvis, June, 'The Prison Experiences of the Suffragettes in Edwardian Britain', *Women's History Review*, Vol. 4, No. 1, 1995, pp. 103–33.

Purvis, June, 'From "Women Worthies" to Poststructuralism? Debate and Controversy in Women's History in Britain', in June Purvis (ed.), *Women's*

History: Britain, 1850–1945 (London and New York: Routledge, 1995), pp. 1–22.

Purvis, June, 'A "Pair of . . . Infernal Queens"? A Reassessment of the Dominant Representations of Emmeline and Christabel Pankhurst, First Wave Feminists in Edwardian Britain', *Women's History Review*, Vol. 5, No. 2, 1996, pp. 259–80.

Purvis, June and Maureen Wright, 'Writing Suffragette History: The Contending Autobiographical Narratives of the Pankhursts', *Women's History Review*, Vol. 12, Vols 3 & 4, 2005, pp. 405–33.

Purvis, June, 'The Pankhursts and the Great War', in Alison Fell and Ingrid Sharp (eds), *The Women's Movement in Wartime: International Perspectives 1914–1919* (Basingstoke: Palgrave, 2007).

Rappaport, Helen, *Encyclopaedia of Women Social Reformers*, Vol. 1 (Santa Barbara: ABC-Clio, 2001).

Rendall, Jane, *The Origins of Modern Feminism: Women in Britain, France and the United States, 1870–1860* (Basingstoke: Macmillan, 1985).

Rendall, Jane, 'A Moral Engine'? Feminism, Liberalism and the *English Woman's Journal*', in Jane Rendall (ed.), *Equal or Different: Women's Politics 1800–1914* (Oxford and New York: Basil Blackwell, 1987).

Rendall, Jane, 'The Citizenship of Women and the Reform Act of 1867', in Catherine Hall, Keith McClelland and Jane Rendall (eds), *Defining the Victorian Nation: Class, Race, Gender and the Reform Act of 1867* (Cambridge: Cambridge University Press, 2000), pp. 119–77.

Rendall, Jane, 'John Stuart Mill, Liberal Politics and the Movements for Women's Suffrage, 1865–1873', in Amanda Vickery (ed.), *Women, Privilege and Power: British Politics 1750 to the Present* (Stanford: Stanford University Press, 2001), pp. 168–200.

Rendall, Jane, 'Who was Lily Maxwell? Women's Suffrage and Manchester Politics, 1866–1867', in June Purvis and Sandra Stanley Holton (eds), *Votes for Women* (London and New York: Routledge, 2002), pp. 57–83.

Richards, Jeffrey, *Imperialism and Music: Britain 1876–1953* (Manchester: Manchester University Press, 2001).

Roberts, Michael J.D., 'Feminism and the State in later Victorian England', *The Historical Journal*, Vol. 38, No. 1, 1995, pp. 85–110.

Roper, Michael, 'Slipping Out of View: Subjectivity and Emotion in Gender History', *History Workshop Journal*, Vol. 59, No. 1, 2005, pp. 57–72.

Rosen, Andrew, *Rise Up, Women!: The Militant Campaign of the Women's Social and Political Union 1903–14* (London and Boston: Routledge & Kegan Paul, 1974).

Rover, Constance, *Love, Morals and the Feminists* (London: Routledge & Kegan Paul, 1970).

Rowbotham, Sheila, *Hidden from History: 300 Years of Women's Oppression and the Fight against it*, 3rd edn (London: Pluto, 1977).

Rowbotham, Sheila, *Dreamers of a New Day: Women Who Invented the Twentieth Century* (London and New York: Verso, 2010).

Royle, Edward, *Victorian Infidels: The Origins of the British Secularist Movement 1791–1866* (Manchester: Manchester University Press, 1974).

Royle,. Edward, *Radicals, Secularists and Republicans: Popular freethought in Britain, 1866–1915* (Manchester and New Jersey: Manchester University Press and Rowman & Littlefield, 1980).

Rubinstein, David, *Before the Suffragettes: Women's Emancipation in the 1890s* (Brighton: Harvester, 1986).

Schwartz, Laura, 'Free Love and Feminism: Secularist Debates on Marriage and Sexual Morality, England c.1850–1885', *Women's History Review*, Vol. 19, No. 5, 2010, pp. 775–93.

Scott, Benjamin, *A State Iniquity: Its Rise, Extension and Overthrow* (New York: Augustus M. Kelley, 1968).

Shanley, Mary Lyndon, *Feminism, Marriage and the Law in Victorian England, 1850–1895* (London: I.B. Tauris, 1989).

Smith, Angela K, *Suffrage Discourse in Britain during the First World War* (Aldershot and Burlington: Ashgate, 2005).

Smith, H.L., *The British Women's Suffrage Campaign, 1866–1928*, 2nd edn (Harlow: Pearson, 2007), chapter 5.

Smith, M. van Wyk, *Drummer Hodge: The Poetry of the Anglo-Boer War (1899–1902)* (Oxford: Clarendon Press, 1978).

Spender, Dale (ed.), *Feminist Theorists: Three Centuries of Women's Intellectual Traditions* (London: The Women's Press 1983).

Spongberg, Mary, 'Female Biography', in Mary Spongberg, Barbara Caine and Ann Curthoys (eds), *Companion to Women's Historical Writing* (Basingstoke: Palgrave Macmillan, 2005).

Steedman, Carolyn, *Childhood, Culture and Class in Britain: Margaret McMillan, 1860–1931* (New Brunswick, New Jersey: Houghton Mifflin Company, 1990).

Steedman, Carolyn, *Past Tenses: Essays on Writing Autobiography and History* (London: Rivers Oram, 1992).

Stevens, W.B. (ed.), *History of Congleton* (Manchester: Manchester University Press, 1970).

Strachey, Ray, *'The Cause': A Short History of the Women's Movement in Great Britain* (London: Virago, 1978).

Strauss, Sylvia, *'Traitors to the Masculine Cause': The Men's Campaigns for Women's Rights* (Westport and London: Greenwood Press, 1982).

Tanner, Duncan, 'Ideological Debate in Edwardian Labour Politics: Radicalism, Revisionism and Socialism', in Eugenio F. Biagini and Alistair J. Reid (eds), *Currents of Radicalism: Popular Radicalism, Organised Labour and Party Politics in Britain, 1850–1914* (Cambridge: Cambridge University Press, 1991), pp. 271–93.

Taylor, Barbara, *Eve and the New Jerusalem: Socialism and Feminism in the Nineteenth Century* (London: Virago, 1983).

Taylor, Barbara, *Mary Wollstonecraft and the Feminist Imagination* (Cambridge: Cambridge University Press, 2003).

Tickner, Lisa, *The Spectacle of Women: Imagery of the Suffrage Campaign, 1907–1914* (London: Chatto & Windus, 1987).

Tosh, John, 'The Making of Masculinities: The Middle Class in Late Nineteenth-Century Britain' in Angela V. John and Claire Eustance (eds), *The Men's Share?: Masculinities, Male Support and Women's Suffrage in Britain 1890–1920* (London: Routledge, 1997).

Tyldesley, Bert, *The Duke's Other Village: The Roe Green Story* (Neil Richardson, 1993).

Tyrrell, Ian, 'Transatlantic Progressivism in Women's Temperance and Suffrage,' in Gutzke (ed.), *Britain and Transnational Progressivism* (Basingstoke: Palgrave Macmillan, 2008), pp. 133–48.

Vicinus, Martha, *Independent Women: Work and Community for Single Women, 1850–1970* (London: Virago, 1985).

Walkowitz, Judith R., *Prostitution and Victorian Society: Women, Class and the State* (Cambridge, Cambridge University Press, 1980).

Walkowitz, Judith R., *City of Dreadful Delight: Narratives of Sexual Danger in Late-Victoran London* (London: Virago, 1992).

Woolf, Virginia, *To The Lighthouse* (London: Penguin, 1992).

Woolf, Virginia, 'Sketch of the Past', in Jeanne Schulkind (ed.), *Moments of Being: Autobiographical Writings* (London: Pimlico, 2002), p. 139.

Wright, Maureen, '"An Impudent Intrusion"?: Assessing the Life of Elizabeth Wolstenholme Elmy, First-Wave Feminist and Social Reformer, 1833–1918', *Women's History Review*, Vol. 18, No. 2, 2009, pp. 243–64.

Wright, Maureen, 'The Women's Emancipation Union and Radical-feminist Politics in Britain, 1891–99', *Gender and History*, Vol. 22, No. 2, 2010, pp. 382–406.

Yeo, Eileen Janes, *The Contest for Social Science: Relations and Representations of Gender and Class* (London: Rivers Oram, 1996).

Unpublished articles and theses

Bulmore, Barbara, 'Moravian Education at Fulneck Schools, Yorkshire, in the Eighteenth and Nineteenth Centuries'. Unpublished PhD thesis, University of Manchester, 1992.

Dingsdale, Ann, 'Generous and Lofty Sympathies': the Kensington Society, the 1866 Women's Suffrage Petition and the Development of Mid-Victorian Feminism', Unpublished PhD thesis, University of Greenwich, 1995.

Fielding, Muriel, 'Elizabeth C. Wolstenholme Elmy: A Forgotten Feminist'. Unpublished MLitt dissertation, Victorian Studies, 1988. Women's Library, London Metropolitan University.

Lemoine, Sheila C., 'The North of England Council for Promoting the Higher Education of Women, 1867–1875/6'. Unpublished MEd thesis, University of Manchester, 1968.

Mercer, John, 'Buying Votes: Purchasable Propaganda in the Twentieth-Century Women's Suffrage Movement'. Unpublished PhD thesis, University of Portsmouth, 2005.

Worzola, Diane M.C. 'The Langham Place Circle: The Beginnings of the Organized Women's Movement in England, 1854–1870'. Unpublished PhD thesis, University of Wisconsin-Madison, 1982.

Index